Operations Strategy

Chandrasekaran N.
Professor, Operations Management Area
IFMR Graduate School of Management
Krea University

Chandiran P.
Associate Professor and Chairperson
Centre for Logistics and Supply Chain Management
Loyola Institute of Business Administration (LIBA)
Loyola College Campus

CENGAGE

Australia • Brazil • India • Mexico • Singapore • United Kingdom • United States

CENGAGE

Operations Strategy

Chandrasekaran N.
Chandiran P.

ISBN-13: 978-93-5350-350-5
ISBN-10: 93-5350-350-7

Cengage Learning India Private Limited

T-303, 3rd Floor
DAV Complex, Plot 3
Mayur Vihar Phase 1
Delhi-110091

Cengage Learning is a leading provider of customized learning solutions with office locations around the globe, including Australia, Brazil, India, Mexico, Singapore, United Kingdom, and United States. Locate your local office at: **www.cengage.com/global**

Cengage Learning products are represented in Canada by Nelson Education, Ltd.

For product information, visit **www.cengage.co.in**

Printed in India
First Impression 2020

A teacher enjoys his profession when he co-creates knowledge with students. He dedicates to youth by sensitising the value of commitment and pride in the learning process as they together progress! My students have always been my source of strength. I dedicate this work to them.

Further, I dedicate this work to my daughter, ***Sangeethaa****, spouse* ***Prabha*** *and mother* ***Annapoorani***

– Chandrasekaran N.

I dedicate this work to my parents, ***Palaniappan*** *and* ***Chinnakannu****, my wife* ***Santhy****, my daughter* ***Kavya*** *and my son* ***Mukundan***

– Chandiran P.

Contents

Preface

Firms that pursue operations strategy create a competitive advantage and set themselves up to be game changers in the industry. Technology explosion and use of advanced communication technology in manufacturing and service industries impact the longitudinal horizon of decision time frame. Such technology growth brings enormous opportunities and challenges in designing new products and services, innovation, supply network, facility location, and size of plant and facility. Operations managers need to be sensitive to such opportunities and look at the evolution of the industry in which they operate. They must be conscious of game-changing initiatives and observant of competitive forces that intensify their business risks. Globalisation, outsourcing, and cost economies have further redefined the landscape of operations management.

The objective of this book is to provide a holistic text on operations strategy with a focus on decision areas, decision environment, implementation, and performance management. The book focusses on contextualising to readers in the subcontinent to understand the environment and learn to respond to changing conditions. Further, it discusses the inbound and outbound strategies of global and Indian firms, respectively.

The book is structured in a systematic manner with precise learning objectives. It aims to help business students learn Operations Strategy as part of their curriculum. At the same time, it is equally suitable for those seeking to develop an understanding of Operations Strategy to participate in analysing firms' performance, industry structural factors, and conduct of firms concerning innovations, technology, and market to be served.

Chapter Organisation

The layout of the book is designed such that each chapter builds on the learning of the preceding chapters.

Chapter 1 introduces operations strategy and its positioning along with business and other functional strategies. This chapter highlights the importance of competitive positioning and how operations strategy can be handled to be a driver of competitive advantage.

Chapter 2 discusses different concepts and techniques involved in developing operations strategy. The focus of this chapter is to introduce a detailed approach to strategy formulation and implementation. It links overall corporate and business strategy to a functional strategy. The readers will familiarise themselves with the linkages and will be facilitated to fix the requirements.

Chapter 3 discusses concepts and decision making relating to the size and location of plants as an essential aspect of operations strategy. Any strategist would feel the need to align this operations perspective in an overall strategic decision framework, as this could be one of the competitive drivers for a firm. The chapter presents a few examples of game-changers in the Indian industry.

Chapter 4 explains the importance of a firm to align with its extended entities in fulfiling an ultimate customer demand—the purpose for which a firm exists! As part of this, discussion concepts like outsourcing and choice of strategic alliance that can be built among suppliers and distribution network are discussed. The extent, nature relationships and need to nurture relationships are also covered. Again, this chapter is core to operations strategic perspective in overall effort to gain competitive advantage.

Chapter 5 discusses the core area of operations strategic perspective towards driving a firm to achieve a competitive advantage. There are numerous aspects which are considered while selecting a technology and production process. Further, with new trends of technology explosion, firms choose automation and advance product-process mix subject to market requirements like cost, dependability, flexibility, quality, and speed. The chapter cites a few cases on the above.

Chapter 6 discusses the importance and relevance of new product/service development. It explains about innovation and how firms that innovate can create an edge for themselves in an industry. It may be noted that the development and innovation strategies must be in synchronisation with the market requirements like cost, dependability, flexibility, quality, and speed.

Chapter 7 explains the importance of sustainability of environmental factors during the production and distribution of goods and services. Globally, trends are moving towards the adoption of "Green Principles" and orienting all stakeholders towards the sustainability of resources endowed. Hence, in this chapter, focus has been on sustainability as an operation strategic perspective towards competitive conditions.

Chapter 8 discusses the importance of an alternate strategic perspective, namely resource-led strategies. Aspects like the choice of material, split location, or even people resources are cited as game-changers for a firm to achieve competitive advantage.

Chapter 9 covers the aspects of approaches to improve performance and controlling operations. It also discusses models of excellence and their linkages to operations management. It is not enough that a firm has high competence in developing a pathbreaking strategic perspective in the operations area. Such a strategy must be effectively implemented, monitored, and course-corrected. This chapter discusses the approaches and techniques for the same.

Chapter 10 explains the need for global orientation in operations. The perspectives and drivers of global operational strategy to be pursued explain the importance of a firm to look at inbound and outbound operational, strategic initiatives to go beyond domestic markets or resources for the supply side. As one looks at globalisation of operations, several factors enable the same, while a few could be challenges which a firm may have to face. The chapter brings out such factors that could facilitate globalisation and highlight cases of successful firms.

The book includes nine case studies which present active learner with opportunities to understand and apply operations strategy to deal with the critical concerns.

- *Performance Improvement through Vendor Rationalisation: ABC Tractor Ltd (ATL)* discusses issues relating to just in time (JIT) and supplier relationships. ATL envisioned improving its supply chain function, and quality initiatives and cost managements were to follow in such a rationalisation project.
- *Wireless Industry Analysis and Service Operations Positioning of T-Mobile: A perspective* explains industry analysis, trends in technology, and operations strategic perspective. It throws an opportunity to understand strategy formulation and industry analysis in decision making.
- *Super Auto forge: Technology and leadership led growth* is focussed on the integration of operations perspective and market requirements of the company and relates the same to its growth. It discusses some key strategic initiatives like the implementation of quality management processes, continuous improvement through learning and HR practices adopted by the company.
- *Reliserve Distribution Management Ltd: Surge in demand for a short window and service challenges* is focussed on opportunities for supply chain service providers towards fulfiling the demand of service by e-commerce players. It discusses opportunities and challenges in serving demand which swings in a pattern within a year. However, investment and fixed overheads are committed over a long-time period.
- *Logistics-Excellence in Chennai: Customer profitability and operations strategy* discusses a supply chain service provider who is operating as Importer of Record and doing fulfilment services for large hardware

computing company. With changes in demand and pressure to be responsive in the supply chain, it is interesting to observe how this company handles financial stability.

- *L-X Logistics India: Time-sensitive spares and uptime service of automatic teller machines* discusses the challenges faced by the operators of third-party service providers who maintain uptime by delivering consumable spares to service technicians at ATM location. This case discusses the aspects of service contract and environmental changes impacting business.
- *Aligning Supply Chain of Sweet Corn Processor for Growth* helps to understand niche agribusiness supply chain and application of strategic thinking towards managing growth, especially in a different product category in India.
- *Sapthagiri Street Food Vending: Positioning and entrepreneurial clarity* discusses the supply chain network defining nodes and flows of physical, financial, and information for food retail, which is on a cart selling at roadside. Such an activity is a part of the livelihood business for many tiny entrepreneurs. The case helps to understand their operations model and critical success factors in sustaining the business.
- *Management of Pharmaceutical Drugs in Resource-constrained Not-for-profit Healthcare in Uttar Pradesh* focusses mainly on issues concerning forecasting and inventory management practices in a not-for-profit organisation. Such challenges are common for many businesses. The relevance of discussing this type of organisation is to emphasise that the operations strategic perspective is essential for such organisations as well.

This book includes a licence key for our digital learning app, Cengage app, that provides access to flashcards and self-assessment activities to help readers relate to concepts and check their understanding.

Chandrasekaran N.

Chandiran P.

Acknowledgents

I am grateful to the divine grace for endowing me with the ability to work on this book.

I would like to thank my parents and teachers for making me capable of accomplishing the modest goals I have set for myself and for teaching me to be objective, devoted, and resolute in my effort.

I am grateful to IFMR Graduate School of Business, Loyola Institute of Business Administration, and Management Development Programme (MDP) participants from different companies for allowing me to develop myself in this area. I am also thankful to my students for their probing questions and sharp insights on many of the topics covered in this book. I would also like to acknowledge the support of Dr. K. Ravi Kumar, Professor Emeritus at Marshall School of Business, University of Southern California, Dr. T. V. Subramanian, Professor Emeritus at IFMR Graduate School of Business, Professor P. S. Anantha Narayanan, Professor G. Balasubramanian, Mr. S Seetharaman, Chairman Super Auto Forge (P) Ltd, Professor Sundaram, Professor M. Ramasubramaniam, Mr. Debasis Mohanty, and that of my colleagues, Professor Vijaya S. and Professor Suresh Venkataraman. I would also to thank Mr. Srinivasan H. R. and Fr. Christie for their support and encouragement. There are other colleagues and friends in the industry who had continuously been supportive of my writing and giving feedback on some of the specific contents. I am grateful to them as well.

I would like to appreciate and acknowledge the team of Cengage Learning for their support throughout the journey of completing this book, and for giving it a form with persistent attention to quality and features.

I am grateful for the constant encouragement and support that I have received for my work from my daughter, Sangeethaa and spouse, Prabha.

Chandrasekaran N.

First and foremost, I thank God Almighty for giving me the strength and ability to complete this work. I would like to thank my parents and teachers, who have shaped me and made me continue to learn forever and for their guidelines and teachings.

I am grateful to Loyola Institute of Business Administration (LIBA) for supporting this project. I would like to express my thanks to my director, Fr. C. Joe Arun, SJ, for his motivation and support. I would like to acknowledge the support of my colleagues at LIBA, especially Dr. M. Ramasubramaniam, Dr. M. P. Pandikumar, and Dr. P. C. Laksmi Narayanan. I also thank Fr. Christie, SJ for his support and encouragement. I would also like to acknowledge Dr. Rammyaa, Mr. Theophilius, and Professor Sundaram for their encouragement. I sincerely acknowledge the persons who have helped me in the initial years of my career, my research guide Dr. K Suryaprakasa Rao, Professor N. Ramaswamy, Dr. S. N. SoundaraRajan, Dr. Shanthi Nachiappan, Dr. Angelin, and Dr. Rajmohan.

I greatly appreciate the assistance and support provided by the team of Cengage Learning during this work.

I am also grateful to my students, MDP executives and executive program students, for their queries which help me learn continuously.

As always, my wife, Santhy, my daughter, Kavya and my son, Mukundan provided me with moral support throughout the development of this work.

Chandiran P.

CHAPTER

1

Strategic Perspectives in Operations

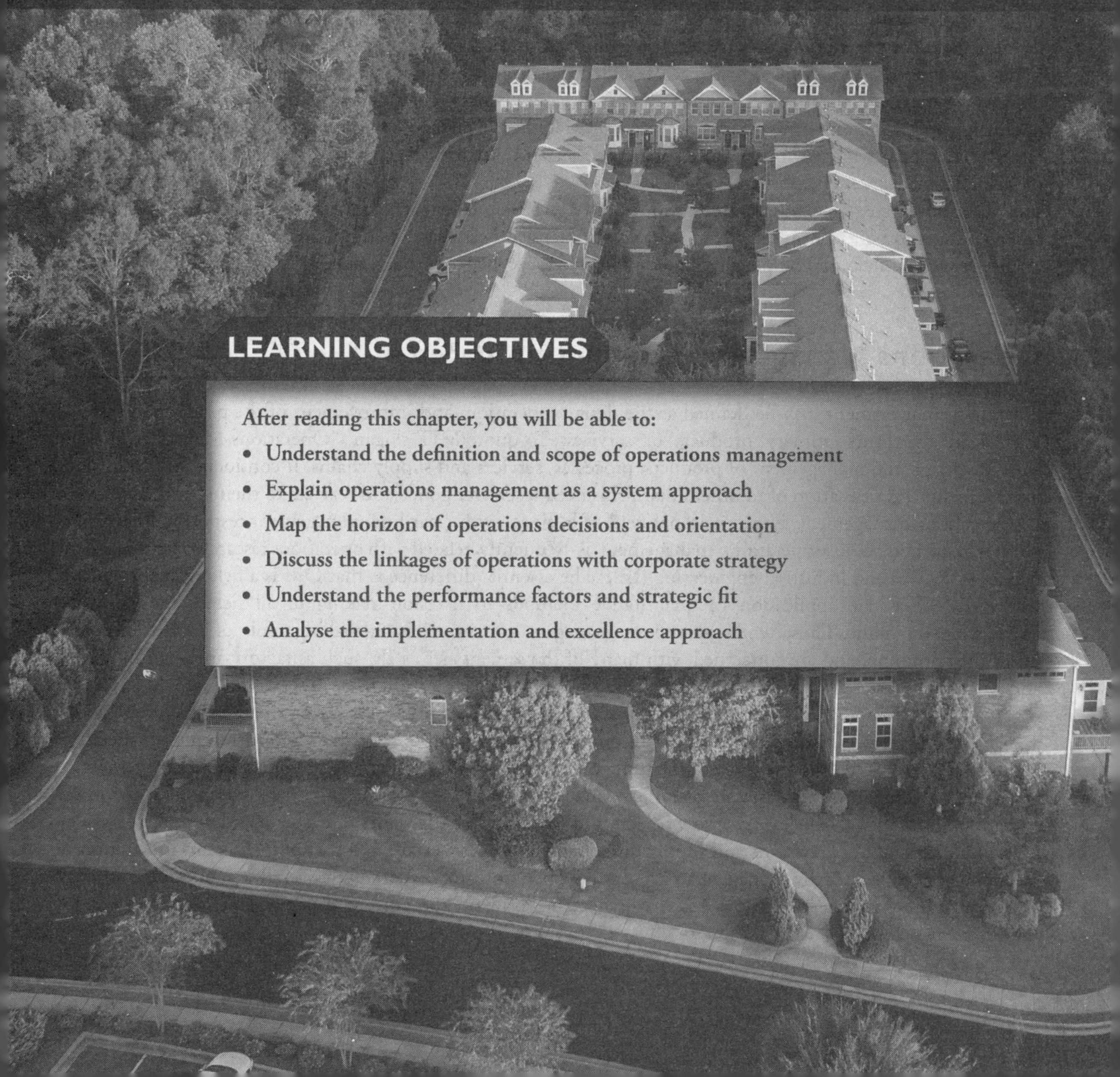

LEARNING OBJECTIVES

After reading this chapter, you will be able to:

- Understand the definition and scope of operations management
- Explain operations management as a system approach
- Map the horizon of operations decisions and orientation
- Discuss the linkages of operations with corporate strategy
- Understand the performance factors and strategic fit
- Analyse the implementation and excellence approach

Introduction

John Abraham, who was educated in one of the best engineering colleges in Tamil Nadu, moved to the USA in 1980s to pursue his post-graduation in Industrial Engineering at a premier university and later, took up a job in the USA. He got married and settled there. After twenty five years plus, in 2017, he visited Tamil Nadu, India for a batch reunion. He was taken aback to see his friend and competitor at school and engineering, Ram Narayan, who studied MBA from a premier institute in India now being Executive Director of a large conglomerate which manufactures and sells international brands in India through joint ventures and alliance. John inadvertently asked Ram, "How come such a change in India? I do not see any longer brands which I was familiar with like BPL, Onida, Kelvinator, Bajaj Scooters and Ambassador cars of Hindustan Motors? I have been reading about the presence of Samsung, Whirlpool, Haier, Honda Motors, Hyundai and Volkswagen. But how did they manage to produce in India? What are those operations strategies which changed Indian customers' choice? Is it just opening up of the economy? Then, existing players could have also made it big. Did international players bring unique technology, process, quality perspective, supplier and distribution networks, flexibility, speed to market and cost leadership? How did Indian customers react to such opportunities brought by new set domestic and international players? How was operations excellence achieved? Ram responded, "Operations excellence and strategising growth in creating and sustaining demand in newer market!" He then explained about an Indian company by the name Lava International which is into feature phone market and set to emerge as a promising Indian brand in the mobile handset market (Exhibit 1.1).

Operations strategy, thus, is an area of study and a professional engagement wherein there are opportunities and challenges to build a firm. Any firm that has transcended over years of competition and sustained in market would have certainly built competence and demonstrated excellence through operations strategy.

Operations Management: Defined and Scope

Operations management may be defined as the design, operation, and improvement of the production systems that create the firm's primary products or services. To quote MIT slogan, "Operations Management deals with the design and management of products, processes, services and supply chains. It considers the acquisition, development, and utilisation of resources that firms need to deliver goods and services to their clients want".

Operations management is a functional field of business with clear line management responsibilities. This point is important because operations management is frequently related with operations research or management science (OR/MS) and industrial engineering (IE). The essential difference is that OM is a field of management, while OR/MS is the application of quantitative methods to decision-making in all fields, and IE is an engineering discipline. Thus, while operations managers use the decision-making tools of OR/MS, such as linear programming, and are concerned with many of the same issues as IE, such as factory automation, layout and work study issues, OM's distinct management role distinguishes it from these other disciplines.

Predominantly, operations management focusses on the management of systems or processes that create goods and/or provide services. In the process, it draws inter disciplinary support of tools and techniques for decision making. Here we would discuss some of the functional linkages with production and operations management.

Assume a company which is into manufacturing of brake linings that are used as a component for brake system for automotive vehicles like two wheelers and four wheelers. It wants to evaluate and develop a strategy for manufacture of brake systems and supply directly to automotive sector as a part of its forward integration of business. In such a case, the management would like operations to validate with overall organisational strategy and ensure fitment. The operations team will need to evaluate the current capacity and identify areas for improvement.

Exhibit 1.1

Lava International Ltd.: Smart Operations Strategy Led growth

Disclaimer: This is indicative based on open source information and not exhaustive. There is no confirmation on our observations by the company and hence recommended only for academic discussion.

Indian mobile phone industry has experienced a phenomenal growth over a decade and half reaching across different levels of society with a wide range of choices. MNCs, international players mainly from China and domestic companies have jumped into the fray.

One such company is Lava International Ltd., a Noida based Indian company in the business of designing, making and marketing mobiles phones in India and abroad. The worth of the company was about ₹6500 crore as reported in one of the business magazines. To give an idea about its size of operations, the company sold about 10 million smart phones and over 17 million feature phones in FY 2017. The market share of Lava feature phone market is 7.2 per cent. Table 1.1 gives market share of mobile phones in India.

TABLE: 1.1 Top five smartphones and feature phones market share (Units) 2017

Smart phones		Feature phones	
Company	**Market share in %**	**Company**	**Market share in %**
Samsung	24.7	Samsung	20.5
Xiaomi	20.9	Transsion	1.7
Vivo	9.4	Micromax	8.7
Lenovo	7.8	Reliance Ind.	8.3
OPPO	7.5	Lava	7.2

Source: IDC 2017. Notes: IDC Quarterly Mobile Phone Tracker, Feb 12, 2018.
Adapted from Business India, 18 June – 1 July 2018, P. 49.

In the last five years, the company reported overall sales growth of about 90 per cent CAGR, out of which 66 per cent is contributed by feature phones and 248 per cent by smart phones segment. This is phenomenal performance compared to industry growth rate of 6 per cent which means the company has cannibalised a few players. It has sold about 110 million handsets in the last five years. It is also important to note here that the share of smartphone in domestic market sales mix in terms of value mix has increased from 17 per cent in 2012-13 to 51 per cent in 2016-17 and reported to have moved up to 57 per cent in first nine months of FY 2018. This clearly shows that operations strategy of Lava International Ltd. is to grow its position in feature phone market and more aggressively in smartphone market. The sales mix strategy is not just a market and competitive position but a lot to do with operations strategy and orienting operations in sync with other functional strategies like marketing and overall corporate growth strategy.

Let us now look at some of the important operations strategies that the company has pursued.

1. The company has become the only Indian company to launch "Designed in India" mobile phone with its own design team. It has set up its design centre at Noida with a team of 30 designers and engineers who have been

trained on industrial, mechanical, hardware and software of mobile phone.

2. According to Hari Om Rai, CMD, Lava International, "It is a critical step towards building the mobile components and parts using the ecosystem in the country. Over the last few years, Lava has built its capability and expertise in mobile design". The design team spent one year in China. The initial investment of ₹250 crore is being made towards developing its design capability and looking forward to roll out advanced at various price points.
3. The Research and Development centre in Shenzhen, China has over 700 engineers, covering the entire gamut of mobile designing. It has been there now for close to a decade. This shows that Lava International focusses on product development, innovation and building capability indigenously to capture a growth market. The company has an R & D centre at Bengaluru since 2016.
4. According to published report based on dealer feedback, the company has a strong supply chain network. This is more with forward or downstream linkages towards its distribution and dealer network. Lava has a single layer distribution model wherein over 1200 distributors are there pan-India who are directly managed. This can be time consuming but could be a strategic differentiator as in this case!
5. On the upstream and backward linkages, apart from design and component sourcing, key supply chain network design framework is that setting up manufacturing facilities in India. Rai, CMD at Lava International, mentioned that mobile manufacturing is shifting in a big way to India from China. More than 75 per cent of mobile shipment is made domestically and this is likely to go up to 90 per cent. In line with this, Lava is in the process of investing over ₹2600 crore in ramping up manufacturing facilities in the next five years. It will then localise 70 per cent of its mobile handset production from the current 25 per cent. The company is setting up two greenfield facilities, one at Tirupati, Andhra Pradesh and the other along the Yamuna Expressway near Greater Noida.
6. The company is also consolidating its product portfolio. It had more than 50 products — about 20 smartphones and about 35 feature phones— a few years ago. Currently, it has about less than 15 phones, 5 smartphones and about 9 feature phones. The focus is more on quality and providing customers with improved features.
7. Lava International is well entrenched into South and South-East Asian markets. It launched smartphones in Thailand in 2015 and moved up to number two position by 2016. It is second largest feature phone in the Asia market. The company's international operations are spread over 13 countries, including Thailand, Nepal, Bangladesh, Sri Lanka, Indonesia, Mexico, Middle East and Russia. It has entered into Egypt and thereby opened up in African market as well.

If one was to objectively analyse business and operations performance of this company, operations strategy has played a key role in growth of business. The company has set a clear vision and chalked out its growth strategies around product rationalisation, design improvement, quality focussed facility location, well-structured supply network, collaborations and internationalisation.

References

1. "A force to reckon with; Lava is set to emerge as a promising Indian brand", *Business India* dated 18 June – 1 July P 48 – 50.
2. http://www.lavamobiles.com/aboutus ; accessed on 10 August 2018.
3. https://www.ibef.org/industry/manufacturing-sector-india/showcase/lava-international-ltd ; accessed on 10 August 2018.
4. https://www.thehindubusinessline.com/info-tech/lava-to-invest-over-rs-2600cr-in-manufacturing-units-in-5-yrs/article22549621.ece ; accessed on August 10. 2018.

Operation managers would need to work with marketing team to know what the customer requirement would be, understand the market, validate market size and share data assumed with the marketing team. They would also require working with the finance department on validating assumptions of cost of capital, fund flow and risk features assumed in evaluation. Further, operations team will have to work with the human development department on issues relating to workers' attitude and capability for added range of product and also the capability of salesforce and incentives when product range is expanded. Thus, an operations management team is strategic initiative requires support of other functions as well.

This is not only true for long-term decisions but also for short-term decisions, such as flexibility plan adjustment in production planning and scheduling, supplier relationship management, adjusting capacity with inventory plan and selling incentives. Fulfiling these objectives requires using multifunctional approach to make all the operations management decisions.

If we look at the core of operations management, it involves transformation of inputs into outputs through scientific and systematic processes. In this process, the goal of operations management is to produce the right product/service at the right time, in the right quantity, with the highest quality, at the lowest cost, and with the shortest delivery time. The production and operations management may focus on delivery of outputs and the marketing and distribution function could take over from there.

However, the contemporary thinking is that supply chain orientation must clearly bring in operations, finance and marketing and distribution functions keeping the ultimate customer as the fulcrum of the business. Hence, operations management must look at comprehensive processes till products and services reach the ultimate customer. Figure 1.1 depicts the transformation processes of operations management function.

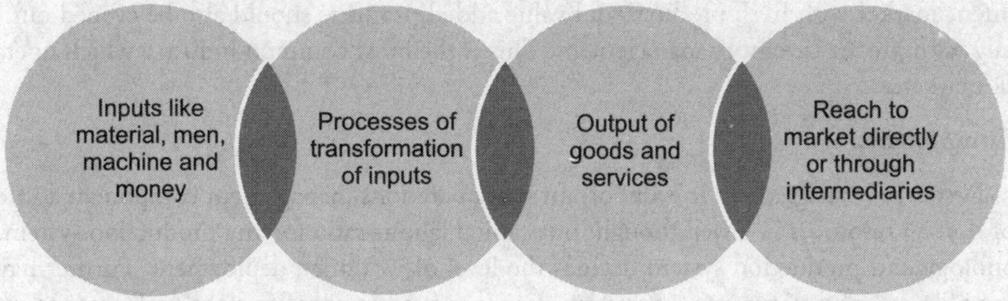

FIGURE 1.1 Operations management process

Operations Management: A System Approach

The term 'system' is meant as "Anything formed of parts placed together or adjusted into a regular and connected whole". Further, it is viewed as a whole entity with a slight amplification is provided by adding that each of the parts or subsystem is independently operational and collectively they function towards achieving a common objective. We live in a social system, are governed by democratic system, have public health system and communication system.

In an analogous way, the operating system of a manufacturing or service organisation consists of a set of highly interactive sub-systems. Each of these sub-systems as stated earlier is identifiable as an independently operational system. An operations manager must be aware of the significance of the total system with a common objective — organisational profitability and productivity.

The various components of operations management system are:

1. Production (goods/services): This is core of operations as a product or service is what the customer pays for and value creating activities are towards the same.

2. Product/service Design: Design is fundamental to a product or service as it features product or service with its components to create value to a customer.
3. Production Planning and Control: This is again an important component of operations management as a facility which is created for generating goods and services utilised on a plan for delivering the same to customers. There could be seasonality or variations in demand and supply based on the nature of product and other factors, including climatic conditions, societal, culture and so on. Production planning and control supports deployment of facility in production for meeting annual demand.
4. Plant Maintenance: This is again another component of operations which ensures that production or service facility is maintained well for continuous planned deployment for delivering the output. The function would require proactive planned maintenance and contingency or sporadic failure address system in case of such happening.
5. Realisation Process Design: Process design includes addressing every stage in a plant value adding stations which are balanced and optimally structured so that cost is minimised and zero wastage is achieved. For example, if there is a sugar plant, it has milling sections, process sections like clarification, crystallisation, centrifuge station and packaging. Each of the stations needs to be balanced for managing a varied input handling from crushing of cane to packing of sugar which would be a challenge of operations to ensure synchronised functioning of all process stations.
6. Inventory Management: As explained earlier in production planning and control, there could be seasonality or variations in demand and supply. For example, in dairy, processing milk is available more during winter, from October to March, which is called flush season but demand is low. However, demand is high during summer, lean period, when supply could be low. So the process must carry butter oil and milk solids to supplement market with fresh products and value added products should also be evened out. This is possible only with proper inventory management. This is the most common industry which operates in made to stock market.

Supportive Components:

1. Human Resource Management: It is important that operations management component addresses deployment of human resources in a well thought out capital labour ratio for any production system. The choice of technology and production system decides the level of workmen deployment. Further having decided on threshold level of deployment, operations manager need to identify right performance incentives and compensation to achieve best of productivity of resources.
2. Financial Management: Finance supports flow of goods and services in the value creating stream of activities. It is important to note that finance plays a significant role in operations management as the core function may manage physical component of a product or both tangible and intangible components of a service. However, finance is required for payment of resources and receipt of value in pecuniary terms from the customer. As the time gap involved with respect to value creation and appropriation in financial terms vary, someone needs to fund. For example, sugar may be sold and value realised from the stock. However, funding needs to happen from purchase of cane, processing and stocking and may be even further during distribution.
3. Marketing: Marketing function and operation management need to work in a synchronised way. Marking input by way of sales forecast is a key input for production planning. Similarly, marketing provides important feedback on product or service design and customer value recognition. Also at various stages, marketing provides competitor intelligence for cost management. Hence, a firm needs to be a component of operations management.
4. Information System for Monitoring and Control: Information system is all pervasive and fully present through all stages of operations management to provide feedback and pass on information to successive stages of operations.

Thus, operations management involves a whole gamut of issues relating to product, production, processes, resource management, and relationship with suppliers and customers in fulfilling a customer demand. It requires effective coordination with international functions of the firm like finance, marketing, information technology, human resources and corporate service like strategic visioning and direction team. It is all about transforming resources like men, machines, material and money towards serving actual and potential customers.

TABLE 1.2 Horizon and orientation of operations management decisions

Decision nomenclature	Time span	Capital involved	Management bandwidth	Examples
Operations	Block time of a shift, say 2 or 4 or 8 hours depending upon JIT supplies and shift timing to a week	Using available resources as per the master schedule running the operations with deployed machines/process centres and manpower	Floor level or operating unit supervision; junior to middle level operations managers handle running and senior managers attend on escalations	Line feed in a manufacturing factory, stores management and kitting, branch banking activities like customer service when one joins the queue, cheque processing, clearing of financial instruments, attending to patients at ward in a hospital and so on
Tactical or planning	Planning bucket of 3 months to 18 months, few services have a planning period of a month, most of those who plan for 3 months have monthly reviews	Focusses on using the best available machinery, equipment and long-term capital to match supply and demand…resource management could be possible with available limits…	Production planners, sourcing managers, supplier relationship managers, outsourcing service managers and so on…predominantly middle to senior level managers working for achieving annual budgets and drill it down to planning bucket	Production plan, material resources plan and distributions resource plan, demand estimation and so on in manufacturing, processing or assembly plants and service organisations like banking, insurance, healthcare, hospitality and so on.
Strategic	Long term, say, three years or more	All resources including plant and machinery, key processes, information systems, new location can be added. May require large capital outlay.	Senior and top management and many times, require approval of Board of Directors. Capital purchase committee does a thorough examination of such decision situations.	Adding a new line to an assembly or process unit, purchase of new equipment, reducing range or category of service in a retail bank branch' adding a specialty treatment in a hospital and so on.

Horizon of Operations Decisions and Orientation

One may observe that in production and service businesses, range of decision situations is vast and varies widely on three important criteria:

1. Time Span – Immediate to long term in terms of action and impact.
2. Financial Capital – From using existing assets for revenue creation to budget asset and working capital allocation to requirement of capital for equipment and long-term investment for operations area like a new line/facility, R&D and so on.
3. Managerial Width: From shop floor management to deep understanding of linkages of different decision areas of operations and linkages with other functional areas at middle and senior level to finally, long-term decisions of high capital and risk involved wherein senior and top management, including at times, board level professionals.

Decisions can be put through three buckets namely short term ranging from a shift to a week, medium term ranging from a quarter or 3 months to six quarters or 18 months and long-term decisions would have impact of over 3 years and above. Table 1.2 captures horizon of and orientation of operations management decisions.

It is not that the decisions are to be seen in silos and are disintegrated. In fact, they are inter-woven! The success of operations strategy fundamentally rests on effectiveness of operations tactical or planning decisions and operations execution.

Linking with Corporate Strategy

Strategy is commonly used to communicate a plan, policy, approach or a tactic. Most widely used analogy of strategy has been a chess board. We used to wonder why only the game of chess is related to strategy. Is not a cricket team or a football team or a tennis player strategising an approach to a match? There is sense in using chess board as a symbol of depiction to strategy as the game requires every move to be thought from self-initiative and possible response of opponent to emerge as a winner. Today's business enterprise managers should focus on their capability to win in marketplace amongst competitive forces.

Strategy, thus, should have basically three perspectives in any decision situation. First, time horizon should be long term. Many times we must understand that short and medium term decisions are more of operational and planning focus, respectively. Second perspective of strategy is that it is not easily reversible. This may be common in many decision situations. Here it means that effort and resources of reversing a strategic decision are more. For example, in a personal decision like acquiring professional skills to become a doctor, one would consider it strategic as it involves long-term commitment to learn and practise and if you like to change the profession, it is going to be time-taking to unlearn and learn new professional skills. This brings to the third perspective of strategy, namely substantial involvement of capital costs. Any strategic decision would involve capital costs either explicitly or implicitly. In business, all decisions are focussed on impacting income and expense statement and balance sheet. Unless a capital asset is created with a matching liability and assets are productive to generate income and profits, the liability can be paid off over years and surplus adding value to the firm. Thus, strategic management involves planning, organising, directing and controlling long-term decisions of an enterprise which are not easily irreversible, and involves substantial capital costs facilitating to achieve corporate objectives.

Earlier, long range planning was commonly used to refer planning of strategic initiatives. Focus then was more on planning and controlling resources for growth. The terms like business policy, corporate strategy and policy and corporate planning were also commonly used.

Strategic management is about setting objectives for corporate or its business units or functions to achieve a better alignment of business priorities to achieve respective decision goals. This involves systematic analysis of the external and the internal environment to evaluate current strategy and initiate new strategic moves. According to Porter, strategy is about creating a different position in a competitive environment through planning and structured proactive initiatives. John Kay (2000) also mentions that strategic management is about using careful analysis to understand and influence a company's position in the marketplace. According to Hamel, a corporate can foray on winning strategy by combining foresight and vision. Thus, one can see strategic management as systematic process and other view being handling uncertainty and achieve chosen position in a competitive environment.

Strategic decision can be classified on a hierarchy of decision making and its relations to strategic orientation, as shown in Figure 1.2. The depiction in the figure is for a large group whose strategies originate from an investment company which sets its vision for building a business empire and earns a decent return on overall investment in a portfolio of businesses of products and services. Each of the entity then becomes an area of focus and has to be managed by professionals and guided by a board. This entity is what is here referred as "corporate" that would be in the businesses of manufacturing/marketing products and/or services in multiple geographies or in a location. Each of these can be called a strategic business unit (SBU). Strategic initiatives at SBU level strategies are in synchronisation with corporate level. Further next level of hierarchy is that of functional strategies like that of finance, marketing, HR, operations and systems, and so on. Functional strategies can be related to the SBU and can be driven commonly by a corporate functional team. This would be under matrix organisation structure. Thus, operations strategy as a subject matter of decision making is linked across levels and important for all stakeholders.

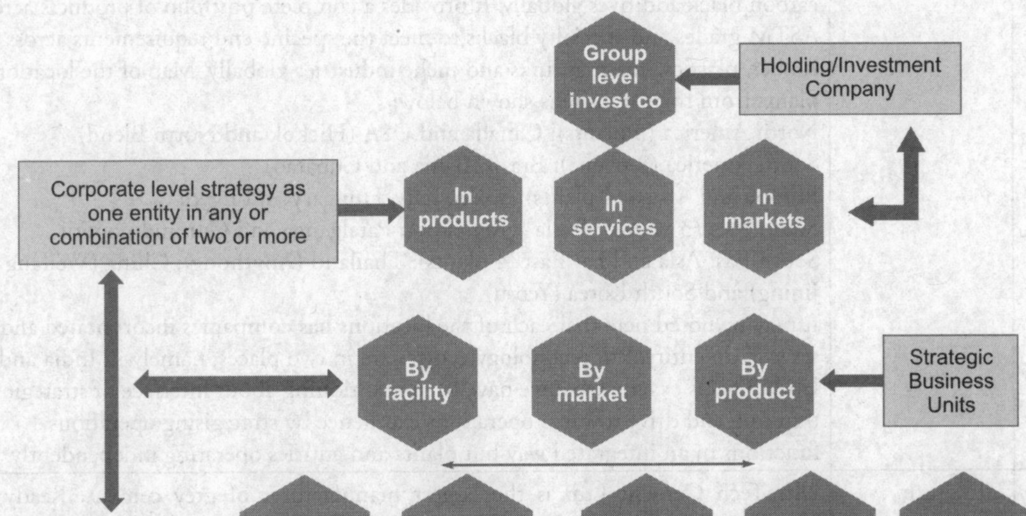

FIGURE 1.2 Linkage of operations strategic orientation across levels in corporate

The above can be explained by the following example. Aditya Birla Group is in the League of Fortune 500 with a turnover of about US $44.3 billion. The group has an employee force of 120,000 belonging to 42 nationalities. Over 50 per cent of its revenues flow from its overseas operations spanning 35 countries. It would be complex to imagine how the investment company standardises its strategies across companies, nations and markets to achieve fair return on investment. Some of the highlights of the group companies are shown in Table 1.3:

TABLE 1.3 Aditya Birla Group

SNo	Company	Remarks
1	Novelis – Aluminum products	Novelis is the leading producer of flat-rolled aluminum products and the world's largest recycler of aluminum. The segments include beverage can, automotive and high-end specialty markets. The company is operating an integrated network of technically advanced rolling and recycling facilities across North America, South America, Europe and Asia. Novelis leverages its global manufacturing and recycling footprint to deliver consistent, high-quality products around the world. Globally ranked 1st in this product.
2	Grasim Industries Ltd.	Grasim Industries Ltd. ranks among India's largest private sector companies. Its consolidated net revenue was ₹562 billion (US$8.6 Bn.) and had a consolidated net profit of ₹37 billion (US$ 565 Mn.) in FY 2018. It is the largest global player in viscose staple fibre and the only one in India. It has as its subsidiary UltraTech Cement, which is the largest cement producer in India, in a highly competitive and aggressive inorganic growth driven market. Grasim is also the largest caustic soda producer in India. Incidentally, this company forms nearly 20 per cent of A B Group.
3	Birla Carbon	Birla Carbon is one of the largest manufacturers and suppliers of high-quality carbon black additives globally. It provides a complete portfolio of products across ASTM grades and specialty blacks to meet the specific end requirements across rubber, plastics, coatings, inks and niche industries globally. Map of the location of plants from their website is shown below: North America (3 plants): Canada and USA (Hickok and North Blend) South America (2 plants): Brazil (Bahia and Cubatao) Europe and Africa (4 plants): Spain, Italy, Hungary and Egypt South Asia (3 plants): India – Renukoot; Patalganga and Gummdipoondi South East Asia and Far East (4 plants): Thailand (Angthong); China (Weifang and Jining) and South Korea (Yeosu) It may be noted here that each of the locations has companies incorporated and serve as an entity. But technology centres are in two places, namely in India and USA. This is exactly what we have been mentioning about interface of strategic thinking and drive towards operations excellence by strategising operations functions in an integrated way but plants and entities operating independently.
4	UltraTech Cement	UltraTech Cement Ltd. is the largest manufacturer of grey cement, Ready Mix Concrete (RMC) and white cement in India. It is also one of the leading cement producers globally (4th largest in the World excluding China). The company has an installed capacity of 96.5 million tonnes per annum (MTPA) of grey cement. UltraTech Cement has 19 integrated plants, 1 clinkerisation plant, 25 grinding units and 7 bulk terminals. Its operations span across India, UAE, Bahrain, Bangladesh and Sri Lanka. This would explain complexity of its operations in a competitive market.
5	Aditya Birla Nuvo	It is a conglomerate and details are given in Figure 1.3 with consolidated revenue more than ₹30,000 crore as of 2018.

Source: http://www.adityabirla.com/about-us/overview Accessed on 13 September 2018 and individual company web sites of the group.

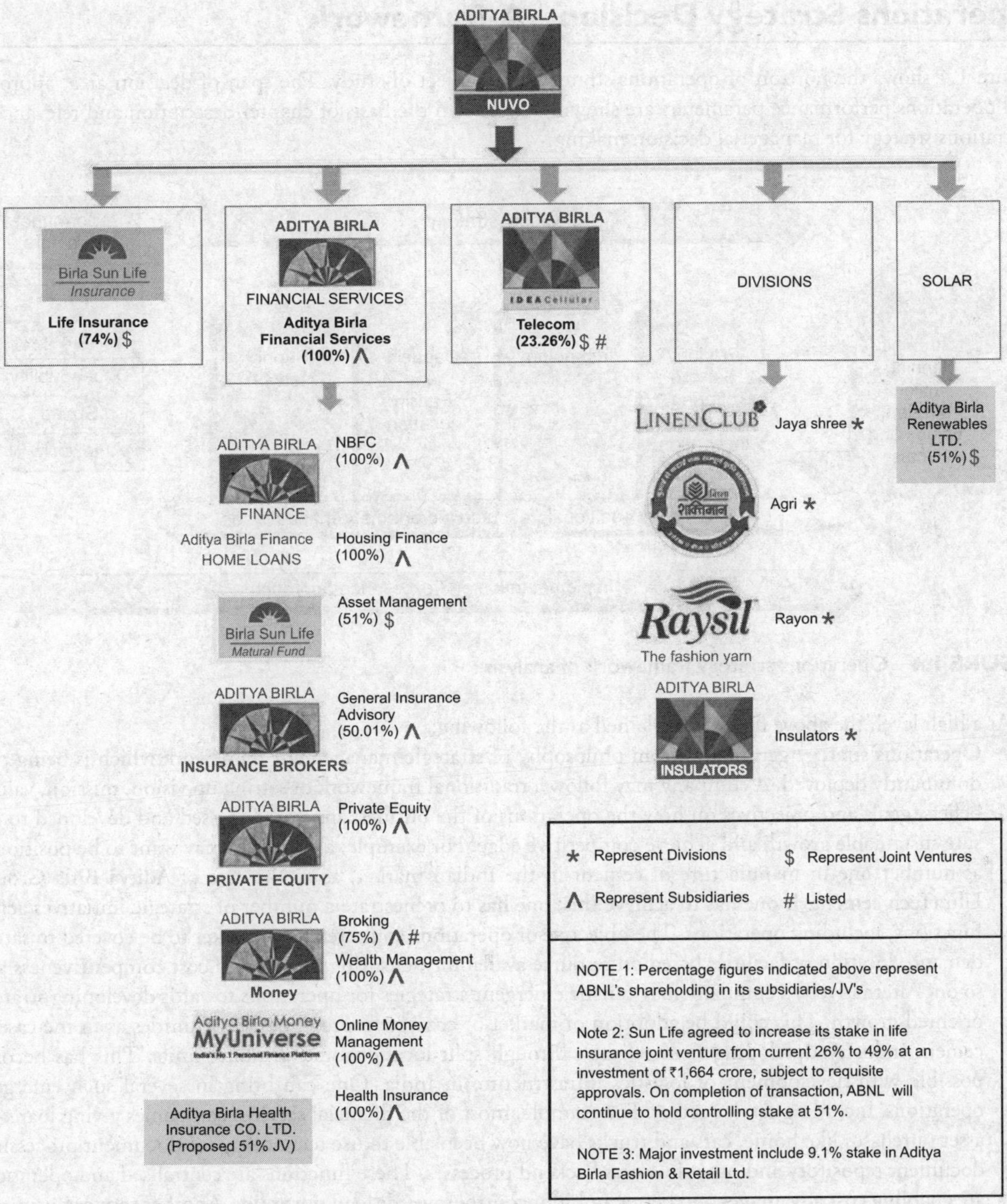

FIGURE 1.3 Aditya Birla Nuvo group chart

Source: http://www.adityabirlanuvo.com/About_us_Overview.php Accessed on 13 September 2018.

Thus, one can relate linkages of corporate strategy along with operations strategy at multiple level of investment and management of manufacturing and service business.

Operations Strategy Decision – A framework

Figure 1.4 shows the horizon of operations strategy as a subject of study. The span of decision area, approach and operations performance parameters are shown. These form the basis of chapter description and relevance of operations strategy for managerial decision making.

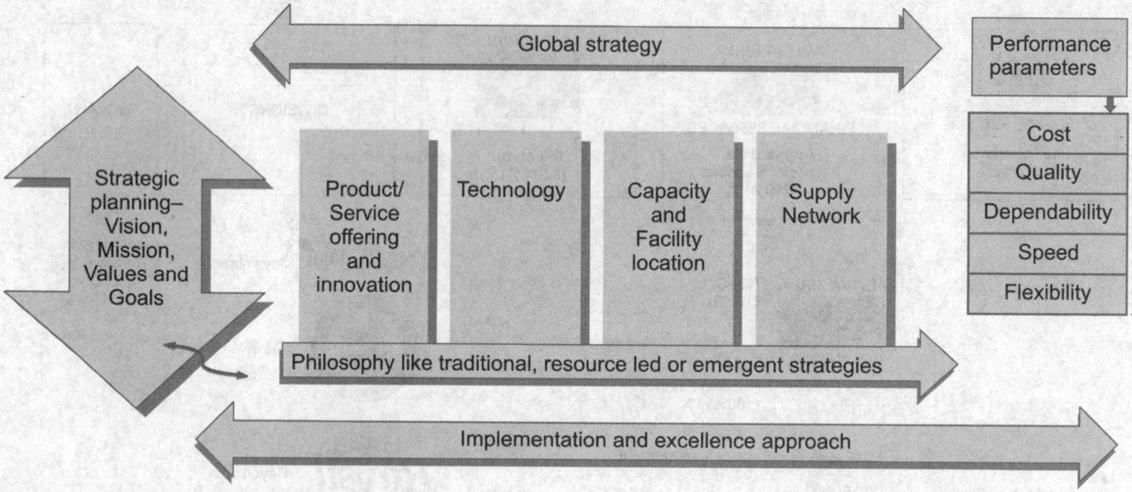

FIGURE 1.4 Operations strategy framework of analysis

At a high level, the above figure is explained as the following:

1. Operations strategy germinates from philosophy of strategic management framework which is being predominantly deployed. A company may follow a traditional framework of setting up vision, mission, values, beliefs, goals and objectives on how the operations of the business must be focussed and developed to ensure sustainable growth and achieve competitive edge. For example, a company may want to be positioned as number one in manufacture of cement in the Indian market, as in the case of Aditya Birla Group's UltraTech cement. If one has to achieve this, one has to orchestrate a number of strategic initiatives across functions, including operations. The objective of operations could relate to market to be covered to satisfy demand, location of facilities based on resource availability, ensuring quality and cost competitiveness and so on. Alternatively, a company may pursue emergent strategies for operations towards developing strategy oriented growth. This could be adoption of market or ecosystem provided opportunities as in the case of cement industry developing market reach through split locations and grinding units. This has become possible with development of logistics infrastructure in India. One can bring in several such emergent operations, including service sector. For example, most of the financial services companies giving loans for asset purchases like home, cars and trucks have now been able to use technology for document processing, document repository and other business backend processes. These functions are centralised and operations are enabling cost advantages and better ambit of control towards loan portfolios. Another service businesses in similar space are mutual funds and investment management that are benefiting by the advantages of technology. Technology helps in having quality research reports and information processing for effective investment management. Further proliferation of technology has helped for better connect with retail investment community and serving has brought scope for managing large portfolios. Thus emergent strategies in operations are deployed. One can look at Blue Ocean strategies like completely new strategic horizon built on a competitive frame. Use of robots in manufacturing plants and distribution centres, laser technology

in healthcare, virtual space learning in education and digitalisation in public distribution are some of the examples. An operations manager who is oriented in managing his business strategically must be clear of strategic focus to base and ensure openness for each of the philosophy of strategic thinking.

2. Decision areas: Though there are innumerous strategic decision situations, we have selected four key areas of operations strategy decisions for detailed understanding in this book. These are four pillars of operations strategy and there are a few support areas around the same which are also depicted here.
   a. Product/service offering and innovation: This is one of the foremost decision situations in operations strategy. Product/service offering could be demand driven or supply driven. Both require competitive conditioning for achieving sustainability.

      For example, a generic commodity like sugar or cement may be mostly demand driven. But it requires some supply conditions as well like locational advantage, efficient processing for cost and quality competitiveness and so on. On the other hand, Apple Inc and Dell computers have demonstrated how supply, distribution and product innovation and streamlining operations can provide strategic advantage to a player. Apple Inc's innovation on iTunes for music and later iPods, laptops and phones took market by storm, making the company top among Fortune 100. Apple IOS and strategies around the same were critical of its success. Similarly, Dell Computers with pull based supply chain network for mass customisation of laptops and computers bought by customers was a phenomenal strategic move which was a game changer in the industry then. Customers were delighted that they could configure their product and get it delivered in less than a week (5 days was the service time).

      Similarly in India, one could see products and services being offered with strategic bent of mind and there had been a few phenomenal innovations.

      One may look at some of the product and service offering and relevance of operations strategy. One of the interesting products is elevators and escalators in India in the last two to three decades. High rise building in India are of recent phenomenon and elevators and escalators in commercial places had been far less and few till recently. When there was market change of using better floor space index and authorities permitting high rise building of four floors and above, the market was on a boom. But this opportunity is much localised. This is because in case of international standards, high rise are of different level. When companies like Schindler came into India, they had to adopt their product offering to Indian conditions. Their product engineering, designing and supply of components may not have been synchronised to this market, whereas a local player like Johnson Lifts was well-established. It was a challenge for the latter as well as they had to compete with international players and ensure that their market share is not being taken over by competition.

      Another interesting product is about water which is potable and consumed by humans and used in institutional processing. There are two set of products which have caught up well in business to consumers (B2C) segment, namely water purifiers and/or filtered water which is installed for retail households and used for consumption. The other is the packaged water which is popularly branded as "mineral" water. Two decades ago, these products were there only for affluent. Today, every common man has access to these products and prefers premium packaged water bottle brands like Aquafina and Kinley belonging to companies like Pepsi and Coke India. Water purifiers are again in a highly competitive space where these two brands with large bubble pack compete along with filter installations of Kent, Aquaguard, Havel's and so on. One may go on listing more such products!

      In service business as well, such initiatives regarding offering and innovation have been successfully implemented. In the last three decades, Speed Post by Postal department has been one of the highest valued fair priced services in the offering for delivering documents and small parcels. The department has been able to network its extensive postal office network, sorting stations and assets for transportation and human resources. There are a number of healthcare, insurance, financial services, education and so on where such instances are observed.

      Thus, strategising portfolio of products and services to be offered and ability to innovate new products and services would be key strategic role of operations management team.

b. Technology: Selection of appropriate technology for manufacture, processing or assembly and even for service business is an important operations strategy decision. Technology chosen would impact quality of output, manufacturing/assembly or process efficiency, and resource productivity. Economies of scale in production and other functions are traditionally linked to deployment of appropriate technology. Few examples of technology driven operations strategy which has led to a change of competitive landscape are given below.

In case of cement industry in India, technology adoption happened in phases. First in early stages, companies were manufacturing cement using wet process, wherein raw material was made into slurry and then in a kiln, clinker formulation were to happen. This was inefficient as it used substantial amount of power to vaporise water particles to ensure binding power. Then, the industry had pursued technology upgradation, in a short duration which was in late 1970s, a process called semi dry process. The World Bank encouraged Indian cement firms during this time to adopt from international technological base, namely dry process where water consumption was nil for milling section and power consumption was reduced drastically. Further it helped in adoption of automation of process section after discharge from kiln. All these technological advancements increased the normal capacity of the plant. Firms which could adopt this operations strategy, could grow faster and establish lead position in competitive conditions of the industry.

Interesting technological advancement can be seen in manufacture of sugar. This is not with respect to processing of cane juice but the auxiliary power generation which is used for providing energy to mill drivers and steam to vessels for condensation and crystallisation. Earlier era of manufacture used low pressure boiler and the technology was designed to use bagasse from crushing cane to be burnt for being self-reliant towards electric power and steam for the plant. Since 1970s, 400 plus sugar plants in India have switched to high pressure boilers and deployed matching steam turbines so that they jointly generate electricity which can be supplied to the power grid. Under current circumstances, this technology option for auxiliary plant has become a competitive driver for sugar manufacturing.

In number of warehouses, one can look at automated loaders, stocking stations and retrievers replacing humans and improving efficiency. Further, robotics deployment is expected to be significant in years to come especially in advanced countries where labour is scarce. The trend has already started. Similarly, one can see that automation in line assembly of plants is increasing phenomenally to improve productivity, resource efficiency, consistency of output and quality improvement reducing rejections. This is seen in manufacture of electronic goods like mobile phones, laptops, home electronics and consumer durables. Similarly, line upgrades through automated processes and robots are being implemented in automotive sector, especially in developed countries. Germany, Japan and the United States of America are likely pioneers in taking this trend ahead with changing landscape of technology adoption in operations.

Service operations are also widely benefiting out of technology advancement for improving operating efficiency. Easiest to visualise is the banking transaction which has changed over a decade wherein e-cheques are more common than physical cheques for payments. Increasingly, customers are relying on ATMs rather than the teller at the bank branches! All such developments have an impact on operations strategy of the banks and improved their competitive capability. Similarly, managing savings and personal investment has changed as today they are done through websites, portals and virtual access modes using mobile phones. Data are available dynamically to take decisions. Further quality of advisory service towards managing savings and investments has improved significantly. This is mainly because firms give such support services at a click of button on a computer and the same are accessible in smartphones as well. Investor community is better connected through social media and thus operations strategy of any firm providing such service needs to be cognizant of technology proliferation. Healthcare and education are also deploying technological advancement in operations for servicing the customers. Quality of service and customer experience is directly related to technology deployment for operations. When did you last hear about an invasive cataract surgery in an urban area in India? They are rare nowadays.

c. Capacity and facility location is another important set of operations strategy decision that a firm would take towards achieving competitive edge. Capacity and facility location are to be seen as both independently and mutually influencing factors. As an operations strategist, it is important to understand capacity sizing decisions as there is a need to understand market forces and capacity decisions determine supply factors. At the same time, it is also influenced by cost of production as fixed cost contribution is linked to capacity size and after a point, per unit of fixed cost lowers and marginal factors are more of ability to generate demand and marginal costing determined by variable costs. In most of the industry, the capital cost of setting up a normal capacity of plant and the incremental capital cost is generally less than proportionate. We would see detailed analysis later when we discuss the determination of size of plant. Operations strategists must keep these perspectives as one plan for long term decisions.

   Location is another important strategic decision in the area of business and operations perspective is critical for the same. Location determines inbound material logistics and costs thereupon and similarly outbound goods shipment cost and service conditions. Theory would say typically locate a weight losing product close to source material and goods which are driven by volume metric close to market. Though such directives are important and realistic, and detailing of location factors are driven by innumerous and competing factors including global, regional, and domestic and site level conditions. An operations strategist must evaluate locational factors and relate capacity decisions so that logistics costs as well as aftermarket service cost are optimised. Capacity decision and location decision are interrelated, especially in those commodities which may need to be located close to customer centres.

d. Designing supply network is another important strategic decision which an operations manager would be involved in. It is one where a focal firm establishes a supply network to satisfy customer demand. This network has upstream linkages of supply of material, components and services, intra firm assembly, manufacture, process or conversion and downstream movement of products through channel partners to the ultimate customer. Typically, supply network is referred with a firm that takes ownership of creating value around a product or service to an ultimate customer. However, a focal firm could be a trader of material who imports raw material and supply to many producers who in turn develop a new supply network around a product using that imported material. For example, in India, there used to be importers of coal when buyers used to use coal for captive power generation for their manufacture or processing. In such cases, two supply networks were linked but not a common one. Similarly, a retail chain can sell downstream products of manufactured consumer goods and compete with manufacturers supply network as well. Thus, operations strategists must understand that firms compete through supply network and challenge/opportunity is in creating such network which optimises value creation for customers and value appropriation for all intermediary participants across the network.

   Thus, the four decision areas namely product/service offering and innovation; technology deployment; capacity and facility location; and supply network design are significant drivers for establishing competitive advantage by an operations strategist.

3. Philosophy like traditional, resource led or emergent strategies is a binder for the above four decision areas. A firm could decide to follow a traditional strategic planning methodology like building a vision, mission and goal and from working on a SWOT matrix, selecting a strategy to implement based on the same and execute the strategy through well-defined strategic management process. Alternatively, a firm can go by resource led operations strategy. For example, IT services industry in India has gained by locational advantage of time zone to serve Western European and North American markets and comparative cost efficiency of workforce. This again within India got clustered in states due to good human resources as a result of development in educational institutional resources and ecosystem. Similarly, growth opportunities in minerals and mining sector happened because of resource base and the ability to exploit the same commercially. An interesting fact is that though minerals and high value stones are widely available in Central Africa, not all of them could exploit the value as efficiently as South Africa. Middle East and Russia are able to exploit the availability of crude and energy resources as well as the USA in the energy sector. Thus a firm can map

resource advantage and pursue operations strategy accordingly. Apart from these two viewpoints, strategic decision orientation, a third view point, is emergent strategies wherein firms are forced to pursue highly responsive and market led opportunities which could be due to technology development or customer preference or both. In India, we have observed that in consumer electronics, especially home electronic durable goods like air conditioners, refrigerators, televisions and music systems, proliferation of product functionality and choices have taken the market by storm. Firms which could adopt emergent strategies are those who survived and grew while many succumbed to competition. Similar conditions prevail in financial services, insurance and personal wealth creation where new products and services are considering customers and the ability to pursue strong operations strategy along with marketing strategy is what makes a firm stay ahead in competition! One can list numerous such emergent strategies in communication industry, mobile phones and so on. An important note here is that spirit of strategic thinking and choices are not limited by framework and under no condition one would supersede others. It is important to pursue a balanced approach.

4. Another important aspect in the framework of operations strategic decision is that of global strategy to be pursued by the firm. Around two or three decades ago, such a global business decision would have been construed more as a corporate or a business decision. A functional area approach to globalisation of business gained momentum in the era of technology explosion in business. Digitalisation drive and rationalisation of World Trade Agreements have created a congenial environment of globalisation of business. Before these developments, only selected international firms who had capital, established marketing infrastructure and policies and well-structured corporate leadership could pursue such strategies. IT growth showed how startups and small and medium scale companies or niche product/service firms can pursue global strategies successfully.

   Given this context, we may now discuss global strategy as a part of operations framework. First, decision area is that of product and/or service offering and innovation for a global market. For an operations strategist, it would be a challenge to develop a unique product or service that could be accepted across markets at a price point to provide normal profits if not excessive one! To overcome this challenge, one should focus on leading markets and after initial success, it is customised for entry into markets on relative importance and entry opportunity guided by environmental factors like socio, economic, political, ecological and so on. There are numerous examples of such products like that of Apple Inc, Samsung and so on. One can relate many other examples to this like that of computers, laptops, automobiles mainly cars, agricultural machinery and equipment, banking, insurance, financial services, transportation services, software and so on. It has been a challenge for operations strategist to custom fit the product. For example, tractors sold in USA cannot be manufactured or marketed in India because land conditions and holdings are limitations for India compared to USA. Similarly, in service business like luxury holidays and vacation service such complexity exists. The range of operations which are possible in such vacation (leisure) hotels in two markets would vary widely. Even if it is possible that international holiday travelers are likely to use such a service, operational constraints would fail to create the same ambience to ensure same value for money spent across locations. Thus, a global strategy for such services tries to harmonise customer experience in different locations and is required to localise global offering.

   This is how global operations strategy would consider product and service offering and innovation.

   Next, global strategy must synchronise with the choice of technology. Though there is a tradeoff between capital intensity and other resource component, especially of labour, in selecting technology, global strategy would arrive at an optimal resource mix for an appropriate technology choice for the global presence. For example, a car manufacturer based out of Chennai in India focusses on domestic as well as overseas market. It may have to clearly understand the focus of overseas market. Is it going to be emerging markets which are similar to that of India in auto sector or to low end small car segments of global market? Or would it put some of the popular models on global market to take competition head on? Technology selection and post-sale service would be critical in such approaches.

Another intriguing question on global operations strategy is that of determining location and capacity sizing. Though basic factors like resource endowments, demand and supply conditions, logistics infrastructure and managerial talent could drive decision making, environmental factors like macro-economic conditions, sociological, legal, cultural and environmental conditions would drive such decisions. There would be a few prime drivers of the decision for locating production facility in a centre and distribution points. However, a final choice of allocation of demand to supply points as a part of operations tactical decision and strategic decision to put up a facility are more guided by other auxiliary factors too! Further, the firm's stakes are high and competitive edge is determined by managing a portfolio of products and locations for fulfiling customer demand points, for given set of operations performance parameters.

Global operations strategy decision would also involve supply chain network alignment and how to establish network of nodes and flows for serving an ultimate customer in a global supply network perspective. Most of the other decision areas are predominantly related to focal firm and its customers.

Perforance Factors and Strategic Fit

Any strategic initiative is meaningful only if it is linked to outcome and measured. Some of these parameters are cost; quality; dependability; speed and flexibility. It is always difficult to state precisely in which order all these are to be picked. Do operations strategists focus on all five parameters? Is there a link between industry maturity and choice of performance metrics with respect to operations strategy? Do firms within an industry have differentiated focus on these parameters when they have to decide on a strategic fit? What kind of business environmental factors drive such a strategic fit? Finally, what is the role of culture and leadership in linking strategic focus and choice of parameters in a firm?

It may be noted that the five measurement factors, namely cost; quality; dependability; speed and flexibility could be divergent and competing to make a choice. For example, focus on excellence in quality process which is the benchmark for standards could be at a cost and may be divergent to cost focus in the industry where mediocre peer standards would also be acceptable to customers. The problem could be because of product classification to satisfy a want versus product aesthetic to serve the need for a certain segment of customers. The latter may tend to be a standard in due course! The path towards is the contradiction in operations strategy and challenge is how to take both divergent factors or pursue either of the strategic goals.

Let us look at the case of Apple Inc, whose products and services which are at premium compared to many such similar product and service providers. But that is the strategic positioning taken by Apple and their operations strategy, especially development of new products and services and protecting them with intellectual property rights. And owning proprietary helps them to hold a niche position. If one may look, there is a huge dependability factor in Apple Inc products which is positive for customers and the product performance has been reflective of the same. However, speed to market and flexibility to avail service may not be easy unless it is through the proprietary platform. Thus, it is not necessary that strategic fit of operations strategy must be singular focussed and fits in all decision areas and performance factors. As long as it gives a competitive edge and overall sustainability to the firm, portfolio of choice may be pursued.

On a link between industry maturity and choice of performance metrics with respect to operations strategy, there is a strong association between the two. After any industry reaches a level of maturity in its lifecycle wherein demand and supply is stabilised and product and service features provide little scope for increasing the intensity of competition, the firms would settle for choice of operations strategic decision areas and performance factors so that they hold on to their market share and profitability. For example, automotive industry, as of the decade 2010, is far more settled though new product development for Industry 4.0 like driverless cars and auto pilot mode. Contemporary features are highly componentised with the use of electronic parts with levels of components and easily controlled and tracked. Second, cars are quality focussed and most of them have adopted certain quality processes and implemented them across supply network. These are more mandatory competitive features rather than differentiators! One observes similar trends in banking and financial services industry in India in the current stage where technology deployment and web based services have been the way forward. These firms have introduced dependability factor, speed to market, cost focus, quality and to certain extent flexibility. If any player wants to survive in this industry, he must achieve such a level of maturity to stay in the competition! Thus, industry phase would be a factor. There are a number of introduction and growth stage examples which can be thought of and would be discussed appropriately in the book.

Further, within an industry, firms have differentiated focus on these parameters when they have to decide on a strategic fit. As mentioned earlier, Apple Inc has focussed on leadership based on quality and dependability while another firm like Samsung might have focussed on speed to market, cost and flexibility as key factors. For the latter, quality and dependability would be at certain threshold level. Not that the latter has compromised but has created conscious strategic positioning to serve different segments of the market. These are visible in different industries.

In India one can observe home furnishing industry having different levels of positioning like while certain brands are at premium segment based on quality and dependability factors, others may be cost focussed and could be serving a larger market segment. Similarly, there are innumerable examples in service industries like hospitality, restaurants, healthcare and education and so on. It may be noted here that these are driven by the overall strategic positioning that a firm would like to take. Moreover, it has to be interfaced with other functional strategies like that of marketing and finance. Marketing identifies white spaces in the market and drives operations while finance guides on financial viability and funding options for pursuing such operating strategies.

Next, business environmental factors drive such a strategic fit. Business environmental factors are political, societal, economic, legal, environmental and technological. Political factors impact operations strategic decision areas like design of supply network, locations and so on. Firms may find certain countries and economies that may not be politically stable, though cost focus in such geographies could be an advantage. In earlier era, firms would have avoided certain countries because of such political conditions and their leaning towards communist policies. Now that it has changed, still certain regions have limitations on political factors. Such factors can limit flexibility as a performance factor as labour laws and duties and taxes can follow protectionism. Thus, not only political and economic factors matter but other environmental factors may also impact the firm. Ecological/physical conditions may not encourage operations in certain locations and hence operations strategy must reckon the same. Growth of IT services industry in India was largely favoured by locational advantage in the longitude which helped to serve North America and Western Europe. Availability of infrastructure like education, mainly scientific resources helps US pharmaceutical companies to stay ahead in competition. Country like India has a large number of graduates in science, especially in chemistry, which supports operations strategy of locating generic drug companies. While mentioning about economic conditions, apart from taxes and duties, other macro policies like credit policy, management of inflation, foreign exchange, corporate income tax and fiscal incentives would matter. One may have noticed how setting up of free trade zones and other economic incentives for attracting investment has influenced operations strategy. Performance factors like cost focus must consider such conditions. Thus, business environment would influence the choice of operations strategy and balance of performance factors for the same.

Finally, culture and leadership have linkage with strategic focus and choice of parameters of a firm. Many firms have achieved excellence in quality process and thereby, an operations strategy differentiator because of culture imbibed in excellence and role of leadership in driving the same. It is commonly observed in many automotive companies and auto tier I and II companies in India. Annexure 1.1 gives the list of companies and leaders who have won the award. Similarly, culture and leadership drive towards cost management as well. It is noticed how Toyota, in spite of quality focus, consistently through its expert production management system, namely Toyota Production System (TPS), has been effective in cost management. There are a number of other firms in India as well who have achieved such success.

Thus, operations strategy decision areas need to look for strategic fit and structure its performance factors accordingly.

Implementation and Excellence Approach

Operations strategic framework can be complete only when implementation of decision areas and performance metrics with excellence approach as a part of process are adhered to. It is bit of conflict in us when we combine implementation and excellence approach in operations. The reason being quality as a performance factor imbibes excellence approach for top notch companies. Then, why should we club implementation and excellence approach? The rationale being that while quality and excellence approach can be clubbed only by a few top firms, it is important that all firms while implementing operations strategy follow rigor of an excellence approach as defined by different framework. More than being an achiever, striving for being extraordinary operations strategy focussed company in the chosen product or service and market is important for every firm and hence the stand is taken.

Strategy implementation requires policy, linking of budgets and strategy, deployment information system and feedback mechanism, culture, leadership and regular assessment on predefined interval to ensure strategic initiatives are creating competitive edge and a sustainable growth for the firm.

Review meetings at different level from line to board are important. Further, it should have top down and bottom up approaches for effective operations strategic management. There must be a cross-functional team responsible for the same and the operations head must also be a part of the overall corporate strategy and strategic business unit level initiatives. Many successful organisations have used tools like balanced score card effectively which would be discussed in this book.

SUMMARY

Operations management is defined as the design, operation, and improvement of the production systems that create the firm's primary products or services. Decisions can be put through three buckets, namely short term ranging from a shift to a week, medium term ranging from a quarter or 3 months to six quarters or 18 months and long term decisions would have impacted over 3 years and above. Looking at the hierarchy of decisions, operations strategic decisions are those which have long term impact; involving substantial amount of capital and decisions are generally not easily reversible or involve another strategic intervention for reversal or rework on decisions. The success of operations strategy fundamentally rests on effectiveness of operations tactical or planning decisions and operations execution. Operations strategic decision framework involves creating vision; mission, goals, objectives, values and beliefs. Then, certain decision areas like facility location; selection of product and service to offer and innovation; capacity planning; technology choice and designing a supply network. One may look at global strategy as encompassing all these areas of decision making. It is noted here that a strategic choice could be based on traditional strategic decision making processes or through emergent strategies or any of the contemporary philosophies of strategic decision making. Then such process needs to look into performance factors like cost, quality, dependability, flexibility and speed. Some of the factors could be divergent when operations strategic decisions need to be taken in any of the areas mentioned earlier. This is where appropriate strategic fit needs to be driven and a cross-functional team must work for ensuring that appropriate strategic orientation is achieved for ensuring competitive edge and sustainability of growth. Finally, implementation of the plan and an excellence approach need to be adopted as being defined by different benchmarking and quality frameworks.

Key Ters

1. Operations management: Operations management is concerned with converting materials and labour into goods and services as efficiently as possible to maximise the profit of an organisation.
2. Operations strategy: A plan specifying how an organisation will allocate resources in order to support infrastructure for manufacture or process of products and/or services. An operations strategy is typically driven by the overall business strategy of the organisation, and is designed to maximise the effectiveness of production and support elements while minimising costs.
3. Tactical planning: Tactical planning takes a company's strategic plan and sets forth specific short-term actions and plans. It is more for allocation of resources to a production and/or distribution plan.
4. Emergent strategy: Emergent strategy is the process of identifying unexpected outcomes from the execution of corporate strategy and then learning to integrate those unexpected outcomes into future corporate plans.
5. Blue Ocean strategy: Blue ocean strategy generally refers to the creation by a company of a new, uncontested market space that makes competitors irrelevant and creates new consumer value often while decreasing costs. It was introduced by W. Chan Kim and Renée Mauborgne.
6. Cost focus strategy: Porter called the generic strategies "Cost Leadership" (no frills), "Differentiation" (creating uniquely desirable products and services) and "Focus" (offering a specialised service in a niche market). He then subdivided the focus strategy into two parts, "Cost Focus" and "Differentiation Focus." Thus cost focus strategy is offering no frills product or service to a niche market.
7. Excellence model: It is often described as outstanding practices in managing an organisation and achieving results, all based on a set of fundamental concepts or values. These practices have evolved into models for how a world class organisation should operate.
8. Flexibility in operations: The operational flexibility is defined as an index which integrates both the mix and volume flexibility. Operative data and the associated costs are used to determine the optimal level of operational flexibility in the flow shop manufacturing system. It works equally for service operations as well.
9. Quality systems: A quality management system (QMS) is a formalised system that documents process procedures, and responsibilities for achieving quality policies and objectives. A QMS helps coordinate and direct an organisation's activities to meet customer and regulatory requirements and improve its effectiveness and efficiency on a continuous basis.
10. Dependability in operations: This is to measure how dependable the company is when it comes to timely delivery of products to its customers. The product's ability to function in an intended way consistently over a reasonable period of time is also a measure of its dependability.
11. Global operations strategy: Global operations strategy as defined in business terms is an organisation's strategic orientation of its operations to globalisation. A business can employ a global operations strategy to reap the rewards in a worldwide market by managing demand and supply through deployment of resources across markets and regions.
12. Vision: Vision statement describes the desired future position of the company.
13. Mission: A mission statement defines the company's business, its objectives and its approach to reach those objectives.
14. Goals and objectives: A goal is a description of a destination and a long-term outcome to be achieved. An objective is a measure of the progress that is needed to get to the destination. Objectives tend to be single achievable outcomes. They are concrete in statement and purpose.
15. Values and beliefs: Values describe what an organisation desires or seeks to achieve. Values such as "loyalty", "truthfulness", "charity", "integrity" and "honesty" are a few examples. On the other hand, beliefs are judgments about ourselves and the world around us. They are usually generalisations.

CONCEPT REVIEW QUESTIONS

1. What do you understand by operations management? What is the scope for a firm to drive competitive advantage?
2. Elucidate with example the importance of operations management in manufacturing as well as service business. Highlight areas of commonness and differentiation between the two.
3. What do you understand by operations strategy? Explain the scope and importance of the same for a firm.
4. Briefly explain operations strategy framework that may be used by a firm to manage its operations.
5. Describe strategic management and its process. Also explain corporate level, strategic business unit level and functional level strategies with an example.
6. Describe time span of decision and hierarchy with example, especially in the area of operations.
7. Discuss four key operations strategic decision areas and give examples that you are familiar with.
8. What are the performance factors which an operations strategist must focus on while crafting operations strategy? Explain with example.
9. "Performance factors could be competing and pose challenge for a firm's strategist to prioritize". Elucidate with an example.
10. "Firms in the same industry need not have similar operations strategy decision focus and drive of performance factors". Elucidate with an example.
11. Describe global operations strategic initiatives which a firm can take. You may cite an example.
12. "Implementation and excellence approach are of paramount importance for effective operations strategy". Analyse.

CRITICAL THINKING QUESTIONS

1. Using the information given in the exhibit on Lava International in the beginning of the chapter, analyse competitive advantage the firm has carved for itself in the segment it has focussed on, in light of the operations strategy pursued. You may use industry competitive information available online.
2. Cement industry has used split location to serve deficit market from supply centre using locational conditions and supply network. Explain in detail with an example like that of Ramco cements or any other which you may choose.
3. Nokia had set up a plant in Chennai in India. What were the business environment factors that were favourable for the choice? Why did the firm close the same later? Critically analyse the same from an operations strategist's perspective. Bring in globalisation related issues in support of your analysis.

PROJECT ASSIGNMENTS

1. Select an industry with which you are familiar. Choose the top three firms and analyse the operations strategic orientation these companies might have followed. Discussions are for an academic purpose and hence make required assumptions to support your analysis. Use data and information from online sources.

2. Visit a leading food restaurant chain in your city. For example, at Chennai, Hotel Saravana Bhavan or Sangeetha Vegetarian Restaurant or Adyar Ananda Bhavan. Identify the key performance factors it has which in your opinion can be considered as a part of its operations strategy. Try to do a validation check with stakeholders like customers, restaurant manager or owner and with competition.
3. Choose a manufacturing company which is a leader in its chosen area of operation. Analyse its operations, strategic orientation from corporate, SBU and unit level and draw your inference on how and why you think the firm has a competitive advantage over other players in the industry.

REFERENCES

1. Iyer, Ananth V., Seshadri, Sridhar and Vasher, Roy (2009). *Toyota Supply Chain Management*; Tata McGrawHill Education Private Limited.
2. Bhrgava R. C. and Seetha (2010). *The Maruti Story*; Collins Business.
3. Chandrasekaran N. and Ananthanarayanan P. S. (2011). *Strategic Management*; Oxford University Press of India.
4. Liker, Jeffery K. (2004). *The Toyota Way, Toyota Supply Chain Management*; Tata McGrawHill Education Private Limited.
5. Dornier, Phillippe-Pierre, Ernst, Ricardo, Fender, Michel, and Kouvelis, Panos (1998). *Global Operations and Logistics*; Wiley India.
6. Porter, Michael E. *Competitive Advantage*, Free Press, 1985, Export edition 2004.
7. Holstein, William J. "Six Keys to a Winning Manufacturing Strategy -How John Deere bucked industrial trends to become an international growth star", *Strategy + Business,* 28 May 2008.
8. Kaushik, Manu. "Darkness to light; How a smart turnaround strategy helped Havells to make a comeback", https://www.businesstoday.in/magazine/case-study/smart-turnaround-strategy-helped-havells/story/197235.html.
9. http://www.isqnet.org/deming-prize-winner/ accessed on 21 October 2018.

Annexure 1.1 Companies and leaders who have won Deming award from India

India	
Year	**Details**
2015	1. THE DEMING GRAND PRIZE
	National Engineering Industries Limited (India) Mr. Rohit Saboo, President and CEO
	2. THE DEMING PRIZE FOR INDIVIDUALS
	Mr. Tadaaki Jagawa Advisor, Toyota Motor Corporation
	Executive Adviser to the Board, Hino Motors, Ltd.
	3. THE DEMING PRIZE
	Cataler Corporation (Japan)
	Mr. Hiroaki Sunakawa, President
	CPRAM Company Limited, Ready to Eat Food Business (Thailand)
	Mr. Wisade Wisidwinyoo, President
	GS Yuasa Corporation, Industrial Battery Production Division, Industrial Batteries & Power Sources Business Unit (Japan)
	Mr. Jun Tabuchi, Division Manager, Industrial Battery Production Division, Industrial Batteries & Power Sources Business Unit
2014	1. The Deming Prize for Individuals
	Dr. Kazuyuki Suzuki
	Professor, the University of Electro-Communications (Japan)
	2. The Deming Distinguished Service Award for Dissemination and Promotion (Overseas) -
	Mr. Kan Trakulhoon
	President & CEO, Siam Cement Group (Thailand)
	3. The Deming Prize
	GC America Inc. (U.S.A.)
	Mr. Yutaka Suzuki, President & COO
	Sekiso Corporation (Japan)
	Mr. Shinji Yamada, President
	Mahindra & Mahindra Limited, Mahindra Powerol Business (India)
	Mr. Ashok Sharma, Chief Executive
2013	THE DEMING GRAND PRIZE
	Rane Brake Lining Limited
	THE DEMING PRIZE
	RSB Transmissions(I) Limited, Auto Division(Jamshedpur(Unit 1), Pune & Pant Nagar Plant)

2012	THE DEMING GRAND PRIZE
	Tata Steel Limited (India)
	Mr. H M Nerurkar, Managing Director
	Rane (Madras) Limited (India)
	Mr. L Ganesh, Chairman Lucas-TVS Limited (India)
	Mr.T. K. Balaji, Managing Director
	DEMING DISTINGUISHED SERVICE AWARD FOR DISSEMINATION AND PROMOTION (OVERSEAS)
	Mr. Janak Mehta
	Chairman & Managing Director, TQM International Pvt. Ltd.
	THE DEMING PRIZE
	SRF Limited, Chemicals Business (India)
	Mr. Roop Salotra, President and CEO
	Mahindra & Mahindra Limited, Farm Equipment Sector, Swaraj Division (India)
	Mr. Bishwambhar Mishra, Chief Executive
2011	Sanden Vikas (India) Limited
2010	National Engineering Industries Limited (India)
2008	Tata Steel Limited (India)
2007	Asahi India Glass Limited, Auto Glass Division (India)
	Rane (Madras) Limited (India)
	Reliance Industries Limited, Hazira Manufacturing Division (India)
2005	Krishna Maruti Limited, Seat Division
	Rane Engine Valves Limited
	Rane TRW Steering Systems Limited, Steering Gear Division
2004	SRF Limited., Industrial Synthetics Business
	Lucas TVS Limited
	Indo-Gulf Fertilisers Limited
2003	Brakes India Limited., Foundry Division
	Mahindra and Mahindra Limited, Farm Equipment Sector
	Rane Brake Lining Limited
	Sona Koya Steering Systems Limited
	Birla Cellousic, Kharach-A Unit of Grasim Industries Limited (India)
2002	TVS Motor Company Limited
	Hi-Tech Carbon GMPD
2001	Sundaram Brake Linings Limited.
1998	Sundaram-Clayton Limited, Brakes Division

Source: http://www.isqnet.org/deming-prize-winner/ accessed on 10 August 2018.

CHAPTER 2

Developing and Managing Operations Strategy

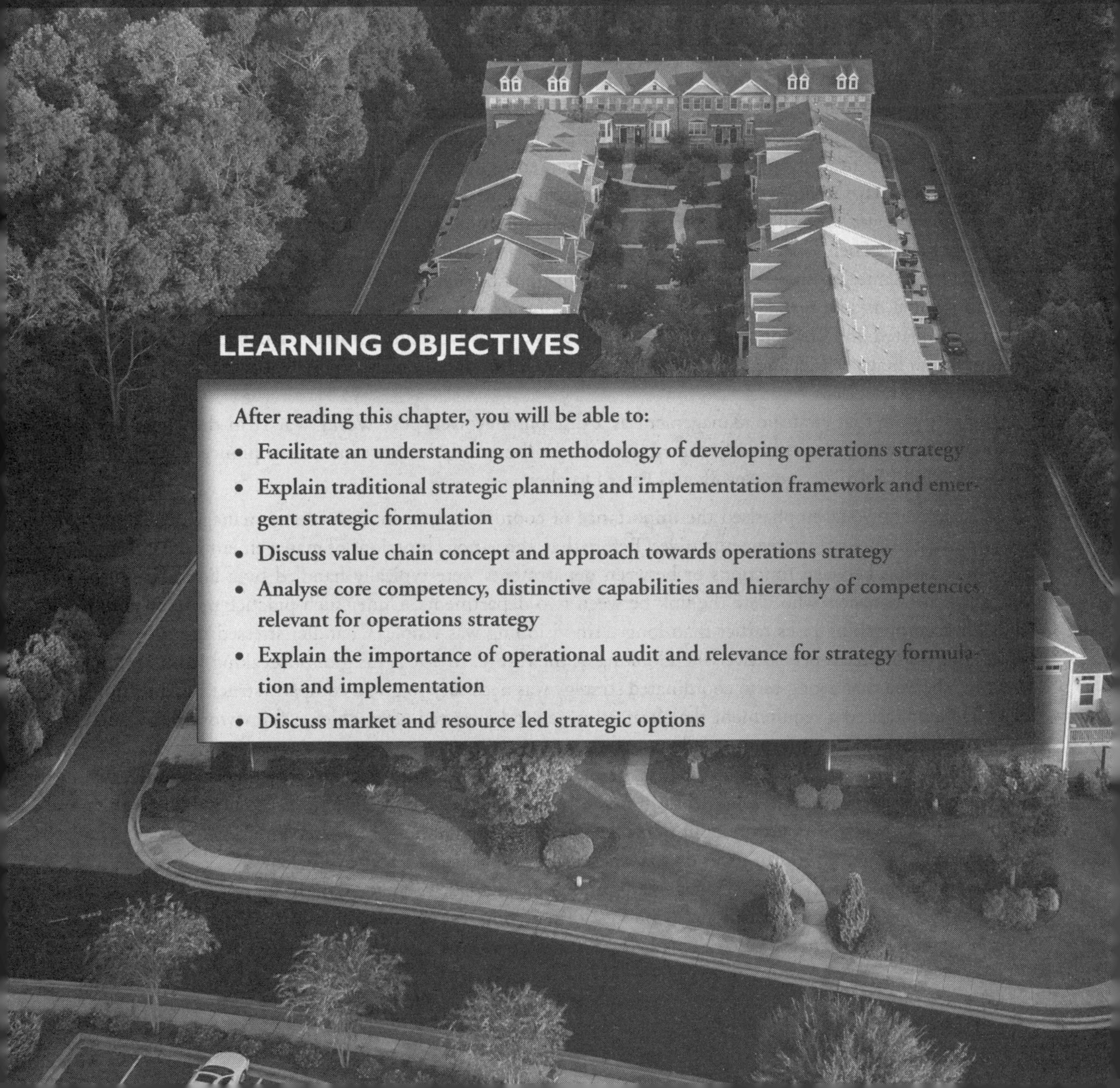

LEARNING OBJECTIVES

After reading this chapter, you will be able to:

- Facilitate an understanding on methodology of developing operations strategy
- Explain traditional strategic planning and implementation framework and emergent strategic formulation
- Discuss value chain concept and approach towards operations strategy
- Analyse core competency, distinctive capabilities and hierarchy of competencies relevant for operations strategy
- Explain the importance of operational audit and relevance for strategy formulation and implementation
- Discuss market and resource led strategic options

Introduction

Strategic management involves formal analytical approach to economic perspective of a corporate growth and profitability. This will be true for functional areas like operations, marketing, finance, human relations and information technology. One may have to have an approach, including social aspects like culture, leadership and competence required, to face uncertain situations and ensure growth in manufacture of products and distribution of products and services. With varying definitions and approaches, different approaches will be discussed here. This ranges from traditional aspects of starting from structured approach towards operations strategic management to modern aspects to facilitate a learner for a thorough understanding on the subject and pursue more analytical approach to decision making.

Methodology of Developing Operations Strategy

Typically, as a functional strategy, this may go through traditional strategic planning process which could be top-down method. Corporate strategy team could have a group of members who can participate to develop operations strategy. This group will have members from corporate strategy team, SBU level member, SBU leadership team members like plant head (overall plant in-charge), marketing head, manufacturing head and finance head. The group may also have invitees from quality, supply chain and representatives of workmen on select basis for soliciting their views. Typically, in a top-down approach, ambitions for operations excellence would be set by the Corporate Board. Then, operations strategists go through a formal traditional strategic management process to implement the same. At times, there would be bottom-up approach, wherein an operating team member or any other functional middle management person or even outside stakeholders like suppliers come up with an idea which is evaluated and developed. There are innumerable cases wherein customers' feedback and participation have helped in new product and service development. Here, we are discussing frameworks that are typically used by operations strategists.

One may note that strategic management as a discipline evolved post World War II in the 1950s and 60s. Although there were numerous early contributors to the literature, the most influential pioneers were Alfred D. Chandler, Philip Selznick, Igor Ansoff, and Peter Drucker.

Alfred Chandler (1962) emphasised the importance of coordinating various aspects of management under one encompassing number of strategic initiatives. Before that, the various functions of management were independent silos. Interactions between functions or between departments were typically handled by a boundary position, that is, by the managers who were the link between two departments. Under such practice more of immediate focus for accomplishing tasks rather than long-term visioning was visible. Chandler stressed the importance of considering a long-term perspective when looking at the future. In 1962, his groundbreaking work *Strategy and Structure*, showed that a long-term coordinated strategy was necessary to give a company structure, direction, and focus. He emphasised a requirement that strategy needs to be crafted after which a framework of organisation hierarchy, policy and execution must follow.

According to David (1989), strategic management is the conduct of drafting, implementing and evaluating cross-functional decisions that will enable an organisation to achieve its long-term objectives. This is the most widely used view where various functions of management are brought under one domain using knowledge so that respective management level can focus on managerial effectiveness and resource efficiency.

Around the same time, strategic management process-oriented views emerged in the literature. The lead among them was *Philip Selznick* who introduced the idea of matching the organisation's internal factors with external environmental circumstances (1957). This core idea was developed into SWOT analysis by Learned, Andrews, and others at the Harvard Business School General Management Group. Strengths and weaknesses of the firm are assessed along with the opportunities and threats from the business environment.

Igor Ansoff (1965) further worked on Chandler's ideas by creating a strategy grid that compared market penetration strategies, product development strategies, market development strategies and horizontal and vertical integration and diversification strategies. According to him, management could use these strategies to systematically prepare for the future opportunities and challenges.

Peter Drucker (1954) propounded the concept of management by objectives (MBO) that stressed the importance of setting objectives and work around to achieve those objectives. The procedure of setting objectives and monitoring progress towards them should pervade the entire organisation, top to bottom. Later, he came up with an outstanding contribution by predicting the importance of what today we would call intellectual capital.

Another key development in strategic management came up in 1970s where size, growth and portfolio theory had their influence. The Profit Impact of Marketing Strategies (PIMS) project was started by Sidney Schoeffler working at General Electric in the 1960s. Later in 1970s, Harvard's Management Science administered by the American Strategic Planning Institute took over since 1975. The study identified several strategic variables that typically influence profitability. Some of the most important strategic variables studied were market share, product quality, investment intensity, and service quality which were found to be impacting profitability.

In the 1970s, management researchers extended the theory to product portfolio decisions and managerial strategists extended it to operating division portfolios. Each of a company's operating division was a component of asset in a portfolio. Portfolio theory by BCG and GE focusses on managing investments and operations of each component so that portfolio returns are maximised, and risk reduced.

Another interesting development was that of Japanese model of management and linkage to strategy. The success of Japanese firms was attributed to high capital intensity and productivity; economies of scale; low cost structure; high employee engagement; quality management and high customer focus approach.

Richard Pascale (1981) along with Anthony Athos in *The Art of Japanese Management* claimed that the main reason for Japanese success was their superior management techniques. They divided management into seven aspects, namely strategy, structure, systems, skills, staff, style, and shared values. The first three of the seven Ss were called hard factors and the remaining four factors (skills, staff, style, and shared values) were called soft factors. According to Pascale, the difference between decision making styles was hierarchical in America, and consensus in Japan. He criticised the American businesses because they did not focus on the long-term vision, preferring to apply management fads and theories in silos.

The Industrial Organisational Approach is based on economic theory — dealing with issues like competitive rivalry, resource allocation, economies of scale assumptions — rationality, self-discipline behaviour and profit maximisation. This has traditions of Chamberlin, Joan Robinson and Joe S. Bain who worked extensively on imperfect and monopolistic competition and how firm behaviour influenced profitability of firms and industry. Later in 1970, Richard Caves published a work on the structure of U.S industry which formed the basis for Structure – Conduct – Performance paradigm on which Michael E. Porter developed his work on competitive strategy and later, competitive advantage which are landmark developments in strategic management. Fundamentally, these frameworks are based on economic principles which has focussed on profits or profit equivalent creating intangible assets in case of not for profit organisations. The sociological approach deals primarily with human interactions assumptions — bounded rationality, satisfying behaviour and profit sub-optimality.

Contemporary management thinkers like C. K. Prahalad, in early 1990s, mentioned about core competency as critical for a corporate growth and focus on strategic initiatives. Later, he propounded Bottom of Pyramid theory where an enterprise must look at large volume driven low value but mass production base as engine of growth. Including him, a new generation of theorists discussed about sustainable resources and initiatives, such as green, responsible procurement and ethics across supply network as being the challenge of future because of the issue of limited resources today.

Thus, strategic management involves formal analytical approach to economic perspective of a corporate growth and profitability and soft approach including social aspects like culture, leadership and competence required to face uncertain situations and to ensure growth. With varying definitions and approaches, an analyst must use a balanced approach with emphasis on traditional aspects of starting from structured approach to strategic management to modern aspects to facilitate a learner to have a thorough understanding on the subject and pursue more analytical understanding.

After going through the commentary of different management experts on the importance of strategy, the relevance of strategic management is clear. In the era of technology explosion, process rigor and knowledge centric work culture, strategic initiatives alone can catapult a firm to leadership level in an industry.

Apart from external factors, the following internal benefits also drive a company for adopting a strategic framework:

1. Formal strategic management process allows a firm to anticipate, initiate and influence actions ahead of market. Managements need to be proactive instead of reactive. Senior management executives must figure out constantly such challenges based on competitive intelligence and hence structured strategic sessions become relevant.
2. Formal approach brings enhanced commitment as the system takes care of setting of objectives, initiatives, targets, action plan and review. When this process is open and transparent, it brings commitment from all stakeholders involved in strategic management process.
3. Similarly, a formal approach ensures greater productivity not only in strategic management meetings but also across functions. Managers beyond their attention on strategy, also focus on implementation. Thus, effective strategies and better implementation makes this relevant.

Steps in Strategic Manageent Proces s

Traditionally, strategic management began with developing vision, mission and goals for the company. But today, by and large, a top-down method is adopted through most of the companies, although in certain cases bottom–up approach is also an essential approach. This is followed by SWOT analysis wherein the firm looks at external environment, namely political, sociological, cultural, environmental and legal relevant for the organisational goals. Similarly, an in-depth analysis of internal factors, especially on resources and competency is critical. This would help one to identify the gaps and work on the same so that the organisational goals are met.

Contemporary strategic management thinkers lay a lot of stress on resources-based strategy as resources acquisition and allocation are immensely important for the success of an organisation.

Henry Mintzberg suggests that the traditional way of thinking about strategy implementation focusses only on deliberate strategies. Minztberg claims that some organisations begin implementing strategies before they clearly articulate mission, goals, or objectives. In this case, strategy implementation precedes strategy formulation. According to him, such strategies that unfold in this way are emergent strategies. Implementation of emergent strategies involves the allocation of resources even though an organisation has not explicitly chosen its strategies. Organisations under current circumstances are compelled to use both deliberate and emergent strategies.

Globalisation and open markets during the last three decades have brought a host of entrepreneurs. To pre-empt competition, corporates empirically start allocating resources and start implementing strategies on an emergent basis. Subsequently, full comprehension of business and competition leads to deliberate strategy formulation involving corrections to emergent strategy.

Strategic management in India is more critical and compelling because of liberalisation, globalisation, entrepreneurial development, technology absorption and breakthrough. The IT revolution has shrunk the world and has brought the developed and developing countries closer and has made them more interdependent.

Communication has become instant and has opened new opportunities in transferring operational businesses. Two other important factors which led to application of contemporary management practices in India is availability of qualified manpower from premier institutions and commitment to quality process which requires the rigor of planning and implementation.

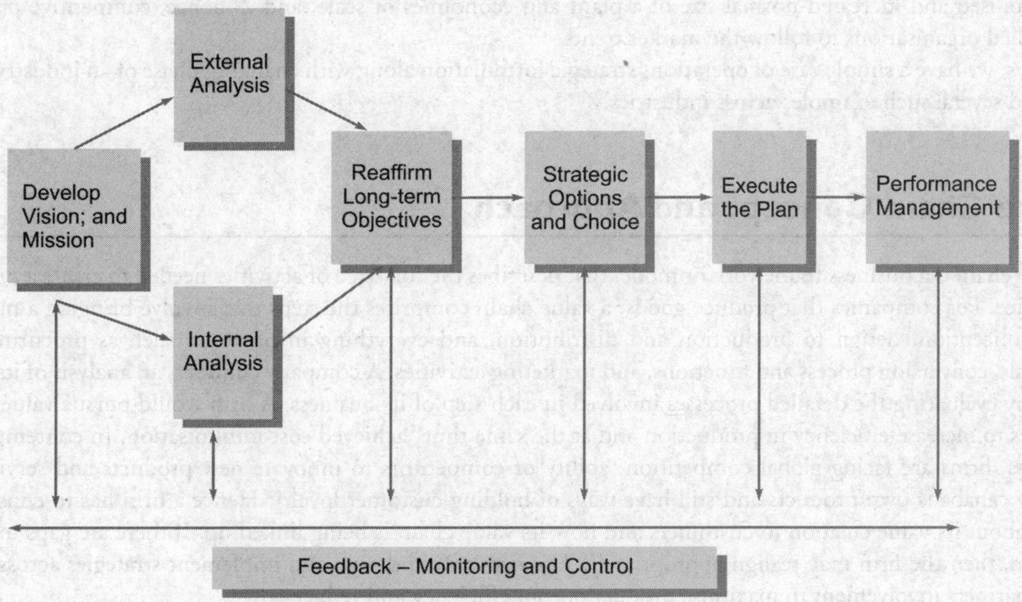

FIGURE 2.1 Strategic management process

The above approaches apply for operations strategy decision as well. For example, a sugar plant was operating at a capacity of 2500 tonnes of cane crushing per day. Being a seasonal industry, it used to operate for about 230 days in a year. Sugar production months are between October and September synchronising with monsoon. Plants typically start around October last week and go up to April end and complete about 180 days of crushing. They try to do a special season of 50 days in August and September. This plant wanted to develop a joint product of generating co-generation of power by deploying high pressure boiler and matching turbine so that it can export to grid excess power which can go up to 25 MW regularly on operating days. If it can use alternate fuel, it can operate captive power plant up to 340 days in a year and during sugar off-season, it can export 28 – 29 MW. To initiate this operations strategy, the company must do the following:

1. This is a plant level functional strategy and operations strategy formulation and implementation must be at the level of plant which could be a strategic business unit.
2. This decision is primarily an operations strategic decision involving the engineering process and utility managers along with cane manager who is responsible for procurement of raw material. However, ultimate decision ownership will be with plant head.
3. Capital budgeting team along with finance prepare a feasibility report having both technical and financial feasibilities and submit to board or its investment committee which would appraise board on the decision. A key decision like this which involves transition from one facility and in the same location replacement happens for a new set of plant and equipment for crushing double the quantity of cane, processing of juices and crystallisation of sugar and along with operation of high-pressure boiler and turbine, scraping the old low-pressure boilers.

4. This is a critical operations strategy for business restructuring and ensuring sustainability of the plant in a competitive horizon.

Though this involves traditional strategic management process, it is also a part of emergent strategy for two reasons— 1. technological advancement in handling high-pressure boilers for power generation in sugar plant has stabilised and increased normal size of a plant and economies of scale, and 2. hence, competitive pressure compelled organisations to follow the market trend.

Thus, we have a simple case of operations strategic formulation along with changing phase of an industry. One can find several such examples across industries.

Value Chain Concept and Approach

A value chain is a business framework or model that describes the full scale of activities needed to create a product or service. For companies that produce goods, a value chain comprises the steps that involve bringing a product from conception, design to production and distribution, and everything in between, such as procuring raw materials, conversion process and functions, and marketing activities. A company conducts an analysis of its value chain by evaluating the detailed processes involved in each step of its business. A firm would pursue value chain analyses to increase efficiency in production and at the same time, achieved cost minimisation. In contemporary business, firms are facing global competition, ability of competitors to innovate new products and services to quickly canabalis own products and still have ways of holding customer loyalty. Hence a firm has to constantly probe about its value creation to customers and how its value chain is being linked up. If there are gaps in value creation, then the firm may realign appropriately. The firm would design and implement strategies across value chain partners involvement to maximise product output efficiency and reduce costs.

Value chain analysis helps in increasing efficiency in production and at the same time, achieving it with minimum cost. With global competition, many competitors bring out new products, which will affect the firm's sales of its own products. Therefore, the firm must continuously innovate and come out with new products and services with efficiency and cost minimisation. The firm should realign its value chain activities to remain in the market.

More importantly, it must also ensure that enough action is taken to make customer group realise that value creation alignment has been done so that all stakeholders would benefit. Value-chain analyses can help with this as well. The goal of a value chain is to deliver the most value for the least cost in order to create a competitive advantage.

Background

Michael E. Porter, Harvard Business School, introduced the concept of a value chain in his book, *Competitive Advantage: Creating and Sustaining Superior Performance* (Free Press, 1998). "Competitive advantage cannot be understood by looking at a firm as a whole," Porter wrote. "It stems from the many discrete activities a firm performs in designing, producing, marketing, delivering and supporting its product."

It's important to maximise value at each specific point in a firm's processes. The value creation might originate from human resources, product design, technology adopted, its production processes, its supply chain processes, and its marketing and loyalty programmes.

Components of a Value Chain

In his concept of a value chain, Porter splits a business's activities into two categories, primary and support, sample activities of which are listed as follows. Specific activities in each category will vary according to the industry.

Primary activities consist of five components, and all are essential for adding value and creating a competitive advantage:

1. ***Inbound logistics:*** Functions like receiving, warehousing, transportation, and managing inventory.
2. ***Operations:*** Processes and technologies for converting raw materials into finished product.
3. ***Outbound logistics:*** Activities and processes to distribute a final product to a consumer like transportation, distribution centre activities and packaging.
4. ***Marketing and sales:*** Strategies to enhance visibility and target appropriate customers, such as advertising, promotion, and pricing.
5. ***Service:*** Programmes to maintain products and enhance consumer experience like customer service, customer problem solving, maintenance, repair, refund, and exchange.

Support Activities

The role of support activities is to help make the primary activities more efficient. When you increase the efficiency of any of the four support activities, it benefits at least one of the five primary activities. These support activities are generally denoted as overhead costs on a company's income statement:

1. ***Procurement:*** How a company obtains raw materials.
2. ***Technological development:*** Used at a firm's research and development (R&D) stage—designing and developing manufacturing techniques; and automating processes.
3. ***Human resources (HR) management:*** Hiring and retaining employees who will fulfil business strategy; and help design, market, and sell the product.
4. ***Infrastructure:*** Company systems; and composition of its management team—planning, accounting, finance, and quality control.

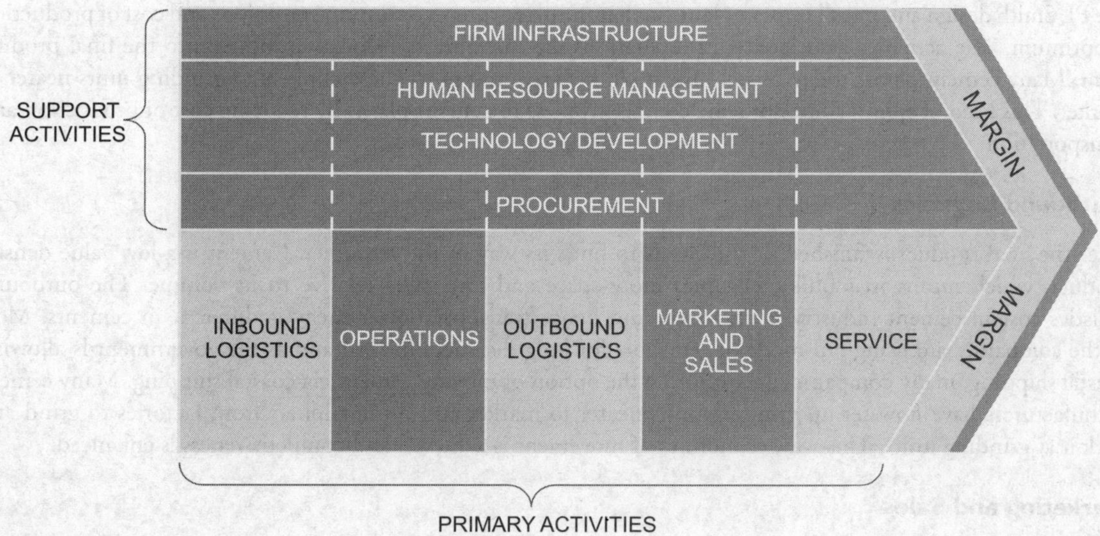

FIGURE 2.2 Porter's value chain

Key Takeaways

- Value chains help increase a business's efficiency, so the business can deliver the most value for the least possible cost.

- The end goal of a value chain is to create a competitive advantage for a company.
- Value-chain theory analyses a firm's five primary activities and four support activities.

Examples of Value Chains

The value chain can be best explained with illustration from cement industry in India. The first are primary activities, which include the five main activities. All five primary activities are directly involved in the production and selling of the actual product. They cover the physical production of the product, its sales, and exchange to the buyer as well as after sale service and support. The five primary activities are *inbound logistics*, *operations*, *outbound logistics*, *marketing and sales* and *service*. Even though the importance of each category may vary from industry to industry, all of these activities will be present to some degree in each organisation and play at least some role in competitive advantage.

Inbound Logistics

Inbound logistics is where purchased inputs, such as raw materials are often taken care of. For cement units, the important raw material is limestone which is available from limestone quarries. These materials are heavy and bulky and hence the inbound logistics cost are high. To reduce these costs, many companies locate their cement plants near to limestone quarries and transport limestone mostly through conveyors and trucks. Many cement companies either set up new plants near quarries or buy existing plants to reach geographically dispersed markets. Because of this function, it is also in contact with external companies, such as suppliers.

Operations

Once the arrangement is made to bring raw materials to plant, operations can convert the inputs in the desired product. Cement factories convert raw materials like limestone and gypsum into cement. Consulting companies like FL Smith design and install cement plants so that the plant runs in optimum conditions and cost of production is optimum. The activities associated with operations are therefore transforming inputs into the final product form. Many cement plants today make cement clinkers and transport these clinkers to grinding units nearer to market. This kind of split facilities provide competitiveness to cement plants by reducing cost of production and transportation.

Outbound Logistics

After the final product is finished, it still needs to finds its way to the customer. Cement is a low value density product, which means it is bulky, occupies more space and low value relative to its volume. The outbound logistics cost in cement industry is very high and hence transportation strategy is different in cements. Most of the companies are using rail mode of transport for long distances in land and as the government is allowing coastal shipping, many companies are exploring the option of moving cement via coastal shipping. Many cement manufacturers have now set up grinding units nearer to market and bring clinkers from factories to grind and pack it at grinding units. This way, economies of movement is achieved and competitiveness is enhanced.

Marketing and Sales

The products need to be distributed to market through different channel partners and marketing and sales takes care of these activities. It is the job of marketers and sales agents to make sure that potential customers are aware of the product and are seriously considering purchasing them. Cement companies also create and build brands though cement is difficult to differentiate as unique value provider. Different companies have developed brands and they advertise and promote their brands. With development of market maturity, the customers now demand ready-mix concrete, and hence distribution and marketing becomes more important. Cement companies are locating their ready-mix concrete plants within city and supply to project sites through specially built mixer-truck facilities.

Service

In this competitive scenario, customer support and service is critical to win over customers and hence, after-sales service and field support is important. Due to social media and Internet, complaints from unsatisfied customers are easily spread and shared and the consequences on the company's reputation might be vast. Cement industry also has developed call centre support system and field engineering support system to service customers better. Amazon.com also has a huge call centre system to support its customers.

Support Activities in a Value Chain

The second category is support activities. They interact across the primary activities and aim to coordinate and facilitate their functions to the maximum by providing purchased inputs, technology, human resources and various firm wide managing functions. The support activities namely, *procurement*, *technology development* (R&D), *human resource management* and *firm infrastructure* interact with primary functions and add value in the process. The dotted lines highlight the fact that procurement, technology development and human resource management can be linked with specific primary activities as well as support the entire value chain.

Procurement

Procurement is an important support activity for primary activities in creation of value to customer. A firm requires inputs for manufacturing/assembly/processing to produce an output. Hence, procurement of materials and services at a reasonable landed cost is a key function of a manager to ensure proper value add in. Not only the cost but also the right quality and sustained sourcing of material from buyers engaging supplier relations are a part of this activity. In case of cement industry, a plant may be located close to limestone mines. They need other materials including coal or combustion fuels for captive power generation and gypsum and other materials. Further a cement plant may need maintenance, repairs and overhauling materials and spares. Apart from these, there are capital equipment purchases. Thus, procurement is therefore needed to assist multiple value chain activities between both primary and support activities.

Procurement of raw materials, components and consumables, compliments the core value activity of manufacturing and service processes. By proper strategic approach, a manager can save lot of money in procurement, which supports value creation. Procurement ensures availability of materials at the right time, controls quality of inputs and saves cost with right suppliers. Procurement also builds supply chain relationship with partners and suppliers, which ensures alignment and consistency in supply of materials. An automobile firm should collaborate with suppliers to provide continuous support to its assembly line. The firm should work with immediate tier I suppliers for regular supplies with quality. The firm should also work with second level and territory level suppliers so that the risk in procurement can be reduced.

Technology Development (R&D)

Every value activity embodies technology, be it knowhow, procedures or technology embodied in process equipment. The cement manufacturing technology has improved over a period and all cement plants are investing in different kinds of technologies. The array of technology used in most companies is broad. Many cement companies are working on automated truck calling system/traffic management system, where with the use of machine learning and predictive analysis of truck status through RFID and GPS, whole truck movement inside the plant will be optimised where system will take most optimal decision on its own to manage traffic movement so there will be more ease to logistics. There is no doubt that digitalisation and automation is having an incredible impact on cement logistics across the globe and is here to stay. Companies are faced with many options as new products and applications enter the market and gain acceptance in the industry. Having a purposeful strategy for supply chain digitalisation and automation is now essential to assess the new technological landscape and chart a way forward to reap the benefits and stay ahead of the competition.

Human Resource Management

HRM consists of activities involved in the recruiting, hiring (and lay-off), training, development and compensation of all types of personnel. Human resource is the source of achieving competitive advantage because of its capacity to convert the other resources into output. The competitor can emulate other resources like technology and capital but the human resources are unparalleled. According to Barney, proponent of resources based theory, human resources lead to competitive advantage when they are precious, unique and well-organised. Cement plants emit lot of polluting particles and workers normally work in a vulnerable environment. Cement companies should provide safety support to all workers and also provide better environment for them.

Firm Infrastructure

In this framework, firm infrastructure would refer to all those support activities, mainly engaging with environment linking internal and external to the firm. It also refers to methods and ways like strategic management and planning.

It refers to all base activities of the firm, which enable smooth operation of the firm. It also involves support activities involving external entities like government and other statutory bodies. It involves planning and implementation of processes required for traditional strategic management processes. Further this includes statutory financial basic aspects like accounting and financing functions, including recording, maintaining and reporting of financial statements as per law. One can note that the firm is infrastructure would include any such similar function like coordinating with government and industry bodies that enable value chain activities. It may be noted that these are threshold activities and not enablers of competitive advantage to a firm.

Hierarchy of Competencies and Linkages to Operations Strategy

A firm has several resources especially human involved with material, machines and money to process inputs for output. A cluster of activities are involved and competence refers generally these skills and capabilities of the companies. These have been acquired and evolved through learning or combined experience. Such experiences and abilities reached a level to perform an activity consistently well which is seen as an advantage within the company. It establishes a cost advantage and translates into a valuable competence.

One may wonder how line job in an apparel manufacturing industry works with precise efficiency giving cost advantage, reliability, consistency and predictability in order fulfilment. The same kind of competent set of activities have come up establishing leadership in other business like BPOs, KPOs, banking and financial services, leather finishing and goods manufacture, consumer electronics and manufacture of mobile phones and so on. If we closely observe, there would even be a specialisation of labour engaged in delivering such value.

A core competence is that internal activity which a firm excels at compared to other activities performed internally, which is a key for giving cost advantage. Mainly this could be in operations activities like new product or service development; just-in-time inventory system; line feed; exclusive supply network; seamless production planning and zero error or near zero error system and so on. Such competency could have been giving resource advantage as there had been a learning curve effect and resources per se have become exceptionally valuable. Market values such resources significantly, if it is key workmen and managerial professional. The core competence may not directly give strategic advantage but through cost leadership, differentiation and focus could help to achieve the same. Thus, over time, core competence will result in not only reducing cost per unit of product or service but also in achieving economies scale by increasing normal size of a facility. This is when the real benefit of core competency comes alive by aligning with other competencies and careful deployment of operations strategy.

Next level of competency in the hierarchy is that of distinctive competency. Core competency can be widely available across firms in an industry and be common, as learning across and adoption was rather simple and straight forward. For example, large scale entry level recruitment of developers and training them to be market ready for billing was a successful core competency which many Indian IT companies deployed as core competency in the last two decades. Each one of them, especially among the top eight had this capability to attract talent. Similarly, most of them had quality process and relevant certification as a core competency through process management. A particular company will have only one competency as core and that will be exceptional and will differentiate from other internal competencies/activities! It never came as directly competitive advantage. On the other hand, a distinctive competency is the ability to be able to get competitive advantage for a reasonable time or at least that is being reversed engineered and adopted by competitors. For example, a banking and financial services product company had a distinctive competency of solution developers because of their combined experience in working in large number of countries' banking system and contributed to solutions development. This gave them an edge as a company and was finally taken over by another leading ERP product and solutions company as a value add in their offering. The other competitors could not adequately attract talent and build similar product or service in a reasonable time frame. That is where unique competency helps in the market.

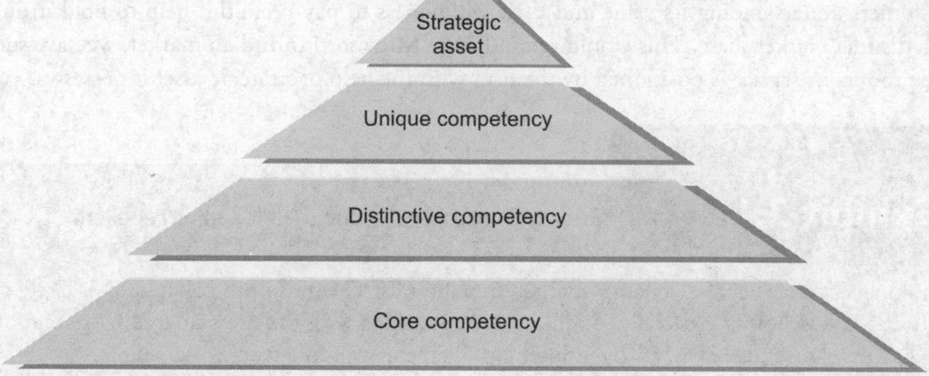

FIGURE 2.3 Hierarchy of competency

Similarly, one can look at such distinctive competency achieved in product and other service industries. Some of the government banks and insurance companies have such a distribution network, especially of locating branches in rural and semi-urban towns of India which cannot be matched by new generation players. Some of the competitors have taken it up and matching the same over the years. In product market, brands like Dabur, Mysore Sandal soap and Bullet bikes have set up competitive advantage because of perception they have created about their products. This leads up to the next level of competency hierarchy which is unique competency. A distinctive competency protected in the market for a longer tenure which could be because of exclusive distribution rights, Intellectual Proprietary Rights (IPR) and ability to maintain secrecy on product engineering, formulation and processes.

In case of unique competency, it is either protected through law or secrecy or trade practices by a firm to achieve competitive advantage in the market. A mosquito repellent in India was long known by the brand name till competition came up with similar product after passage of substantial time by which the first mover had a competitive advantage. Mosquito repellent market is a large and competitive market in India. Godrej is a leading player in this market. (Exhibit 2.1).

Home storage solutions Godrej has been leading and has unique perception about product reliability. This is just not perception but even physically seen in product quality by customers of household safety solutions.

Ability to build in such product features is critical for developing unique competency and stay ahead of competitors for long. It is important to note that unique competencies are established in the market and competitive advantage in operations arises of these. Unique competencies could also arise because of the ability of a firm to exploit physical location and access to premium resources. Using them, they develop a product or skillset to achieve unique competitive advantage. One of the leading industrial houses has key unique competency in managing coffee estates in three districts of South India. There they have developed capability to manage estates which have premium location in terms of access to irrigation, labour and ability to attract managers. Similarly, a Western Indian brand in tea manages exceptionally in procurement, transportation and distribution of tea in Western Indian states, namely Gujarat and Rajasthan and competes with MNCs. This is possible because of the unique competency the company has in operations!

The top most level of competency hierarchy is referred to as "Strategic Asset". Such a competency which is above unique competency is beyond IPR and Copyrights protection. It has been created, nurtured and enjoyed by a firm because of the supremacy in product composition, design, manufacture or process. Competition fails to crack the same. For example, in beverages market among cola brands like Coke and Pepsi, command premium across globe and competition has not been able to go past them. Another classic reference of strategic asset is that of KFC. Likewise, one can list some products and services that have stayed ahead of competition for secular period. Customers understanding its value and their willingness to pay premium help to hold it on top of the market with distinct market share. This would remind us of Microsoft! In Indian market, we have such example wherein the product or service is positioned by the firm with the help of strategic asset it possesses.

Exhibit 2.1 Godrej Consumer Products – Mosquito repellent

Household insect repellent is a large market in India. Indian households, especially middle and lower segments, are badly affected by household insects like mosquitos, cockroaches, flies, rats and bandicoot causing infections and diseases especially in the monsoon season and poor sanitary conditions in many cities. Though Swatch Bharat movement is sensitising the same and trying to impact, it will take some more years to be clean across the country.

Given this background, the total household insect repellent market in the country is around 6000 crores. It is mentioned that Godrej accounts for 60% share with its GoodKnight, Hit and other brands. The mosquito coil market is likely to be on a decline with the users upgrading to mat or liquid repellent products to avoid smoke.

Godrej, a market leader in the home insecticide category in the country, is aiming at gaining significant share of the ₹600 crore mosquito repellent agarbatti market in the next few years. This market is currently dominated by the unorganised sector. Godrej is likely to launch a product made from neem and turmeric as consumers are becoming aware and sensitive to these products.

Source: //economictimes.indiatimes.com/articleshow/69789945.cms?from=mdr&utm_source=contentofinterest&utm_medium=text&utm_campaign=cppst

Exhibit 2.2 Shree Khedut Sahakari Khand Udyog Mandli Ltd

Shree Khedut Sahakari Khand Udyog Mandli Ltd. located at Baben-Bardoli is the first sugar factory started in co-operative sector in Gujarat in the year 1955. The society is the largest cooperative sugar factory in Asia. It was started with crushing 850 TCD (tons cane per day) and presently the capacity of the plant is 10000 TCD. It achieved this level by 1992-93. The factory has won number of accolades. What is important is that while many sugar plants have gone through the stress of sugar cycle and some of them have even been extinguished or promoters having sold their stakes, Bardoli sugar plant under cooperative structure is still going strong and serves the purpose of benefiting local cooperative sugarcane farmers. It may be noted here that although number of sugar plants have moved in for joint product like power generation, Bardoli sugar plant is managing without such related diversification to accommodate a joint product!

Source: http://bardolisugar.com/AboutUs.aspx. Accessed on 11 October 2019.

Success of Amul is not only product development but more importantlym, the ability to run successfully as a cooperative even in this modern era and keep the brand afloat. The strategic asset the firm possesses is the ability to stay cohesive and at the top through co-operative culture in running a commercial enterprise which leads the dairy sector over four decades.

Another classic example of strategic asset possessed by a firm in similar nature is that of Shree Khedut Sahakari Khand Udhyog Mandli Ltd. which is referred as Bardoli Sugar plant near Surat. (Exhibit 2.2)

Thus, success of the plant and its competitive advantage is mainly because of strategic asset of their inbound material procurement through cooperative system. The strength continues over six decades!

Thus, competency hierarchy distinguishes four different levels from must have a core competency to creation of strategic asset in operations perspective. It could be relating to product design, process or manufacturing system, ownership rights with a procurement process (inbound distribution of material) or just organisational excellence in operations like success of execution and ownership process and disengaging ownership and professional operations managers allowing the latter to run professionally!

Operations Audit

Operational audits are a forward looking process rather than doing an ex-post analysis and fault finding. Though latter is one such audit more for validation or error analysis, main purpose of operations audit in many organisations' ongoing search for operations excellence through business process is improvement of initiatives. The findings of operational audits are intended to diagnose which areas need attention for enhancing resource efficiency and customer value through value added activities of operations team. Further, it also helps to safeguard assets by understanding potential future risks due to obsolescence of technology, overuse and natural nearing of terminal life time requiring replacement.

According to one Internal Auditor Professional forum, the definition of an operational audit is, "A systematic process of evaluating an organization's effectiveness, efficiency and economy of operations under management's control and reporting to appropriate persons the results of the evaluation along with recommendations for improvement."

Financial audit is statutory obligation to different stakeholders, especially to capital providers. As a part of financial audit, contemporary practice requires several validations which need to be supported by internal and external (selectively) management audit which would complement financial statutory audit on matters relating to business processes and system for effective decision making. The primary information sources are policies and achievements related to the objectives of the organisation.

Operational audits are an intense inquisitive analysis into different aspects of management. Turnaround time for an internal audit can vary from a few weeks to many months, depending on scope, complexity, and size of the organisation. Typically, operational audit breaks into processes, subprocesses and SBUs to make it time sensitive and componentise the whole process of assessment. Though operational audits are often carried out by an internal auditor in most of the traditional firms, contemporary business provides scope for operational audit through several external agencies. For example, ISO 14001 and ISO 45001 or EHS audit or Business Excellence award application can provide opportunities through an external agency. Benchmarking initiatives also provide opportunities for internal audit, especially when such initiative is taken involving industry wide participation. Quality management processes which are discussed later in this book would also help to understand how operational audits are facilitating improvements in operational, tactical and strategic decision making.

It may also be noted that the traditional framework of strategic management process emphasises the importance of monitoring and control mechanism in strategy formulation and implementation. Such framework would work only if operational audits are conducted systematically and inputs are provided to strategy implementation team on required action for course correction.

Innovations and Ability to Create New Product and Services

Products and services firms will have to be creative and innovative to be market leaders. At times, they may have to create a new market (Blue Ocean Strategy) which is not being currently served. In 1978, for the first time, home pregnancy tests kit was made available in drug stores. Imagine the kind of comfort which customers had by reduction in anxiety levels. Further research in this product has now made it a healthcare product commonly available. One can say the same about many other healthcare and clinical laboratories equipment and testing that have been influenced by market. Operations theatre are no longer same, thanks to innovations that are being constantly pursued. Keyhole and non-invasive surgery are medical advancements wherein researchers wanted to think ahead of market felt needs. In fact, such Blue ocean strategic moves in product innovation has clearly helped advancement of the medical science and society.

One of the classic cases which is discussed in India is about Jaipur foot (Exhibit 2.3).

Exhibit 2.3

Jaipur Foot: Rehabilitating amputees and Polio Patients in India

Since inception in 1975, Bhagwan Mahaveer Viklang Sahayata Samiti (BMVSS) has rehabilitated more than 1.78 million amputees and polio patients by fitting/providing artificial limbs (Jaipur Foot variety), calipers, and other aids and appliances, mostly in India and in 27 countries across the world. The idea of creating BMVSS, the Jaipur Foot organisation, was born out of a trauma on the hospital bed which Dr. Mehta founder of the organisation experienced for five months after meeting with an accident. He started this to serve the underprivileged with artificial limbs. One can see how he has understood a need and created a market. Over the years, BMVSS focussed on research and development, and tries to combine service with science. It has forged agreements with Stanford University, USA; Massachusetts Institute of Technology (MIT), USA; the Indian Space Research Organisation; and Indian Institute of Technology (IIT), Jodhpur and many more centres of excellence. The Stanford-BMVSS Jaipur Knee, which is the product of research due to a formal memorandum of understanding between BMVSS and Stanford University, was hailed by *Time* magazine, USA (23 November 2009 issue) as one of the world's 50 best inventions in 2009.

Source: www.jaipurfoot.org Accessed on 11 October 2019

One can find similar examples in capital equipment industry, consumer goods industry and service business operations. It is important to note that operations strategist must constantly endeavour to create new products and services through innovation and move the horizon where customers and other stakeholders could see value. Creating new categories of demand and market is also one of the key functions of the operations strategists.

Resource Led Operation Strategies

Firms have positioned their operations strategy around the resource endowment which could be due to geographical location, societal advantage or other demographic profile like age composition often population, work ethics and so on. If we observe agribusiness industries, plantation of white sugar in India are around places where cane is cultivated closer to river beds or any other water source. Large and successful factories are those who could use the resource base better. Similarly, we can observe that cement plants are located close to limestone resource basins. Power plants are located where coal is available from the ground or can be imported easily as sea port handling costs are low and appropriate rail links are available to move into hinterlands.

India's advantage for growth of software service business is due to time zone difference, English speaking youth population and ability to drive policy framework for growth in certain urban centres. We have seen growth of banking and financial services in India in the post-independence era, because market was underserved till then. Bank nationalisation and later, privatisation and digital penetration gave the market an opportunity. Resource advantage was the ability of managerial professionals to quickly scale up such demand for resources and train service people to fulfil such growth. This was a classic case of operational strategy wherein market requirements and operations perspective for strategic orientation created a symphony to take banking for lower strata of the society.

One can list numerous such examples and a chapter in this book discusses the same.

Order Winners and Qualifiers

In this subsection, we would like to introduce order winners and qualifiers as we are discussing operations strategy with market orientation and perspective.

There are certain criteria required to be winner in the marketplace. Terry Hill (2000) divided qualifiers from winners.

An order qualifier is that characteristic of a product or service that customer would expect to be available. One may term it as threshold requirement or feature of a product or a service. All firms competing to fulfil a demand must have it in their offering.

Therefore, firms must have imbibed the qualifiers to get into or stay in a market. Qualifiers are needed to be as good as their competitors. Failure to do so may result in lost sales and exit from the marketplace. Order qualifiers have to be clearly well-established at the best of quality, cost, effectiveness and speed to market so that customers consider the product or service among the basket of options to fulfil a demand.

However, to provide order winners, firms must be differentiators in the market. It sets up the firm differently from the host of competition.

It may be noted that order winners and order qualifiers need not be only linked to product or service features. There could be factors like price as one of the qualifiers in certain cases, especially of those catering to popular category of demand. Ironically, when such a feature like price is seen by a group of customers as a qualifier, a firm which incurs comparatively higher cost either may have to sell at a loss or lose the qualifier.

Order winners and qualifiers are normally market-specific and time-specific. As technology develops and customer preferences change, qualifiers and winners would change. Mostly winners are driven by firm's corporate and operating strategies. Lot occurs because of product and service innovations leading to new products/features and significant improvement in processes leading to cost advantage. Till competition follows, those could be winners and later, it becomes denominator across competition. For example, in a smartphone industry, quality of touchscreen is now a qualifier than a differentiator. In a car industry, ABS or air bags are becoming qualifier in

India which was available only in higher versions a decade back. One can similarly look in number of industries. Mechanical products and common service industry could have longer tenure of qualifiers and winners compared to technology-based industries.

Understanding the relevant order qualifiers and order winners is important for operations and supply chain managers to formulate strategy and execute their business plan. Operations strategists must scan the industry and help a firm to drive its business for establishing competitive advantage. In any industry, one can clearly map successful firms' ability to consistently create winners. An analyst may relate hierarchy of competencies a firm achieves and aspects of wines and qualifiers as well.

SUMMARY

In this chapter, we have seen how operations strategists can pursue traditional strategic management formulation and implementation framework. This may have to be aligned with other functional strategies as well as with SBU level and corporate strategy. Firms may have to ride on emerging opportunities in the market or through innovations in operations. It could be industry wide change in technology, enhancement of normal size of a plant or facility and thereby economies of scale, achieving economies of scope through better utilisation of existing assets for multiple product categories and so on. Emerging strategic orientation is the key considering changing customer preferences with shorter life cycle of products, breakthroughs in technology impacting supply side and changes in policy framework, especially with ease of trade regulations.

We further discussed value chain framework and value network and their importance for an operations strategist to optimise value of creation through manufacture, assembly, process and distribution. We also discussed about competency hierarchy and how a firm can move up in it. Operations strategists play a key role in facilitating a firm in achieving sustainable competitive advantage by creating appropriate competency level in the industry in which they operate. Leaders and pioneers set up high standards and engage through unique competency and strategic assets which they have built over long term.

Importance of operations audit was mentioned, and this followed up with discussion on innovations creating new market space. Operations strategy is all about aligning market requirements in terms of products and services under five qualifying factors from operations perspective, namely cost, dependability, flexibility, quality and speed. Whether one follows a market led approach or a resource led approach or a combination, operations strategists must strive for creating competitive advantage and sustainability of a firm.

Key Terms

1. **Benchmarking:** Benchmarking is the practice of comparing business processes and performance metrics to industry's bests and best practices from other companies. Dimensions typically measured are quality, time, cost, and so on which are important for establishing competitive advantage.
2. **Blue Ocean strategy:** Blue Ocean is a term referring to the uncontested market space of an unknown industry or innovation.
3. **Core competency:** A core competency is a concept in management theory, introduced by C. K. Prahalad and Gary Hamel. It can be defined as "A harmonised combination of

multiple resources and skills that distinguish a firm in the marketplace" and therefore, are the foundation of companies' competitiveness.

4. **Distinctive competency:** Distinctive competence refers to some characteristic of a business that it does better than its competitors. Since the business can do something better than other businesses, that business has a competitive advantage over other businesses.
5. **Emergent strategy:** Emergent strategy is the process of identifying unexpected outcomes from the execution of corporate strategy and then learning to integrate those unexpected outcomes into future corporate plans.
6. **Operational audit:** Operational audit is a systematic review of effectiveness, efficiency and economy of operation. It is a future-oriented, systematic, and independent evaluation of organisational activities.
7. **Order qualifier:** An order qualifier is a characteristic of a product or service that is required for the product/service to even be considered by a customer. Therefore, firms must provide the qualifiers in order to get into or stay in a market.
8. **Order winner:** An order winner is a characteristic that will win the bid or customer's purchase.
9. **Quality management:** Quality management is about managing all the activities and tasks needed to maintain a desired level of excellence. This includes the determination of a quality policy, creating and implementing quality planning and assurance, and quality control and quality improvement.
10. **Strategic asset:** Strategic assets are those assets or competencies possessed by a firm for it to maintain its ability to achieve future outcomes for a long-time horizon and competitors could imitate the same.
11. **Value chain:** A value chain is a set of activities that a firm operating in a specific industry performs in order to deliver a valuable product (i.e., good and/or service) for the market. The idea of the value chain is based on the process view of organisations, the idea of seeing a manufacturing (or service) organisation as a system, made up of subsystems each with inputs, transformation processes and outputs. Inputs, transformation processes, and outputs involve the acquisition and consumption of resources — money, labour, materials, equipment, buildings, land, administration and management.

CONCEPT REVIEW QUESTIONS

1. Explain traditional framework of strategic formulation and implementation and its relevance to operations strategy.
2. Discuss emergent strategies in operations in the last three or four decades. You may use an example.
3. Explain the concept of value chain and its approach towards operations strategy formulation.
4. Discuss different levels in hierarchy of competencies and relate it to operations strategy formulation.
5. What are some of the innovations and new product strategies which were driven by operations perspective namely new product offering and service and how it impacted the industry?
6. Explain with examples, order qualifier and order winner.
7. Elucidate the importance of operational audit and its relevance to operations strategy formulation.

CRITICAL THINKING QUESTIONS

1. "A firm has to balance traditional strategic planning process and emergent opportunities to stay competitive. If they must be ahead of competition, they may have to look at Blue Ocean strategy like venturing into something not still surfaced." Elucidate with an example from one of the industries and firms you are familiar with. You may consider healthcare, pharmaceuticals, IT, communication (mobile) and entertainment.
2. Analyse hierarchy of competency which a firm might have created as distinctive but remained as core as competitors could acquire the same. You may also consider a situation in which a firm can move up in hierarchy of competency to stay as key or dominant player in a chosen industry.
3. Discuss the role of external agencies like quality certification, industry wide benchmarking and excellence award as enabler of operational audit. How should a company systematically benefit through the same?
4. Porter called the value producing activities of one organisation, "a value chain" and the network organisations involved in the production and delivery of an offering to the end customer, "a value system". Elucidate that under such value system it is likely that value creation by network partners may not allow super normal profit earned by any single constituent of the system.

PROJECT ASSIGNMENTS

1. Identify a business of your choice and understand how they are implementing operations strategy. Find out their recent key strategic decision in operations domain and map the following:
   a. Linkage with overall business strategy
   b. Linkages with other operations decision perspective like facility, location, size, supply network and organisation process development.
   c. How such a decision impacted day to day operations and tactical decisions during implementation stage?
2. Use open source information and analyse changing trends in operations strategy due to technology development in a chosen industry or service like banking and finance, insurance and supply chain outsourcing, KPOs and BPOs. Choose any one industry and write a detailed note as a strategist to your top management.

REFERENCES

1. Porter, Michael E. (1998). *Competitive Advantage: Creating and Sustaining Superior Performance*, Free Press.
2. Chandrasekaran N. and Ananthanarayanan P. S. (2011). *Strategic Management*, Oxford University Press of India.
3. Hill, Terry (2000). *Manufacturing Strategy: Text and Cases.* 3rd ed. Boston: Irwin McGraw-Hill.
4. https://www.jaipurfoot.org/who_we_are/our_history.html. Accessed on 11 October 2019.
5. http://bardolisugar.com/AboutUs.aspx. Accessed on 11 October 2019.

CHAPTER

3

Capacity Strategy

LEARNING OBJECTIVES

After reading this chapter, you will be able to:

- Understand the levels of capacity decisions
- Learn the measurements of capacity
- Explain capacity sizing from long term perspectives
- Discuss the dimensions of capacity strategies
- Analyse capacity strategy in service systems and queuing theory

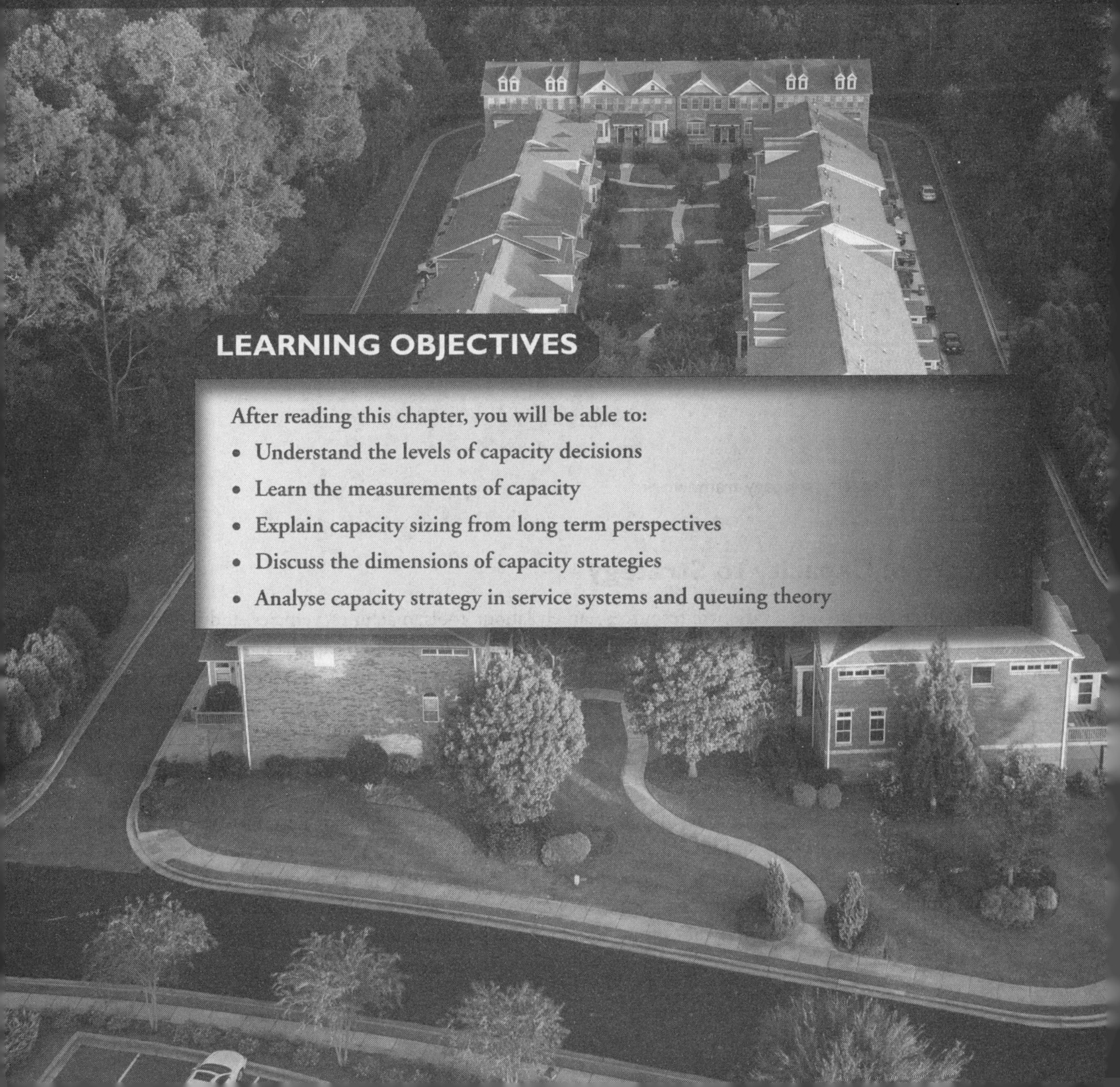

Introduction

Capacity sizing is the most important strategic decisions in the area of operations management towards excellence in business. It is a fundamental and top management decision. This strategy should be in line with organisational growth strategy. Capacity should be built to meet the demand most efficiently all the time. Too much capacity and too less capacity are dangerous for long term sustainable business. Many times one may wonder how Hyudnai decided to set up a plant at Chennai for 700,000 cars facility first and expanded by nearly the same size as Plant II in the same location. Similarly, one may ponder how ICICI Bank converted from development financial institution into a universal bank with branches across India and arose to the level of second largest bank in India.

The following highlights the importance of capacity strategy in operations:

(i) Capacity decisions are long term oriented and related to growth of the organisation.
(ii) These decisions bear lot of risks and hence careful analysis is required.
(iii) Capacity building involves financial outflow for the organisation.
(iv) Competitive strategy of the organisation influences capacity strategy.
(v) Built capacity can be order winners for organisations.
(vi) Capacity decisions are mostly irreversible.

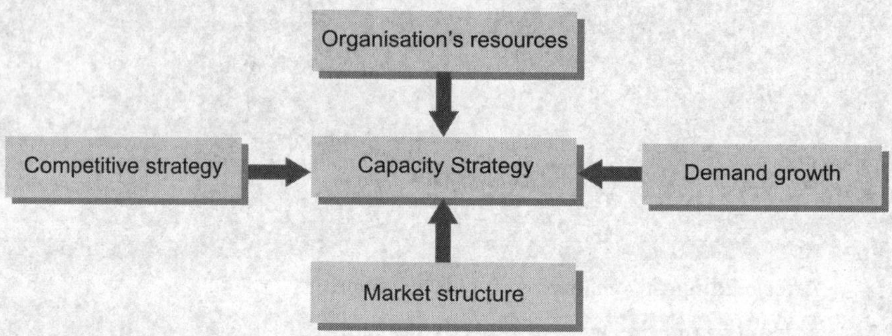

FIGURE 3.1 Capacity strategy framework

Linkages of Capacity to Strategy

Every operations system uses a variety of resources namely labour, tools, machines, vehicles, and facilities. All these resources are used in some proportions to form a production or a service system capable of producing certain level of product or service output. Capacity requires a fixed investment for repetitive use by the system until it requires replacement. So, capacity is a production resource which attracts investment. And such capital deployment is for long term and cannot be easily reversed but repositioned at a substantial additional capital. Hence the decision is critical for organisation growth as it absorbs a key resource namely capital but gives opportunity to market goods and/or services.

Capacity also denotes the maximum output of services units or products generated by a system. So, capacity is mix of physical assets, people and methods to produce certain number of products over a period of time or to serve certain number of customers over a period of time. It is also termed in terms of inputs such as how much crude oil can be processed in a refinery or what are the number of beds a hospital can provide. This way of representing capacity is due to variety of outputs like multiple products and variety of customers.

Capacity is a critical resource for producing products or services that meet the timing expectations of the customers. Capacity is the outcome of resources that can produce a specified volume in a specified amount of time. Capacity is time sensitive and if needed it should be reserved in advance. Capacity is also expensive sometimes and hence capacity decisions are highly sensitive and scrutinised always.

Capacity strategy can be summarised with the following key points:

(a) It decides number, location and size of the plants.
(b) In deciding the reconfiguration of capacity when demand and supply environment changes and also when competition changes.
(c) Deciding effective capacity requirement when there is a structural change in the industry like merger and acquisition.
(d) It decides the degree of flexibility in capacity adjustment in short term.

Levels of Capacity Decisions

Capacity decisions are normally classified into three levels namely strategic, tactical and operational. This classification is arbitrary, and respective time span varies from industry to industry.

A car company decides capacity of a production facility at three levels. When it begins operations, it should decide the production capability to meet demand for the next five to eight years in the market. It must decide location, infrastructure, equipment, machineries, and other facility related decisions with respect to long-term demand. For example, Hyundai Motors in India decided to have a facility at Chennai and started operations in 1998. The company must have forecast demand for automobiles for the next ten years then and had decided on capacity.

Similarly, the company need to have medium term plan in terms of what models, and how much to produce and also to decide how to increase production in medium term. They might have used extra time and shift to produce more or cut down one shift to reduce production so that they can meet the demand in medium term of six months to one year. In day to day operations, the plant manager needs to decide the sequence of production and any changes to be made in schedule. Due to shortages of some component, the manager needs to decide to produce Model A instead of Model B in the line in short term.

It is important when deciding on long term capacity of a plant, it must be sure that this capacity is flexible in medium term and short term.

Levels of capacity decisions depend on the time horizon of planning. They are classified as strategic, tactical and operational decisions.

Strategic Level

In the long term, the importance of capacity planning is on deciding the right amount of capacity available to meet the future projected growth in demand for product or services. The time period is typically 2 to 5 years and it varies with industry. An organisation normally makes certain investment on capacity. Once the capacity is utilised fully due to demand growth, firms need to take decisions in advance for augmenting capacity. This means expanding with additional production capacity at the same place of existing plant or putting additional plants near to new markets or taking over additional capacity through mergers and acquisitions. Key decisions made are:

- How much additional capacity to be built?
- Using capital budgeting, one may have to select the best option for investment.
- Many tools are used which includes break-even analysis, discounted cash flow techniques, decision trees and other investment planning tools.

Tactical Level

In the medium term, the capacity decisions are pertaining to balancing demand with supply in intermediate period. The intermediate period is typically two months to six months. This planning with respect to supply is also called aggregate planning or sales and operations planning. It is concerned with determining quantity and timing of production along with inventory policy to meet demand for the immediate future. These plans need to be matched with top management strategic plan and it should work within available capacity and resources.

This planning combines demand of similar products (for example, all variants of washing machines) and plan for resources to produce in a given time span. One looks at aggregate demand and plan for overall capacity in terms of possible options in resources. This is why it is called aggregate planning.

The decisions involved are related to how much of each of the following resources should be used:

1. Labour hours
2. Machine hours
3. Inventory
4. Subcontracting
5. Overtime and shifts

From demand side, it is also possible for the firm to shift the demand from peak period to non-peak period through promotions so that demand and supply can be matched.

Operations Level

These decisions are confined to utilising the available resources to the maximum possible and not allowing any resources to remain idle. These decisions are pertaining to short period of days to a week. This is also called scheduling. It involves adjusting the production against unforeseen developments like equipment breakdowns, surge in demand and poor planning. Waiting line models and scheduling tools are used to manage capacity in short term.

Measurements of Capacity

To understand the expression of capacity in a production or service centre is crucial. There is no single way in which it is used across industries and services. In case of certain products, it is based on output. For example, it would be number of cars produced in a shift, tons of steel produced per day, tons of clinker or cement produced per day and so on. In certain industries, it could be based on inputs like tons of cane crushed in case of sugar plant, in a BPO it would be number of seats, in a hospital it could be number of beds and in case of restaurants it could be number of seats or meals served, in an entertainment hall, number of seats available and in case of a retail, number of footprints and so on.

This becomes little more complex when in same line different products can be produced by changing over product mix. For example, in an industrial bakery, it could be manufacture of breads, biscuits, cakes or quick bites. Their common denominator may be used for defining and managing capacity. It could be as simple as cost of goods sold that is being produced in a shift or a day. The idea of defining capacity is to manage assets more appropriately and provide value to stakeholders.

Measures for Manufacturing

For most of the manufacturing systems, the output rate capacity is used to measure capacity. For a facility having a single product or a few homogeneous products, the unit of measure is straightforward (barrels of beer per month, Mega Watts per day, watches per shift and so on.)

For a facility having a diverse mix of products, an aggregate unit of capacity must be established using a common unit of output (sales rupees per week).

Measures for Service Facilities

For most of the service facilities, Input Rate Capacity is used to measure capacity, commonly used for service operations where output measures are particularly difficult. Some of the examples are:

- Hospitals use available beds per month.
- Airlines use available seat-miles per month.
- Movie theatres use available seats per month.

Other Measures

Capacity Utilisation Percentage

Capacity utilisation percentage relates actual output to capacity defined. For example, actual automobiles produced in a quarter divided by the quarterly automobile production capacity. Sometimes, it also relates actual input used to input capacity. For example, actual accountant hours used in a month divided by the monthly account-hours available.

Capacity Cushion

An additional amount of capacity added on to the expected demand to allow serving the similar amount of excess demand. This leads to understanding two system effectiveness measures namely efficiency and utilisation. There is something called design capacity. This means that the equipment or facility or manpower time is set to achieve a desired output. For example, a doctor is available in a clinic for eight hours in a day. But effective time available for consulting patients could be seven hours. The latter is called effective capacity. Thus, efficiency is the ratio of actual output to effective capacity. Capacity utilisation is the ratio of actual capacity to design capacity.

Efficiency = Actual output/Effective capacity

Utilisation = Actual output/Design capacity

It is important to focus on right measures and budget for capacity utilisation and managing assets utilisation for providing market rate of return to investment by capital providers. Sometimes, operating managers may tend to focus on monitoring efficiency parameter based on effective capacity and tend to ignore utilisation based on design capacity. Such practice may lead to poor utilisation of assets and capital.

The following illustration will highlight the importance of monitoring capacity utilisation in a firm whether it is in manufacturing or service business.

ILLUSTRATION 3.1

A hotel has 240 rooms built; two restaurants of each capacity 120 seat covers and three banquet halls of average 100 occupants each per function. The facility can merge if there is a large function. Normally, capacity is designed as a business class hotel with one night one person occupancy; two meal serving namely one for lunch and one for dinner and breakfast is completely complimentary; and banquet hall for a function in a day.

MIS report to the CEO at the end of September 2015 showed that there were 240 room nights lost because of maintenance. Designed capacity as per plan was to lose 90 room nights for maintenance on a perpetual basis. Actual room nights sold was 5400. He asked his analyst to provide analysis and rationale.

Solution:

Number of rooms built	240
No of days in the month of September	30
Planned maintenance of a room in a month	90
Available capacity in a month	7110
Actual number of rooms under maintenance in September	240
Effective capacity	6960
Room nights sold in September	5400
Efficiency	78%
Utilisation	76%

Analyst reported 2 per cent loss in revenue. This was due to delay in maintenance service and handover rooms back to front office for sale in case nearly 60% of room nights which were lost and another 40% due to unexpected random failures. The CEO could now review the budget estimates, capability of maintenance crew and revisit age versus failure analysis.

Sizing Capacity Cushions: Generally, it is recommended that the average utilisation rates should not get too close to 100 per cent. When they do that, then it is usually a signal to increase capacity or decrease order acceptance so as to avoid declining productivity. The capacity cushion is the amount of reserve capacity that a firm maintains to handle sudden increases in demand or temporary losses of production capacity; it measures the amount by which the average utilisation (in terms of *effective* capacity) falls below 100 per cent. Specifically,

Capacity cushion = 100% – Utilisation rate (%)

Since 1950s, manufacturers have maintained an average cushion of 18 per cent, with a low of 9 per cent in a year to a maximum of 27 per cent in another year which was 15 years apart from the earlier one. This could be linked to business cycle then. The appropriate size of the cushion varies by industry. In the capital-intensive paper industry, machines can cost hundreds of millions of dollars each; cushions well under 10 per cent are preferred. Electric utilities also are capital intensive but consider cushions of 15 to 20 per cent in electric generating capacity to be optimal to avoid loss of service to customers at times of demand peaking and shooting over normal conditions.

Businesses find large cushions appropriate when demand varies. Large cushions also are necessary when future demand is uncertain, particularly if resource flexibility is low. Another type of demand uncertainty occurs with a changing product mix. Though total demand might remain stable, the load can shift unpredictably from one work centre to another as the mix changes. High degrees of product customisation also lead to uncertainty.

Supply uncertainty also favours large capacity cushions. Capacity often comes in large increments as lumpiness of additions of facility is common due to technical conditions. So expanding even by the minimum amount possible may create a large cushion. Firms also need to build in excess capacity to allow for employee absenteeism, vacations, holidays, and any other delays. Penalty costs for overtime and subcontracting can create the need for further increases in capacity cushions.

The argument in favour of small cushions is simple. Unused capacity costs money as there is always certain amount of fixed cost attached to it. For capital-intensive firms, minimising the capacity cushion is vital. Since the mid-1970s, airlines have expanded capacity by cramming about 20 per cent more seats into the same size aircraft. Studies indicate that businesses with high capital intensity achieve a low return on investment when the capacity cushion is high.

Capacity Sizing from Long Term Perspectives

After having understood definitions and appropriate measurement of capacity, it is important to understand different criteria which are used for arriving at capacity for establishing a facility whether it is a plant or service. Typically, capacity size determination is a strategic decision. This means that it takes into consideration long term factors; invests substantial amount of capital and decision is not easily reversible or there is a high cost involved in reversing the same. Hence an operations manager must understand the factors that determine capacity sizing decision.

Key Factors Determining Capacity

Capacity decisions depend on—

(a) Demand conditions

When a firm decides on capacity creation, it projects the future demand trends. Normally, while deciding capacity creation, it is important to understand what would be future demand for the product or service. Though no one can preciously estimate future demand especially on a longer horizon, it is important to have a visibility on a band how demand would be in the years ahead. As this is a strategic decision, it is difficult to widely vary effective capacity to meet demand. For example, an IT company is looking at creating its own infrastructure for servicing its clients at USA and Europe. One of the key aspects of such planning is what would be the number of seats it should have. Currently, the company has 600 seats and expects that the business measured in terms of revenue would grow at approximately 25% CAGR. Table 3.1 gives growth plan.

TABLE 3.1 Growth plan

Year end	1	2	3	4	5
Employees	600	750	1000	1200	1500
Revenue in crores	400	550	750	1000	1200

This would be a challenge for capacity planner to accommodate as growth is happening in stages and there is substantial difference from Year 1 to Year 5. To make it simple, he would see if they can grow in two stages. First, they plan up to Year 1 and in Year 2, revisit to firm the plan for further period. Suppose, if the demand fails to grow at 25% and a global recession hits market in Year 3, it could complicate demand estimate and thereby capacity planning. It is to be noted here that demand factors significantly influence capacity sizing decision.

(b) Supply factors

Supply factors again could be determinant of capacity sizing. Any facility whether it is manufacturing or service or even an equipment to operate we require a number of inputs. Some of the inputs could be critical. Capacity sizing will have to necessarily take into consideration availability of inputs or raw material for setting up a facility and then its size. In the above example, the IT company discussed above may not find problem in getting resources if it is located in a tier I city or in any of the major metros. However, if the company is going to be located in Tier II or Tier III town, supply conditions could be challenging. Another example we can think of is that of a dairy plant to be set up in a private sector. If the promoter wants to set up a 200,000 litres per day processing facility, then he must be able to organise competitively and procure so much milk from different villages preferably in a radius of 100 kms, else cost of procurement operations and its risk could be high. Thus, supply conditions could be a determining factor for capacity sizing.

(c) Technological factors

While setting up a plant and machinery or even service business where technology supports scaling, such businesses are likely to be influenced by technological factors. Technological changes constantly improve technical sizes and processes and hence when capacity is being decided, it is important to decide on appropriate technological conditions in which plant and machinery is being installed. This will have high impact on productivity. For example, in apparel manufacturing number of garments produced can go up significantly based on technology deployed in cutting, tailoring, pressing and packaging sections of a unit. Similarly, in case of a process plant in a chemical plant capacity of vessel, heat exchangers and incinerators which have volume, pressure, density and type of material used can significantly impact capacity sizing. One can think many other production conditions where technological factors including sophistication of technology and volume, area and density metric defining capacity sizing.

One can understand the same set of factors impacting service businesses as well. Look at health care service wherein hospitals and doctors are able to perform more sophisticated intervention with change in technological factors. Right from ophthalmology, dental to critical operations like cardio intervention, technology adoption has redefined size of facility and hence capacity is being redefined. One can observe the same in case of banking operations which nearly automated to high levels has increased capacity to process instruments and enable a number of transactions to a high level. To cite instances, number of customers handled in a branch and number of home loans released have all significantly gone up. Ability to understand such technological factors while sizing is critical for capacity planning and strategy for operations.

(d) Capital availability

Another important factor in deciding capacity sizing is availability of capital. Though different options could be available for setting up plant and machinery or a service facility, availability of capital plays an important role in deciding size at any given time when investment is made. Capital has two components namely equity which includes owners fund and debt fund. Amount of debt fund which can be raised depends upon equity brought into the project and ability of the project to support maximum debt. Every business has its own norms on ideal debt equity ratio. Businesses with high operating risk measured by variability in earnings before depreciation, interest and taxes will go in for a conservative debt structure (financial leverage) because of risk in payment of interests. Alternatively, firms with low operating risk may go for higher leverage when there is stability in earnings. Generally, a leverage of twice of equity is thought of a limit and firms are more within this limit.

For example, the IT company capacity planning discussed above, at the end of the third year would require approximately 1,00,000 sq.ft of area which can be built in outskirt of a metro or tier I city at a facility cost of about ₹20 crore or so. Equity which may have to be brought in may be to the extent of ₹10 crore from this business for this real estate build up. If full capacity at the fifth year projected business is required, then it may be around 2 times of the size in the third year at 25% CAGR which means the company has to bring in about ₹40 crore of capital. This gives an idea of capital availability deciding capacity sizing decisions.

(e) Scope for flexibility in deployment - Varieties of SKUs and products to be produced in a line:
Another important factor which is critical in deciding a plant or service facility capacity decision is the scope for flexibility in deployment of the equipment or facility to adopt changes in production or revenue generation. To cite an example, in the hotel capacity illustration which we discussed earlier, we mentioned about banquet halls of three numbers of each 100 seats capacity. Ideally, this facility must be flexible where it can take demand for 100, 150, 200, 250, 300 or sometimes even as low as 50 to make revenue and cover capital costs of facility instead of allowing the revenue opportunity to go. Most of the time, capacity when after deployment of facility, if it is not utilised, then it is unproductive. In certain cases like hotel and airline, it is perishable as well. Many of the food and beverage businesses are component based assembly facility looking at creating production line level flexibility to change SKUs or product for better utilisation of capacity.
One can think of such opportunities arising in service sector as well. In service sector capacity is more defined by service providers or operators and in contemporary business they are demanded to be multi skilled and can handle multiple tasks. For example, in banks today a counter must be able to handle variety of functions like issue of instruments, processing of customer requests for service, teller services and so on and no longer take care of dedicated service as a specialisation. Thus, flexibility in resource handling and using of equipment and machinery is a key aspect of capacity planning.

(f) Competitive conditions
Another important factor or driver of capacity sizing is competitive conditions. There are certain fundamental factors in competitive space which drive capacity sizing decisions. If it is an imperfect market where there are large number of suppliers and any supplier could not influence the market, then normal capacity in such manufacture based on technical features is taken as capacity driver. For example, in a busy high street where there are a number of eating joints serving the market, any other player who wants to enter under normal circumstances should go based on the average capacity of an eating joint which could be, say 60 seats or so. Similarly, if we are looking at mini cement plants in India which thrive among oligopolistic market where large players have capacity of more than 6000 tons per day or 2 million per annum, a mini plant technically will not look beyond 600 tons per day which is a standard for such plants. A number of mini cement plants operate at that level exploiting limestones reserve available locally and serving a local market.
One can discuss innumerable examples of such competition driven capacity sizing. However, there could be a large player who can take the market by sway or a group of a small number of firms can have huge market share. For example, in Chennai, ITC Grand Chola hotel came up with a property in Central Chennai which has large ultra-modern facility for banquet and well-designed restaurants which redefined hotel industry at Chennai. On the other hand, if we look at mobile service providers like Airtel, Vodafone and Tata who intensively compete with high level of business rivalry are too large and make competition tougher. Unless any operator pitch at that level, it would be difficult to service. One can look similar oligopolistic practice in domestic airline business where a few players like Indigo, Spicejet, Jet Airways and Air India compete and there are players with much lesser capacity trying to enter and grow. Thus, competitive conditions would be a key driver of capacity.

(g) Cultural orientation
Cultural orientation may also drive capacity decisions. Though this may not be a key driver, yet it has a role to be played in certain businesses. This happens where culturally in certain business, promoters tend to be of small and medium sized firms and family wants to control the business. Capacity decisions are also driven by the same consideration. This happens in traditional businesses like textile manufacture, retailing, household furniture, home furnishing, apparel manufacture for both domestic and export, engineering industries, castings and forgings, logistics like warehouse operations, transport services, people logistics services on road sector, and so on. Normally, even when they see opportunities to grow they create multiple entities and

manage risk within an entity instead of consolidating horizontally. Cultural orientation and attitude towards managing business risk are key drivers of such capacity choice exercised by these firms. Though there have been some changes in the last decades, it is likely to be predominantly driven by such conditions as long as they are viable and successful in value creation.

(h) Stage at which economy is passing through:
From a conceptual perspective, the **business cycle** is the upward and downward movements of levels of GDP (gross domestic product) and refers to the period of expansions and contractions in the level of economic activities (**business** fluctuations) around a long-term growth trend and its impact in each industry.
Every economy goes through phases of growth in gross domestic product (GDP) over a period of time. This is generally considered on a long term. The upward movement of business cycle is towards peak of growth and downward movement is towards trough of business cycle. These are called expansions and contractions in the level of economic activities. During this movement towards peak and troughs, normal trend fitted will have periods of recession and recovery.

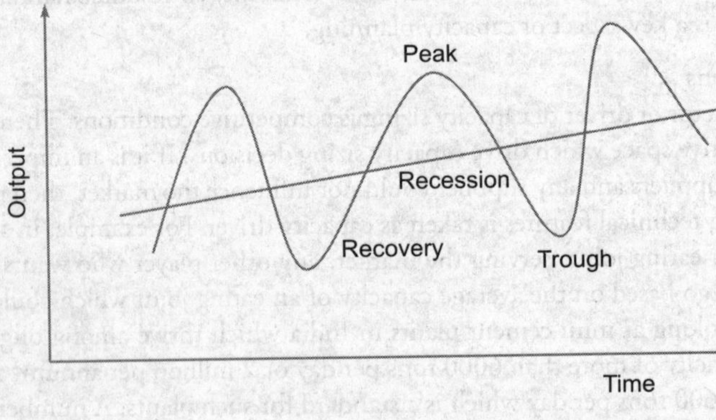

FIGURE 3.2 Business cycle

Similarly, industry can have its own cycle where industry demand growth could be cyclical. Then phases could be of growth; stable and decline. When a firm decides on setting up capacity, it must study the business cycle and industry phase at which the firm considers its decision to create or add capacity, estimate the longevity of the phase and its risk profile and decide on capacity sizing.

Dimensions of Capacity Strategies

Operations managers must also examine three dimensions of capacity strategy before making capacity decisions:

1. Number, size and location of plants
2. Timing and sizing expansion, and
3. Clustering.

1. **The Number and size of plants**
   The number and size of plants vary due to various long-term strategic factors. For example, the company MRF Tyres in India have seven manufacturing facilities across South India mostly catering to Automobile OEMs. Ford India invested with only one plant at Chennai and recently expanded its operations with second plant in Gujarat.

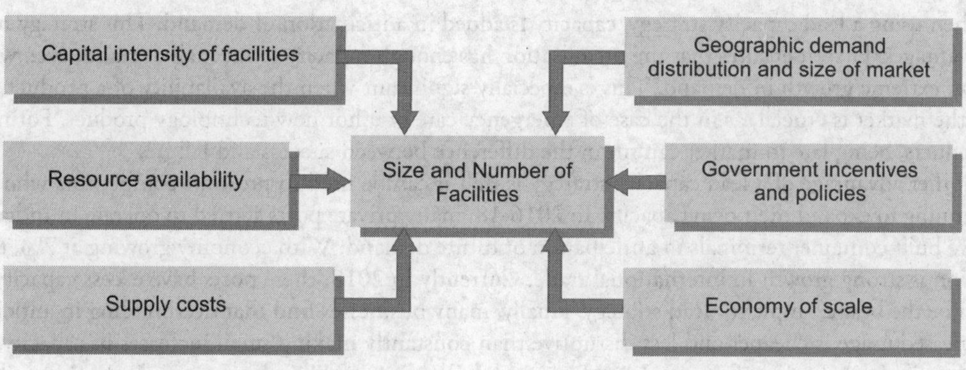

FIGURE 3.3 Size and number of facilities

Capital Intensity of Facilities and Economy of Scale: If a facility attracts huge investments like car assembly plant, organisations mostly restrict number of plants to one and they look for economies of scale at that location.

Resource Availability: Organisations also look at resource/capital availability for multiple plants and decide accordingly. If resource is a constraint, most of the organisations look for few plants and sometimes outsource production from other plants.

Supply Costs: The cost of supply also decides location and number of plants. For products like soaps and detergents, the raw material availability is not restricted by any factors and hence multiple factories are located and serve regional markets. For product like automobiles, the suppliers location is very important in terms of nearness and hence they are located in auto-hubs where suppliers' concentration is available.

Demand Distribution and Size of Market: If the demand is widely distributed across the country, then multiple plants are advisable to reduce outbound costs given that inbound costs are minimum. Power plants are located region wise so that transmission loss can be reduced. Consumer goods like packaged food, shampoo, soaps etc., attract large volumes and hence plants are located region wise and mostly outsourced by marketing companies.

Government Incentives and Policies: Due to strong investment friendliness of state and central governments, many regions attract investments in manufacturing and service business. The state also provides many subsidies to organisations to attract investments. This leads to multiple plants with strategic initiatives including expansion, growth and diversification into related businesses.

2. **Timing and Sizing of Capacity Expansion**

Planning for expansion of capacity is complex decision making due to characteristics of capacity expansion. There is a gap between time of making a decision to expand capacity and the time at which expanded capacity becomes operational. This project lead time creates an uncertainty in decision making. Also, when expansion takes place, the economy of scale should be considered. Incremental small addition in capacity may not provide the economy of scale and hence capacity should be increased in significant scale. These two factors create complexity in decision making related to capacity.

Oftentimes capacity decisions are made to accommodate future growth in demand of product lines. As the demand becomes more uncertain, the decision to increase capacity face uncertainty and risk. The question managers must deal with is how quickly or frequently to increase capacity. Three common strategies for timing capacity expansions are the lead, lag, and match strategies.

When using a lead capacity strategy, capacity is added in anticipation of demand. This strategy has several advantages. First, it ensures that the organisation has enough capacity to meet all demand, even when there is an extreme growth in demand. This is especially significant when the availability of a product or service in the market is crucial, as in the case of emergency care or a hot new technology product. For many new products, being late to market can mean the difference between success and failure.

Another advantage of a lead capacity strategy is that it can be used to preempt competitors who might be planning to expand their own capacity. In 2016-18, many private ports started to operate in India and they have built container terminals in anticipation of future demand. With economy growing at 7%, the expectation is strong growth in international trade. Currently in 2018, these ports have excess capacity and this can be the best example for lead strategy. Finally, many businesses find that overbuilding in anticipation of increased usage is cheaper and less disruptive than constantly making small increases in capacity. Reliance Industries has built its refinery at Jam Nagar with large capacity. With increase in demand for oil products they face less disruptions. Of course, a lead capacity strategy can be risky, particularly if demand is unpredictable or technology is evolving rapidly.

The opposite of a lead capacity strategy is a lag capacity strategy, whereby organisations add capacity only after demand has increased more than its ability to fulfil demand. Three clear advantages of this strategy are a reduced risk of excess capacity or capacity chunk, greater productivity due to higher utilisation of capacity, and the ability to put off large investments as long as possible. Organisations that follow this strategy often provide mature, cost-sensitive products or services. Many government agencies try to avoid adding extra capacity and their requisite costs until absolutely necessary. Most of the public transportation systems and corresponding infrastructures like roads, bridges, airports mostly follow lag strategy. But, one can easily see the drawbacks of a lag capacity strategy, the most evident being the reduced availability of products or services during periods of high demand.

Most organisations do not follow one strategy. For one thing, different products and services require different approaches. Consider ZARA, a fashion retailer who always keep excess capacity for hot fashion items and produce in-house. But for standard items, it outsources to contract manufacturers in China and possibly in other Asian countries. In a state run hospital, where you are the chief executive officer, you will follow a lead capacity strategy for expanding critical emergency services, especially if yours is the only hospital in the region. You will not apply the same rationale to noncritical services.

The timing and sizing of expansion are related; that is, if demand is increasing and the time between increments increases, the size of the increments must also increase. The lead strategy, which stays ahead of demand, minimises the chance of sales lost to insufficient capacity. The wait-and-see strategy lags behind demand, relying on short-term options such as use of overtime, temporary workers, subcontractors, stock outs, and postponement of preventive maintenance to meet any shortfalls. However, these options have their drawbacks. For example, overtime requires payment of time-and-a-half wages for some employees and may result in lower productivity or quality during overtime hours; union agreements may even limit the amount of allowable overtime. Nonetheless, some mix of short-term options might make the wait-and-see strategy best in certain situations.

Several factors favour the lead strategy. Expansion may result in economies of scale and a faster rate of learning, thus helping a firm reduce its costs and compete on price. This strategy might increase the firm's market share or act as a form of preemptive marketing. By making a large capacity expansion or announcing that one is imminent, the firm uses capacity to preempt expansion by other firms. These other firms must sacrifice some of their market share or risk burdening the industry with overcapacity.

The conservative lag strategy is to expand in smaller increments, such as by renovating existing facilities rather than building new ones. Because the wait-and-see strategy follows demand, it reduces the risks of over expansion based on overly optimistic demand forecasts, obsolete technology, or inaccurate assumptions regarding the competition. However, this strategy has different risks, such as being preempted by a competitor or being unable to respond if demand is unexpectedly high. The wait-and-see lag strategy has been criticised as a short-term strategy typical of some U.S. management styles. Managers on the fast track to corporate advancement tend to take fewer risks. They earn promotions by avoiding the big mistake and maximising short-term profits and return on investment. The wait-and-see strategy fits this short-term outlook but can erode market share over the long run.

Management may choose one of these two strategies or one of the many between these extremes. With strategies in the more moderate middle, firms may expand more frequently (on a smaller scale) than with the lead strategy, but do not always lag behind demand as with the wait-and-see strategy. An intermediate strategy could be to follow-the-leader, expanding when others do. If others are right, so are you, and nobody gains a competitive advantage. If they make a mistake and overexpand, everyone shares in the agony of overcapacity.

3. CLUSTERS

Clustering is the phenomenon whereby firms from the same industry gather together in close proximity. It is particularly evident in industries like automobiles, textiles, and banking. Banking centres in cities such as London and New York have thrived for centuries. Hundreds of banks cluster there, close together and within easy walking distance of each other. This makes it easier for customers to choose between them, and might be thought to act against each individual bank's best interests.

By sticking together, firms are able to benefit from such things as the neighborhood's pool of expertise and skilled workers; its easy access to component suppliers (Toyota's suppliers generally cluster round the mother company's factories, wherever they may be); and its information channels (both formal ones like trade magazines and informal ones like everyday gossip in neighbourhood bars). In earlier centuries of industrialisation in England, clusters were common.

Clusters are also common in India especially in the new era where induced efforts are made for promoting cluster oriented growth. The following are some examples:

(a) Chennai, Pune and Gurgaon are automotive cluster
(b) Tiruppur and Ludhiana - Readymade and knitwear clusters
(c) Surat-Textiles and diamond cutting and polishing clusters
(d) Ludhiana-Bicycles parts cluster

In retail business and service sectors, critical mass is important and hence they locate close to each other. In Chennai, one can take the example of jewelries in T. Nagar. Within a radius of 1 km, one can find more than 50 gold jewelers/retailers and all are doing business over a long period. The Mall concept, where all retailers are located in the same place is also another example.

Modern high-tech clusters often gather around prestigious universities on whose research they can piggyback. Silicon Valley is near Stanford University, for example, and similar high-tech clusters are gathered around MIT near Boston in the United States and around Cambridge University in Britain. In India, many new technology start-ups came up near Indian Institute of Technology, Chennai, and they thrive with support from IIT.

That clustering is not a phenomenon whose time has passed is demonstrated by California's Silicon Valley. New IT and internet firms continue to gather there in spite of the high prices of local property and the danger of earthquakes. Ironically, they find that much of the most valuable information that they obtain comes not electronically but from face-to-face meetings.

Michael Porter, a professor at Harvard Business School, has looked recently at this seemingly paradoxical revival of industrial clusters. In theory, he says, location should no longer be a source of competitive advantage in an era of global competition, rapid transport and high-speed telecommunications. The world's increasingly global businesses should by now be above and beyond geography.

Porter gives several (non-silicon) examples, including the wine-growing industry in northern California and the flower-growing business in the Netherlands. The Netherlands would not be the natural first choice for anyone starting a flower-growing business today, were it not for the fact that the business is already there. This is a huge competitive advantage for a new entrant, who can benefit from such things as the sophisticated Dutch flower auctions, the flower-growers' associations and the country's advanced research centres.

Capacity Strategy-Queuing Theory and Service Systems

Capacity in services is the ability to deliver service over a specific time period. For service, the time period can vary from years (e.g. the decision to build an airport) to hours (e.g. staffing a retail check-out counter during non-peak hours). The objective of strategic capacity planning is to determine the level of service capacity with the level of resource mix. The resource mix might consist of facilities, machines and labour.

It is highly challenging for service firms to plan long-term capacity. Service systems are open systems and thus it creates disturbed flow of demand to use capacity. This results in idle capacity in short term. Because of this, service capacity is always measured in terms of inputs. (e.g., warehouse space). The capacity decisions are further complicated by another dimension that in most of the services, customers are participants in service process and their involvement is mostly high in service delivery process. This results in under-utilisation of capacity.

Capacity strategy is highly related to application of queuing theory. General assumption is that one should increase the utilisation of capacity to the maximum so that the asset utilisation improves over a period of time. This is a common practice in manufacturing plants as well as service set ups.

Queuing Models in Capacity Planning for Service Industries

Queuing theory is often useful for designing service systems. Waiting lines have a tendency to form in a wide variety of service systems (airport ticket counter, telephone calls to a cable television company, hospitals, railway reservation counter). The lines are symptoms of bottleneck operations. Queuing theory is useful in helping managers choose a capacity level that will be cost effective through balancing the cost of having customers wait with the cost of providing additional capacity. It can aid in the determination of expected costs for various levels of service capacity.

No doubt those waiting in line would all agree that the solution to the problem is obvious: simply add more servers or else do something to speed up service. While both ideas may be potential solutions, there are certain subtleties that must be dealt with. For one thing, most service systems have the capacity to process more customers over the long run than they are called upon to process. Hence, the problem of waiting is a short-term phenomenon. The other side of the coin is that at certain times the system is empty, and servers are idle waiting for customers. Thus by increasing the service capacity, the server idle time would increase. Consequently, in designing service systems, the designer must calculate the cost of providing a given level of service capacity against the potential cost of having customers wait for service.

The planning and analysis of service capacity frequently lends itself to queuing theory, which is a mathematical approach to the analysis of waiting line problem. These waiting lines are commonly found wherever customers arrive randomly for services (e.g. supermarket checkouts, theaters, toll gates, post-offices, ration shops, etc.). In business situations, the customers are not people, but orders waiting to be filled, trucks waiting to be unloaded, jobs waiting to be processed, or equipment waiting for repairs.

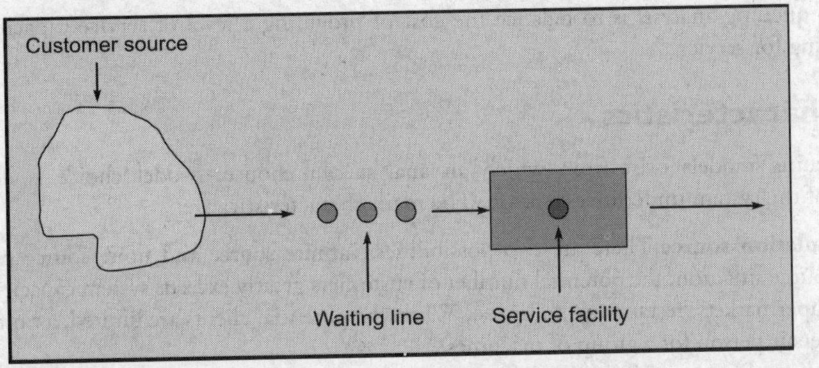

FIGURE 3.4 Simple queue system

Why is There Waiting?

Many people are surprised when they learn that waiting lines tend to form even though a system is basically underloaded. For example, a fast-food restaurant may have the capacity to handle an average of 200 orders per hour. Yet experience waiting line even though the average number of orders is only 150 per hour! The key word is average. In reality, customers arrive at random intervals rather than at evenly spaced intervals, and some orders take longer to fill than others. In other words, both arrivals and service times exhibit a high degree of variability. As a result of this variability, there are times when the system becomes temporarily overloaded, and that gives rise to waiting lines. By the same token, there are other times when the system is idle because there are no customers. Thus, although a system may be underloaded from a macro standpoint, because of variability in arrivals and service, there will be times when the system is overloaded from a micro standpoint.

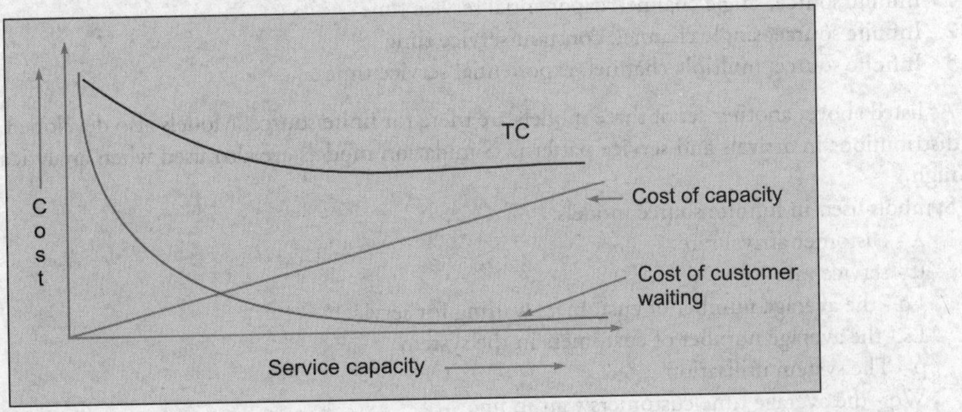

FIGURE 3.5 Tradeoff between service capacity and cost

Goal of Queuing Analysis

The goal of queuing is essentially to minimise total costs. There are two basic categories of cost in a queuing situation: those associated with customers waiting for service and those associated with capacity. Capacity costs relate to maintaining the ability to provide capacity (for example, the number of check-outs in a super market, number of reservation counters). Waiting costs include the salaries paid to employees, waiting space cost and customer dissatisfaction.

The goal of queuing analysis is to balance the cost of providing a level of service capacity and the cost of customers waiting for service.

System Characteristics

Numerous queuing models exist from which an analyst can choose. Model choice is dependent on the characteristics of the system under investigation. The main characteristics are:

1. **The population source** There are two possibilities: infinite source and finite source populations. In an infinite source situation, the potential number of customers greatly exceeds system capacity. (Service is unrestricted-supermarkets, restaurants, tollgates.) When the potential clients are limited, a finite source situation exists (a repair person for a group of machines).
2. **The number of servers (channels)** The capacity of queuing system is a function of the capacity of each server and the number of servers being used. Systems can be either single or multiple channels.
3. **Arrival and service time patterns** Most commonly used models assume that the customer arrival rate can be described by a Poisson distribution and that of the service time can be described by a negative exponential distribution. But these can change into other probability distributions.
4. **The queue discipline (order of service)** All of the models assume that service is provided on a first-come, first-served (FCFS) basis (banks, stores, ATMs). Examples of systems that do not follow by FCFS rule include hospital emergency rooms, rush orders in factory and computer processing of programs.

Queuing Models

Queuing models are discussed in detail in this section.

1. Infinite source, single channel, exponential service time
2. Infinite source, single channel, constant service time
3. Infinite source, multiple channel, exponential service time

As listed above, another set of three models are there for finite source. Models also developed for various types of distributions in arrivals and service patterns. Simulation models are also used when analytical models are not enough.

Symbols used in infinite source models:

λ - customer arrival rate
μ - service rate
Lq - the average number of customers waiting for service
Ls - the average number of customers in the system
ρ - The system utilisation
Wq - the average time customers wait in line
Ws - the average time customers spend in the system
$1/\mu$ - service time
M - the number of servers/channels
L_{max} - the maximum expected number waiting in line

Measures of system performance:

1. The average number being served: 'r' = λ/μ
2. The average number in the system: Ls = Lq + r

3. The average time in line: Wq = Lq/r
4. The average time in the system, including service time: $Ws = Wq + 1/\mu$
5. System utilisation: $\rho = \lambda/(M\mu)$

Formulas for basic single server model:

1. Average number in line: $Lq = \lambda^2/\mu(\mu - \lambda)$
2. Probability of zero units in the system: $P_0 = 1-(\lambda/\mu)$
3. Probability of 'n' units in the system: $Pn = P_0(\lambda/\mu)^n$

EXAMPLE 3.1

An airline is planning to open a satellite ticket desk in a new shopping plaza, staffed by one ticket agent. It is estimated that requests for tickets and information will average 15 per hour and requests will have a Poisson distribution. Service time is assumed as exponentially distributed. Previous experience with similar satellite operations suggest that mean service time should average about three minutes per request. Determine the following.

1. System utilisation
2. Per cent of time the server (agent) will be idle
3. The expected number of customers waiting to be served
4. The average time customers will spend in the system
5. The probability of zero customers in the system and the probability of four customers in the system

Solution:

l = 15 per hour

m = 1/service time = (1 customer/3 minutes) ¥ 60 minutes per hour = 20 customers per hour

System utilisation: r = l/(Mm) = 15/1(20) = 0.75 = 75%

Idle time = 1– r = 25%

Lq = l²/m(m – l) = 15 ¥ 15/20(20 – 15) = 2.25 customers

Ws = Wq + 1/m = Lq/l + 1/m =2.25/15 + 1/20 = 0.20 hours or 12 minutes

P_0 = 1–(l/m)= 1 – 15/20 = 0.25

P_4 = 0.25 (15/20)⁴ = 0.79

Increasing Production Capacity Reduces Manufacturing Lead Times

Only slight increases in production capacities can lead to significant reduction of manufacturing lead times. With significant reduction of work-in-process inventory, more orders can be processed.

Queuing theory can be used to analyse waiting-line production problems.

A production manager believes that reducing the plant's production lead time will give the firm a significant competitive advantage. Two days is the lead time goal that he wants to achieve. Currently, production jobs are arriving at the rate of 6 per day and the operation can process an average of 6.125 jobs per day. What is the current average lead time for a job? What is the necessary production rate to achieve the two-day lead time goal?

l- customer arrival rate or jobs arrival rate = 6 per day

m- service time or process rate = 6.125 /day

Ws – the average time jobs spend in the system

Ws = 1/(m – l) = 1/(6.125 – 6) = 8 days

So, the current lead time per job is 8 days.

Number of jobs in the system Wq = l/(m – l) = 6/(6.125 – 6) = 48 jobs.

Now lead time goal is 2 days (Ws). Substituting in Ws formula and calculating the required process rate 'm'

m = (1/Ws) + l = (1/2) + 6 = 6.5 jobs per day

Also the number of jobs in the system also will get reduced.

New Wq = 6/(6.5 – 6)= 12 jobs.

So, it is concluded that, by increasing the capacity by little, one can reduce the lead time significantly. Many organisations practise this and they get befitted from this strategy.

It may be noted that ZARA Fashion Retailor applied queuing principle in its capacity decision for a distribution centre. Even though there's ample capacity in their distribution centre during most of the year, ZARA still opened a new 100 million Euro, 1,20,000 square metre logistics centre in Zaragoza in 2003. ZARA's strategy is in line with queuing theory principles. The waiting time and inventory shoots up when capacity is tight and demand is varying. ZARA, being in fashion industry and responsiveness is the priority, is tolerating lower capacity utilisation of its factories and warehouses.

SUMMARY

Capacity planning and management is one of the important strategic decisions which operations manager may have to consider. Capacity defines how much a work station or a service facility can handle in a given unit of time. Capacity can be technically defined as the output under input conditions that happen based on design. The installed capacity of a plant is achievable capacity of multiple stations to give an output. Installed capacity can be in terms of output units or throughput used for producing certain output. However, effective capacity could be different from installed capacity as set conditions may not be able to achieve installed capacity.

Various key drivers are discussed that could set upper limits for a plant. Key drivers include demand factors; supply factors; technological factors; capital availability; scope for flexibility in deployment and competitive conditions and so on. A firm can take traditional strategic planning process for capacity decisions or can take emergent decisions or take a blue ocean strategy through innovation and exploring unexplored terrains.

Further, approach to strategising capacity sizing decision may be understood from resource led, market led forces and need for balanced capacity in a multi station facility. These could be based on weight losing nature of the material (resource led); need to be closer to market (market led) or multi station process or line which would have varying designed capacity at independent stations and choose an option which optimises overall capacity in terms of output or throughput for achieving an installed capacity level or best of effectiveness of capital invested (balanced capacity).

Then, steps in capacity planning process are explained which are similar to steps in traditional strategic management process. One may have to evaluate current capacity levels and identify gaps. Then this must be assessed based on future requirements of capacity based on business plans. After analysing technical market and financial implications, a sensitivity analysis must be carried out. A choice for implementation has to be exercised and then a specialised team takes over implementation. On installation, operations manager takes care of regular monitoring of effectiveness of capacity installed. This would be a continuing process.

Service capacity decisions will have to consider certain service related unique factors. These include perishability of capacity if unutilised; volatile nature of demand; need to offer where customer is and supply chain goals of responsiveness and cost management in deciding capacity sizing of service offerings.

Thus, this chapter gives a framework under which capacity sizing decisions are made.

Key Terms

Capacity: The upper limit on the load that an operation facility can handle is called capacity.

Capacity planning: The objective of capacity planning is to achieve a long run match between supply capabilities and demand requirements in terms of products and services.

Design capacity: This means that the equipment or facility or manpower time is set to achieve a desired output.

Capacity utilisation: Capacity utilisation is the extent to which an enterprise or SBU or a line uses its installed productive capacity. It is the relationship between actual output that 'is' actually produced with the installed equipment, and the potential output which 'could' be produced with it, if capacity was fully used. Utilisation, is thus, actual output divided by design capacity.

Efficiency: Efficiency is measured as actual output divided by effective capacity.

Fixed cost: It is a periodic cost that remains more or less unchanged irrespective of the output level or sales revenue, such as depreciation, insurance, interest, rent, salaries and wages.

Internal rate of return: It is defined as the discount rate at which the present value of all future cash flow is equal to the initial investment or, in other words, the rate at which an investment breaks even. A firm would undertake all projects or investments available with IRRs that exceed the cost of capital.

Bottleneck: The bottleneck is defined as the process step (station) in the production line or service centre with the lowest capacity (the "weakest link"). Although the bottleneck is often the process step with the longest processing time, it is important to always look at the capacities for making a judgment.

Process capacity: The process capacity is always equivalent to the capacity of the bottleneck. It is useful to calculate a comprehensible number, such as customers per hour or parts per day.

Payback period: The length of time required to recover the cost of an investment. It is arrived by dividing cost of project by average annual cash inflows.

Throughput ratio: Throughput ratio is the rate a plant or service centre is able to produce a product or service for a given unit of time. Those with high throughput (output) levels are able to be more competitive than lower throughput firms because they are able to produce a given product or service more efficiently.

Variable cost: Variable costs are those costs that vary depending on a company's production volume; they rise as production increases and fall as production decreases. Variable costs can include direct material costs or direct labour costs necessary to complete a certain project.

CONCEPT REVIEW QUESTIONS

1. Describe the importance of capacity planning decision from business perspective with suitable examples.
2. Explain the following:
   a. Design capacity
   b. Installed capacity
   c. Effective capacity
   d. Capacity utilisation
3. Describe the key drivers in arriving at capacity sizing decision. Illustrate with examples.
4. What are the different approaches to capacity decisions? Give example for each of the approaches namely resource led, market led and balanced capacity.
5. Describe different steps in capacity planning.
6. What are unique aspects of service business and how do they impact capacity decisions? Illustrate with examples.
7. Explain the following:
   a. Market evaluation for capacity sizing
   b. Financial evaluation and different techniques

c. Technical factor analysis for determining capacity size

d. Importance of sensitivity analysis

CRITICAL THINKING QUESTIONS

1. Imagine that you are consultant engaged by a promoter whose family owns a large piece of land in the heart of the city. There is a scope to set up a five star hotel in joint venture with an international chain using this as resource. How would you strategise the proposal? What are the key service capacity to be identified and advice on steps to develop a plan for capacity decision?
2. If you are in charge of operations of a component business, which supplies to a scooter manufacturer. There is a sudden increase in demand. Your CEO suggests that you can buy the component and supply after ensuring quality as he was not sure of sustained increase demand. He wants to observe for the next two years. This may require buying out from contract manufacturer at ₹150 per component for incremental demand of 3,00,000 units for whole year. Their current capacity is 15,00,000 units. The cost of manufacture at their unit is ₹108 per unit. If he has to add capacity, he may have to invest ₹3 crore. This will be depreciated on a straight line method over 10 years. Assuming he may bring all capital through equity and his effective tax rate is 30%, how would you approach this decision? You may assume cost of capital to be 12 per cent for your decision making.
3. Imagine you are consultantly approached by an FMCG company selling its products in different parts of India. Considering the fact that Goods & Services Tax is likely to be implemented soon, they want to consolidate their RDCs in one location. The current locations are Chennai, Bengaluru, Kochi, Coimbatore, Madurai, Manipal, Hyderabad, Vizag and Pondicherry. With likely uniform tax regime, how would you approach a solution? Before getting into detailed financial evaluation, you may provide a theoretical construct of the solution.

PROJECT ASSIGNMENTS

1. Think about setting up a green field international airport in a potential city. Develop the capacity strategy for the new airport.
2. Develop capacity measures for the following industries.
   (a) Retail services
   (b) Airlines
   (c) Food delivery start-ups
   (d) Warehousing company
   (e) Health fitness centre
3. Find out an industrial cluster near you and identify the driving factors shaping that cluster.
4. Recently, a new kind of delivery logistics emerged in developing and developed economies called Crowd Logistics. The new start-ups use ordinary people for logistics on unit rate basis. How can capacity be built in this business model? What kind of issues will you face with respect to capacity when demand varies?

REFERENCES

1. Simchi-Levi, David (2010). "Operations Rule", MIT Press.
2. Ferdows, Kasra, Lewis, A. Michael and Machuca, A. D., Jose., "Rapid Fire Fulfillment", *Harvard Business Review*, November 2004.

CHAPTER

4

Supply Network and Supply Chain Strategies

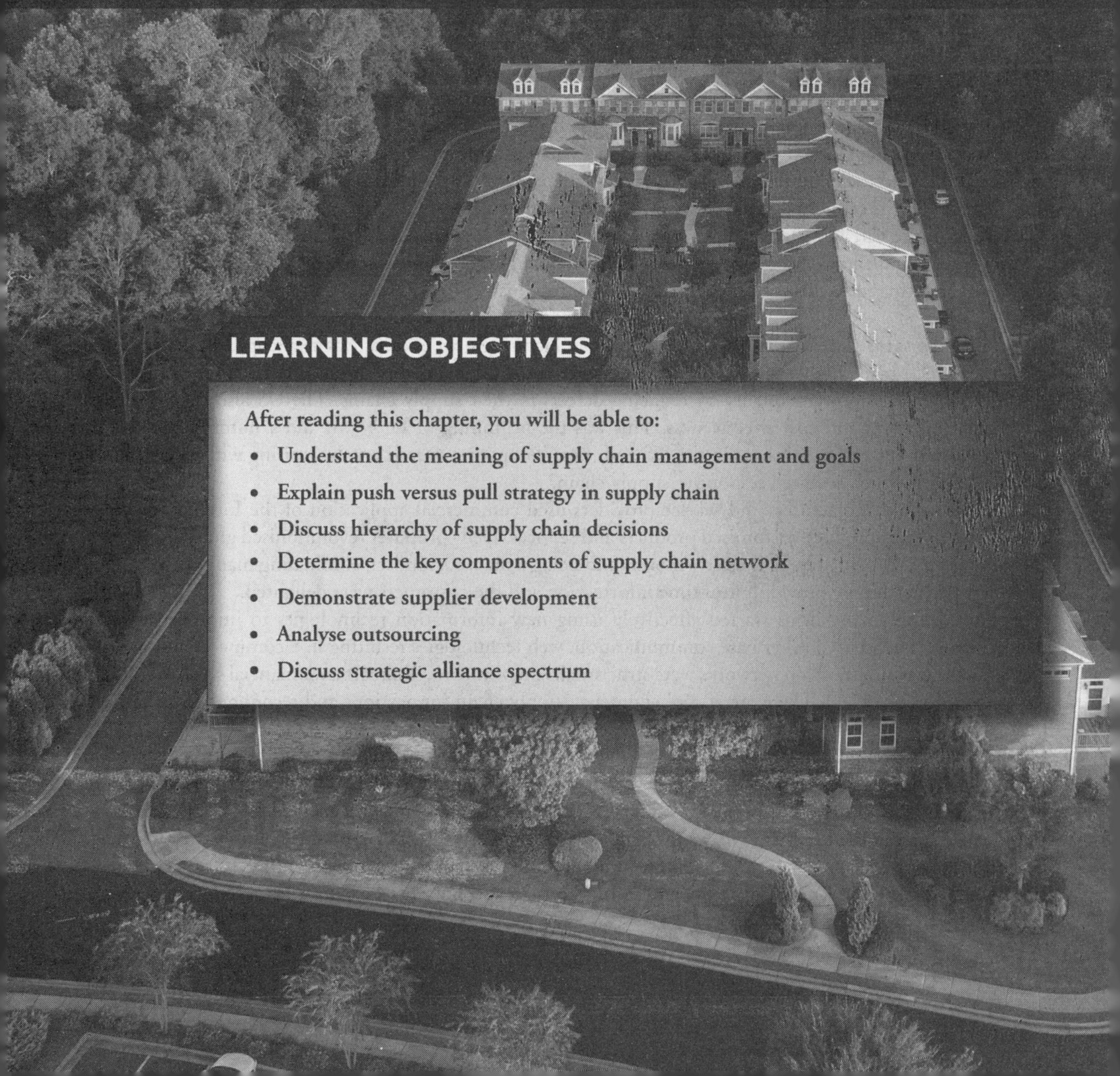

LEARNING OBJECTIVES

After reading this chapter, you will be able to:

- Understand the meaning of supply chain management and goals
- Explain push versus pull strategy in supply chain
- Discuss hierarchy of supply chain decisions
- Determine the key components of supply chain network
- Demonstrate supplier development
- Analyse outsourcing
- Discuss strategic alliance spectrum

Introduction

In modern business, one can see how new ideas and technologies have revolutionised supply chains. Firms are competing on supply chain networks rather than on products, services and geographies! Industrialisation led to capital-intensive mechanised production systems which replaced labour-intensive production systems. Infrastructure development like railroads, national highways, port development, aerospace and new communications media expanded markets and made supply chains effective and efficient. Population growth, formation of regional and international trade unions have also accelerated growth of communities which galloped demand for goods and services. And now digital world has combined the globe into almost one market. Unless, firms and their operations strategy reach certain level of maturity in logistics and supply chain domain, firms would find competitive challenge for survival.

In the early 1900s, Ford successfully established automotive company in the US with car manufacturing being vertically integrated and mass production enabled. Henry Ford created the first moving assembly line. This reduced the time required to build a Model T from 728 hours to 1.5 hours and ushered in the mass production era. Over the next 60 years, American manufacturers became adept at mass production and streamlined supply chains with the help of scientific management methods and operations research techniques.

Post World War II, economies were resurrecting and new World Economic Order was emerging. European economies, especially Germany, Belgium and France were gaining prominence because of the development in manufacturing and trade. Similarly, in East, especially Japan was emerging strong and rising like a phoenix from dust of wars with its economy being led by growth in manufacturing.

Starting in the early 1970s, Japanese manufacturers like Toyota changed the rules of production from mass to lean. Lean manufacturing focusses on flexibility and quality more than on efficiency and quantity. Significant lean manufacturing ideas include Six Sigma quality control, just-in-time inventory and total quality management (TQM).

Around the same time in the 1970s, the US manufacturing's superiority was challenged by firms in many industries which made higher quality products at lower costs. Global competition forced the US manufacturers to concentrate on improving quality by reducing defects in their supply chains. The US also started focussing on quality initiatives and cost effectiveness. This was the beginning of IT boom and a number of technology companies started having their base in the US and these companies started revolutionising with new generation business models which required responsive supply chain.

In 1990s, the manufacturers and service providers used commercial application of the Internet, technology and started to mass-produce customised products and services. Dell computer revolutionised global business with the same approach, being one of the early movers and being a mass customiser, eliminating many channel players, built new partnership by providing real time information and the customers were delighted.

Following this, many firms started effectively using new information technologies to improve service and delivery processes. Secured cyber base communication, web technologies resulting in e-commerce and e-business changing the way supply chain networks were structured. Amazon.com, Walmart and financial services companies led the way for a new era. There are also phenomenal supply chain innovations and reconfigurations impacting business models and thereby fortunes of stakeholders positively.

Today, one is living in an era of digitalised revolution in marketing and selling goods to customers across the globe. One would also see within a national, state and district boundaries that B2C selling of physical goods is happening. Further, one would also notice selling of services and supply network enabled seamlessly for customer fulfilment. One can see healthcare utilising digital supply network for fixing appointment, connecting medical doctors, surgeons and a hospital theater or consulting room booked and patient being offered a service. There are sites which enable even payment gateway and record keeping and link to e-pharmaceutical service wherever it is legally permitted.

Exhibit 4.1

Sale of mobile phone on a marketplace like Amazon in India (Illustration for academic purpose only and not validated business process)

This is presented from a customer perspective and Amazon is the focal firm which owns this supply network. Amazon lists various vendors like Apple, Samsung, Redmi, Honor, Vivo, Oppo and so on. (See Screenshot 4.1).

Customer can review the model, compare prices, also refer to customer feedback and make a decision. There are certain orders which will be billed on the brand directly but fulfiled by the marketplace, here by Amazon from its fulfilment centre. In such cases, the marketplace, namely Amazon, stock goods in a distribution centre and assure supply. Rest of the products for which supply is made from the vendor, there is a time window of service confirmed by the vendor which is shared with the customer for tracking. It may also be noted that Amazon may have its own dedicated delivery set up or service partner who would deliver to customers. On the other hand, in case of vendor directly delivering to the customer, it may still use Amazon platform for information sharing and delivery can happen either with their own network partners or through Amazon is delivery partner.

Source: Open access and experience sharing of customers. Accessed on 19 February 2018

Example shown in Exhibit 4.1 covers innovativeness and genius structuring supply chain networks which have become possible with explosion in technology, adoption across network, people capability and structuring of business process. Even product/service flows are synchronised with informational and financial flows for efficient and effective supply chain. At the end of the day, it not only benifit the focal organisation but also every stakeholder, including the customers, and it is shared in an equitable way. Hence, one could observe that supply chain has evolved dramatically over the period and keeps challenging business for its success.

Supply Chain Manageent

A number of authors and institutions have presented various definitions of supply chain management (SCM) over years. Many times, it is seen as logistics, operations management, procurement or a combination of the three (Lambert et al 2000), but today, the broader definition by Global Supply Forum is generally accepted, "Supply Chain Management is the integration of key business processes from end user through original suppliers that provides products, services, and information that add value for customers and other stakeholders". This definition mentions about key business processes like buying, movement or storage and their integration, without limiting any one activity. Also, using terms like original suppliers and adding value to customers and stakeholders which are quite interesting and appreciable.

Another interesting description is that, "SCM is the term used to describe the management of the flow of materials, information, and funds across the entire supply chain, from suppliers to component producers to final assemblers to distribution (warehouses and retailers), and ultimately to the consumer". This highlights managing three flows, namely physical, informational and financial flows across the chain and also about a purpose being relevant to the ultimate customer. The object of SCM is the supply chain which represents "… Network of organizations that are involved, through upstream and downstream linkages, in the different processes and activities that produce value in the form of products and services in the hands of the ultimate customer" (Christopher, 1998). This connotes that a supply chain involves two or more organisations for serving the ultimate customer, which happens by articulating the flow of material, finance and information. It may be worth reiterating here that the key to existence of supply chain is the presence of ultimate customers and value to them.

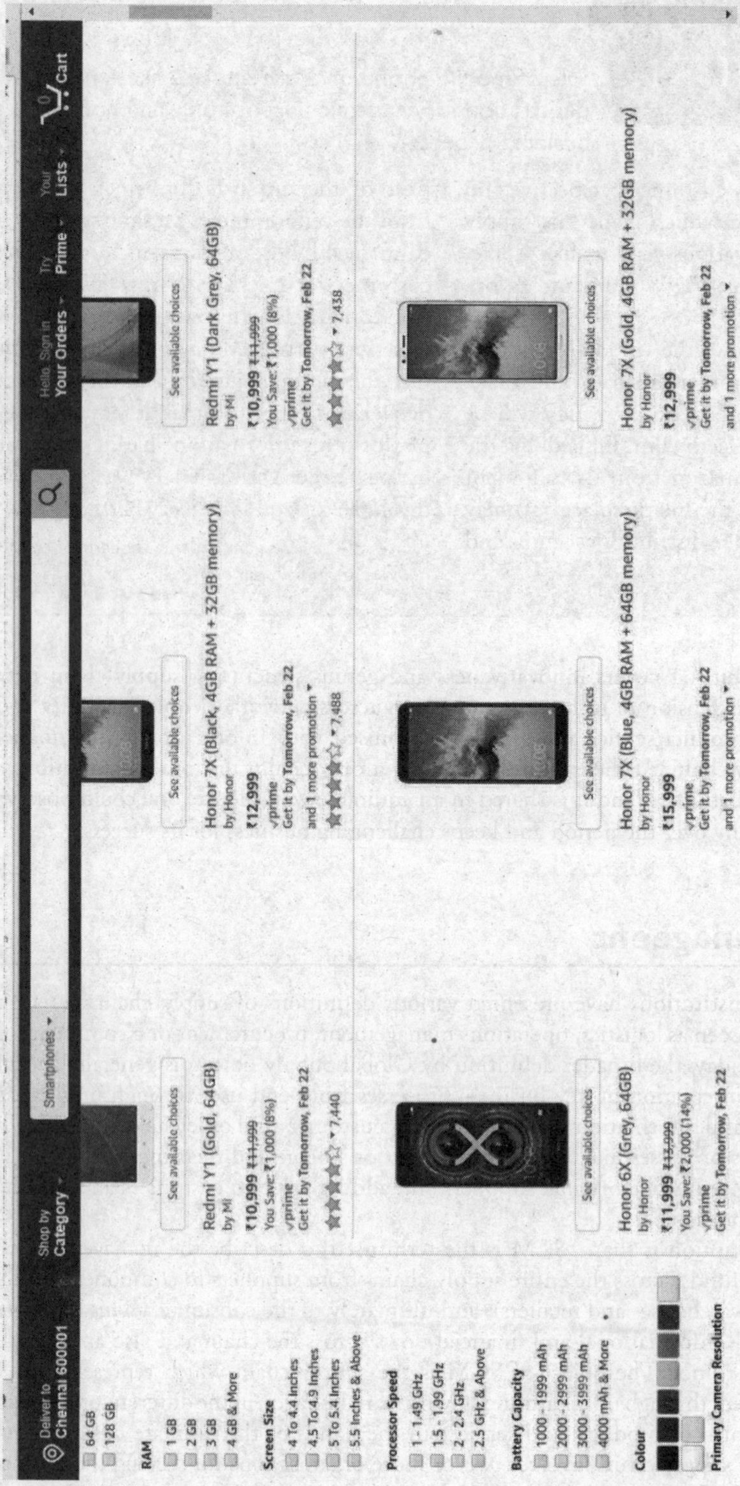

SCREENSHOT 4.I

A network of organisations, generally, links up nodes and flow of multiple entities. Some of the flows could be divergent while the others could be convergent. An organisation would focus on flow of goods and services to a set of customers for which a value is being enabled.

There has been a tendency to use nomenclatures, logistics and supply chain management interchangeably. In fact, some professionals treat approach to each of these interchangeably also. It may be useful to understand the focus areas of both of these where one would find commonality and niche of each of these. Evolution of each of these has the advantage of the other as it has been mentioned earlier how logistics functions existed in earlier era and its contribution in public life, military operations and business.

Value Chain, Value System and Supply Chain

As one observes relationship about logistics and supply chain management, it may be useful here to discuss another useful concept, namely "*Value chain*" developed by Michael E. Porter (1985) and relate it with supply chain. According to Porter, value chain analysis can be used to identify an organisation's internal business processes and how they interact. An organisation in its purpose of creating value to different stakeholders performs numerous activities which are a part of processes. These could be to develop, produce, sell, and distribute its services and products.

Again, value activities are those which create value for the customers. Customer perspective, in certain cases, is given more importance rather than cost parameter; an organisation may have a tendency of increasing cost as a premium product or service. According to this, value is more important than the cost. Customer's value is captured by way of revenue which would be cost plus margin.

TABLE 4.1 Value chain of a washing machine manufacturer

Category	Activities	Washing machine example
Inbound logistics	Associated with receiving, storing, and disseminating inputs into the product, such as material handling, warehousing, inventory control, vehicle scheduling and returns to suppliers.	Receiving of components like motors, electrical switches, controls, metal sheets and paints.
Operations	Associated with transforming inputs into the final product form, such as machining, packaging, assembly, equipment maintenance, testing, printing, and facility operations.	Assembly of components and conversion into final product.
Outbound logistics	Associated with collecting, storing, and physically distributing the product to buyers, such as finished goods warehousing, material handling, finished goods inventory control, delivery vehicle operation, order processing and scheduling.	Movement of finished goods into mother warehouses, dealers and own stores.

(*Continued*)

Category	Activities	Washing machine example
Marketing and Sales	Associated with providing a means by which buyers can purchase the product and inducing them to do so, such as advertising, promotion, sales force, quoting, channel selection, channel relations and pricing.	Marketing functions like pricing, promotions, appointment of channel partners and sales force management.
Service	Associated with providing service to enhance or maintain the value of the product, such as installation, repair, training, parts supply and product adjustment.	Installation of product at customer's place on purchase, warranty management and parts availability.

According to Porter, there are five generic categories of primary activities involved in competing in any industry, as shown in Table 4.1. Each of the above in Table 4.1 is divisible into a number of distinct activities that depend on a particular industry and firm strategy. One may observe that two of the five, namely inbound logistics and outbound logistics, are key focus areas of logistics management and play a significant role in value chain activities. Though operations which are a part of manufacturing and marketing and sales and service are a part of marketing function and also involve supply chain and logistics focus. Hence, primary activities of value chain have strong connection with logistic and supply chain management.

Instead one could argue that essence of value chain arises from efficient management of supply chain. Value chain for competitive advantage could only be possible if there could be application of strategies like cost leadership, differentiation and focus applied to primary activities. For example, in the same industry like auto manufacture, few players are able to deploy just-in-time (JIT) inventory management more effectively in reducing cost and providing value to customers compared to competitors. This is possible because of the focus they provide for inventory management function compared to competition which could be due to strategic initiatives deployed over years. Key point is that synchronisation of logistics perspective is important for managing value chain activities.

Support activities, according to Porter, can be divided into four categories, namely (i) procurement, (ii) technology development, (iii) human resources management, and (iv) firm's infrastructure including general management, planning, finance, accounting, legal, government affairs and quality management. Of these, procurement is more of a logistics related function. He defines procurement as the function of purchasing inputs used in a firm's value chain and not as the purchased inputs per se. According to him, the cost of procurement activities itself usually represents a small if not significant portion of total costs, but often has a large impact on firm's overall cost and differentiation. Improved purchasing practices can strongly affect the cost and quality of inputs, as well as of other activities associated with receiving and using the inputs, and interacting with suppliers.

If one looks at the value chain activities, they are mainly inward looking and organisation centric. As one is familiar with Porter's framework on industry analysis in which he discusses five forces models, he reckons power of buyers and sellers and intensity of rivalry among firms in an industry to succeed. It is natural for him to extend or move value chain analysis forward, the spectrum of relationships for competitive advantage.

According to Porter (1985), a firm's value chain is embedded in a larger stream of activities termed as "*value system*". Value system links up value chain of the firm with the value chain of supplier and with that of channel and buyer (Figure 4.1). In the upstream linkages with suppliers, a firm must synchronise its value chain with that of the supplier.

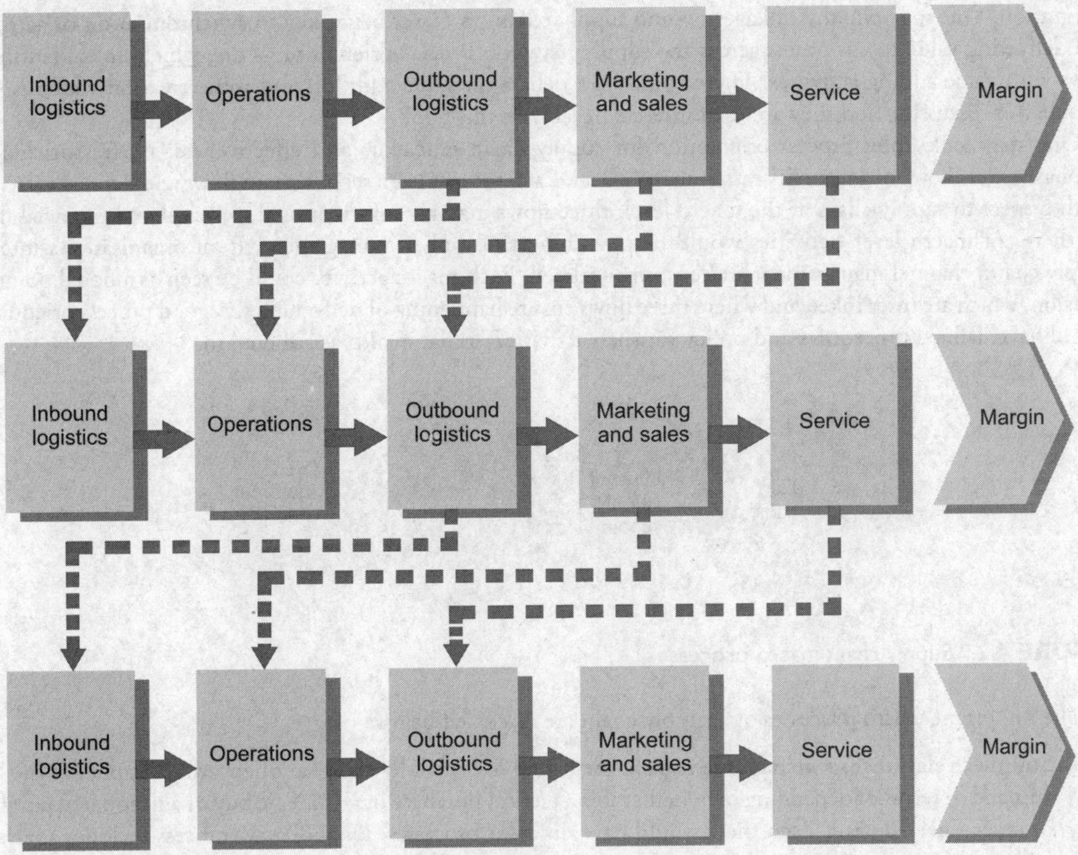

FIGURE 4.1 Value System and its linkage to supply chain network

When one looks at the value system, it is not just movement of goods from a supplier. It is more as a buyer from upstream understanding value creating activities of supplier, including margin, which is critical for competitive advantage. In the same way for downstream linkages at node, value mapping and understanding is critical. Competitive advantage could be gained and sustained not merely by understanding one's value chain but the whole system is critical. This is what the supply chain concepts focus at. Today, companies no longer compete on product or service but mainly on the strength of the supply network. Hence, it is important for a supply chain manager to understand the nuances of value chain and value system and work with strategic management orientation for driving success.

Hence strategically managing suppliers, channel partners and customers, which are key to supply chain management, are the essence of value system. It is important to note interfaces of concepts and framework and not to be carried away with the idea that one could replace the other framework.

Supply Chain Macro Process

In continuation with our discussion on value system, it could be useful to have an understanding of macro processes of supply chain. This would show interfaces among supply chain network and need for seamless integration. One may cite the linkages among supply chain processes being key to synchronisation of activities and delivering value to customers across the supply network. Process orientation is one which links identifiable flows with value adding activities. There could be a debate on value addition and value creation which is kept outside this discussion and they are used interchangeably in this book.

One may look upon process orientation for supply chain efficiency and effectiveness. Process orientation emphasises on "how" of an activity rather than "what". Each process has a set of certain flows and defined activities. With respect to supply chain at the macro level, three flows, namely informational, physical and financial flows are there. At macro level, activities would be pertaining to supplier management, focal organisation's internal supply chain, channel management and customer related. Each macro activity could be seen as a nodal point for decision, which are interlinked and where three flows ensure happening of deliverables. A good process orientation would have defined procedures and policy for such activities so that quality is adhered to.

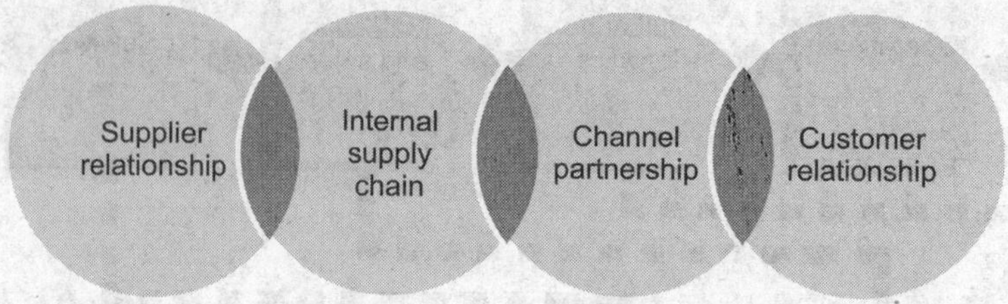

FIGURE 4.2 Supply chain macro processes

The important macro processes of a supply chain are discussed below:

(i) **Supplier relationship management process:** Figure 4.2 includes the goal of ensuring supplies at the best cost and in terms of depending on whether it is a tactical purchase or a strategic buy or a negotiated purchase or an engineered item. Each these would have different processes. By and large, process includes analysing information on supplier capabilities and pricing. Strategic buying and engineered item would have more activities in the process of evaluation, especially at the initial stage of collaboration. It must be clearly understood that the whole supplier management process is driven by the nature of purchase and linked to product manufactured. This establishes backward linkages in the supply chain network.

(ii) **Internal supply chain process:** This includes a number of activities with respect to receiving of goods, conversion and despatch of finished goods. During this process, goods are internally value added through in-plant logistics operations like stores management, movement, storage and so on. All these activities are heavily linked to supplier collaboration like JIT, Kanban and design collaboration, etc., and also with channel partners and customers. One may note that automated information flow and physical movement are synchronised for supplier maintained inventory at the plant. Same would be true if one were to consider importance of information flow from customer end to plant operations, especially changes in weekly production in tune with change in market conditions. Financial flows are fundamentally essential in these, and hence functional approach to manufacturing would limit to excellence in manufacturing but may lack supply chain synchronisation unless it is explicitly pursued.

(iii) **Channel management:** The next important macro process is channel management. One can look at this as key distribution functionality. Instead of looking at distribution as a function, one may take a process approach. It is important to note linkages in distribution with multi-tier depending upon type of products moved. In case of FMCG and consumer products group, it may have multi-tier. In case of heavy capital goods, it could be a simple channel structure but with complicated movement and handling activities. The goal in this stage is mainly to reduce channel cost and improve availability to customers. Channel conflicts emerge because of priorities and conflicts in objectives between channel partners and the focal organisation.

Unless, flows are synchronised and trust is created among stakeholders, supply chain would suffer in terms of effectiveness and efficiency.

(iv) **Customer relationship management:** Another important macro process is customer relationship management (CRM). As mentioned earlier, the purpose of a supply chain network is to serve an ultimate customer of the focal organisation. The focal organisation orients itself to synchronise its role agents and processes to serve a customer at a right price. The customer delight happens only if the product meets customer satisfaction in terms of time, quantity, responsiveness and cost. Also aspects like warranty, service support and parts availability are critical. Customer retention and upgrade would be key expectations of the focal organisation which could happen only if flows, namely financial, informational and product are managed effectively. Interdependence among processes and role agents must be well-appreciated and synchronised for effective and efficient supply chain network. CRM from supply chain management perspective must take care of responsiveness, reliability and flexibility. These could be possible only when focal organisation seamlessly integrates all processes.

It is pertinent to note process orientation and the importance of linkages among macro process for running an effective supply chain network. Though task and parameters for accomplishment of task are important for functional approach, primarily supply chain management is entrenched on process orientation and adherence. Successful organisations identify their macro processes and enable them seamlessly. A strategic orientation needs to be in place to ensure that these processes engage all supply network partners in fulfiling customer orders.

Another methodology of process view is discussed by Sunil Chopra and others (2007). According to Chopra, "A supply chain is a sequence of processes and flows that takes place within and between different supply chain stages and combine to fill a customer need for a product". A cycle view is a process in a supply chain that is divided into a series of cycles, each performed at the interfaces between two successive supply chain stages. Alternatively, push/pull views are also processes in a supply chain that are divided into two categories depending on whether they are executed in response to a customer order (pull) or in anticipation of a customer order (push).

There are typically five nodes, namely customer, retailer, distributor, manufacturer and supplier; and four stages in supply chain. Cycle view clearly defines processes involved and the owners of each process. This view specifies the roles and responsibilities of each member and the desired outcome of each process. The four processes in four stages are:

1. Customer order cycle (customer-retailer)
2. Replenishment cycle (retailer-distributor)
3. Manufacturing cycle (distributor-manufacturer)
4. Procurement cycle (manufacturer-supplier)

It can be observed that these are closely linked to the macro processes discussed earlier. One may also note that the number of stages are decided depending upon the value creation of intermediaries. For example, traditional business like dairy industry has numerous of stages as intermediaries. On the other hand, certain businesses like manufacture of capital goods may have less number of intermediaries. However, such operations would also have severe process intensity within the level of operation. The importance of this approach is that it is useful in supply chain operations and establishment of rules and procedures and enables handling performance expectations well.

Similarly, supply chain is mainly driven for serving an ultimate customer and processes get triggered in relation to customer demand. Such process views could be classified either in anticipation of demand or in response to a customer demand. Pull in supply chain depicts execution of demand being initiated in response to a customer order. This process is reactive but brings value creation to customers by allowing flexible configuration of products. The advantage to focal organisation is that it reduces finished goods inventory by postponement. For example, 'Dial a Pizza' is normally a pull based supply chain wherein the focal organisation provides customers flexibility in selecting toppings of their choice. And at the same time, the focal organisation manages inventory better.

Push in supply chain means execution of processes are initiated in anticipation of customer orders. This mainly depicts speculative character of supply chain where production and stocking happens based on demand forecasts. This process would be more driven by economies of scale in operations and for low value items. For example, popular model of two wheelers are produced in India based on demand estimates and await customer initiation of demand to be sold out of the available stock. Hence these are the categories of products which are built to stock.

It is important to understand the boundary of push and pull in any supply chain network. These processes are useful in considering strategic decisions relating to supply chain design as one gets more global view of how supply chain processes relate to customer orders. Based on such global view, facility locations could be split or consolidated and other facets of supply chain can then be designed accordingly. One may also note here that the balancing of push and pull processes and their relative importance will have an impact on supply chain process. Generally, it is believed that push process would be focussed on cost and pull processes would be on responsiveness.

Interface of Technology, Process and People

The era of technology explosion has given way to remarkable experience of revolutionary supply chain with new business models in the last two decades. This is one of the key strategic initiatives which are being increasingly adopted by firms to gain competitive advantage.

About two to three decades ago, global business was experiencing technology development. Technology can be divided again into two (i) information technology and (ii) purely business specific technology. Advancement of each of these independently triggered growth for the other and customers benefitted in a big way. A classic example one could cite is e-business, especially from fruits to apartments, books to boutiques, cards to cars, and so on. One could see success in different models like B2B, B2C, G2C, and so on. These are all possible because technology could be a trigger and at the same time, be amenable to all these.

Business applications have moved from simple use of technology for transactions and management information system to real time connectivity and integration with partners eliminating time and need to stock information and cash. Today manufacturing firms have a supplier network linked through their server and visibility on production plan and schedule are enabled for efficiency and effectiveness in supply chain. It is difficult to imagine life and business without interface of technology, more like a routine and close to being a universal truth. Handheld instruments, smartphones and tablets are revolutionising the way business is transacted.

The capability of people in supply chain domain has also been improving dramatically. Their competencies are critical at operating and planning levels. They must have the ability to take advantage of process and technology advancements. One would wonder how in transformed supply chain such phenomenal changes occurred in India. If one had experienced receiving a courier and small packets earlier, the delivery personnel would bring less organised document at the time of delivery and took confirmation of receipts. One would wonder how such people would confirm delivery to consigner.

Today delivery personnel carry a small handheld device and take the signature on the monitor of the same. One can track the delivery status sitting anywhere in the world on near real time basis. Similarly, a store person who had been handling huge documents for reordering and analysis, now is able to do it using technology. People have not changed but capability has improved dramatically. One can go on listing such examples around us. These could be in public life, services like banking, insurance and education or manufacturing like engineering, pharmaceuticals, and so on. People have become more productive and their capability has moved up notches giving an advantage by way of competing through supply chain and new business models.

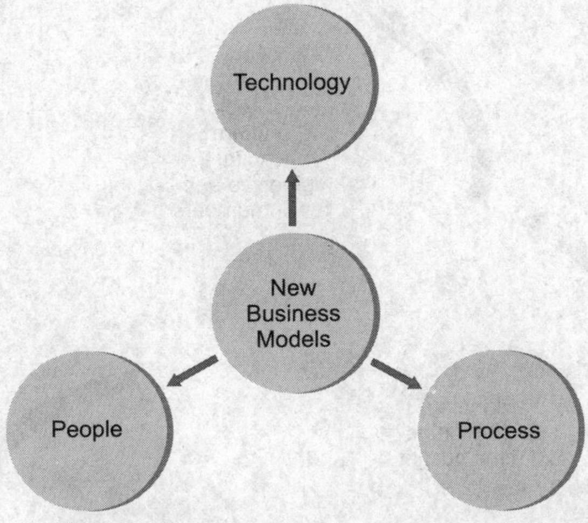

FIGURE 4.3 Relationship among technology, process and people

It is important to note that development of new business models is happening not just because of technology advancement or due to process improvement or quality of people. It is rather due to the ability to interface all these in a systematic way (Figure 4.3). In reality, new models have evolved drastically and have changed from where they had started. Needless to say, improvement in one is leading to the other. One would be amazed in financial services, especially in stock broking where the changes in technology applications have occurred during this decade. Players have the ability to assimilate information and act rapidly because of the information availability, process improvements to transact using technology and skill set of people to assimilate and make use of such changes for good. It has benefitted all stakeholders because of the interface among technology, process and people.

Similarly, one can look at many purchasing decisions at corporate that have improved. It is important to note here that level of interface varies depending upon business. However, it is certain that either directly or indirectly the interfaces among technology, process and people are facilitating configuration of new supply chain and have dramatically improved the supply chain performance.

For example, 'metaljunction' is a joint venture between Tata Steel and SAIL to market secondary steel in India. It is one of the largest e-marketplaces for steel in the world, having sold over 4 million tonnes of steel for its clients. It is reported to be selling at an average rate of 150,000 tonnes per month as of 2012. The buyer community of 5,400 plus buyers comprising traders, fabricators, re-rollers and end-users transact through metaljunction. The operational efficiency, transparency and equal access that the platform provides seems to be widely accepted too. It is reported that metaljunction's clients have experienced significant benefits on migrating to online selling and their price realisations have increased by up to 23 per cent.

Supply Chain Decision Hierarchy

Supply chain management decisions could belong to one of the three levels (i) strategic, (ii) planning, or (iii) operational level, based on the time bucket of decision. Figure 4.4 shows the three levels of decisions in a hierarchy. The decisions on strategic level set the conditions under which planning and operational level is made. Strategic level involves non-routine and critical decisions, planning would include scheduling and structuring a framework for effectiveness and operational level would deal with execution.

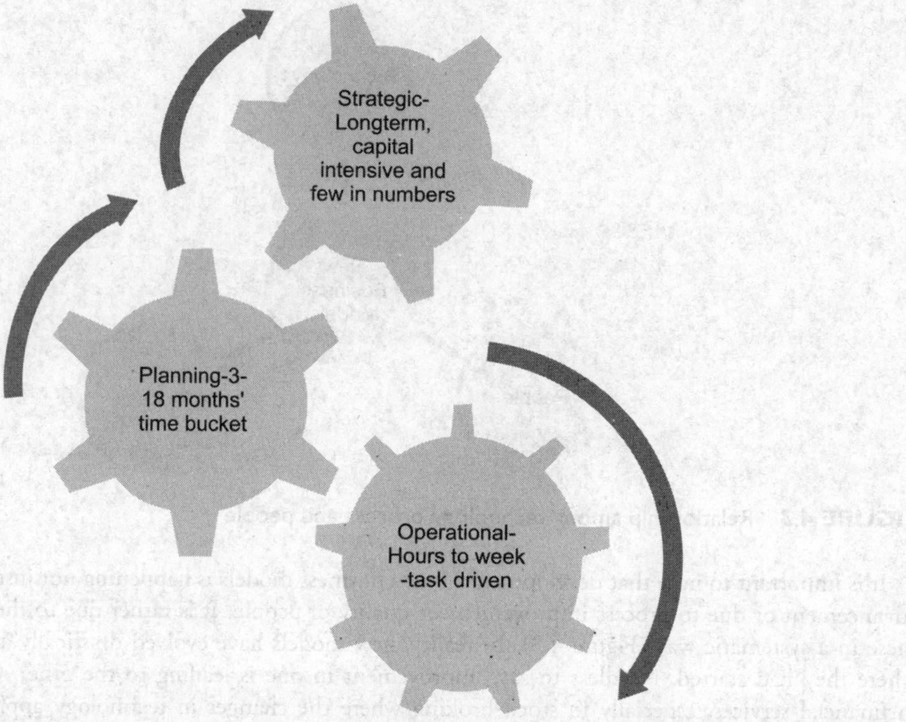

FIGURE 4.4 Hierarchy of supply chain decisions

Strategic decisions have three characteristics, namely long term, capital in nature and may not be easily reversible. These are related to network design wherein facilities like plant and warehouse location are decided. Also, other facets like inventory management, supplier development through alliance network, transportation modeling and so on can be decided at this level. Decisions made on the strategic level are of course interrelated. For example, decisions on mode of transport are influenced by decisions on geographical placement of plants and warehouses, and inventory policies are influenced by choice of suppliers and production locations. Modeling and simulation is frequently used for analysing these interrelations, and the impact of making strategic level changes in supply chain.

At the *planning* level, functions and decisions are arrived at quarter-wise demand estimates, arriving at production plan and tie up with supplier on production schedule, aggregate planning at family level products, quarter wise inventory policy, and so on. This level of decision hierarchy is mainly focussed on resource planning and budgeting for achieving efficiency and effectiveness of supply chain. For example, an automotive plant would arrive at annual budget and indicate same to supplier for their preparedness. Then, it would release a quarter-wise production plan which is near time plan for them to be prepared to supply. This would have more certainty and could be adjusted every month.

At the *operational* level, decisions and activities are more dependent on shift basis and maximum of a week. These are more firm activities which are meant for accomplishing immediate tasks on set parameter and policy. These are routine with a number of functions which could be happening repetitively. The focus is to accomplish without any error or loss of resources. This could be production scheduling, executing delivery, movement of a consignment, and so on.

It is important to note here that the nature of decisions like resource requirement and competence required vary widely among the hierarchy of supply chain. Hence the preparedness and execution capability must reckon the same. Many times, strategic decisions are driven from top management while planning decisions are structured and anchored by supply chain experts. Operational decisions are at ground level and supervisory management becomes responsible and accountable for these decisions in reality.

Supply Chain Structure or Supply Network

The structure of a supply chain network refers to the pattern or manner in which constituent parts are arranged together. The characteristics of such supply chain network anchored by the focal organisation that exercises strategic influence on nature of competitive forces including sharing of profit across the supply chain constituents and level of customer service within the network are referred to as structural factors. Those structural characteristics are believed to play an important role in conduct and performance of organisations participating in the supply chain network and they provide competitive advantage to the focal organisation.

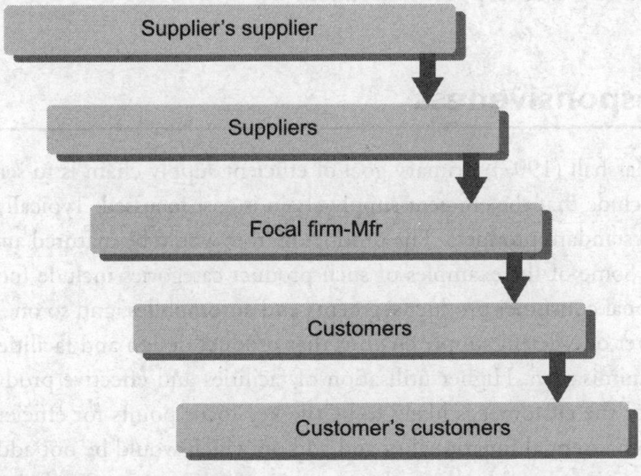

FIGURE 4.5 Making of supply chain structure

In the mindset, Figure 4.5 would immediately reflect on network of organisations in supply chain. It would mean that in terms of focal organisation's supplier, supplier's supplier, intermediaries logistics service providers, customer and customer's customer, and so on. The design of a supply chain must take into account such issues as WHERE and HOW the products are produced, and then ENTER the market, where they are STORED, and how they REACH a customer. Even this approach is manufacture-centric and not really supply chain centric, i.e., customer centric.

One key aspect which is being stressed throughout is to set supply chain from customer perspective. This is mainly because a supply network serves a customer.

The key or starting point for designing a structure is the purpose and command or hierarchy, which is all about striking a balance between minimising cost of storing and moving goods and services of focal organisation from its supplier to customer. In the process, another important aspect which needs attention is level of customer service. Hence, supply chain horizon extends from efficiency on one side to responsiveness on the other side. Many times, these two are extremes and mutually exclusive options. It has been a managerial challenge to bring both extremes close so that a high degree of efficiency and responsiveness can be achieved giving competitive advantage to the focal organisation.

There is no formula or framework which prescribes a right balance. The optimal supply chain structure typically differs not only from company to company but also among product and market groups. This is mainly because each product and market group is unique and a company's competitive approach varies based on resources it commands and other strategic factors like focus and vision. There are a number of factors which influence supply chain structural features like:

1. Character and type of product
2. Nature, type and size of market
3. Distribution channel strategy
4. Facilities locations and options available
5. Customer characteristics and preferences
6. Tax including direct and indirect taxes and levies
7. Strength of logistics services and intermediary options
8. Strength of information and communication channels
9. Level of industry maturity and scope for innovations

Efficiency vs Responsiveness

According to Fischer, I Marshall (1997), primary goal of efficient supply chain is to serve demand at the lowest cost. Hence one may conclude that the efficient supply chain is cost focussed. Typically, this is common in case of necessities, utilities and standard products. The product market would be matured and normal good or service would be commoditised. Some of the examples of such product categories include food items, dairy products, popular models of functional consumer product segments and automobiles, and so on.

The other key parameter of efficient supply chain is that product design and facilities management would be designed towards cost minimisation. Higher utilisation of facilities and effective product design with standard usage and functionality for the customer is likely to be the key focus points for efficient supply chain. Product design focus would be from essential functionality and add on which would be not adding up to the cost as the customer would not be requiring the add on at high price points in these cases. Similarly, inventory level would be cost focussed which means that nodal organisation would reduce inventory. One may question whether facilities minimisation and inventory reduction can go together. It would, if one is looking at only standard and matured product/services market.

Another aspect, namely lead time reduction would also be a part of an efficient supply chain. It would help inventory reduction and cost. However, lead time reduction as efficiency in supply chain is challenging as it could impact responsiveness. Thus, an efficient supply chain is one end of supply chain structure spectrum which works well for demand items which have more certainty, low to medium value items which are standardised and market being matured.

Responsiveness is a measure of speed of reaction to customer demand. It is measured as a unit of time in normal parlance and some authors include it rightfully as a level of customer service. According to Fischer, I Marshall (1997), primary goal of responsive supply chain is to respond quickly to demand. One may also consider, apart from quick response, the ability to serve demand as a factor. Some refer to it as the time to respond. But there are many instances apart from time customer service level that could be important factors. Hence one may conclude that responsive supply chain is time and level of service to customer demand.

Typically, this is common in case of high value items, fashion goods, personalised demand items where customisation is needed and for new products at introduction and early growth stages of product life cycle. The product market would be in early stages and new developments and good or service would be specific to a group or individuals. For example, high engine power and trendy motor cycles focussed on youth segment in India which is high priced. Some more examples for this type include hi-tech goods, medical equipment, garments, fashion jewelry, mobiles, electronic goods, home furniture, and selected automobile segment in passenger cars, commercial vehicles, two wheelers, agriculture equipment including tractors, etc.

The other key parameter of responsive supply chain is that product design and facilities management would be configured towards creating product in modularity and allowing postponement of product completion on demand. Modularity allows product differentiation and high degree of customisation. It may require more common items but allows variety on completion.

Higher flexibility in manufacturing allows for meeting uncertainty in demand. Along with this, accommodating product variation based on demand is the key manufacturing strategy for responsive supply chain. Supplier relationship management is driven based on the ability to respond quickly to demand variation, provide flexibility in manufacturing and have ability to do concurrent engineering. Quality management is one of the key aspects which is more than threshold requirement for responsive supply chain. Similarly, inventory strategy would be focussed on creating buffer to meet service level and enable quick response to demand. This would also help to meet demand and supply uncertainty allowing flexibility in demand.

One may question whether facilities, flexibility and inventory buffering, would result in high investment and commitment of resources. Obviously, such concerns are genuine for any supply chain manager and this has to be supported by functional strategy of effective pricing and having high margins. When one discusses high profit margin, aspect of absolute and relative margins must be considered. Absolute margins refer to gross margin in currency compared to standard items. Relative margins would look in terms of net margins compared as percentage of cost of production or offering of service. Many times, responsive supply chain have pressure on relative margins especially during downtrend in economic cycle where across the board sentiments are weak.

Another aspect, namely lead time reduction irrespective of cost would also be a part of responsive supply chain. This sounds very theoretical and contradicts right management perspective. How can one recommend lead time reduction irrespective of cost? To understand this, one has to interpret this with respect to customer service level and relationship between increasing service level or availability vis–a-vis cost of providing the same. After a point, increasing responsiveness would require more than proportionate increase in costs and would affect margin. Contemporary manufacturing management practices are addressing this issue with new techniques like JIT, lean and so on.

Thus, a responsive supply chain is on the another end of supply chain structure spectrum which works well for demand items which have uncertain characteristics, especially for high value items, products that lend for customisation and market being in early stages of growth stage in product life cycle and or innovation is basic character of the product group like electronics and medical equipment.

Supply chain efficiency focusses on reducing cost which would lead to reduction in customer service level and response time and so on. As mentioned earlier, efficiency focusses on less variants and standardisation of products and manufacturing set up. Hence efficiency leads to responsiveness. On the other hand, responsiveness is speed at which one services the customer requirement. Many times such a speed can be achieved with higher inventory, expensive and reliable movement and so on. Responsive supply chain would mean high on cost.

Thus there is a direct relationship between responsiveness and efficiency as shown in Figure 4.6.

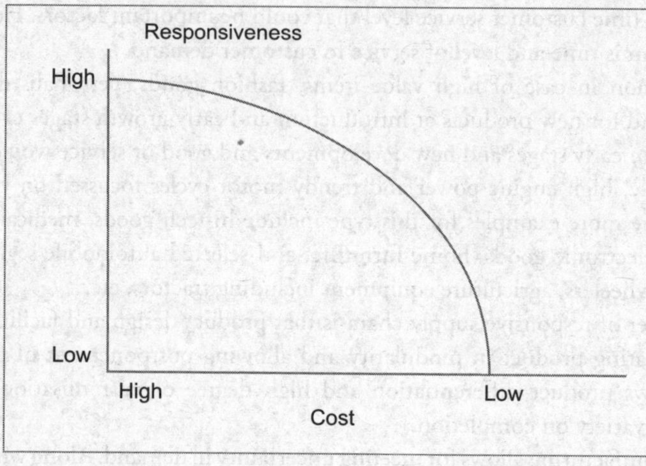

FIGURE 4.6 Cost versus responsiveness frontier

Ideally any supply chain manager would like to reverse the relationship which is a challenge in supply chain management. The objective for all is cost minimisation and increased customer service that a manager would look forward to. As it can be observed from Figure 4.6, beyond a point for a small proportionate increase in responsiveness, there is a need to spend higher proportion of cost and so it becomes less attractive after that point. When a firm focusses on increasing responsiveness, it must question the ability to pass on to customer such disproportionate increase in cost. Different firms approach this differently based on their strategic focus and resource capability.

Push Based Supply Chain

One of the broad classifications of supply chain is *push and pull based supply chain* which is based on process view. Prima facie pull based supply chain relates to responsiveness, whereas push based supply chain is related to cost efficient supply chain. Both push and pull based supply chain are seen as strategy and approach to supply chain configuration, whereas cost efficiency and responsiveness is more like purpose and philosophy of a supply chain network.

Push based supply chain, in simple terms, works in anticipation of customer orders. Because it is engaged in anticipation of customer order, it is seen as speculative supply chain. One needs to understand the following issues in perspective while analysing a push based supply chain.

1. Why should a manufacturer prefer to set up his/her production function and incur huge marketing and sales support in order to woo customers?
2. Are there inherent product, market and industry characteristics which warrant push strategies?
3. Are there certain processes or structural features which facilitate only push strategies?
4. What is the relationship between cost efficiency and responsiveness if push strategies are to be pursued?
5. What are the managerial levers available in order to make push effective and be cost efficient as well?

It is obvious from above that there are aspects of business which require push strategies in supply chain to be deployed. In such cases, the management must ensure that it applies all its efforts and resources in order to achieve the objective of cost minimisation. Business and industry evolution has over the years facilitated for streamlining approaches towards cost efficient push based supply chain strategies. These strategies should be well executed with planning and operations management. Multi-disciplinary orientation is also important for successful implementation. The enablers of push based supply could be due to industry factors, organisation of distribution structure, nature of the product and strength of support services including logistics service providers, and so on.

One of the key enablers of push strategy is the manufacturing strategy of 'Made–to–Stock (MTS)". MTS strategy is one where product is produced to stock for meeting an expected or estimated demand. Based on experience, a production plan is drawn so that at any point of time a sales order might come in and delivery to the customer is done from the existing stock. One may appreciate that MTS strategy works in situations where lot sizes require production in large lots and releases have to be made in batches.

Manufacturing set up for this type demands such kind of runs wherein production function is constrained by lumping into some standard size of operation. Second, there could be continuous process operations like chemicals, cement, sugar, and so on, which would again run based on operating efficiency rather than on demand requirements. Manufacture of such products is driven by production economies and capital machinery set up which have considered certain demand pattern. There are situations wherein it may not be demand pattern but supply of raw material which determines the MTS strategy.

The classic case could be manufacture of sugar and many other agricultural and dairy products which go in as input. Manufacture of white sugar plantation is determined by cane availability and sucrose content in cane which is seasonal. Similarly, dairy products like cream and butter oil are produced and stocked during peak season and recombined as milk during off season. MTS are also followed by many ancillaries and component business to maintain operating balance and viability of business as firms have limited resource capability to manage flexibility and huge variations in demand.

It may be interesting to note that "Make to Availability" is a commitment to the market, or to specified clients, to maintain enough availability at a specific warehouse to be able to deliver immediately upon request at all times. This is different than make-to-stock where no firm commitment is given. It is the point in offering a commitment for availability to allow the potential client to rely on getting fast response whenever needed. This is applicable when the client is able to improve his/her business due to the availability provided.

Cost efficient push based supply chain could be successfully deployed if industry, market and product characteristics warrant the same. Management ability to meet challenges of such strategy and to be innovative has been established over the years and across the markets. Supply chain managers must be conscious of such developments and deploy initiatives for being a competitive player in the market.

Pull Based Supply Chain

Pull based supply chain is configured to execute a customer order being initiated. If such execution is warranted, then there is a need to know the arrival of customer and preparedness to serve the customer with certainty. Pull based supply chain is more a reactionary process as it reacts to customer demand.

Simplest example to relate is 'Dial a Pizza' served on customer demanding a delivery. It must be noted that most of the pull based supply chain are on downward stream wherein an inventory framework and capacity dedication are available. Also, ability of delivery mechanism are to use quick, responsive and customised out bound transportation. Over the years, improvements in industry practices enable pull based supply chain for upstream activities as well. Just in time (JIT) in manufacturing is one of the classic applications of pull strategy in downstream activities, wherein supplier is encouraged to deliver components at production line to save time and inventory and also have flexibility and responsiveness towards servicing customer demand. The enablers of pull based supply could be due to industry factors, organisation of distribution structure, nature of the product and strength of support services including logistics service providers, and so on.

One of the key enablers for pull strategy is the manufacturing strategy of "Made–to–Engineer" (MTE) and "Made–to- Order" (MTO). MTE strategy is one where product is produced after it is specifically designed and based on tender and quotation, and when an order is confirmed. Typically, MTE works for capital machinery and high value capital goods like machinery, power generators, and so on. Many times, a customer directly or through agents initiates the buying intent of the buyers through tenders. After which the responses are evaluated technically and commercially and an order is frozen. This is common in project execution and delivery. This kind of sourcing is based on pull strategy as customer demand is configured.

The question would be who would be the nodal organisation and whose supply chain issues are addressed? In this case, the customer is the nodal organisation whose supply chain issues are addressed specifically. The manufacturer of the capital good is a supplier. When one shifts gear and reflects on supply chain issue of capital goods manufacturer, he/she might organise his/her manufacturing on pull basis from customer order. The context must be clearly understood from supply chain manager of the nodal organisation in handling supply chain decisions.

MTO manufacturing strategy is pull based where the nodal organisation is the manufacturer that has standard product designs and the ability to configure the final demand providing a mass customisation opportunity. An example could be that of fashion jewelry of high end. One can come across a number of such cases in engineering industry, especially in manufacture of capital goods, where the product design and functionality is standardised with little variation to serve final demand. For example, generator sets an auxiliary power generation equipment, electrical fitments, and so on. Food in luxury hotel restaurants is another example of MTO strategy where customer gets high value and pays premium for the same.

Responsive pull based supply chain could be successfully deployed if industry, market and product characteristics warrant the same. Management ability to meet challenges of such strategy and be innovative has been established over years and across markets. Supply chain managers must be conscious of such developments and deploy initiatives for being a competitive player in the market. Pull strategies are increasingly practised in both upstream and downstream supply chain activities. Pull strategies assume more significance at times downtrend business cycle as it gives flexibility with suppliers as manufacturer acts after knowing with greater certainty the demand and wherever possible improves margin with customers.

Trade-off between Push and Pull Strategies

One may note that there are wide differences among firms in different industries/markets and within an industry in adopting push and pull strategies. There are certain general guidelines on trade-off between push and pull strategies which are discussed here.

The processes in supply chain can be divided into a series of cycles, namely customer order cycle, replenishment cycle, manufacturing cycle and procurement cycle. The trigger in each cycle happens because of certain actions or incidence by a player. For example, customer order cycle triggers on arrival of a customer. Hence, for certain action to trigger, aggregation has to take place. In case of manufacturing cycle to be triggered, there must be a demand of goods by the distributors from manufacturer.

Procurement cycle trigger would lead for the material resources plan to be released based on a production plan. Generally, pull strategies are fairly easier to be configured close to customer demand as it happens on initiation of order, whereas push strategies are configured wherever production has to happen based on anticipated demand. So first trade-off is point of incidence of ability to serve on demand and need to anticipate for demand and manufacture to stock.

Further, a trade-off can be thought of as a goal of supply chain network. If the goal is to be cost efficient, then cost efficient push strategy is preferred. Typically, popular segment products are of this nature. For example, bicycles used a by common man can come in this category. In the same industry, when one looks at fitness cycle, kids segment and technically higher level of cycles like geared ones are more based on responsiveness and pull based strategy. Most common day-to-day application of push and pull based is luxury hotel restaurants where in the same building one restaurant would serve buffet meals which have a wide range of choices at low price point but with choice limited to spread of the day. In the same hotel, specialty restaurants offer customer preference at a high price point. There are innovative practices adopted wherein buffet hotel chains now come with the idea of giving preference which are both cost focussed with limited responsiveness and an ability to increase price point.

Another situation where there could be a trigger for trade-off is product configuration and ability to postpone the product completion to customer preference. When products are standardised and demand is stable and predictable, it is better to deploy push based strategies. A number of products like perishable services of air transportation service on fixed schedules, hotel rooms, standardised financial products, home furniture for popular segment, automotives for the same segment and fast moving consumer goods, etc., can be in this category. On the other hand, there are products requiring modularity and need to be configured close to point of consumption. These could be specialty furniture, capital goods, engineering goods, computers for personal, home and office segments and hi-tech equipment including medical equipment, etc. This trade-off must be handled with innovativeness. Literature has abundant material on how Dell computers were innovative when they introduced made-to-order in that segment.

Third trigger of trade-off between push and pull strategies is production options that are deployable for the business. Mass production would facilitate production cost economies with standardisation and facilitate output price at normal profits. On the other hand, if production runs on batches and when set up costs and change over costs are high, cost efficiency is foregone for providing responsiveness and pull based strategies. One can come across many such examples like casting and forgings in engineering industry.

Fourth trigger of trade-off could be linkages among supply chain perspective like inventory policy, sourcing, transportation choices, facilities plan, information systems and linkages of supply chain strategy to overall business strategy. If resources are limited and industry is matured, a firm would prefer push based strategies for cost efficiency. On the other hand, if firm is at product introduction stage, especially of a new product or in highly volatile product shelf life businesses like consumer electronics, mobile phones and apparels, responsive pull based supply chain is preferred. One may ponder on how pull based system could work in mass customers demand goods like ones cited above.

Here, one may apply the cycle view concept and pull work at customer order cycle level where retailers serve through stores and at replenishment stages. Feedback mechanism and agile manufacturing is what would help in such cases.

Identifying Appropriate Push and Pull Strategy

There is nothing like a prescribed push or pull strategy for a business or a supply chain network. Industry practices mature over a period of time leading to evolution of approaches which commonly benefit industry, market and customers. However, the above discussion on trade-off between push and pull strategies gives some guideline. One may also look at the following aspects in identifying appropriate pull and push based strategies:

1. Resource availability with the organisation
2. Strategic vision with respect to business and differentiation initiatives
3. Innovativeness
4. Demand and supply characteristics of products and market
5. Technology and its obsolescence
6. Maturity of logistics service providers and support system

Choice of push and pull strategy is a behavioural attribute of a firm which would be strongly influenced by above industry structural factors, competitive forces and performance attributes. A supply chain manager must be sensitive to these and involve a multidisciplinary approach while addressing choice of push and pull strategies. As mentioned earlier, it should not be seen as mutually exclusive but as complementary to achieve growth through customer satisfaction.

Supply Chain Drivers and Their Importance

Supply chain drivers are key to performance of supply chain constituents and role players across the network. A network is operational only when supply chain drivers are in place. The drivers are components of supply chain structure which lead to effectiveness of supply network. In a way, supply chain drivers are to be viewed as operating tools for implementing supply chain strategies and carrying out operations.

Drivers act as pillars of supply chain on which blocks are laid and operations dwell. These could be logistical drivers like warehouse facilities, inventory and transportation and cross-functional drivers like pricing, sourcing and information. Apart from these drivers, certain external factors like tax system, logistical infrastructure may impact the performance of supply chain indirectly through configuration of drivers. Hence it is important to understand the role of drivers in supply chain performance, their components and how they influence and impact the competition.

Supply chain strategy cannot be independent of other functional strategies or business unit level or corporate level strategies. Alignment of a specific business strategy to a corresponding supply chain strategy is achieved through proper deployment of supply chain drivers. For instance, when a firm introduces a new product group as a part of business strategy with focus on product acceptance and then on market share growth during the introduction stage, it requires a responsive supply chain strategy. Because the linkage to product lifecycle is strong and based on customer response, product reconfiguration and position need to be undertaken. Without responsive supply chain, it cannot be done.

If there is need to be a responsive supply chain, supply chain drivers like facilities, inventory, supplier relationship and transportation are organised accordingly. In the environment of high demand uncertainty of the introduction stage, higher levels of inventory may be utilised to achieve responsiveness by enhancing product availability. Product availability at the introduction stage translates to market share. Similarly, the remaining supply chain drivers of information, facility and transportation are deployed in view of achieving alignment between business and supply chain strategies of the introduction stage. Hence role of drivers become important.

For example, look at a conglomerate with multinational ownership structure in India which adopts a strategy of localised approach for growth and introduces ready-to-eat food business in India. The company may be in a position to exploit economies of scope in distribution as well as in sourcing. As the company has been leaders in FMCG business, foods could be an addition to use the distribution network which requires additional efforts in terms of application of learning and experience, capacity and managerial effort in managing new relationships in channel for widening reach. Since it has good understanding of Indian agriculture, extending sourcing practices for increasing variety of food business is also appreciable. However, the challenge lies in achieving success in the introduction stage of products with variations in cultural and culinary preference of diversified ethnic Indian population.

Supply chain drivers are enable to keep a balance between responsiveness to customer and efficiency in supply chain. This enables the company to be competitive in its chosen strategic arena. One may also note that there is a need for synchronisation of supply chain strategy with functional strategies like product, marketing and finance and competitive strategy. Supply chain structure defines such strategic focus for supply chain which needs to be accomplished through effective deployment of supply chain drivers, namely facilities, inventory, transportation, sourcing, pricing and information.

There are situations where fiercely competing players in an industry like automobile, consumer electronics, FMCG and capital goods firms have different approaches in configuring supply chain drivers. One may note the differences in their facilities location including warehouses, inventory policy, delivery network and transportation and so on. One may also note numerous endogenous factors which impact a firm. These could be product portfolio, budget allocation, market focus, brand strategy and strength of channel partners. For a supply chain manager, it is important to understand endogenous factors like the ones mentioned above and many other exogenous factors which influence choice of a configuration.

Individually, each driver has a role and selection criteria and together they form a framework. While deciding the framework, a few conflict situations could arise and managerial decision would be to arrive at a trade-off in such situations. One broad principle is that these are driven by strategic focus of a firm on supply chain horizon with respect to responsiveness and cost efficiency.

Trade-off situations arise when there is a competing demand for supply network configuration. Any managerial decision involving resource commitment and being strategic in nature with a potential to impact earnings and balance sheet has some peculiarities. Supply chain driver configuration by way of creating facilities or using third-party facilities, inventory policy and distribution network involving transportation and distribution centres is influenced by many factors.

Though it is natural that evolution of an industry would standardise the supply chain drivers' configuration, it seldom can be taken as static framework. One may understand that while arriving at strategic decision on location or structuring of inventory policy based on development of suppliers, a supply chain decision-maker formulates certain scenario for a longer horizon based on many factors, it is important to see how such managers could constantly review these decisions as the factors are dynamic and influenced by competitive situations and/or at least at what frequency such conflicts are to be reckoned and resolved.

These are:

1. **Demand and supply conditions**: Changes in character of demand and supply conditions considerably influence configuration of supply chain driver. One may see these macro factors influencing all players and hence how it could lead to conflict for a firm level decision. In reality, change in macro factor affects firms differently and conflicts are differing in nature. Though recession is a macro event, it affects each firm differently.
2. **Negotiating power of suppliers**: While configuring logistical drivers, namely facilities — manufacturing and DCs, inventory and transportation, one may have to consider the extent of power and its changing character of supplier relationship. If supplier is a dominant player or a single manufacturer who possesses superior technology and the component is critical to product, then manufacturer is driven by supplier decisions. It is important for supply chain strategist to reckon bargaining power of suppliers in different scenarios and understand configuration of drivers accordingly. Adjustments and reworking of strategies are important to establish effective supply network.
3. **Negotiating power of buyers**: Porter's five forces model on competitive analysis explains the importance of bargaining power of buyers. One may look at how it is relevant for configuration of supply chain drivers. In most of the cases, where it is differentiated products, customers are conscious of brand and post-sale service is critical, and so on. Bargaining power of buyers here is high. In such scenarios, supply chain structure is responsive.

   Configuration has challenges because there is a need to establish more facilities and stock inventory, outbound transportation must be customer specific. As long as customer pays for it, it becomes easier. Once volume increases, challenges go up as character of product changes and ability of constituents to service become difficult. Under such circumstances, supply chain drivers' configuration also needs to be re-assessed. For example, change in inventory is a smooth function compared to demand for warehouse space which could be a step function. When buyers are powerful, firms get affected as buyers tend to go in for competitive products. To avoid loss of market share, firm has to increase its cost of service where conflict in supply chain configuration will surface, i.e., cost increases when responsiveness is also tough.

Conditions of strong buyer behaviour arise when the buyer is captive or a single customer (a situation of monopsony) arises. Though the nodal organisation may have structured its supply chain drivers to suit such a condition, any circumstantial situation like spurt in demand also leads to a situation where re-configuration of supply chain drivers would be warranted. Under this circumstance, the buyer expects the firm to strengthen the facility and catch up with demand parameters. Unless the firm responds on time irrespective of cost, it runs the risk of jeopardising the relationship with the buyer.

There are situations where group of buyers have strong bargaining power which may be due to psychological factors or due to some extraneous factors like political power and so on. For example, in India, mass consumers of staple food articles and agro-based commodities like sugar, vegetable oil would have high collective bargaining power as media and government are sensitive to price rise and availability. Hence supply chain managers of such commodity groups must be able to quickly reconfigure supply chain drivers whenever such commodity market is distorted.

4. **Innovations and competitive behaviour**: There are certain businesses in which innovation is a regular feature impacting competitive behaviour of firms. In such businesses, supply chain is configured to be responsive and less cost efficient. However, innovation as a strategy works only when customers are able to absorb cost inefficiency or alternatively firms are able to bring out products which are cost saving and efficient so that the customers realise incremental value at decreased cost.

   In the latter situation, product delay is treated as a strategy and a firm must be able to provide spares and service supports for certain stock keeping units (SKUs). This is possible only when there is a combination of responsiveness and cost efficiency which is a conflict under normal circumstances. Any firm in such a business must be prepared with strategies and policies to combat disruptions due to frequent innovations. Few good examples of such industries are consumer electronics and communication.

   One would also often come across new generation mobile phones, entertainment devices and home appliances with increased functionality and features introduced in the market. A supply chain manager is expected to service the customers who have earlier version of models and also satisfy another set of customers who demand new generation products, which is challenging. This is so because one part of supply network needs efficiency and other responsiveness. Hence innovation as a strategy brings pressure on supply chain configuration.

5. **Resource led:** Resource based factors strongly influence configuration of supply chain drivers. As it is commonly understood, supply chain configurations like facility build, transportation options and inventory consume lot of resources including physical and financial. A nodal firm's command over resources determines the choice of supply chain drivers. However, resource's availability and quality changes dynamically due to firm's earnings and market conditions. Once when there is an increase or decrease in resource command, the configuration needs to be reworked. Any supply chain strategist would aspire to improve responsiveness and cost efficiency when there is an ease of resource availability. However, this needs to be justified by fundamentals of capital budgeting decisions.

   Apart from resource availability and command, market factors would also immensely influence supply chain driver configurations. For example, when competition builds a large facility or increases the number of distribution centres across the channel, a firm is compelled to re-assess configuration of its supply chain drivers. At the outset, this may look more like a problem of competition and less of supply chain issue. However, an innovative supply chain manager must resort to practices which may address competition given his own drawback on resource command.

6. **Technology**: Technology as a competitive force also impacts configuration of supply chain drivers. When one looks at technology, it could be related to pure play technology with respect to products and services and those relating to processing of data and information. Here both are discussed. Product technology is embedded in product features. Here, value is created because of technology applications or through manufacture or process which are deployed in creating products. A supply chain manager must understand

product technology obsolescence factor and new product introduction and accordingly strategise supply chain driver configurations. This is common in many consumer electronics and home appliances segment. Another interesting segment in India where product technology has an impact on supply chain configuration is industrial product segment in office power support systems, especially in battery backups and power support systems. A wide range of UPS systems and power conditioning solutions are marketed by players to applications based on requirements. These are applied for varied kinds of situations from manufacturing units, office, hospitals, data centres, BPO and IT companies, etc.

One may also note how developments in information technology have impacted supply chain configuration. Information is one of the critical drivers and advancement in information technology impacts other supply chain drivers. This happens because the decreasing cost and ease of application of information technology brings in transparency and visibility in supply network. The result is a facility where way of manufacturing and warehousing is reconfigured to reflect this. Nowadays, safety inventory is getting reviewed closely and companies are reducing demand risks with better information availability. Again application of technology has facilitated track and trace in movement which improves transportation efficiency. Thus, supply chain drivers are extremely sensitive to technological advancements as competition quickly adopts new applications for improving value across the system.

7. **Government policies:** Government policies impact supply chain drivers' configuration. Facilities which may be manufacturing and warehousing locations are influenced by government policies. At the global level, since late 80s, government has been focussing on reducing trade barriers and encouraging location of plants. Some of the classic examples are China and India in manufacturing, countries like Thailand and Taiwan in electronics segment and Malaysia and Singapore have also been actively leading such change. Configuration of network changes strategically with change in government policy.

Situations arise domestically as well when there is a change in state level duties and taxes or incentives provided by Central/Federal Government to encourage a region to grow. For example, in India, Uttaranchal State Government announced a number of incentives which encourage some firms to set up their manufacturing base at Uttaranchal. This encourages reconfiguration of supply chain drivers which provides economies in production and distribution.

Sales tax system had also greatly influenced warehouse and distribution centres. Rationalisation of central government and state government sales tax and value added tax had greatly influenced setting up of distribution centres. Due to dual tax structure (CST and VAT), most of the companies maintained carry forward agent (CFA) and warehouse in every state, leading to fragmented, small and inefficient warehouses apart from higher inventories. Implementation of Goods and Services Tax (GST) in 2017 led to consolidation and change in supply chain drivers.

Government policies not only influence facilities location and thereby other drivers but also other drivers. As seen above, tax policies influence inventory configuration. Similarly, implementation of improvements in policies like Just-in-time and VMI has helped in changing the configuration and deployment of third party and fourth party logistics service providers.

Similarly, investments in infrastructure like roads, sea ports and airports have led to change in transportation network. In India, new roads have increased the speed of goods transfer which has knocked off some capacity creation by way of either facility or storage. Ability to deploy high power vehicles has enabled movement of large size cargo and thereby reconfiguration has been initiated.

Apart from these, government policies with respect to investment in Special Economic Zones have led to reconfiguration of supply networks in manufacturing and trade in India.

Thus, government policies influence supply chain configuration and changes in policies constantly drive the need for reassessment and reconfiguration of supply network.

8. **Changing structure of logistics service providers:** Logistics service providers, especially in India, are more of splinter groups and small firms that run on ownership and partnership structure rather than being professionally run through corporate structures. This feature has been increasingly changing during the last decade because of the following reasons:
   a. Globalisation and foreign players are bringing in professional organisations and international players in the forefront.
   b. Consolidation of logistics service providers has been included across the globe and in India as well. At least, companies are getting into strategic alliances if not ownership changes and improving the quality of service.
   c. Intensity of competition impacting small and marginal players to employ professionals and improve systems to thrive has increased.

   Thus, the changing industry profile is demanding reconfiguration of supply network for focal organisations to exploit such healthy change for its competitive strength.

Supply Network Decision: Sourcing

Sourcing or buying decision can be analysed in a two by two matrix with criticality of material and value/cost in another axis and both are judged to be on a scale of high and low as shown in Figure 4.7.

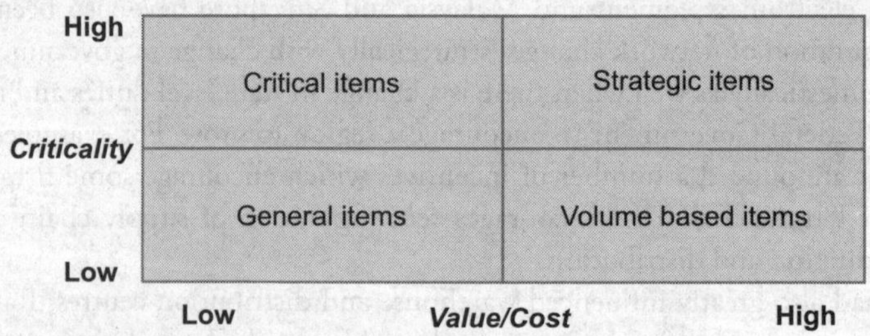

FIGURE 4.7 Product criticality and value/cost relationship in sourcing

1. **Generalised items:** These are low cost/value items that are low in criticality, typically consumables like lubricants in production process. These items typically can be purchased "off-the-shelf" and highly standardised. Also, these items could not be competitive differentiator among peers in business. Firms generally go through administrative buying or off-the-shelf or through web.
2. **Volume based items:** These items are standardised through engineering and may be common among competitive products. Product design and engineering may not be a differentiator. Still it cannot be considered as off-the-shelf item as value could be important for negotiation and for achieving cost advantage. These products may not be critical for performance but important for product functionality and value. Product group like tyres in OE cars can be considered as important component but not a differentiator in technology of focal organisation in the network, namely the automotive company. Typically, these products have multiple vendors and firm deals with buying these components by creating competition among, for cost advantage.
3. **Critical items:** These are products which may not be very high in terms of cost/value compared to overall product cost but would be critical in establishing product functionality. It would be like a brake lining in a car brake system which would be critical for performance of car and safety. Quality in manufacture and improvements may be important for vendor selection. Selection of vendors for such product supply must

be of those who can compete on quality, work closely with OE and can bring continuous improvements. Generally, firms have less number of such suppliers but work closely with them.

4. **Strategic items:** These are all high value/cost items and are critical for performance of product. These decisions are strategic in nature. As such suppliers and components are expensive, important in long term and cannot disown relationship easily as they are a part of business and familiar with critical process or component or both. These are suppliers along with whom focal organisation works on design collaboration, concurrent engineering, prototypes and so on and constantly in dialogue on technology advancements and bringing in additional features to customers. For any such products, there would be either single source dedicated vendor or at best two vendor policies would be followed by the focal organisation. At times, focal organisation also enters into strategic relationship through alliances, joint venture or other forms of investments.

   For example, in a motor car, engine parts which constitute as a group engine and responsible for engine performance would come under this category. One can think of body metal which again needs to be of high quality though it is classified under commodities but requires specific performance standards, especially in developed countries for high speed vehicles. In case of computer printers, drivers and memory are critical for performance of printers and it is of high value. Thus, sourcing of strategic items requires analysis and focusses at higher level of management and must be a part of a strategic plan.

   It may be noted that generalised items could be purchased following administrative processes, volume based items could be between purchases and procurement; critical items need to be planned and procured following procurement process and strategic items needs to be sourced strategically through long-term relationships.

   It is pertinent that focal organisation must nurture good relationship with its suppliers. The relationship matures based on experience and trust created by both transacting parties. Trust is fundamental in relationship building between supplier and focal organisation. If both parties believe that mutual interest of each would be taken care of and actions are initiated for overall supply chain profit improvements, trust must be firm.

   Trust between supplier and focal organisation would facilitate:

   1. Understanding each other's objectives and synchronising towards supply network.
   2. Better sharing of information and smooth communication leading to transparency in actions. This would again avoid speculative initiatives and response by way of back up plans for supply and overstocking and so on. This would also improve productivity as unnecessary efforts are being avoided through communication and synchronisation of activities for meeting demand and supply.

Having said this, organisations do not easily lend themselves for scaling up on trust based relationship. Trust based relationship works mainly when there is mutual dependence and competitive dependence of power is equally relevant for both parties. Trust would also be influenced by power enjoyed by buyer and focal organisation.

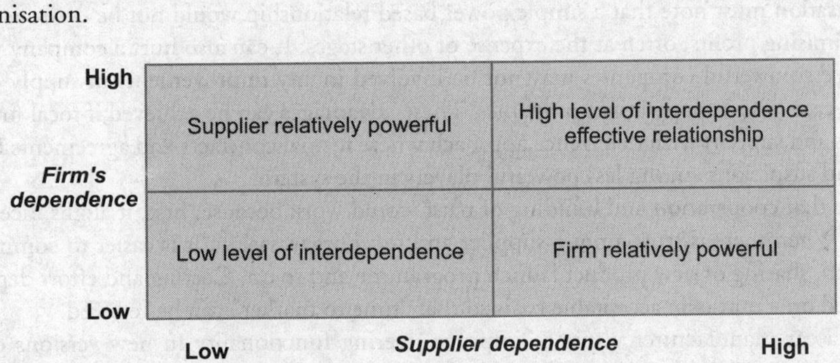

FIGURE 4.8 Interdependence between firm and its suppliers

It may be observed from Figure 4.8 that:

1. When supplier dependence is low on the firm and vice versa, there would be a situation of low level of interdependence between the two. This can be a possible situation when there are a large number of buyers and sellers for the product. It is highly standardised and homogenous with less or no differentiation. Typically, these could be generalised items as described in earlier product criticality and value/cost relationship in sourcing.
2. When supplier dependence is high on the firm, while firm's dependence on supplier is low, there would be a situation of high supplier dependence on the firm and firm has a role of dominant partner. This can be a possible situation when there are a large number of sellers and few buyers like the focal firm, for the product. It is a standardised product and cost could be a differentiator. Typically, these could be volume based items as described in earlier product criticality and value/cost relationship in sourcing. Apart from product volume, even purchase value of huge numbers could lead to low supplier power in a buyer relationship in supply chain network.
3. When supplier dependence is low on the firm, and firm's dependence on supplier is high, there would be a situation of high dependence of the firm on supplier and supplier plays a dominant role. This can be a possible situation when a large number of buyers and few sellers are there for the product. It could be a niche component, design or material with quality and possession being differentiators. By design, focal firm could have created such suppliers in order to control competition. Typically, these could be critical items as described in earlier product criticality and value/cost relationship in sourcing. For example, steering, brake system and clutches suppliers for automotive car manufacturers could be such kind of products where suppliers can fall in this category. Relationship is developed through alliance mode wherein focal firm shares technology and leads in R&D efforts of vendor organisation.
4. When supplier dependence is high on the firm and vice versa, there would be a situation of high level of interdependence and effective relationship between them. This can be possible situation when there are a few buyers and few sellers for the product. It could be strategic items which could be critical for performance and high in value. By design, focal firm could have created such suppliers in order to control competition. Typically, these could be strategic items as described in earlier product criticality and value/cost relationship in sourcing. For example, engine parts and steel body suppliers for automotive car manufacturers could be such kind of products where suppliers can fall in this category. Relationship is developed through alliance spectrum wherein focal firm shares technology and at times is participative in capital and management efforts of vendor organisation.

Thus, buying relationship based on value/cost and criticality and matrix mapping interdependence between focal firm and its suppliers provides guidelines for establishing relationship with suppliers for achieving supply chain objective through integration of supplier relationship management with other components.

A focal organisation must note that a simple power based relationship would not be desirous as it would lead to one stage maximising profits, often at the expense of other stages. It can also hurt a company when balance of power changes. Less powerful companies may not be involved in any improvements in supply chain efficiency. This is similar in case of less cooperative companies! These advantages can be achieved if focal firm initiates trust building exercises and support with deterrence approach where formal contracts and agreements facilitate to clear certain doubts and suspicions among less powerful players in the system.

One may note that cooperation and building of trust would work because, first, it aligns incentives and goals among partners. When there is trust among supplier and focal organisation, it is easier to communicate change in production plan, sharing of new product launch programme and so on. Costing and effort deployment can be shared and worked on a mutually acceptable basis so that "time to market" can be reduced.

For example, a car manufacturer wants to improve steering functionality in new versions of a car. Such a firm has to necessarily work with steering supplier who would be a Tier I vendor to the firm and get involved in product development process through the vendor. Unless there is trust and cooperation between the two players, such car model improvements cannot be done. Obviously, focal firm must align not only the goal of improvement but also incentives or profitability improvements on such initiatives with the vendor. One may note that once there is trust, actions of players are to coordinate and implement as in this case. Resultant effect is that the supply chain performance measured by profitability and productivity chain improves by reducing duplication or allocation of effort to appropriate stage. This would also encourage greater sharing of information as there is adequate trust and cooperation created even on strategic issues and hence planning and operations information flow could be enhanced.

Firms may use deterrence based approach through use of formal contracts to start off trust based relationship. Normally, contracts should not be seen as mutually exclusive for trust based relationship. It may be worth having appropriate contract in place even if there is perfect trust between supplier and firm. One of the problems noticed in practice is that while going is good firms do not have contract in place and once there is a trigger of slightest issue, the relationship and trust get spoiled. This is seen among firms during times of market fluctuations, deviations in goals and suspicion about fair and reasonable sharing of incentives. When there is a contract in place, at least it would mirror agreement entered consciously and resolve souring points of any relationship.

It is also pertinent to note that key aspect in sourcing is that parties would behave in a way that trusting each other would be on self-interest. With increasing pressure on competitiveness, firms are highly self-interested in building trust and relationship with engaging partners. As a part of corporate governance, firms have well-laid out purchase policy and procedures. They are vocal and open about the same as corporate governance code has increasingly been deployed.

Strategic Sourcing

Strategic sourcing includes those activities of purchase department which involve long-term development of vendors wherein effort and resources are invested for achieving competitive advantages in procurement. Such competitive factors could be with respect to cost, responsiveness, focus and breadth of product and markets. Traditional purchase functions meet the needs of the manufacturing or any other internal requirement which would predominantly be a purchasing activity. Such approach sets a narrow focus on transaction, fails to develop long-term relationship for competitive intelligence and is not ideal for long-term growth of the company.

The following are some of the aspects of strategic sourcing which would be discussed here:

1. Decision to make or buy; Criteria for outsourcing
2. Supplier development

Outsourcing

Many manufacturing firms are outsourcing the manufacture of parts and services to focus on their core competencies. They expect their suppliers to deliver innovative and quality products on time at a competitive cost. When a supplier is not capable of meeting these needs, a buyer can bring the outsourced item in-house and produce it internally or switch over to a more capable supplier or help improve the existing supplier's capabilities. All of these can work. The choice depends on price, volume or the strategic nature of the procured item.

For low-value added non-strategic commodities, the cost of changing to a new supplier is low and is therefore the best option. At the other extreme, if an underperforming supplier provides an innovative product or process technology, the buyer may protect the potential advantage and bring the work in-house by acquiring the supplier.

Outsourcing is the act of transferring some of an organisation's recurring internal activities and manufacture and supply of components, parts or services by outside vendors or service providers. Strategic use of outside parties to perform activities which would be non-core activities to vendors is the purpose of outsourcing. Unlike traditional practice of contracting, outsourcing is a strategic management tool that involves organisational restructuring unlike in contracting. It allows the organisation to concentrate on its core competencies, to adopt "best-in-class" practices, be more competitive and thereby reduce cost and advance technologies.

The challenges of outsourcing could be loss of expertise and dependence on vendor for component or contractual jobs which could lead to decrease or total loss of in-house expertise. This may lead to loss of control thereby increasing the organisation's vulnerability as it becomes partially or totally dependent on a service provider. There could also be an increase in risk and uncertainty as dependence on vendor increases. But these concerns could be addressed through relationship management between supplier and focal firm.

There are three phases of outsourcing:

- Internal analysis and evaluation
- Needs assessment and vendor selection
- Implementation and management

Internal analysis and evaluation: It is important that top management is involved in the process of outsourcing components manufacture or value addition through sub-contracting. Internal analysis would focus on identifying organisational goals and understand components or jobs to be outsourced. This has to be preceded by efforts of focal firm's team to identify and understand its core competencies. This exercise will allow organisations to identify non-core activities and functions for outsourcing.

Evaluation must include comparison of cost of activities in-house with that of outsourcing. Then a number of non-financial questions are to be addressed. These include, How critical are these functions/activities? What are the dependencies on these activities? Does this activity tend to become a "mission critical" activity? After having addressed these questions, an analyst must look into long-term cost and investment implications. Total cost of ownership through outsourcing must be done. One also could evaluate work morale and support because of outsourcing non-core manufacture.

Need assessment and vendor selection: A focal firm may use information within the organisation and using its competitive intelligence may identify vendors who could supply components or services. Based on this, a request for proposal or a bid is floated. This would define requirements and terms on which it would be required. Vendor assessment and selection would be a cross-functional team with expertise in legal, finance, human resources and the specific function being outsourced. The team would evaluate vendor's financial stability, cultural fit and proven track record. If possible, contact the vendor's existing clients to understand and verify capabilities. Once evaluation and selection is complete, contract needs to be awarded. Contract would involve negotiation of value, performance criteria and how they will be measured. Success depends on both parties' ability to communicate regularly and openly and express mutual desire to succeed.

Implementation and management: Outsourcing depends on defining the areas or components to be outsourced, establishing mechanism of measurement, training and facilitating change management in supplier – focal firm departments and finally the ability to resolve conflicts to the satisfaction of both parties.

Thus, outsourcing is one of the key strategic sourcing decisions which need focus for supply network effectiveness.

Supplier Development

Supplier development is defined as an activity that a buyer undertakes to improve a supplier's performance and/or capabilities to meet the buyer's short-term supply needs. These activities include assessing a supplier's operations, providing support and incentives to improve performance, fostering competition among suppliers and working directly with suppliers, either through training or other activities. Supplier development requires both firms to commit financial, capital and personnel resources to the work; to share timely and sensitive information; and to create an effective means of measuring performance.

Continuous long-term improvement of supplier performance is only achieved by identifying value creation in supplier and focal firm interface and also tweaking in model wherein supplier relations management could be a key differentiator. Implementing an integrated supply management strategy to maximise internal and external capabilities throughout the supply chain would be vital for translating strategy into action and value for all players in the network. For example, an auto major which is in commercial vehicle segment depends upon improvements on castings and forgings for performance improvements. Also, castings and forgings supply would depend upon model variants which are produced and synchronised with production plan and schedule. This product requires continuous improvement on material used and casting efficiency. Auto major works closely with the supplier from new material development, model developments, improving production facilities for cost reduction and productivity improvement and so on. Unless there is a strategic sourcing initiative, such development could not happen. In this relationship, supplier had engineering, design, volume commitment and also support of joint R&D. In fact, senior management team building can be done by focal firm by transferring a few key executives to the supplier firm which could be a subsidiary.

Although most firms are able to identify suppliers requiring development, few are completely successful in their supplier-development efforts. Most commonly used framework for successful supplier initiatives are as follows:

1. Identification of right components/sub contract function for supplier development. As seen in relationship between value/cost and criticality, supplier development focus is important in areas relating to low value, high criticality items and high value, high criticality items. Managers must assess the performance of suppliers who supply commodities in the "strategic supplies" category. These commodities are considered strategically important, as they might be difficult to substitute or purchase from alternative suppliers.
2. Establishing an effective cross-functional team in a supplier development initiative, with cross-functional experts like supply chain, purchase, commercial, production, finance and marketing depending upon size, volume and nature of procurement.
3. Interaction with supplier top management would be another important criterion. It may be noted that establishing processes and information technology could be important. Over and above, one must establish three keys to supplier improvement— strategic alignment, supplier engagement through measurement and feedback; and being transparent and professional in approach. These become important as many times suppliers are dealt based only on negotiating power, and the commitment for supplier development could be missing.
4. Constant endeavour to identify improvement areas and put in efforts jointly. After identifying promising opportunities of supplier development, managers must evaluate them in terms of feasibility, resource and time requirements and potential return on investments. The aim is to decide what the goals should be and whether they are achievable. Once it is done, specific metrics and targets must be agreed and it may be good to enter into formal contract.

Thus success factors in supplier development are guided by relative positions of strengths, intention and efforts to work together for common goals.

Supplier Development – Concern Areas

Though as an initiative, supplier development is laudable for improving supply network effectiveness, there are certain concern areas which need management attention for making it effective. These concerns could be specific to supplier, focal firm and/or common to both parties.

Supplier specific issues could be related to inadequate commitment, resources like people and technical capability. Commitment depends upon understanding and participation in development initiatives and how it would improve future growth of supplier. For example, in case of Suzuki Motors, manufacturer of Maruti brand of cars or BHEL, the supplier who participates with commitment has grown bigger and some of them have even become large players in components and sub-contracting business. It may be important that the supplier is committed to continuous improvement; both the parties agree on cost reduction targets.

Both parties identify specific opportunities for an improvement within the supplier's manufacturing process. Similarly, most of suppliers lack the resources like engineering capabilities, equipment and people skills, especially of managerial talents that are required to implement the improvement ideas identified in a supplier-development initiative. To overcome this concern, focal firms at initial stages must highlight the need for commitment of resources and initially support supplementing with their resources. Many times, organisations have found training suppliers directly or through third party vendors to be helpful in order to cover the gaps. Some of these trainings are specific skill improvements for identified supplier development initiative and generic training skills to improve supplier standards to scale up to the next level of horizon.

Concerns relating to focal firm who is a buyer in this situation could be reluctance to fully commit to supplier development, primarily when they see no potential benefits. The reluctance could be due to bargaining power enjoyed, competitive condition in supplier's market where there are many players and lack of strategic focus. A focal firm would narrow down supplier development initiatives to a selective set of suppliers who could be relevant strategically in terms of either criticality or value or both. Many buyers optimise their supply bases and use single suppliers to achieve economies of scale. When embarking on such initiative, developing a chosen supplier becomes important. Apart from price, it looks beyond the price of the goods it purchases and examines the impact of its important suppliers on the quality and technology of its parts. Going back to the same example of Suzuki Motors, development of lamps supplier could be important as quality of lamps would impact customer satisfaction in a big way and customer cannot tolerate failure. Thus, a focal firm would use total cost and long-term strategies as criteria for justifying investments in its suppliers.

It may be important for focal firms to set small goals initially for buyers to improve for seeing and believing small successes. When vendors experience focal firm's initiative with minimum demand on resources, time and effort, they develop confidence. Risk of improvement is limited and fear of failure is also within limits to handle. This also provides a window to focal firm to experience from being a buyer to a partner in development. Such exposure to the suppliers will provide the basis for extending the improvement initiatives. Engineering companies and auto components industry go through such processes regularly in vendor development initiatives.

Focal firms would use total-cost-of-ownership (TCO) as a measure to decide on investing on supplier development initiatives. TCO includes all lifecycle costs with respect to product or service acquired. This may include direct, indirect, explicit and implicit costs associated with buying. TCO involves estimating risk component with respect to acquisition and deployment of product or service and included as a part of costing. It is based on the concept that purchase price is a part of TCO. There is a tendency of purchase managers to look at landed price of a material while acquiring. TCO insists to look beyond the landed price.

Typically, TCO begins with requirement specification. All possible elements costs are listed and what are explicit and need to be considered by prospective supplier would be shared. Implicit and hidden costs would be mapped and considered while evaluating bids. However, all elements are identified in the Pre-RFP stage itself. Once when tenders are floated, prospective suppliers and focal firm gather more intelligence on purchase transactions by way of questions, clarifications and support information which would improve TCO computation. It may be noted that TCO elements are prioritised and only items of material substance are prioritised and considered for analysis. Purchase committee would choose that bid which is most economical on TCO basis for awarding the contract. In fact, an analyst in supply chain may note that TCO basis is one which builds long-term view of buy and applied, especially for strategic buying. Both the vendor and focal firm would benefit when they apply this concept, especially when they are looking at enduring relationship. Implementation of TCO basis of selection would help to get out of low-price bid selection mental makeup so that the buyer understands that it is not acquisition but cost of ownership that matters.

Exhibit 4.2 Total Cost of ownership

TCO Elements:
- Define/Buy product or service
- Maintain – post buy activity
- Relocate – post buy activity
- Fallbacks – failure or any such condition, may cover warranty as well
- Implement or install product or service and costs associated with
- Infrastructure
- Secure and insure
- Upgrade – as and when required due to buyer need or technology change
- Replace – normal circumstances or otherwise
- Handoff and dispose – Retire the product or sell off
- Defects = Failure to conform to requirements; compute costs of defects
- TCO analysis drives requirements
- Total cost of the procurement process
  - Direct process costs
  - Methods and tasks
- Reviews/Approvals
- Inspection and acceptance
- Risk trade-offs
- Hard and soft costs
- Staff satisfaction
- Internal customer satisfaction
- Vendor relationship quality

One must also include the following while considering procurement
- Time
- Infrastructure
- Experts support required and value of same in terms of time and effort cost
- Overhead
- Opportunity cost
- Relationship impact including the disputes that could arise, frequency and process of settling the same
- Credibility impact

As it could be observed while computing TCO, quality is an important factor in supplier development. Quality standards are a part of requirement and buyers generally pre-approve vendor after quality processes are adhered to. Once vendor is in pre-approved list, then random quality checks are made and rest goes by certification. This can happen only when there is an evolved relationship between vendor and focal firm. Quality adherence is important as it reduces various facets of risk like that of product, production schedule and so on. It may be important on the part of vendor and buyer to clearly arrive at a contractual relationship with respect to quality requirement so that supply network is not jeopardised. Apart from defining expectations on quality standards, procedures for measurements of performance must be clear.

Thus, a TCO based, quality driven initiative from focal organisation would improve to overcome fears of vendors with buyers.

There are certain concerns with respect to supplier – focal firm interfaces which need to be addressed while embarking upon supplier development initiatives. Concerns may originate in the interface between buyers and suppliers, in areas such as inter-organisational trust, alignment of organisational cultures and ineffective communication of potential benefits.

One of the biggest challenges in supplier development is to cultivate mutual trust. Suppliers may be reluctant to share information on costs and processes, which may be sensitive and confidential. The concern arises from a psychic feeling that focal firm would use such data against the supplier and would not share improvement advantages with them. To overcome this, the focal firm may have to use its strategic position and win over supplier confidence and demonstrate fairness in action by being transparent and open to supplier interaction either individually or in group or both. Focal firm may also inform third parties like industry forums and even supplier forum to handle the same.

For example, some leading public sectors in India like BHEL are believed to be encouraging suppliers and ancillary association and have openness in resolving issues. Supplier's confidential information must be kept exclusive. Sharing confidential information is difficult when dealing with new suppliers in high-technology areas. Thus, many companies safeguard their interests with nondisclosure agreements and even exclusivity agreements. This means that the supplier provides a specific product only to one buyer. Such agreements are necessary when dealing with high-technology products, to ensure a competitive edge for the buyer. However, legal involvement can be minimised. The buyer should consider the supplier as its extension. Formal contracts should be sparingly used. Alliance agreements between the buyer and supplier must be established using a single advisor to minimise legal involvement.

Another factor that may affect supplier is that focal firm interface is poor alignment of organisational cultures and changes that may occur. When conditions change, the existing supplier development approach may no longer be valid. Change in the supply chain or plant locations or any other external or internal factor induced change triggers, then it may affect the supplier development. Supplier development programmes must be designed keeping in mind the local and changing conditions.

There could be insufficient inducement to the supplier because of inadequate understanding of benefits of supplier improvement programme which could be either failure of focal firm to explain the benefits or buyer's inability to understand the same. Generally, a focal firm needs to communicate potential benefits of investing in the supplier development efforts to suppliers. If not, the supplier's total commitment may be lost. Buyers should offer financial incentives and repeat business to suppliers. This effort will gain them suppliers' commitment.

Focal firms while embarking in their supplier development efforts may encounter key problems. These problems often arise during meetings between buyer and supplier management teams, while defining development projects or initiatives, while defining agreement terms and determining metrics for success, and while monitoring project status and subsequently modifying strategies.

To avoid these problems, both suppliers and focal firm must establish transparent and reliable communication. They should openly discuss impediments and resolve issues as soon as possible. The initial projects between the supplier and focal firm should be relatively easy to achieve. This will encourage both to work together in more complex and difficult development initiatives. If the initial targets set for a project are too complex, they usually result in poor follow-up. This is either due to lack of resources or lack of commitment from the supplier's side. The focal firm must sort out problems with the supplier in the initial stages, itself. On the other hand, if a focal firm does not commit adequate resources for its proposed development effort, it is difficult to convince the supplier is top management. Therefore, firms should determine the cost they must bear, and the cost and resources to be shared with the supplier well in advance. Finally, establishing metrics and a time frame for the follow up, as well as sharing the responsibility of problem solving is critical to a project's completion.

Perhaps these suppliers do not recognise the value of improving the quality or delivery performance. Sometimes suppliers do not even realise that they have a problem. The front-end managers of the buyers and sellers do not support supplier development to avoid differences of opinion or ego clashes that may ensue. This issue therefore needs to be handled carefully by close monitoring and prompt action.

Strategic emphasis on the purchasing and supply-chain management is essential for a strong supplier development effort. A strong purchasing mission statement reflects and drives strategic emphasis and alignment.

A focal firm (buyer) may pursue its mission by:

1. Developing a world-class supplier base capable of meeting current and future needs
2. Obtaining the highest quality, most cost-effective goods and services in a timely manner
3. Establishing long-term relationships with supply partners that meet the company's standards and are committed to the manufacturer

Relationship management is critical to the success of the supplier development programme. On a relationship spectrum, strategic decision of supplier – focal firm relationship can progress on an alliance spectrum as shown in Figure 4.9.

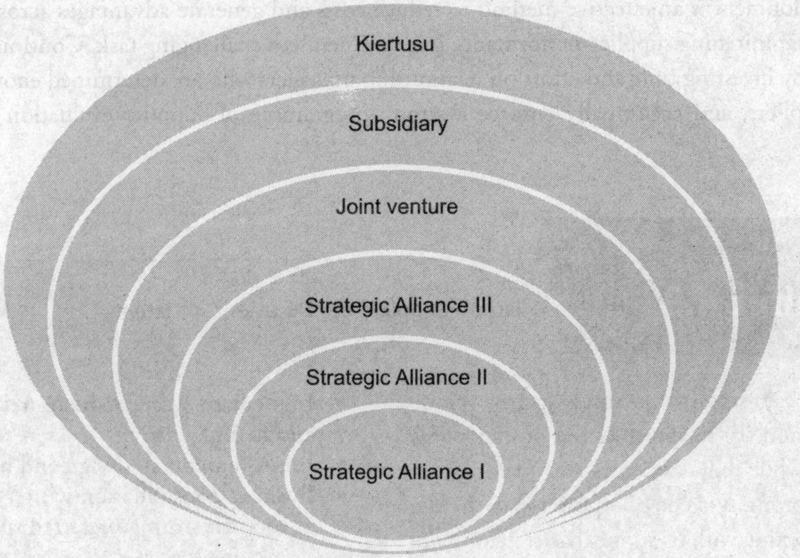

FIGURE 4.9 Supplier – Focal firm relationship stages

Strategic alliance I is an option wherein focal firm is willing to consider vendor along with other vendors for development initiative without any commitment. Subject to fulfilment of quality and other standards, focal firm is willing to support the vendor.

Strategic alliance II is an option wherein focal firm would be willing to support a volume commitment subject to quality and other standards and it would be long-term contract with scope for timely monitoring, evaluation and scaling up standards.

Strategic alliance III is an option wherein focal firm would be willing to support a supplier with technology and financial resource commitment along with level II commitments. This comes only after increased understanding and based on criticality and value factors and most likely vendor could be supplying critical components for product performance.

Joint ventures (JVs) are opportunities of supplier–focal firm relationship to secure business between them and supply for focal firm's requirement. Focal firm and supplier create an entity to monetise the relationship to supply to competitors and larger industry base. The rationale of JV is that component business is different from product business, but component per se has a huge potential and through JV focal firm can achieve certain competitive advantage. For example, an engineering company can invest in a JV with castings and forgings business which would ensure its requirement and as a standalone can supply to market. In a JV, focal firm would not have controlling interest.

There are cases where a focal firm can have a supplier which is a subsidiary which is option V. This is like JV except for the fact that the focal firm scales up investment to a level of majority holding and consolidation of balance sheet is possible. Advantage of subsidiary is that focal firm is majority and would be able to drive strategic initiatives.

Kieretsu is another form of relationship which is common in Japan. It could be horizontal or vertical. In case of supplier based kieretsu, it is vertical where a focal firm develops supplier through investment and also management through deployment of senior management as top management of supplier kierestu company. Thus, investment and pecuniary relationship could impact supplier development. Apart from the above, as mentioned earlier, power based relationship would also impact.

Supplier development is an effective method to reduce costs and generate advantages across supply network. One may note that initiating supplier-performance improvement is a challenging task. Continuous improvement can be achieved by investing time and effort on relationship managers who are determined enough to pay follow-up visits to suppliers, and continually enforce a strong programme of supplier evaluation and performance feedback.

Exhibit 4.3 Visteon supplier development initiatives

Pressure on automotive business across globe pushes the industry to improve the output of its supply base while reducing costs and maintaining consistent output. Visteon Corporation is in the process of working with its supply base to eliminate waste, and improve design and manufacturing quality. Such initiatives would increase the operating margins of Visteon and its suppliers by employing a combination of short-term, quick fixes and long-term collaborative improvements.

The global team of Visteon has set the goals as follows:

- Immediate waste reduction in engineering and manufacturing
- Improvements in design and manufacturing
- Business consolidation with a select number of top performing preferred suppliers

Suppliers that meet their clearly defined requirements enjoy significant financial rewards and enjoy favoured status on future quoting opportunities. The factors which lead to success are meaningful incentives, effective idea generation for supplier involvement and follow through and accountability.

Source: http://www.visteon.com/company/features/101602.html

Other processes:

Since the focus of discussion is more on operations strategy, downstream linkages in supply network like distribution channel strategy and CRM have been kept out of the discussion. Operational strategists need to necessarily work with marketing and business strategists for a complete linkage of strategic initiatives across the supply chain network. Internal supply chain process strategies are discussed in different chapters of the book which are on operations strategies.

SUMMARY

A supply chain involves two or more organisations for serving an ultimate customer which happens by articulating flow of material, finance and information. Supply chain is more outward looking and inter-organisational in approach. Value chain, value system and supply chain management interface complementing approach to value creation to customers by defining activities and system. Value system links up the value chain of the firm with that of the supplier, channel and buyer.

Supply chain macro processes include supplier management, internal supply chain, channel management and customer relationship management. Supply chain management is entrenched on process orientation and adherence. The four processes in four stages of supply network are customer order cycle, replenishment cycle, manufacturing cycle, procurement cycle which is cycle view of supply chain. Push in supply chain means execution of processes, which is initiated in anticipation of customer orders. This mainly depicts speculative character of supply chain where production and stocking happens based on demand forecasts. Trilogy of technology, process and people plays key role in improving supply chain effectiveness.

Supply chain structure is about setting a framework striking a balance between minimising cost of supply chain activities for a defined level of responsiveness. Efficient supply chain is cost centric at one end of the spectrum which works well for standardised items which have more certainty with respect to demand estimate, low to medium in value items which are for standardised goods and services and being in a market which is matured. On the other hand, a responsive supply chain is a measure of speed of serving customers and level of customer service.

Push based supply chain strategy is configured in anticipation of demand. It would be more akin to cost efficient supply chain. Pull based supply chain is configured to execute a customer order as it is being initiated or on arrival of order. Trade-off between push and pull is driven by many factors like structure of the industry, market, competitive forces and performance attributes. Demand and supply factors, technological changes, innovativeness and resources command along with strategic thinking of firm would determine balancing of push and pull strategies.

Supply chain structure defines such strategic focus for supply chain which needs to be accomplished through effective deployment of supply chain drivers, namely facilities, inventory, transportation, sourcing, pricing and information. Each driver has a role and selection criteria and they together form a framework. While deciding the framework, a few conflict situations could arise and managerial decision would be to arrive at a trade-off in such situations.

Sourcing plays a major role in effective supply chain decisions as a focal organisation depends on outsider vendors for material procurement. Sourcing strategies are inter-woven with supply chain strategies and are responsible for achieving supply chain objectives of a firm.

Buying relationship based on value/cost, criticality and matrix mapping interdependence between focal firm and its suppliers provides guidelines for establishing relationship with suppliers for achieving supply chain objective through integration of supplier relationship management with other components. Strategic sourcing involves those activities of purchase department which involve long-term development of vendors wherein effort and resources are invested for achieving competitive advantages in procurement. Such competitive factors could be with respect to cost, responsiveness, focus and breadth of product and markets.

Outsourcing is the act of transferring some of an organisation's recurring internal activities and manufacture and supply of components, parts or services by outside vendors or service providers. Strategic use of outside parties to perform activities which would be non-core activities to vendors is the purpose of outsourcing.

Supplier development is defined as an activity that a buyer undertakes to improve a supplier's performance and/or capabilities to meet the buyer's short-term supply needs. These activities include assessing a supplier's operations, providing support and incentives to improve performance, fostering competition among suppliers and working directly with suppliers, either through training or other activities. Success factors in supplier development are guided by relative positions of strengths, intention and efforts to work together for common goals. Total cost of ownership is one which builds long-term view of buy and applied, especially for strategic buying. It includes all lifecycle costs with respect to product or service acquired.

Key Terms

1. **Supply chain management (SCM):** SCM is the integration of key business processes of a focal organisation on the one side with downstream players to customer and customer's customer and on the other side, upstream players including supplier and supplier's supplier. It also includes managing three flows, namely products/services, information and finance.
2. **Logistics management:** Logistics management is defining a system and managing the same for movement of material, storage of goods in intermediary stages and finished goods to customers in line with the business strategy. Logistics management is inward looking, focussed on cost optimisation and service level for the focal organisation.
3. **Cycle view of supply chain:** Cycle view clearly defines processes involved and the owners of each process. This view specifies the roles and responsibilities of each member and the desired outcome of each process. There are normally four stages and five stakeholders, namely customer, retailer, distributor, manufacturer and supplier. Each two successive nodes are connected to form a cycle.
4. **Push/Pull in supply chain:** Pull in supply chain depicts execution of demand being initiated in response to a customer order. This process is reactive but brings value creation to customers by allowing flexible configuration of products. Push in supply chain means execution of processes is initiated in anticipation of customer orders. This mainly depicts speculative character of supply chain where production and stocking happens based on demand forecasts.
5. **In-bound logistics:** Activities associated with receiving, storing and disseminating inputs from suppliers, inspection, inventory management and transport management and so on are categorised as in-bound logistics.
6. **Out-bound logistics:** Activities associated with order processing, order picking and packing, shipping, delivery vehicle operations and dealer/distributor network and so on are categorised as out-bound logistics.
7. **Hierarchy of supply chain decision making:** This refers to management level at which decisions are made. Supply chain could be strategic, planning and operational based on time window, significance of resource deployment, whether decision is routine or otherwise and criticality. Strategic decisions involve multi-disciplinary team at the senior and top management level as it involves high capital and is not easily reversible in character. Planning decisions are on medium term window (3–18 months time frame) for allocation of available resources; and operations decisions are day-to-day execution of planning decisions.
8. **Value chain:** A value chain identifies primary activities like in-bound logistics, operations, out-bound logistics, marketing and sales and service; and related support activities like human resources, procurement, product R&D, technology and systems development and so on.
9. **Value system:** A focal organisation's value chain is embedded with its forward linked organisations' value chain towards the customer and the backwardly linked organisations' value chain, namely those of suppliers. Together these are addressed as value system.
10. **Business model:** A business model refers to revenues and costs incurred in conducting a business for which an assets and liability structure is created resulting in margins and return on investment. The model is fundamental to product/service offering and approach to competition.
11. **Push strategy:** In a push based strategy, supply chain activities are based on long-term forecasts. The approach could be for achieving production economies feasibly. There could be diseconomies in transportation and inventory related costs. Deployment depends on overall advantage.
12. **Pull strategy:** In a pull strategy, supply chain activities are triggered on arrival of customer rather than on forecast demand. The firm does not hold any inventory and only responds to specific or-

der. This works for hi-tech and high value items, fashion goods and technology intense products and so on.

13. **Make-to-stock (MTS):** MTS strategies in manufacturing are characteristics of industry where there is reliable forecast and production economies are achievable by lumping order size.
14. **Make-to-order (MTO):** MTO strategies are those where production is specific to customer order. Make to Engineering (MTE) is a step ahead of this where customer engineers the product to his specific requirement. In case of MTO, specification, basic product design and engineering is frozen. Variability is provided to customer and hence on arrival of demand, manufacture is triggered.
15. **Focus strategy:** At times, an organisation cannot afford a wide scope cost or leadership or a wide scope differentiation strategy for managing business. Then, a focus is deployed by which an organisation focusses effort and resources on a narrow, defined segment of a market.
16. **Supplier development:** Supplier development is defined as an activity that a buyer undertakes to improve a supplier's performance and/or capabilities to meet the buyer's supply needs.
17. **Outsourcing:** Outsourcing is the act of transferring some of organisation's recurring internal activities and manufacture and supply of components, parts or services by outside vendors or service providers. Strategic use of outside parties to perform activities which are non-core activities is the purpose of outsourcing.
18. **Strategic sourcing:** Sourcing initiatives in supply management has strategic orientation. With a view to develop reliable and effective supply base, a firm must have well-thought and structured sourcing strategies and executed through procurement plan and efficient purchase processes.
19. **Total cost of ownership:** TCO includes all lifecycle costs with respect to product or service acquired.

CONCEPT REVIEW QUESTIONS

1. Analyse supply chain management and logistics management in terms of perspectives with which discipline approach managerial decision. Discuss the same with examples.
2. Define 'value chain'. What are its linkages in upstream and downstream activities? Identify a focal organisation's value chain and elucidate how it works within the industry it operates. Discuss whether value chain could be different among firms within an industry, if so, cite an example.
3. Discuss the role of technology applications and process adherence from real life examples for effective supply chain management.
4. What do you understand by 'macro processes in supply chain' and how are they related? Explain the concept with an example.
5. "Role of supply chain manager is more like a functional manager and has limited scope." Comment on the statement with different industry situations.
6. Describe efficiency and responsiveness in supply chain with examples.
7. Analyse push and pull strategies of supply chain and their advantages and disadvantages.
8. Define a 'supply chain driver'. Explain its relation to supply chain focus with a couple of examples.
9. Explain the role of cross-functional drivers, namely information, pricing and sourcing in supply chain with examples. Discuss how competitive forces can influence deployment of those drivers.
10. Explain the various factors which lead to reassessment of configuration of supply chain drivers. Give some examples.
11. Discuss the role of sourcing and its importance for achieving supply chain objectives. Give some examples.
12. What do you understand by strategic sourcing? Explain key facets of strategic sourcing.

CRITICAL THINKING QUESTIONS

1. Imagine that you are a supply chain manager of an auto major who wants to make his plant competitive, which is located at Chennai. You have tier I and II companies who supply components. How would you strategise strategic sourcing and supplier development in light of need to bring new models every two years and variants every year? You have to demonstrate your value system to your management and win their support for fair approach in sharing supply chain profits. Point out major focal points for your discussion with your management.
2. Assume that you are in charge of supply chain of a retail chain's big store. How would you approach technology, process and people integration for in-store supply chain management? Recommended to visit a store and apply accordingly.
3. Consider a branded fresh coffee retailer who sells coffee beans and grind for selling coffee powder. He also has an instant coffee brand and is a supplier (convertor) to a large brand who sells instant coffee. He also exports coffee powder to Russia and parts of East Europe. What are the key supply chain issues which you focus on and how would you deploy sourcing and procurement strategies? What kind of risks would he face in his business as a supply chain manager?
4. Imagine a situation of hi-tech products like high-end mobile phones. The product is marketed directly through cyber sale, agents and other possible channels. You need to reckon fact that there are diversified channels and products that need to be fresh. How would you go about deploying supply network strategies? Map macro processes of the supply network.
5. You are appointed as chairman of local fruits and vegetable market which acts as a hub in your city. How would you assess the driver and improve effectiveness. You must focus more on cross-functional drivers in improving effectiveness. Few observations include arrivals are in early morning between 3 a.m. and 4.45 a.m. Institutional buyers and resellers buy between 5 a.m. and 7 a.m. Retail and small resellers buy till 1 p.m. At 1 p.m., it is assessed that balance stock available on weekend are low at 15%, whereas during midweek it goes up to 36%. If you are to advise the traders that sell in the market, how would you approach?

PROJECT ASSIGNMENTS

1. Visit a manufacturing facility on your town and map its relevance to supply chain. Also inquire what are the competitive forces which influence this facility? You may also look at competitive advantages the facility may provide in the supply network.
2. Go through web research and analyse growth of consumer electronics and subgroup, namely television industry in India. Analyse competitive factors and supply network aspects like sourcing, supplier development and role of all the nodes in the supply network.
3. Do a structural analysis of Indian fertilizer industry and find out how supply network is configured for a chosen fertilizer brand or unit.

REFERENCES

1. Van Mieghem, Timothy, "Lessons learned from Alexander the Great", *Quality Progress*, Vol. 31, No. 1, January 1998, pp. 41–46.
2. Lambert, Douglas M. and Cooper, Martha C. (2000). "Issues in Supply Chain Management", *Industrial Marketing Management* 29, 65–83.
3. http://www.supply-chain.org/.
4. Christopher, Martin (1998). "Logistics and Supply Chain Management: Creating Value-Adding Networks", *Financial Times* Prentice Hall, Third Edition.
5. Porter, Michael E. "*Competitive advantage*", Free Press, 1985, Export edition 2004; p 36.
6. ibid
7. http://www.mjunction.in.
8. http://www.amul.com.
9. http://cscmp.org/ Council of Council of Supply chain management Professionals.
10. Chopra, Sunil, Meindl, Peter and Kalka, D.V. (2007). "*Supply Chain Management: Strategy, Planning and Orientation*", Pearson.
11. Fisher, Marshall L. "What is the Right Supply Cain for Your product?" *Harvard Business Review*, March – April 1997. pp. 83–93.
12. Christopher, M. (2000). "The agile supply chain, Competing in Volatile Markets". *Industrial Marketing Management* 29, pp 37–44.
13. Christopher, M. and Towill, D. "An integrated model for design of agile supply chains". *International Journal of Physical Distribution & Logistics* 31 (4), 2001. Pp. 234–246.

CHAPTER

5

Technology and Process Strategy

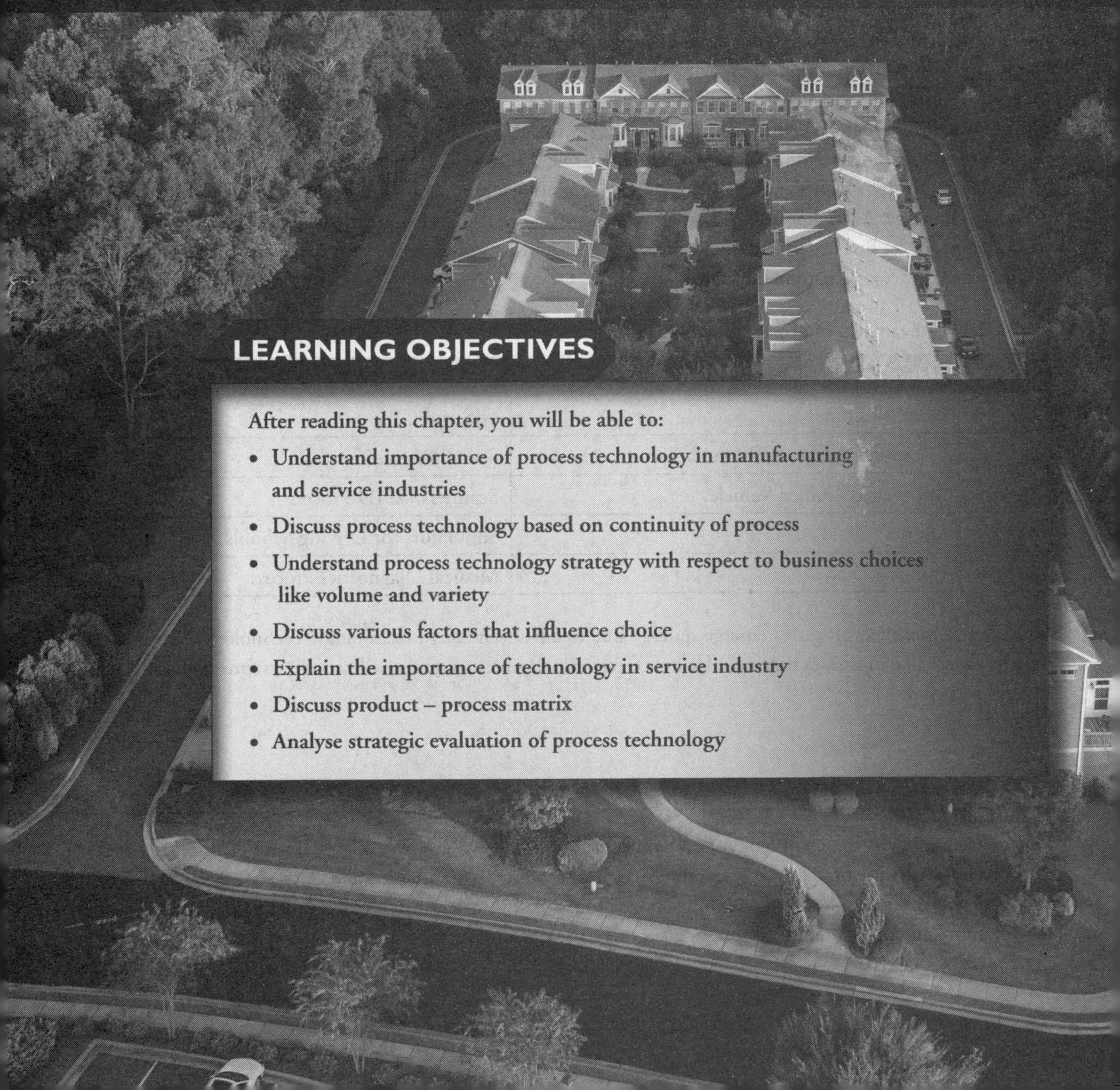

LEARNING OBJECTIVES

After reading this chapter, you will be able to:

- Understand importance of process technology in manufacturing and service industries
- Discuss process technology based on continuity of process
- Understand process technology strategy with respect to business choices like volume and variety
- Discuss various factors that influence choice
- Explain the importance of technology in service industry
- Discuss product – process matrix
- Analyse strategic evaluation of process technology

Introduction

Manufacturing or service operation is an integrated extension of corporate policy to the extent that the total enterprise exists and is organised as a system of transformation (value adding) activities to satisfy pluralistic needs and expectations of stakeholders. Operation is the process of transforming a variety of resources into goods or services. Transformation is not merely conversion of inputs into outputs but also, significant value addition to inputs, by the processes, to create utilities for the end users. Resources include materials, machines, human time, and energy and so on. The output of the operation processes may be manufactured goods, such as automobiles and computers, or services, such as health care or financial transactions. The term 'operations' describes the whole set of activities and processes associated with the production of services and goods. The operations management is about managing the conversion process. In view of the global competition, it is essential to provide goods and services at competitive prices.

These conversion processes which include direct manufacturing processes and service processes along with support processes like transportation, after sales service process, and customer support process are highly strategic in terms of costs and competitiveness. These processes are technology oriented in manufacturing and in high-tech services, the technology has a continuous influence on the effectiveness and efficiency of these processes. Today, there is a strong orientation towards automation of services and technology application changes fast.

Therefore, in this chapter, we deal with process technology and concerned decision in choosing appropriate process technology. As we know already that manufacturing process is designed with focus on how to produce a particular product. But in services, the processes are designed to provide service experience to customers. So, in services, each process is customer oriented.

TABLE 5.1 Examples of process technologies

S.No	Manufacturing	Services
1	CNC Machines	GIS and GPS
2	Computer Integrated Manufacturing	Search Engines
3	Automated Guided Vehicles	Scanners, RFID Process
4	Drones	Simulators for Driving Schools
5	Painting Shop	Medical Diagnostics Process

New and modified processes emerge quickly due to advancement in technology. Technology does not mean only hardware like machines but includes new electronic payment systems, self-service systems and self-check-in systems in airlines.

Process Technology

Process technology is the technology used to produce products or provide services. These technologies include direct technologies used to convert some resources into products (e.g. biscuits) and services (e.g. ATM in a bank) and also indirect technologies used for support processes. Information technology helps in processing many information and data related to suppliers, customers and demand.

Process Technology in Manufacturing Companies

For a manufacturing company, such as Intel, process technology may include basic production equipment and/ or more advanced processes. At Intel, process technology is highly specialised to the semiconductor fabrication process, technologically advanced, very expensive, and used in an extremely complex process.

Process technology is core to converting inputs to outputs in manufacturing businesses, sometimes allowing the firm to differentiate its products or services from its competitors and often requiring a sizable capital investment.

Process Technology in Service Companies

For retailing and distribution companies, process technology comprises the equipment used to move and manage the massive flow or materials throughout the supply chain. In a driving school, simulator technology is used to train drivers before they are allowed to handle real vehicles. Co-creation against co-production is gaining momentum in service process with the help of information technology and artificial intelligence. It is also known that customers are processed in a service system using certain technology process. For example, medical diagnosis is done on customers using certain technological equipments and lab processes. Co-creation and co-production are some new trends happening in service production and delivery, where customers are involved in design and production of services.

In short, process technology is the physical hardware often accompanied by or inextricably intertwined with information technology or software that facilitates the creation and delivery of goods or services.

Process technologies are broadly classified based on

(i) Nature of inputs it processes
(ii) Continuity of the process

Process technologies based on nature of inputs

1. Material process technologies
2. Information process technologies
3. Customer process technologies

Material Process Technologies: These are processes or methods used to convert some physical materials into some physical products. It involves change in shape, size and characteristics of materials. For example, steel rods are converted into fasteners of different sizes, limestone is turned into cement, timber and wood are converted into paper and so on. The technologies involved are many starting from moulding, welding, bending, casting and so on. It also involves chemical, biological and physical processes. Some examples are automated guided vehicles, CNC machines, assembly operations, baking process and so on.

Information Processing Technologies: These technologies are used to collect data and information from customers and other internal sources, process them and provide valuable information for decision making in general. Many organisations deploy appropriate information processing technologies to process large data and information results in software products and services. These are deployed at discrete level like container scanners at port terminals or as a system like Warehouse Management System (WMS) for a warehouse automation. Examples include enterprise resource planning, database systems, expert systems, SCM software, CRM system, suppliers relationship management systems and so on.

Customer Processing Technologies: In services industry, these technologies are common. These are processes used to provide services to customers. A security scanning system in airport is an example. Service systems like airport, hospitals, people transport system, retail systems are some examples. The appropriate technology is deployed to process customers and fasten the service process. Internet technologies are widely used today to process customers faster. Internet banking and ATMs are some examples. Medical diagnostic systems like MRI scan, X-rays and ECG are also customer processing technologies.

Process Technologies/Methods Based on Continuity of Process

Based on process characteristics with respect to continuity of process, technologies can be classified as

- *Continuous Process*
- *Mass Production Process*
- *Batch Production Process*
- *Job Shop Process and*
- *Project Process*

Job Shop Production

Job shop production is characterised by manufacturing one or few quantity of products designed and produced as per the specification of customers within prefixed time and cost. It involves low volume and high variety. A job shop comprises general purpose machines arranged into different departments. Each job requires unique technological requirements, demands processing on machines in a certain sequence.

Job shop production is characterised by:

1. High variety of products and low volume
2. Use of general purpose machines and facilities
3. Highly skilled operators who can take up each job as a challenge because of uniqueness
4. Large work in inventory of materials, tools and parts
5. Detailed planning is essential for sequencing the requirements of each product, capacities for each work centre and order priorities.

Job shop system is highly flexible, better creative products can be produced and variety of jobs can be handled. But this has lowest utilisation of facilities, more inventory and large waiting or lead time.

Batch Production

Production and Inventory Control Society (APICS) defines batch production as a form of manufacturing in which the job passes through the functional departments in lots or batches and each lot may have a different routing. It is characterised by the manufacture of limited number of products produced at regular intervals and stocked awaiting sales.

Batch production is characterised by

1. Shorter production runs
2. Flexible plant and machinery
3. Plant and machinery set up used for the production of an item in a batch and change of set up is required for processing the next batch
4. Less cost and lead-time of manufacturing as compared to job order production

Advantages

Following are the advantages of batch production:

1. Better utilisation of plant and machinery
2. Promotion of functional specialisation
3. Lower cost per unit as compared to job order production
4. Lower investment in plant and machinery

5. Flexibility to accommodate and process number of products
6. Existence of job satisfaction for operators

Limitations

Following are the limitations of batch production:

1. Material handling is complex because of irregular and longer flows
2. Production planning and control is complex
3. Work in process inventory is higher compared to continuous production
4. Higher set up costs due to frequent changes in set up

Mass Production

Manufacture of discrete parts or assemblies using a continuous process is called mass production.

This production system is justified by a large volume of production. The machines are arranged in a line or product layout. Product and process standardisation exists and all outputs follow the same path.

Mass production is characterised by

1. Standardisation of product and process sequence
2. Dedicated special purpose machines having higher production capacities and output rates
3. Large volume of products
4. Shorter cycle time of production
5. Lower in process inventory
6. Perfectly balanced production lines
7. Flow of materials, components and parts is continuous and without any back tracking.
8. Production planning and control is easy
9. Material handling can be completely automatic

Advantages

Following are the advantages of mass production:

1. Higher rate of production with reduced cycle time
2. Higher capacity utilisation due to line balancing
3. Less skilled operators required
4. Low process inventory
5. Low manufacturing cost per unit

Limitations

Following are the limitations of mass production:

1. Breakdown of one machine will stop an entire production line
2. Line layout needs a major change with the changes in the product design
3. High investment in production facilities
4. The cycle time is determined by the slowest operation

Continuous Production

Production facilities are arranged as per the sequence of production operations from the first operations to the finished product. The items are made to flow through the sequence of operations through material handling devices, such as pipeline, conveyors, transfer devices, etc.

Continuous production is characterised by

1. Dedicated plant and equipment with zero flexibility
2. Fully automated material handling
3. Process adherence of a predetermined sequence of operations
4. Component materials cannot be readily identified with final product
5. Planning and scheduling as a routine action

Advantages

Following are the advantages of continuous production:

1. Standardisation of product and process sequence
2. Higher rate of production with reduced cycle time
3. Higher capacity utilisation due to line balancing
4. Manpower is not required for material handling as it is completely automatic
5. Person with limited skills can be used on the production line
6. Unit cost is lower due to high volume of production

Limitations

Following are the limitations of continuous production:

1. Flexibility to accommodate and process numreous products does not exist
2. Very high investment for setting flow lines
3. Product differentiation is limited

Process Technology Strategy

Process technology strategy involves a set of decisions that involves which technology to adopt for production of product/service, (choice of technology), how to deploy the technology in the organisation, when and how to upgrade the technology, and finally, when to abandon the existing one and move to new one.

Operations manager cannot avoid the role of process technologies and its development. They work with them all the time and know how technology improves productivity. They should also be aware of the roles of other functions like engineering, accountancy, human resources and information technology in production. An operations manager need not be an expert in technology and science behind the core process but should be comfortable in evaluating different alternative technologies in terms of growth of the organisation, cost and long-term financial implications, and long-term strategic vision. They need to consult experts and seek relevant information before taking a major decision.

The following factors need to be considered for process technology strategy.

a. How is each technology different from others?
b. How does it work?
c. What future problems we might face if we implement a particular technology?
d. What kind of skill sets are required for operations staff?
e. Capacity and scope for scale up
f. Lifecycle of technology
g. Impact on environment and society

Process Technology Should Support Volume and Variety

Process technologies are different for different types of production systems and products. But they have some characteristics that can distinguish them from one other. These characteristics are highly connected to volume and variety in terms of products. Process technologies vary with volume and variety. High variety-low volume processes require more general process systems with general purpose machines and methods. High volume-low variety processes will have more special dedicated processes capable of producing huge volumes. Within this range, three important characteristics tend to vary with variety and volume.

(a) Technology's degree of automation
(b) Capacity in terms of scale and scalability
(c) Extent of its integration with other technologies in the overall process

These characteristics are discussed in detail under the following headings:

(a) Automation –What Extent one can go?

The rapid growth of technology and its wider applications resulted in rapid industrial automation. Now we have industrial robots, automated guided vehicles, numerically controlled machines, automated quality inspection system and automated process control systems and many more automated systems in factories. Service automation is also happening at a rapid pace which provides competitiveness to service systems. For example, a bank's back office works are automated, most of us do the banking through ATMs and internet banking, and in future, a robot will do haircut and make-up for humans and it will serve food in a restaurant. Maintenance becomes a major management issue when automation is in full force. The implementation of automation definitely attracts huge investments but systems are bound to fail at some point of time due to many reasons. A kind of hybrid system is recommended where manual and automated systems work together. But due to development of better technology, manufacturing sector will face huge level of automation. With the development in Industry 4.0 and Internet of Things, automation will only accelerate in future. Automation will reduce industrial accidents and productivity will also increase.

But in service industry, the hybrid system is recommended wherever possible and complete automation is not recommended due to many reasons. In manufacturing system, if a machine fails, the manager may try to arrange alternative machine or wait for the machine to be serviced. The customer is not present in the factory and hence the manager can afford to wait. But in a service situation, if a machine fails, the manager needs to continue to provide service and hence a combination of manual and automated system is recommended. A balanced allocation of tasks between technology and operator may give competitive advantage for the service system.

Level of automation

Level of automation is a major decision in process strategy. In India, the majority of warehouses are not automated due to labour availability at a lower cost and also social support of employment. But some of the warehousing facilities developed by Amazon are highly automated with robots and drones. Within a given industry, one can find more automation and automated processes in countries like Germany, Japan, and USA, where labour costs are more and less automated processes in countries like China and India. Certain factors influence the level of automation to be implemented in manufacturing and services.

- Commercial factors
- Social and political factors
- Operational factors
- Government and regulatory factors

Commercial Factors:

The common investment related measures and operations efficiency factors like return on investment, gestation period and project flexibility, and lead time must be considered. Maintenance support cost is also considered while going for automation. Larger, complex systems normally require more maintenance with people and cost on the higher side. When adapting to technology automation, flexibility of the process, change in demand, change in customer taste and preferences should be considered.

Social and Political Factors:

Introduction of automation is a process which is always perceived as a threat to current employees in any organisation. Many labour unions in India are against automation. In India, labour unions are affiliated to political parties and hence problems escalate fast and disturb the business. These factors need to be anlaysed, discussed and a mutual agreement should evolve.

Operational Factors:

These factors are concerned with technological and physical constraints on implementation of new process. They are also related to inputs availability like raw materials, infrastructure availability like power, roads, energy and labour availability. The competitiveness factors in terms of cost of production, productivity, economy of scale, flexibility and quality should be considered with new process technology. Safety of workers and man-machine interaction system should be considered. Environmental sustainability should also be considered under operational factors as new technology may result in more pollution and carbon footprints.

Government and Regulatory Factors:

Technology imports, licensing agreements and patents should be handled carefully. Indian Factories Act and labour safety standards should be studied carefully for implementing new processes.

(b) Process Technology – Scale and scalability

Scale is a critical factor in process technologies as well as capacity decisions. By scalability we mean the intrinsic capacity of a system to handle market growth. For a system to be called scalable, growth should proceed unhindered, i.e. the size and volume of processing may expand without significantly affecting the cost of production. It is also interpreted as a measure of contribution margin (revenue minus variable cost) required to produce a good or service unit as the business grows and volume increases. High scalability means the capacity to serve additional customers at zero cost or at extremely low cost.

The concept of the capacity of each unit of technology which determines the capacity of the overall operation process needs to be understood first before we discuss about scalability. For example, in a call centre, a robot executive can handle 50 calls per day on an average, the capacity of the call centre can be calculated with number of robots used. Each unit of technology here is 50 calls. A laundry company buys a laundry machine which can wash 200 clothes per day. If it wants to increase capacity, it needs to buy one more. The unit of technology here is 200. This capacity of each unit of technology influences the scale of operation.

There are some factors that influence the scale of process technology. Larger unit of technology attracts more capital cost but capital cost per unit is small. The operating cost per unit is lower for a larger machine compared to smaller machine. Similarly, advanced larger photocopy machine can produce copies at a cheaper rate. Process technology should match the demand over time. Larger capacity in short run develop capacity chunks. Similarly, integrated larger systems are vulnerable to risk of failure. The scope for upgradation also must be considered before choosing a technology.

(c) Process Technology Integration-Level of interaction of different process technologies within a production system

A production system may contain many sub-systems and hence many sub-process technologies. These technologies need to connect to other technologies and manual processes to produce a product or to provide a service. Smooth interaction and synchronisation is required for complete production. It is also called coupling between process technologies.

Fragmented processes are individual processes, each operates independently and components need to be moved to the next process manually in batches after completion. Integrated processes are those that combine more than one specific unit process into a single piece of equipment or into a group of work stations that are operated under unified control. A number of factors are accelerating the push towards integrated unit processing. These include the need for reduced equipment and process cost, shorter processing times, reduced inspection time, and reduced handling. By their very nature, integrated systems require a higher level of synthesis than a single unit process and also require more capital investments. Therefore, development of integrated processes will generally be more complex than that of individual unit processes, but it could provide simplified, lower-cost manufacturing.

Let us take the example of Precision Gear manufacturing process:

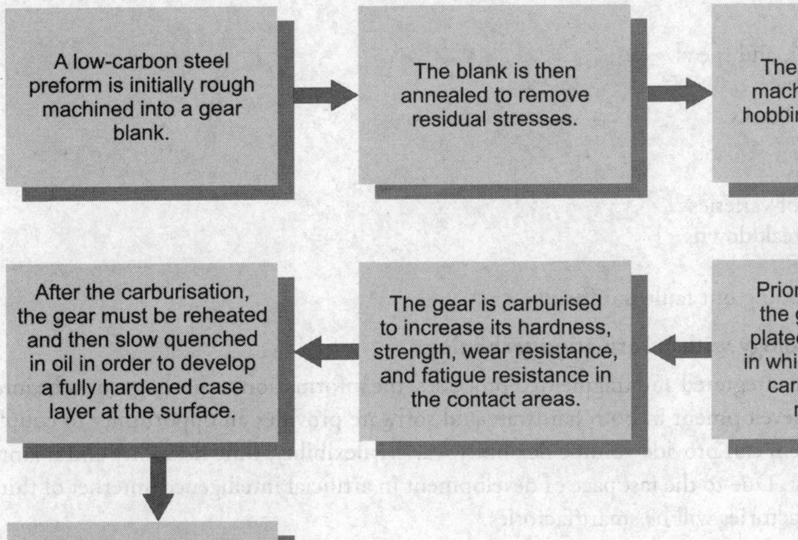

FIGURE 5.1 Conventional process

FIGURE 5.2 Integrated process

There are some traditional advantages as well as disadvantages in conventional fragmented processes:

- Vulnerability to break down is low
- Technology is simple and hence repair is also simple
- Highly flexible in terms of variety and variations
- People intervention is more and hence more robust

Disadvantages:

- More work-in-progress
- Higher direct costs
- Human errors are possible

Integrated processes also have some advantages as well as disadvantages:

Advantages:

- More precision, power, and speed
- Less energy requirement
- Very good for repeated tasks

Disadvantages:

- Less flexible in terms of varieties
- Most susceptible to break downs
- Maintenance is costly
- Due to complexity, finding out fault is difficult

Coupling of Process technology with Information technology

To get the advantages of both integrated and fragmented processes, the information technology must be integrated with physical process. The development in both hardware and software provides an opportunity to couple these technologies so that the system can provide volume flexibility, variety flexibility, time flexibility and maintenance flexibility at a reasonable cost. Due to the fast pace of development in artificial intelligence, internet of things and smart processes, the future factories will be smart factories.

Today, machines are becoming more intelligent with embedded technology, RFID and sensors along with supportive software. The products are becoming smarter and hence process design becomes more flexible due to these developments. The raw products can be embedded with details of operations that need to be performed on it using an integrated chip. The product is handled using intelligent material handling system within factory with readers and sensors. The machines will read the instructions embedded in the product and accordingly do the operation on the product. This makes the product customised and the process more flexible. The scheduling of production becomes much simpler and visible. Industry 4.0 is the ultimate manufacturing automation and it is already making news in global factories. Some of the manufacturing systems in France and Germany already have implemented Industry 4.0 and their experience is positive.

Tehnology in Services

Advances in communications and information technology are having a paradigm shift in which service is offered, especially for customer interface. For example, internet has changed many services like airlines, personal mobility, food delivery and retailing. Mostly services moved from human interface services to technology generated service encounters. Self-service also emerged with assistance of technology. Service automation is happening at a faster rate as one can see in banking services and on-line retailing.

Service has migrated from human interaction to substitution of machines for service employees or where feasible to anywhere-anytime electronic service. This has happened in manufacturing long back. For services, 'the process is the product' because customers participate in the service delivery. As service has meanings like experience, psychological feeling, emotional experience, comfort level and so on, one should be highly vigilant in implementing technology in service encounters. Therefore, success of new technology implementation, especially in front-office, depends on customer experience. The impact on customer is not always limited to a loss of personal attention. New technology forces customers to learn new skills like learning to operate ATM machine or doing banking operation through internet. New technology may make customer interaction less frequent. The contribution and co-operation of customers in co-production of services need to be considered before using a new technology in service process.

Due to technology, many services became self-services where customer also contributes to them. There is a strong effort from customer side to complete the service delivery and process but customers are not given any benefit like discount. Rather, they are charged more due to self-service. This also makes customers to think before adopting new technology and self-service.

Employees are also affected by the adoption of technology in service processes. They may need retraining and orientation so that they can adapt to new technology. Sometimes employees may resist implementation of new technology as it might be perceived as a substitute for people resulting in fear of loss of job from their side. Banks today have automated many services using internet technologies and enjoy less people cost and are able to provide better service.

In many back-office services, the application of technology is easier due to less involvement of customers. Some examples where automation is used are:

1. Core banking in India where transaction between banks became easier
2. Order picking in warehouses

There is less motivation for service innovation and automation due to the fact that many ideas cannot be patented and these can be easily copied. For example, in the online food delivery business model—almost six major players now competing for the same market like Swiggey, Food Panda, Zomoto, Uber Eats and so on.

Product-Process Matrix

The manufacturing and service systems continue to produce goods and services using different processes of conversion. The goods vary from standard commodities like steel, aluminium, sugar and power to goods which are made to order like optic wears, tailored suits, and birthday cakes. In the case of services, it varies from standard services like public transportation to customised services like bridal make-up. Production processes, as described earlier, vary in terms of volume and varieties. Depending upon the requirement of the market, the products and processes should be matched to produce optimally. This results in product–process matrix which assists managers to decide appropriate strategy.

Processes should be having some characteristics which constrain our decisions related to products. The important characteristics are volume, variety and flexibility. Continuous manufacturing process is best suitable for large volume standard products and mass production can be used for high volume, few variety products. More varieties and less volume categories can be dealt with job shop system.

The product–process matrix is a framework that is used to demonstrate the combination of a product's (or product group's) volume and variety characteristics, and the nature of the conversion processes that make it. It was originally devised by Hayes and Wheelwright (1979), who saw it as "one way in which the interaction of the product life cycle and process life cycle can be represented." The product–process matrix is an array whose horizontal dimension represents points on the volume–variety continuum from low volume one off products through to high volume, high standardisation products. Its vertical dimension represents manufacturing processes, from jobbing through batch and mass to continuous.

The product-process matrix triggers the following strategic issues:

(a) Efficiency and flexibility trade-offs
(b) Range of process options available
(c) How a company can manage multiple-plants in terms of market orientation
(d) How competitors may offer their choices

TABLE 5.2 Product–process matrix and its implications

	Project	Job shop	Batch	Repetitive flow	Continuous flow	Mass customisation
Equipment	General purpose, flexible and also some special equipment like Earth movers	General purpose, flexible, more numbers	Some specialised equipment, sometimes organised in groups or cells	Standard special purpose	Standard special purpose with large systems and sub systems	Specialised, but allows for rapid changeover closer to customer
Labour	Specialised by function, often within machine operation (e.g. Q-crane)	Broadly skilled but focussed on few machines	Less broadly skilled; may need technical skills for changeovers	Trained in one special operation and need and troubleshooting and problem-solving skills	Process technical skills and troubleshooting and problem-solving skills	Flexible multi-skilled
Information requirement	Coordination and planning, specification management, costing, procurement and project sequencing	Product specifications, job tracking, planning, routing and scheduling, job costing	Batch tracking, planning and scheduling, materials planning	Output rate planning, materials planning, quality management	Output rate planning, materials planning, quality management	Customer requirements, materials planning, process flow and scheduling
Inventory requirements	Mostly WIP (Work in process), some RMI (Raw Material Inventory)	Mostly WIP	Mostly WIP, sometimes some FGI (Finished Goods Inventory) if build-to-stock	Mostly RMI and FGI; fast process so little WIP	Low levels of RMI to feed process; may have FGI if make-to-stock	Low levels of RMI to feed process; little FGI as is made-to-order
Costs	Fixed low to moderate; variable high	Fixed low; variable high	Fixed moderate; variable moderate	Fixed high; variable low	Fixed high; variable low	Fixed high; variable low
Automation	Moderate	Moderate	Possible	Complete automation	Complete automation	Complete automation

The product-process matrix illustrates the general rules of manufacturing or production processes. Finding and using the appropriate process is necessary to ensure quality and keep cost low enough to match market demand and volume. It is unusual, however, that a product will fit so neatly into one process or another and many products and services depend on several processes for their creation. These hybrid processes, consisting of combination of mass production and job shop production, are becoming more and more common. The steel, which goes into cars and heavy equipment, for example, is created through a continuous process. If you order specialised stereo equipment for your car, it may be produced through batch processing. Although eyeglasses are built in a job shop, the frames may have been created on an assembly line and the glass blank for the lens through a continuous process. For many manufacturers the goal is to create high quality products with the efficiency of a continuous process, while building in as much flexibility as possible in order to allow for more and more customisation. At the same time, small volume producers search for methods to produce greater volumes of specialised products at lower prices. In order to achieve this mass customisation, manufacturers must understand the dynamic of the product-process matrix.

The product-process matrix framework helps organisation strategically in many ways:

(i) It helps in streamlining the existing products and processes so that their mutual fitness can be improved.
(ii) It helps to identify and map the scope for flexibility within the process for varieties and volume.
(iii) It also helps the organisation to identify bottlenecks in reaching efficiency in operations.
(iv) It also helps in mapping the transition through different process approaches like batch production to mass production for a product category over its product life cycle (PLC).

Many organisations who produce low volume high variety goods with customisation rarely migrate along the diagonal to mass production. For example, make to order furniture companies want to limit their volumes but they provide variety, craftsmanship and customisation and are also priced at a higher level. For them, it is not necessary and this way they gain competitive advantage. Similarly in services, a restaurant specialising in Mexican food, concentrates only on varieties on Mexican cuisines and they cater to specific high income customers.

The technology intensity is normally low for job shop kind of system and systems are designed with sub-systems which are loosely coupled. The automation is limited and interaction between technology and human is more. Technology intensity can be more for mass production as well as mass service offerings (bank automation using ATMs).

Moving on the diagonal-Strategic perspectives

Traditionally, organisations start with small unit using simple process, with less automation and more people. They move along the diagonal when demand for their services or products increases. It is not always a smooth ride and has a lot of challenges. The following factors influence the movement in terms of speed and hindrances.

(a) Demand growth in the market
(b) Characteristics of product or service
(c) Varieties and volumes of demand
(d) Availability of suitable scaling up technologies
(e) Logistics cost

The demand growth is easy to understand as organisation scales up when there is more demand for their products/services. Organisations concentrating on low demand still look for better technology for producing varieties. When niche demand grows across geographical boundaries, it is required to replicate their units to reach other markets.

Product or service characteristics sometimes influence the scaling up along the diagonal of product-process matrix. Perishable products cannot be produced at centralised large factories but need to be produced closer to the market. For example, Pizza delivery companies strategically locate their kitchens at many places within a city to cater to local area. Each unit is operated at medium level of scale and there is no need for large scale production. But there are a few exceptions—a sweet and snack retail chain called Adyar Anandha Bhavan in Chennai, Tamil Nadu produces certain categories of sweets and snacks in a centralised factory and distributes to all retail outlets. They use more automated technology in production and handling and also in distribution. Most of the service units are local and small and hence technology adoption is relatively low and their unit of technology is also small.

If organisations produce more varieties with significant volume, the scaling up is meaningful and better technology can be adopted. For example, a variety of biscuits produced by Britannia. It must definitely use appropriate process technology to produce large volumes of all varieties.

In some cases, even the demand is more, for scaling up, the technology might not be available or it may require huge investments. In few cases, the economy of scale gained by technology upgradation might be compensated or nullified by increase in logistics cost.

Levels of customisation and postponement strategy:

Apart from traditional production processes, due to advancement in technology, new strategies are evolving in process and methods. When we try to balance mass production and customisation, new approaches are evolving. Depending on the levels of customisation, there are four types of production processes.

1. **Make to stock system:** This production system is for products with large demand and low varieties. All consumer goods are produced based on forecasting and distributed to the market. The demand mostly remains stable and shows growth every year. No customisation is practised.
2. **Assemble to order system:** This system features customisation of products towards the end of the process. Still customisation is limited to few varieties. A t-shirt printed with LOGO and customer name is an example. Similarly, Dell assembles computers based on ordered configurations.
3. **Make to order system:** This system works based on orders and its specifications. It uses standard components and processes but customisation pushed back to intermediate level. Engine valves are produced based on order from automobile manufacturer and batch size is small to medium and varieties are more.
4. **Engineer to order**: This is a highly customised production system from start to end, the product is manufactured as per customer specifications. For example, BHEL company makes boilers as per the order. It designs as per specifications, and fabricates and delivers to the customer. Similarly, a company called FL Smidth designs and installs cement plants for its clients.

Postponement strategy and technology:

Postponement strategy lies in organising the production and distribution of products in such a way that the customisation of these products is made as close to the point when the demand is known as soon as possible. It means differentiating the service or product closer to the customer. It is also treated as one of the levers to attack variability of demand and supply. This strategy is applied in the following situations:

(a) When demand is highly fluctuating and unpredictable, when demand insists surges when demand peaks for short lead time and when differentiation (same product needs to have different performance characteristics for different markets) is demanded in the market.

(b) Products with high monetary value (due to high inventory cost and high cost of over supply) and high component commonality/modularity.

(c) Availability of proper technology so that customisation is possible.

Due to advancement of technology in different fields, postponement strategy became a major success in various sectors. For example, Asian Paints, a domestic paint company developed a technology to show that paints of any colour in any quantity which can be made as per order at retail level. They developed a concept called Color World, where a retailer can make any colour paint with the help a mixer and a computer. This process technology helped Asian Paints to improve their supply chain operations and gain competitive advantage. IKEA, a Swedish company stocks furniture in components level and customers are required to assemble them at their homes when they buy them. IKEA invested in modular design as well as making common components for furniture. Benetton, a fashion garment retailer, practises postponement approach to reduce the lead time, an important performance measure in fashion industry.

Manufacturing New dimension-3D Printing and Customisation

Another technology development that will create revolution in manufacturing is 3D printing. From making prototypes of kidneys and hearts to actual aircraft parts, it dominates niche areas. It will co-exist with current manufacturing system but in the long run, 3D could integrate with automated manufacturing system. Companies like GE and Airbus are already using parts made by 3D printers. It is also called additive manufacturing and it seems to be the future of manufacturing. This involves a process by which a product, designed using computer and softwares like CAD can be manufactured using repetitive deposit of materials, one above the other. Products of different categories using different materials can be made. Toys, cakes, prototype models, critical spare parts can be made using 3D printing. In 2015, Airbus opted for 3D printing of plastic components and internal cabin parts as suppliers were delaying the delivery. Narayana Health has been using 3D printing technology for making prototypes of organs so that these can be used for teaching and demonstrating complex surgeries.

Benefits of 3D Printing:

- It reduces wastage of material
- It is suitable for customised manufacturing and numbers needed are limited
- Critical components and patented products can be manufactured

Demerits:

- Not scalable
- High cost of printers
- Materials for printers not standardised and require new supply chains

Strategic Evaluation of Process Technology

The most famous methods of evaluating capital investments like process technology are net present value (NPV) analysis or discounted cash flow (DCF) methods. NPV is based on expected gain from the investment with certain rate of return. DCF is based on expected cash inflows and choosing discount rate. Due to rate of change in technology and industrial competition, these methods are becoming irrelevant in evaluating strategic importance of different process technologies. Many factors need to be considered apart from financial returns on timeline.

(i) Long term capability of creation of technological developments as opposed to short term financial results
(ii) Feasibility in terms of implementation
(iii) Importance of product quality and service quality
(iv) Need for flexibility in operations
(v) Demand for short production cycle time and lead time
(vi) The risks involved in chosen technology
(vii) The risks involved in not upgrading to new processes and technologies
(viii) Loss of competitive advantage

These above factors are not quantifiable in terms of costs and benefits. But these need to be considered for evaluation of process technology before we take a decision.

Strategic nature of investment made in Process Technology

Investments in technological change should be considered in terms of the following criteria:

(i) They are critical to the organisation's total performance
(ii) They involve large amount of financial resources
(iii) They are long term in nature
(iv) Mostly, they are irreversible

Returns on strategic investments cannot be evaluated easily as this investment is made to create strategic competitive advantage in the market. The organisation needs to consider its strategic goals and how it wants to create strategic advantage. Three common generic strategies proposed by Porter (1980) are:

(a) Cost leadership
(b) Differentiation
(c) Responsiveness to market by creating flexibility in the process

The evaluation of technology option is not that easy given the above background of its nature. It is suggested to have a basket of techniques both financial and strategic in nature to evaluate technology options. The following framework is suggested for this.

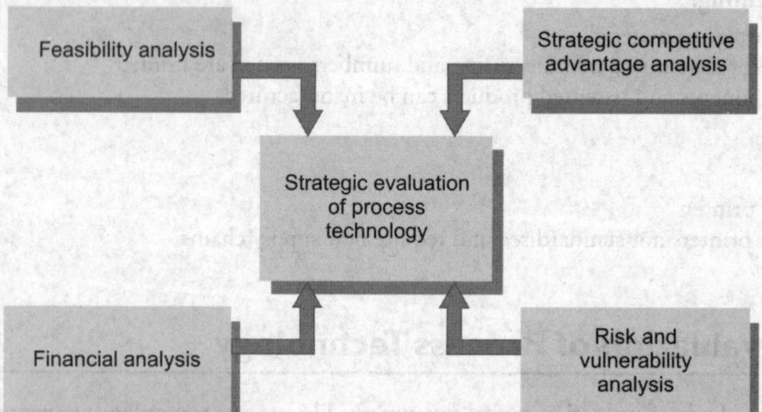

FIGURE 5.3 Evaluation framework for process technology

Financial Analysis

While choosing a particular process technology, most important question a manager faces is how much financial investment it will require and if we can mobilise it. When organisation invests in a new process technology, there is a stream of cash outflows over a period of project implementation. Similarly, there is a stream of improved cash in-flows over the same period. These financial flows need to be evaluated using any of the investment analysis techniques like net present value method so that some objection evaluation can be completed. But there is a problem with this analysis. Many investments in technology do not result in immediate benefits. Some of the benefits are occurring in long term and are intangible. The evaluation should consider the indirect benefits like improvement in morale of employees, less downtime, low maintenance problem, better productivity and flexibility in the system.

Life-cycle cost: This cost is summation of all the costs that will be involved in implementing and executing new process technology. This includes technology costs, people cost, maintenance cost, training costs and these costs occur over the lifetime of the process.

Since well-established financial evaluation techniques to evaluate technology investments are readily available, it is not covered in this book.

Strategic Competitive Advantage Analysis

Strategic competitive advantage analysis is based on how competitive position of the company changes with respect to process technology upgradation. This analysis is based on Porter's work on competitive strategy (Porter, 1980, 1985). The activities of the value chain provide competitive advantage for the company. The value chain of the firm needs to be evaluated with respect to change in technology.

Technologies used in various value chain activities result in creation of products, (production) movement of products to customers (outbound logistics), sourcing of materials (inbound logistics) and other support processes like information technology. These processes are interrelated and hence their technologies should be compatible. Dell's use of technology in sourcing and VMI and in order processing resulted in huge cost advantage and customer service advantage for Dell. Their Direct to Customer model was enabled by internet and other support technologies.

Technology advancement may create competitive advantage in the following ways:

(i) Lowering of production cost and generating economy of scale
(ii) Possibility of creating a unique product which is different from competitors
(iii) Due to change in process technology, competitiveness may be created in terms of time, cost, quality and flexibility for the company
(iv) It also may create first mover advantage like i-Phone for Apple Inc.
(v) New process technology may change the competitive structure of the industry

The new processes should be evaluated based on above competitive achievements that technology can develop in future for the organisation. The choice of process technology should be analysed on all competitive priorities and based on organisations competitive strategy, the choice must be made.

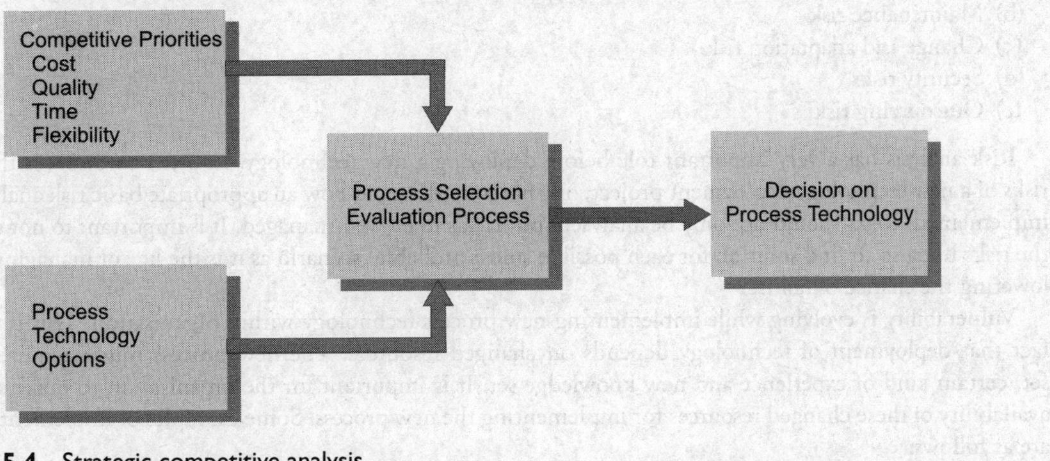

FIGURE 5.4 Strategic competitive analysis

Feasibility Analysis

Even if financial resources are available, technical requirements to implement new process technology need to be analysed. The technical manpower resources and other resources required to implement new process sometimes may not be available and hence feasibility is a question mark. The following important issues are raised in this regard.

(a) What technical human skills are required to implement new process technology?
(b) What kind of change in resource requirement is expected in a timeline while implementation?
(c) Whether this technology demands some scarce natural resources?
(d) Whether this technology has any potential impact on environment and sustainability?

Every process technology will need a skillset within the organisation so that it can be implemented successfully. The additional cost of training, recruitment and compensation needs to be considered before considering the new technology. If the existing workforce is capable of adopting, then there is no issue.

While implementing a new process, new skill and resource requirement may emerge which results in more cost. Some years ago, many organisations had implemented ERP systems. The long period of implementation resulted in change in technology here and there and demanded more resources from organisations. The period of implementation and environment changes needs to be considered.

Today, with huge pressure on organisations to be environmentally sustainable, they must take precautions in implementing new process technology. New processes should not strain our scarce natural resources. For example, a new chemical process expects to consume more water and if there is no way organisation can regenerate water themselves, then the situation is water resource negative. Also, if the technology is connected to mining of some rare materials and if the mining is not environmentally sustainable, it is better to avoid that technology.

Risk and Vulnerability Analysis

New process technology should be evaluated on possible failures and cost escalation risks. The possible risks are listed here:

(a) Cost escalation risks
(b) Maintenance risk
(c) Change and adaptation risk
(d) Security risks
(e) Outsourcing risk

Risk analysis has a very important role before deploying a new technology. In order to discover the possible risks of a new technology deployment project, one has to understand how an appropriate basic risk analysis can be implemented. Risks should not only be analysed, but it has to be well-managed. It is important to not only know the risks but also to find solution for each possible (most probable) scenario as it is the key of managing risks and lowering the chance of failure.

Vulnerability is evolving while implementing new process technology within organisation. This is due to the fact that deployment of technology depends on changed resources. The new process might require new skill set, certain kind of experience and new knowledge set. It is important for the organisation to make sure of the availability of these changed resources for implementing the new process. Some examples of implementation risks are as follows:

Integration with Existing System: The risk is related to transient stage from old technology to new technology. A transaction between a legacy system and ERP fails in production.

Benefit of Realisation Risk: A salesforce automation tool changes its user interface with the practical case that it will improve customer satisfaction. At launch, social media is filled with complaints about the change. Customer satisfaction plummets and executives order the implementation backed out.

Availability Risk: Implementation of unstable technology causes a manufacturing system to repeatedly crash.

Information Security Risk: A web browser implements a new feature that contains information security vulnerabilities that lead to widespread security attacks.

Process Risk: An ERP system is launched without sufficient consideration of production processes such as sales and operations planning resulting in costly disruptions to a firm's supply chain.

Training: A new production line is launched with technically correct systems and equipment but quality control tests fail at a high rate because operational staff weren't trained properly.

Partners Risk: A bank launches a new stock trading service. Orders are executed but settlement fails due to integration issues with a partner. The partner lacks resolve to fix the issues on their side and is difficult to push.

Risk Assessment

The new technology assessment step helps determine if the submission involves new technology, new operating conditions, or both, and categorises the new technology for further evaluation. Here conditions mean existing and potential internal and external forces. Internal conditions include workforce capability, culture, and so on. The external conditions involve suppliers, demand nature, third party capabilities and government policies. The process failure risk should be assessed by this framework to identify risk areas. There are four categories to consider in the first part of the new technology assessment:

(a) Known Technology, Known Conditions
(b) Known Technology, Different or Unknown Conditions
(c) New Technology, Known Conditions
(d) New Technology, Different or Unknown Conditions

Category One involves known technology used in known conditions and requires no additional analysis. Categories Two and Three involve changes to either the area/conditions or the technology. Analysis of new technology in these two categories focusses on the changes in the technology or the condition. Category Four involves changes to both the area/conditions and the technology, therefore, more in-depth analysis is suggested.

Some of the risk assessment methods are given below:

Hazard Identification, Failure Modes and Effects Analysis (FMEA), Preliminary Risk Analysis (PrRA) • Hazard and Operability (HAZOP) Analysis • Change Analysis • Interface Analysis • Event Tree Analysis (ETA) • Trend Analysis • Management Oversight Risk Tree (MORT) • Fault Tree Analysis (FTA) • Pareto Analysis • Probabilistic Risk Assessment (PRA) • Layer of Protection Analysis (LOPA) • Relative Ranking/Risk Indexing • Safety and Risk Evaluation using Bayesian Nets (SERENE) • What-if Analysis • Pairwise Comparison • Integrated System Hazard Analysis

New Process Change on the Horizon-Industry 4.0

Industry 4.0 and the Industrial Internet of Things (IIOT) have become one of the most discussed business and technology concepts recently. McKinsey defines Industry 4.0 as digitisation of the manufacturing sector, with embedded sensors in virtually all product components and manufacturing equipment, ubiquitous cyber-physical systems, and analysis of all relevant data. (McKinsey Digital, 2015). Germany has launched Industrie 4.0 initiative in 2011 as a part of its high tech strategy. Since then, it has gained more attention and it became the main topic on the World Economic Forum 2016's agenda.

There are different names for Industry 4.0 like Smart manufacturing, Industrial Internet and Fourth Industrial Revolution, etc. Driven by the internet of everything, Industry 4.0 will release high potential impact on manufacturing with relatively low cost. All manufacturing and related industry units at one point of time will become digital companies, where machine will interact with machines, products and components interact with machines and robots and highly enabled digital human-machine interaction.

The following are driving forces which are mostly technical in nature for Industry .4.0:

Big data and analytics, autonomous robots, smart factory, simulation, cyber-physical system (CPS), the industrial internet of things, internet of services, cybersecurity, the cloud, additive manufacturing and augmented reality. Recently, the developments in analytics with machine learning, deep learning, and algorithms related to artificial intelligence combined with the growth of robotics, automated machines and handling systems created a new powerful manufacturing revolution.

CPS is a system that connects physical world with virtual world. It is an integration of computers and physical processes. It consists of two sub-systems, one is physical network of machines, components inbuilt with sensors, readers and other communication infrastructure and another is cyber network which can control the physical network.

Internet of Things: This concept is the initiator of Industry 4.0. This is a network of different devices like machines, equipment, products and other communication devices connected by seamless internet. This means that the devices can communicate with one another and can be coordinated with human interface devices. Products are becoming smarter and hence processes are also getting smarter.

Internet of Services: This is based on the idea that different services may be made available through web technologies which means companies can develop new kind of value added services. Information technology enabled services like business process outsourcing and software as a service (SaaS) are connected through internet of services.

Smart Factory: Products and services are connected through internet or through blockchain technology which enables automated and optimised production system resulting in smart factories. These kind of factories can be of de-centralised, type closer to market because of flexibility in terms of volume and variety is possible.

Process of Co-Production and Co-Creation in Service Context-Role of Technology

Customer involvement in any service process is always high and that makes the service unique. At the same time, customer involvement might become customer intervention and delay the service process resulting in poor service delivery. Many researchers have studied this phenomenon of customer intervention and suggested various solutions. These solutions range from complete accommodation of intervention to totally banning the customer intervention in service processes. But on the whole, organisations want to reduce the intervention. However, recent developments in customer expectations have changed this perspective. Customer expectations from a shopping experience, restaurant service, healthcare service and hospitality service or theme park rides are continuously changing and service organisations strive to anticipate such dynamic expectations and respond to these expectations. These can be done by involving customers more in service processes. There are two approaches currently adopted by organisations, co-production and co-creation.

Co-production: The customer is now becoming an integral part of many service processes. In some services, the physical presence of a customer is enough and the service provider performs all operations. But in many other services, the customers are required to involve and participate in service operation processes to complete the service delivery. The degree of customer participation varies but still customer inputs are obligatory in service processes. Self-service technologies motivate customers to get involved in co-production. Co-production by customers normally does not affect the sequence and tasks involved in service delivery process. They only participate in some of the sub-processes of service operations. For example, in a self-service retail store, a customer wants to buy some vegetables. He/she selects the particular vegetables, put them in a paper bag, he/she himself weighs it in the machine, and pastes the price sticker on it before he arrives at check-out counter. This is called co-production.

Co-creation: It is based on service dominant logic which means customers not only are involved in the process but also collaborate to modify and refine the process. The service provider learns from customer and is able to customise the service offer with the help of customers. The emphasis is on joint effort and collaboration in value creating activities. This also leads to creation of new service products and better revenue for the service provider.

In both co-production and co-creation, process technologies like self-service technology (SST), automation and other sophisticated technology are applied to improve service delivery process. Organisations should analyse the suitability of technology for each category of co-creation and co-production and accordingly adopt technologies.

One of the uniqueness of services marketing as distinct from product marketing is the key role that people play and the importance of the holistic experience when customers evaluate services. Yet SST replaces the customer–service employee experience with a customer–technology experience. People are replaced with machines and technologies. There is a danger that organisations might see SST as a cheap way of 'co-creating' value with customers when in fact what they are doing is simply shifting responsibility for service production to their customers, who are of course external to the organisation, which is difficult to control and monitor.

Such an arrangement sometimes is dangerous for organisations due to the following factors:

a. It turns customer into partial employee.
b. Not all customers are equally capable and adaptable to this situation.
c. While customers may be cheaper, they are also harder 'to train' and 'manage' than employees, and they can be influential to other customers.
d. Expertise of customer varies and hence quality also varies.

One side-effect of self-service technologies is that customers handle more of the simple issues themselves and pass on to customer service executives the tough ones. Today's executives at front line are struggling with these complex problems. Also companies focus on new self-service technologies neglecting the investment in frontline service talent. Self-service experience has improved dramatically in recent years, the live service interactions or moment of truths have drastically reduced the good experience for customers.

SUMMARY

Process technology is the technology used to produce products or provide services. These technologies include direct technologies used for converting some resources into products and services and also indirect technologies used for support processes. Process technologies are classified on the basis of nature of inputs as well as on the basis of continuity of process. Process technology strategy deals with a set of decisions that involves selection of appropriate technology to adopt the process, deployment of new process technology in the organisation, upgrading it and finally when and how to abandon existing technology and transit to new one. The process technology choice should consider volume and variety, degree of automation required, scalability issues and level of integration in the process. Product-process matrix helps in formulating strategies during scaling up as well as during the different critical stages of product life cycle. The important evaluation techniques to choose process technology are grouped under financial analysis, feasibility analysis, risk analysis and strategic competitive analysis. The new developments in the area of process technology are Industry 4.0, 3D Printing, Industry Internet of Things and Robotic automation.

Key Terms

1. **Process technology**: Process technology is the technology used to produce products or provide services. These technologies help in conversion of inputs like raw materials into some outputs of useful products.
2. **Material Process Technologies**: These are processes or methods used to convert some physical materials into some physical products.
3. **Information Processing Technologies**: These are technologies used to collect data and information from customers and other internal sources, process them and provide valuable information for decision making in general.
4. **Customer Processing Technologies**: These are processes used to provide services to customers. Customers are products and processed using technology.
5. **Job-shop production**: It is characterised by manufacturing one or few quantity of products designed and produced as per the specification of customers within prefixed time and cost.
6. **Batch Production**: It is a form of manufacturing in which the job passes through the functional departments in lots or batches and each lot may have a different routing.
7. **Mass production**: Manufacture of discrete parts or assemblies using a continuous process are called mass production.
8. **Continuous production**: Production facilities are arranged as per the sequence of production operations from the first operations to the finished product.
9. **Process technology strategy**: It involves a set of decisions that involves which technology to adopt for production of product/services (choice of technology), how to deploy the technology in the organisation, when and how to upgrade the technology, and finally when to abandon the existing one and move to the new one.
10. **Product-process matrix**: The product–process matrix is a framework that is used to demonstrate the combination of a product's (or product group's) volume and variety of characteristics, and the nature of the conversion processes that make it.
11. **Scalability**: Scalability is the intrinsic capacity of a system to handle market growth. For a system to be called scalable, growth should proceed unhindered, i.e. the size and volume of processing may expand without significantly affecting the cost of production.
12. **Postponement strategy**: Postponement strategy lies in organising the production and distribution of products in such a way that the customisation of these products is made as close to the point when the demand is known as possible.

CONCEPT REVIEW QUESTIONS

1. What is process technology? Explain its importance from strategic perspective.
2. Explain the types of process technologies based on inputs.
3. What are the types of production systems?
4. How to decide the level of automation in processes?
5. How process technology strategy and scalability are related?
6. How to decide the level of integration in process technology adoption?
7. How product-process matrix helps in process technology strategy and decision making?
8. Explain the methods of evaluation of process technologies.
9. Explain the latest trends in process technology?
10. What is postponement strategy? In what conditions is this a more suitable strategy?
11. Explain the role of technology in service processes.
12. Explain the role of technology in co-production and co-creation.

CRITICAL THINKING QUESTIONS

1. Think about automation in restaurant business. Critically examine how a restaurant goes about adopting a new process technology.
2. How do you balance technology and labour in the context of co-production and co-creation with respect to the following sectors:
   (a) Hospitality sector
   (b) Retail
   (c) Healthcare
3. Several industries—including those that produce furniture, houses, interior decorations, sailboats, and fashion clothing—have never progressed down the diagonal of the product-process matrix to become highly standardised and efficient. Why do you think this is so? Is this a serious problem?

PROJECT ASSIGNMENTS

1. Collect details about process technology initiatives of Indian railways. Prepare a report on how Indian railways will be able to improve its services in different fields with process technology strategy.
2. In electronics and semi-conductor manufacturing, technology changes very fast. Visit the websites of few technology companies and aggregate their strategies on process technology adoption.

REFERENCES

De Jong, Jeroen P. J., and Bruijn, Erik De., "Innovation lessons from 3-D printing", *MIT Sloan Management Review*, Winter 2013.

Hofmann, Erik and Rusch, Marco "Industry 4.0 and the current status as well as future prospects on logistics", 89 (2017) 23–34.

Frei, Frances X., "Breaking the trade-off between efficiency and service", *Harvard Business Review*, November 2006.

Industry 4.0, How to navigate digitization of the manufacturing sector, McKinsey Digital 2015, McKinsey & Company.

Reeves, Martin, Zeng, Ming and Venjara, Amin. "The self-tuning Enterprise", *Harvard Business Review* South Asia, June 2015.

Porter, Michael E. and Heppelmann, James E. "How smart, connected products are transforming companies", *Harvard Business Review*, October 2015.

Chathoth, Prakash, Altinay, Levent, Harrington, Robert James, Okumus, Fevzi, and Chan, Eric S. W. "Co-production versus co-creation: A process based continuum in the hotel service context", *International Journal of Hospitality management*, 32 (2013) 11-20.

D'aveni, Richard. "It's happening, and it will transform your operations and strategy", *Harvard Business Review* South Asia, May 2015.

Davenport, Thomas H. and Kirby, Julia. "Beyond Automation", *Harvard Business Review* South Asia, June 2015.

Singh, Shelley. "Manufacturing's third dimension", *The Economic Times*, 31 May 2016.

Dixon, Matthew, Ponomareff, Lara, Turner, Scott and DeLisi, Rich. "Kick-Ass customer service", *Harvard Business Review*, January-February 2017.

Product and Service Development and Innovation

CHAPTER

6

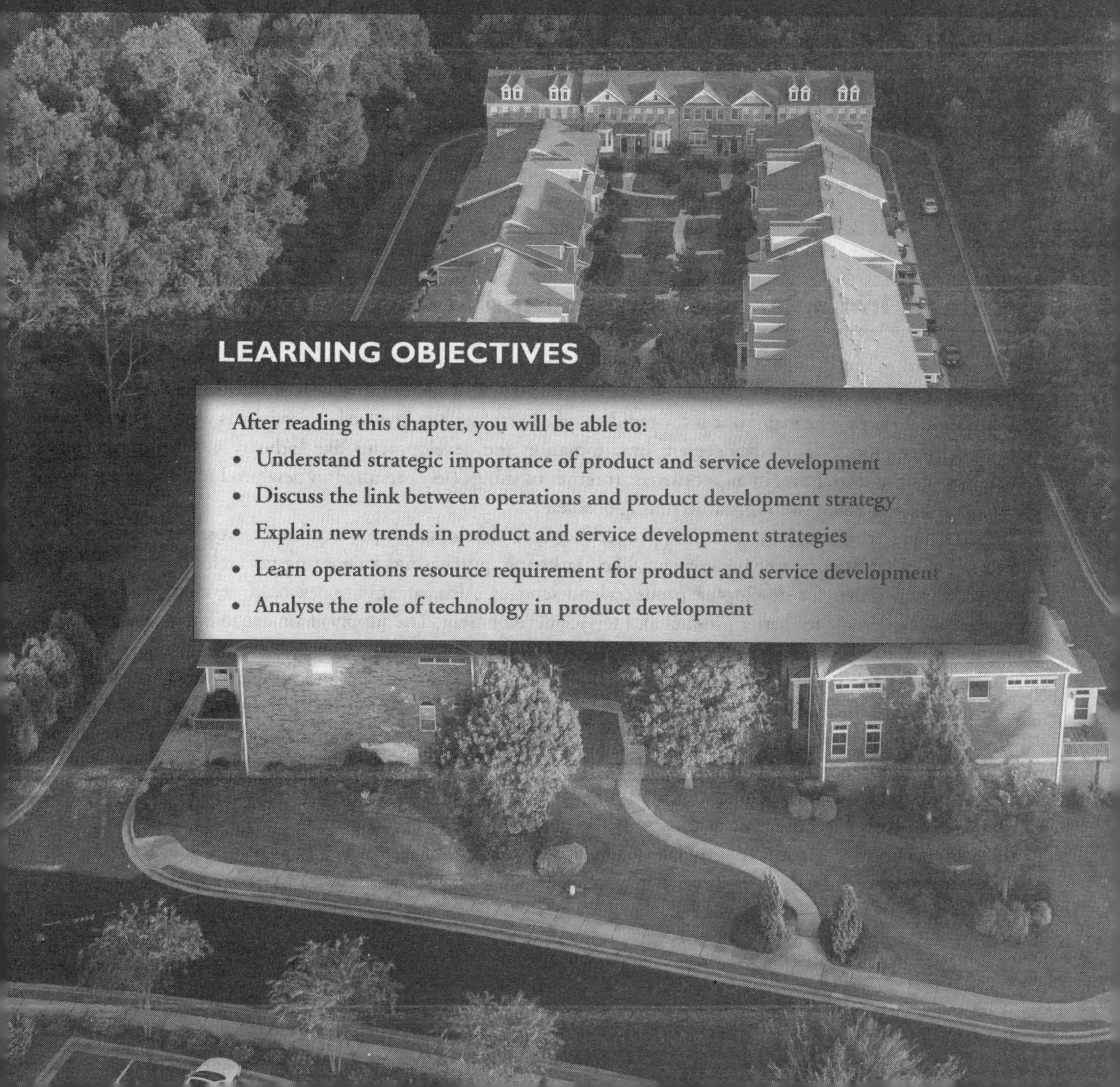

LEARNING OBJECTIVES

After reading this chapter, you will be able to:

- Understand strategic importance of product and service development
- Discuss the link between operations and product development strategy
- Explain new trends in product and service development strategies
- Learn operations resource requirement for product and service development
- Analyse the role of technology in product development

Introduction

Successful products and services determine the long-term success of the organisation. New products and services are important drivers of revenue for any organisation as old products and services may become obsolete with time. Whether it is a consumer product company or a services company, new product and service development process is important for the survival and growth of the company. However, this process is a complex one. While on one hand, it requires the organisation to focus on market in order to find and leverage business opportunities for their products and services, on the other hand, it also requires inward focus on its resources, talents and people skills so that the organisation can develop new services and products and commercialise the same.

Three important developments recently put a lot of pressure on product and service innovation. Time to market has reduced tremendously which means that new product development time should be compressed. Product life cycle is shrinking which means new innovative products should be introduced more frequently. Finally, product technology is continuously changing and hence, process also need to be changed. So, the link between the product and production process is becoming closely linked which means the process also has to be designed parallel with product. There is also another trend which is highly disturbing. The product life itself is shrinking and customers are no more interested in product repair and extending its life. This means more products will reach disposal point early, which means more environmental problems. Recycling of old products may be an option and it put extra pressure on design of products with more focus on design for recycling and remanufacturing.

Strategic Importance of Product and Service Development

The framework given in Figure 6.1 describes the importance of product and service development strategically for an organisation. A number of strategic factors influence the operation resources required to develop new products and services. The major one is the rapid change in technology involved in product as well as production/service delivery process. The advancement in automation and developments like Industry 4.0 introduced new possibilities and uncertainties in all industries. Internet of things (IoT) resulted in new products and networked services whose technology also is fast becoming obsolete.

The changes in technology put new product/services development process under cross-functional rapid process. The other functions of organisation like marketing, purchasing, accounting research and development need to work together for developing products and services. Also, organisation should develop competencies internally and externaly for better product and service development. The supply chain capability is also used as a competing tool for this purpose.

From market perspective, competition is intense from both international and local players. Customers are empowered with information and their preferences are specific. More customised offerings are expected in the market. Also, markets are now micro-segmented due to customised needs and wants. Organisations need to adopt their products to the needs of different markets. Another challenge is shrinking product life cycles resulting in frequent product launches. Competition also follows this and launches alternative products and services. The pressure is also very high in terms of time to market. Organisations need to shrink the period from concept to launch by innovative, networked and rapid development of products. Many organisations adopt concurrent engineering practices to reduce the time to market.

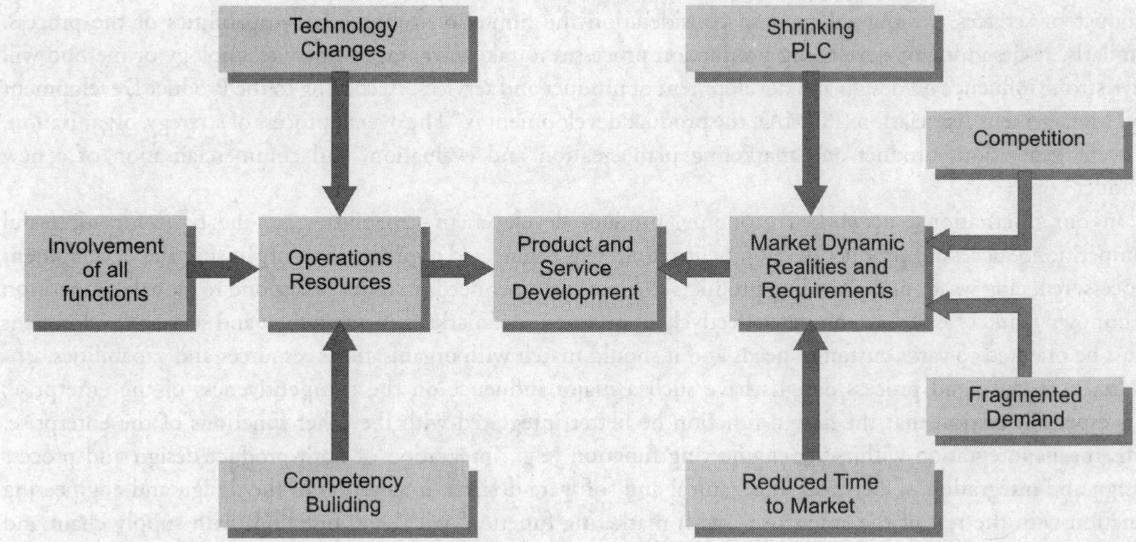

FIGURE 6.1 Strategic importance of product and service development

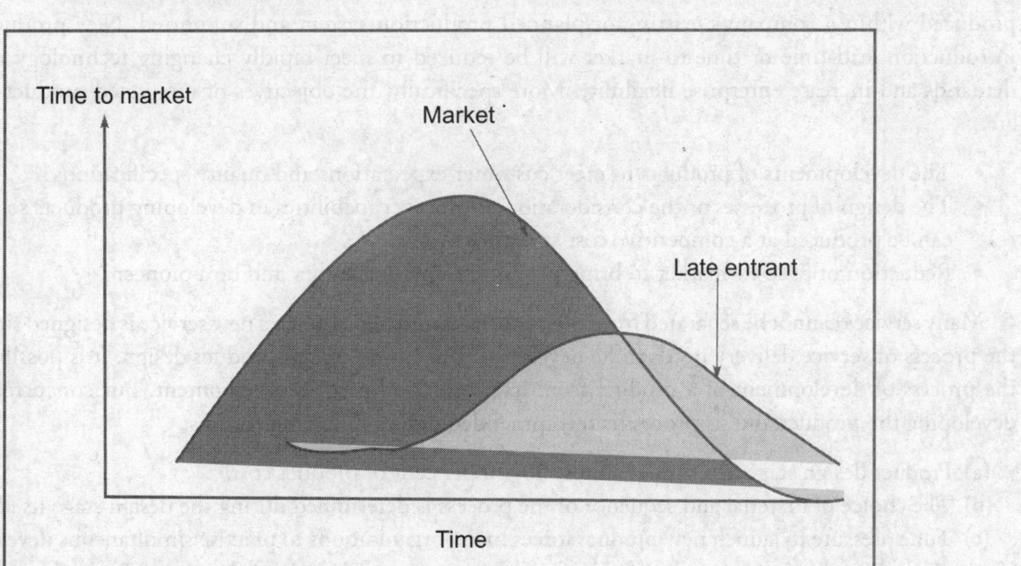

FIGURE 6.2 Time to market

Integrated Product/Services Design and Production Process

The production or service delivery process is highly related to product and services design. In many organisations, product design and process are organised separately which is incorrect. It would be impossible to develop new product or services without taking into consideration the limitations, merits and capabilities of the process. Similarly, re-designing or developing production processes to take advantage of new technology or method will have strong influence on design and development of product and services. According to the Product Development and Management Association (PDMA), the product development is "The overall process of strategy, organisation, concept generation, product and marketing plan creation and evaluation, and commercialisation of a new product".

In our international networked economy, product development capabilities are the basis for successful competition. Successful product development requires re-engineered approaches to organising the development process, reducing waste, and providing products to meet customer needs in order to respond to global competition in our own markets as well as compete effectively in international markets. New product and service development must be oriented towards customer needs and it should match with organisation's resources and capabilities.

Since product and process designs have such a major influence on the competitiveness of the enterprise, it is especially critical that the design function be better integrated with the other functions of the enterprise. This means integration within the engineering function (e.g., integration of both product design and process design and integration of electrical, mechanical and software design), integration of the design and engineering function with the rest of the enterprise—with marketing function, with sales function, with supply chain and finance function and integration of the engineering function with external organisations (distribution network and suppliers network).

This integration will result in the release of more mature product designs which can be more effectively produced within a company's existing or planned production system and supported. New product design and introduction lead-time or time-to-market will be reduced to meet rapidly changing technology and customer demands and increase enterprise flexibility. More specifically, the objectives of integrated product development are:

- The developments of products to meet customer expectations and quality specifications
- The design of processes or the consideration of process capabilities in developing products so that products can be produced at a competitive cost structure
- Reduction of time-to-market to bring products to market earlier and be a pioneer

Many services cannot be separated from their processes and hence when a new service is designed simultaneously, the process of service delivery needs to be developed. But in the case of product design, it is possible to separate the process of development of a product from its production process development. But concurrent method of developing the product and its process is recommended due to following reasons:

(a) Product design stage determines almost 50–60 per cent of product cost.
(b) The choice of material and sequence of the process is determined during the design stage itself.
(c) Time pressure to launch new product forces many organisations to practise simultaneous development. This will reduce the time to market and hence improve competitiveness of their products in the market.

Operations and Supply Chain Perspectives on Product Design

The consumer perspectives on product design may consist of factors like easy to handle, features, cost, and cosmetic look of the product and so on. Operations and supply chain managers also have role to play and show interest in product design because subsequently these managers will be responsible for making products available in the market. Research and development department normally works on new products and design products. If the same product is commercially successful, millions of these products need to be produced in a geographically distributed factories, using skilled and semiskilled labour, procure and coordinate the flow of parts coming from all over the world, and ship the products so that they arrive on time, undamaged, and at the lowest possible cost to the market.

The interest of operations and supply chain management in service design is even greater.

This is because the service design is often the operations process itself. To take an example from warehousing services, when a warehousing firm agrees to provide storage and distribution services to a large customer, it has to make decisions regarding the number of aisles needed, location of warehouses, buy or lease space required and so on. Today, logistics services are bought as a package and hence the role of logistics manager gains more importance in logistics service design.

With this in mind, the operations and supply chain perspective on product design concentrates on seven important dimensions.

(a) Repeatability
(b) Testability
(c) Serviceability
(d) Traceability
(e) Product volumes
(f) Logistics cost
(g) Match between the design and existing capabilities

Repeatability, Testability, and Serviceability

Repeatability, testability, and serviceability are dimensions of product design that affect the capacity and capability of operations to produce the product in large scale in the first place and to provide ongoing support afterward. Repeatability deals with the issue of repetitive production and volume requirement. This issue is addressed using robust design where product can withstand extreme conditions and variations and perform as per specifications during manufacturing process as well as during use. Product designs that are robust are better able to meet tolerance limits making it easier for the operations and supply chain functions to provide good products on an ongoing basis.

Testability refers to the ease with which critical parts and assemblies or functions can be tested during production. When product moves from one stage of process to another, the suitability for further processing must be enabled and product design should support this.

Serviceability is similar to testability. In this case, serviceability refers to the level of ease with which parts can be replaced, serviced, or evaluated. Many modern computers and electronic products are now built on modular design and to repair a product, the modules need to be replaced with new one. Today cars are coming with a computer and hence a car mechanic can troubleshoot the car with the help of computer monitoring system.

Serviceability is of particular interest to organisations that are responsible for supporting products in the field. When products are easy to service, costs can be under control, and service times become more predictable, easy to schedule service calls resulting in higher productivity and greater customer satisfaction.

Traceability

It refers to tracing the origin of components and parts when products fail in factory or in field. This helps in improving the product design and its reliability over a period of time. Today, especially in automobile industry, each component is pasted with bar code or RFID tags and sometimes sensors so that field service people can trace the source of failed components and parts. This helps in training of suppliers in rectifying problems and avoiding future mistakes. This will help in improving overall service and product quality.

Product Volumes

Once a company decides to go forward with a new product or service, it becomes the duty of operations and supply chain managers to make sure that the company can produce the required volumes. This will result in

(a) Expanding the firm's own operations by building new facilities.
(b) Hiring and training of additional workers, and buying new equipment.
(c) Requiring collaborative planning with key suppliers.

Depending on the market demand, the type of production system to be adopted will be determined. Process technology also has influence on product design and both should match.

Logistics Costs

Products can also be designed to minimise material handling, transportation and warehousing costs. Oddly shaped or fragile products can quickly drive up transportation costs. In contrast, products that can be shipped in standardised containers to take advantage of lower transportation rates can hold down the costs of distribution. The nature of products in terms of its weight per unit, value per unit, density of the unit, state of product (liquid, semi-solid, gas) and shape of the product all influence the logistics cost. Products like tyres come in different sizes and their transportation is always uneconomical as tyres are round in shape resulting in large space in the truck being unutilised. Value to volume ratio is also important in logistics. If it is high, the logistics cost is economical.

Product packaging is also related to logistics cost. Packaging must be in synchronisation with product design and it should consider logistics constraints. Packaging must serve multiple purposes. It should help marketing and sales in terms attractiveness and easy to handle. It must serve ease of transportation and storage without any damages and leakages. Ikea designed furniture in modular method and various models of finished products can be assembled using common parts of the furniture. This approach has provided Ikea, a huge competitive advantage in terms of logistics cost. Ikea can keep stock in terms of components which reduces inventory costs. It can transport these components more economically to the market than finished products which are in odd shape. It has improved availability of its products at retail dramatically due to this design and hence resulted profitability.

Match with Existing Capabilities

Finally, operations and supply chain managers are always looking for avenues in terms of how well new products or services can fit with existing products or capabilities. A new product or service that allows a producer to use existing materials and production facilities is usually easier to support than one that requires new ones. This will also reduce cost. Similarly, services that can use existing capacities and capabilities are especially cost efficient. It is obvious that companies should consider such factors as production volumes and existing capabilities when designing new products or services.

Level of Product/Service Change and Its Importance

The outcome of new product development process need not be a complex new product but rather some modifications to existing products or upgradation in terms of features. Similarly, for services also, it need not be a new major innovative service but modifications to existing service system. The market for mobiles is an example for different levels of product development in the last 10 years. Any product launched in the market, needed a frequent upgradation for survival. Similarly, in the food delivery online business, the service package is continuously upgraded to provide better options for customers.

Many organisations have standard operating procedures like 'engineering change order' to modify existing products as per requirements of the market. But these changes should be communicated to all functional areas. Because any change in existing product or development of new product will affect all parts of the organisation in some ways. For example, a change in design of a product might require a different material which may not be available currently and hence will delay its launch.

TABLE 6.1 Level of product/service change-implications

	Level of product/service change			
	Cosmetic change	Product extension	Major change	New category
External perspective	Package, logo, color changes	More varieties, functionality, features	Significant changes, next generation type	New product, pioneer product, market expectation
Internal action	Little changes w.r.t. last stage of production	Some design changes, additional materials	Addition of a component	NPD Process and new product
Example(Product)	Package change in a FMCG product	Adding a sound feature in a phone	Change in software	i-PAD and i-phone
Example(Service)	Renovation in terms of lighting in a restaurant	Offering drive in service	Food delivery service	Taxi aggregation

Product and Service Development as a Process

The new product development process, or NPD for short, consists of every activity associated with developing an idea, developing a product/service based on that idea, and creating a marketable product/service that generates revenue and profit. Many think that NPD is solely the responsibility of R&D. While R&D certainly has the biggest and most visible role, management must realise that NPD is a key business process, not just an R&D function. Today, product development is a function of all functional areas of the organisation.

Concept of the Development

The NPD development process is commonly represented by a funnel. Initially, all ideas generated by different functional areas are processed at the opening of the funnel and filtered. The ideas have to be screened and prioritised as every organisation has limited resources and cannot possibly, or should, develop every idea into a product.

The real world of product development tends to be much more chaotic and the process is better visualised as we see in road traffic. As development proceeds in most companies, problems pop-up to surface with projects. There are design loopbacks, forcing the project team to retreat to the previous phase. Project teams face uncertainty due to problems with existing projects and result in delayed start of a new project. In the early phases, a project may get ejected from the process and be put on hold, and some other projects may be inserted.

Idea generation

The first step is basically involved with the systematic exploration for new product ideas. A company has to generate many ideas in order to find one that is worth pursuing. The major sources of new product/service ideas include internal sources, employees, customers, competitors, distributors and suppliers.

Almost 60 per cent of all new product ideas come from internal sources, according to one study. Companies like 3M and Toyota have put in special incentive programmes or their employees to come up with workable ideas.

Almost 28 per cent of new product ideas come from watching and listening to customers. Customers even create new products on their own, and companies can benefit by finding these products and putting them on the market. New ideas or improvement ideas can be generated by systematically studying customers regarding how they buy, where they buy, how they store the product, how they use the product and how they dispose the product.

Idea Screening

The second step in new product development is idea screening. The purpose of idea generation is to create a large pool of ideas. The purpose of this stage is to filter and reduce these down to just those ideas that are genuinely worth trying. Companies have different approaches for doing this from product review committees to formal market research. It is better to have a checklist and evaluate each idea on these checklist parameters and try to converge on few workable ideas. Companies should assess the marketing potential as well as resource capabilities before accepting an idea.

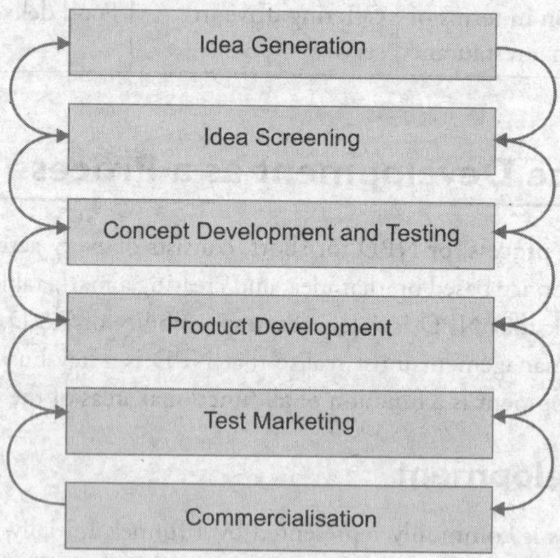

FIGURE 6.3 New product development process

Concept Development and Testing

The third step in new product development is concept development and testing. An attractive idea has to be developed into a product concept. A product concept can be developed in the form of following:

(a) Drawing of the proposed product
(b) Working prototype using other parts
(c) A modified old material form

These concepts are tested with a sample of customers and feedback is collected to improve the concept. Testing helps in correction in terms of our idea, solution combination and material combination.

Product Development

Here, R&D or engineering develops the product concept into a physical product. This step calls for some investments. The 3D printing helps in quick development of product and it can be modified easily when required. It will show whether the product idea can be developed into a full-fledged workable product with available resources and materials. The prototypes are tested for their functionality, robustness and comfort level in handling. They are also tested for safety, reliability and performance.

Test Marketing

If the product passes the functional tests, the next step is test marketing the product in the field settings. The product is launched in a limited market area and promotion and distribution is restricted to that area only. The product performance in terms of sales, repeated sales, variants requirement, feedback from customers, traders and other channel partners is collected and analysed. This activity provides lot of inputs for the organisation in terms of channels required for marketing and distribution, promotion mix required and the overall marketing strategy. The test marketing mostly preferred for relatively significant new categories. Sometimes, market research companies assist organisations to do simulated test marketing in an artificial environment.

Commercialisation

The final step in new product development is commercialisation. Introducing the product to the market—the organisation needs to prepare budget, marketing and distribution plan, and pricing strategy and promotion strategy. The company will have to decide on the timing of the launch (seasonality) and the location (whether regional, national or international). The launch decision depends on many factors like market conditions, peak season times like festival periods, reach of media and so on.

Today, in order to increase speed to market, many companies are dropping this sequential approach to development and are adopting the faster, more flexible, and simultaneous development approach. Under this approach, many departments of the company work closely together, overlapping the steps in the product development process to save time and increase effectiveness. Concurrent engineering is one approach which reduces time to market.

How Do We Measure NPD Success?

NPD success is often measured by whether the new product meets:

1. Performance, product cost, and product quality objectives
2. Project cost objectives
3. Schedule targets

While these are obviously important, it misses the point of why new products are developed in the first place—to satisfy customer needs better than competitive products and generate enough revenue and gain in market share. Market success is the ultimate performance measure of new product development. Even with many product launches fail, one success will compensate these loss and hence return on investment.

Concurrent Engineering

Concurrent engineering, also called simultaneous engineering, is a process for designing and developing products in which different phases of new product development overlap with each other rather than a sequential process. For instance, the design team for a new mobile phone can work on the exterior of the phone while technicians test its features in an electronics laboratory. Although the initial implementation at concurrent engineering can be challenging, the practices result in several competitive advantages.

Concurrent engineering relies on team building and problem solving approach using certain specific techniques. Any new project on product development should be handled by a multi-disciplinary task force and the task force normally consists of

a. Product design engineers
b. Manufacturing engineers
c. Marketing personnel
d. Purchasing
e. Finance
f. Principal vendors

This cross-functional team is permanent throughout the project. There are many advantages because of concurrent engineering:

Faster Time to Market

A major advantage that concurrent engineering offers is that it allows companies to compress the time gap between new product conceptualisation and launch of the product. Being pioneer to launch a product is huge advantage for the company. When product development stages run consecutively, the time taken is larger and feedback also happens sequentially. Due to this system, cross-functional team works on the process and is able to communicate clearly with faster rate. Concurrent engineering allows workers on several stages to work simultaneously, compressing the time to market.

Enhanced Quality

Since cross-functional team is working in concurrent engineering, it is easy for the team to sort out their differences and enable workers and managers to discover any production issues earlier in the process. This leads to a higher-quality product and better production process. These practices also reduce design revisions, unworkable prototypes and excessive testing to arrive at the highest-quality product in the shortest time. In the auto manufacturer example, any issues involving the aerodynamics of the car are uncovered earlier in the process by the testing team, which allows the design and prototyping teams to work towards solving the problem.

Lower Development Costs

The bulk of a company's costs associated with creating a new product involve the design and development processes. Managers can use concurrent engineering as a powerful tool for reducing those early development costs. Since concurrent engineering practices decrease the time spent in the design and development phases, companies can deliver a product faster, better and cheaper than their competitors. In the auto manufacturer example, concurrent engineering practices allow the design, prototyping and testing teams to produce a factory-ready car design in much less time and at a lower cost to the company.

Increased Productivity

While consecutive engineering requires that workers on a later stage wait for those in earlier stages, concurrent engineering allows workers the opportunity to be productive immediately and throughout the process. This process allows workers to focus on the project as a whole, rather than focus solely on their area of specialty. In the auto manufacturer example, the design, prototyping and testing teams all work together on the same problem at the same time to find the best solution.

Market Dynamics and Requirements on Product and Service Developments

Organisations face hard competition in international and domestic markets. They must be able, cost-efficiently, to serve customers better and respond quickly to changing market situations. This competitiveness is closely related to product development process and it should be possible to change the product's design or development processes quickly even at short notice. Competitive priorities in operations consists of quality, cost, flexibility, responsiveness and time and these priorities become core strengths for the organisation to face the market challenges. These same competitive priorities can be applied to new product/service development process as well.

Quality and New Product Development Process

New product quality definitely has a major influence on the market success and revenue potential of a new product. The quality of the product is influenced by quality of resources used for development process. Major resource is the manpower and other supporting technology. Many firms currently use cross-functional team for new product development. Research study reveals that quality is positively related to information integration in the team, customers' influence on the product development process, and quality orientation in the firm. (Sethi, 2000). This means quality of research and development teams, design engineers, and marketing people should be improved to improve the overall quality of the process. The concepts of total quality management (TQM) should be applied both at the level of the whole company and at the level of the R&D and product development team. Total quality describes the culture, attitude and strategy of the organisation that aims to provide and continues to provide, its customers with products and services that satisfy their needs. The quality culture should be built in the organisation as well as in the team. In the case of networked product development, the product lifecycle management (PLM) processes should be in place and monitor the quality of processes.

Speed of Product and Service Development

Long product development cycle times for products are a thing of the past. Organisations are forced to reduce the development cycle time by competition and customers. From durable to fashion categories, the development cycle or time to market continue to decrease due to market expectations. Still reducing time to market for new products is a complex task. The NPD process was handled not in an effective way in the past. The process might have been handled inappropriately leading to delays, ineffective work methods, and repeated manual creation. Decreasing time to market means elimination of slack that existed in co-ordination between different functional areas, improvement in information synchronisation and substantial increase in information processing from different sources.

Benefits of reducing time to market:

Early bird advantage:
New product can be launched in the market well ahead of the competitor and hence organisation can sustain good revenue for a longer period. If the product is the first of its type in the market, the market share will also be more due to pioneer advantage. Early launch also attracts premium pricing compared to competitors. Apple Inc., enjoyed this advantage for a longer duration when they launched iPhones and i-Pads.

Supports frequent product launches:

Due to shortened time to market, organisations can launch many products in short notice and keep the company in touch with market always. Due to the advantage of shortened development time, it is possible to observe the performance of competitor's products in the uncertain market and launch our products strategically to increase our success rate.

Advantage in Technology dependent market:

If the underlying technology is changing rapidly in a market, it will help organisation to increase revenue. The frequent launches of new products combined with frequent update of technology will open up new opportunities for the company.

Flexibility in Product/Service Development

Flexibility in product/service development process is the ability to adapt to external and internal changes normalised by the cost of adaptation. The common list of external changes are

- Competition changes
- Customer preference changes
- Self-service technology changes

Internal changes could include:

- Emergence of superior materials
- Technology changes
- People competency changes

Flexibility is core success formula in high-tech markets, where the ability to accurately forecast future situations is very limited. If the rate of change of technology is high, the customer preference also shift rapidly and it is very difficult to predict competitor's action. Process flexibility is essential to adjusting course in mid-stream when change arrives. Flexibility can be built into several areas in the process environment like

- Product design architecture
- Choice of technology
- Business process and structure of organisation
- Product development process

Importance of flexibility:

Importance of flexibility in development process can be explained with the following examples. Some changes in the market make current development of products/services irrelevant. For example, when Nokia was developing new smartphones, Apple and Samsung had already launched their smartphones and pre-empted the competition. Similarly, due to inter-connectedness of product and services in terms of technology, some new services become extinct very quickly. For example, in 1995-96, India saw the introduction of paging service in major cities and towns. Many organisations entered into this market, invested in building networks and towers and started to provide services of paging. But mobile service, a highly related service to paging, was introduced in India during 1996-97. This led to immediate decline of demand for paging services and by 1998, use of paging and pagers had completely stopped in India.

The above examples provide lessons for product development process refinement and how it must build flexibility in the process so that quick and responsive modifications can be made in product/services.

Benefits of flexibility in process:

- o It reduces product development risks
- o It reduces cost of major modifications in product designs
- o It avoids major market and internal failures

Flexibility in process is not required in all elements of NPD process. Product design and development process should use postponement strategy for building flexibility as well as efficiency in the process.

Cost of Product and Services Development

In new product development projects, there are two category costs that a manager should worry about. One is product cost and other is development process cost. Product cost includes materials, manufacturing, delivery, installation and warranty. Normally, a target product cost is fixed and product development process should stay in line with the target cost of the product. Target product cost is based on estimate of revenue, profitability and life of the product. Another important version of the cost is estimated product cost. This is based on engineering estimates, process design, quotations from suppliers, and so on. Uncertainty in product cost estimate is a function of degree of completion of the design and process and the fraction of new versus existing components in the design.

The development team should also make a 'should cost' estimate of the product. This cost estimation is based on world class manufacturing practices and benchmarking from other industry. The gap between the 'should cost' and 'estimated cost' will give hints about shortcomings in manufacturability and efficiency of the process planned.

Many organisations ignore tracking of product development cost because successful products bring them excellent ROI. So, compressing time to market at the expense of extra cost is justified. However, this practice is dangerous when company grows and many new product development projects are simultaneously executed by the organisation. The cost complexity increases and it is difficult to control the cost. The product development process cost includes the following:

- Cross-functional team labour, overhead, fringe benefits
- Consultants and subcontractors cost
- Prototype and testing material
- Tools for testing
- Depreciation of capital equipment
- Infrastructure cost
- Cost of inputs for product development

It is important to note that cost of development process in inversely proportional to time to market, flexibility in the process, and quality of the outcome and process.

Operations Resources Requirements for Product and Service Development

In product development, seldom does an organisation have all of the required resources to develop and commercialise new products. It is common now that one can outsource some designs to external special professional designers. Similarly, many resources are available within the organisation and some are available outside the organisation. Organisation has to strategically decide about how much internal resources should be used and how much should be outsourced and finally how much and what areas are to be on partnership or collaboration arrangement. Suppliers, customers, alliance partners and other partners in the supply chain together with the organisation's internal resources form a virtual cross-functional team for product development process.

An organisation must determine what capabilities are required for the project and where the resources should come from. The decision about in-sourcing capabilities or acquiring them outside depends on the organisation's business, technology, market and their strategies. Core competencies and core activities must be in-sourced and non-core activities can be outsourced. Sometimes a software might be required for support and this can be outsourced.

New Product Development Capacity

Development process is a service process organised as a project. A team is formed for a specific project and it works on the project and delivers a new product. Capacity is determined by the talent of people, knowledge base, earlier patents and new patents, strength of R&D along with supplier capability, partner's capability, and also effective communication between different elements. It is possible to maintain an inventory of concepts, databases, ideas, and knowledge for a new product design. This will help in some form for new product development and sometimes reduce time to market.

Capacity leading strategy should be used in product development and one cannot wait for the market changes and initiate capacity building for new product development. Capacity building is an ongoing process for organisations where product life cycle is short. They need to build cross-functional teams for many new product projects and hence their manpower planning is also fine-tuned to this process.

Unstable Demand for Development

The demand for new product development or services is not always constant so that the capacity can be utilised fully. Organisations who deal with FMCG products need not have a high level product development process. This industry requires some cosmetic changes in its products and their packaging and invests more on brand building. Industries who are in high technology markets, spend lot of resources on new product developments and subsequent launches. Even in some large organisations, the rate of introduction of new products is not constant. This results in launching of new products as a bunch at some point of time and no launches in other times. This poses a problem in terms of planning and organising of resources. The capacity of development is not like a water tap, where depending on requirement you get the output. Some flexibility is possible by outsourcing some expertise or hire some talents. But to bring stability, we need a team with stable capacity.

Role of Supply Partners in Product Development

Capacity of development process can also be built within the company's supply chain and helps in compression of development time. Supply chain collaboration with suppliers can be extended to product design functions, especially if the product is complex. Many major automobile companies collaborate with suppliers and suppliers work with lot of independency and bring out new ideas in improving existing products and also bring out new product ideas. Suppliers as partners can offer critical technology, know-how, production capacity, new ideas, access to markets, and some special expertise.

In Japan, traditionally, many production networks are operated by major automobile majors like Toyota, Nissan, Honda and electronic manufacturers like Tokyo Electric company, Toshiba, Panasonic. These networks are called production keiretsu. Japanese companies have long practised keiretsu, the linking of companies into industrial groups. A financial keiretsu links companies together with cross-holding of shares, sales and purchases within the group, and consultation. A production keiretsu is a web of interlocking relationships between a big manufacturer (Toyota) and its suppliers. Beneath Toyota, Toshiba, Sumitomo Chemical, Mitsui Bussan, there are hundreds and thousands of smaller firms. These invisible companies are suppliers and assemblers who put together products for a single end-product manufacturer. The parent company can leverage its Keirutsu and a large part of design work can be farmed out, freeing up staff at the parent company for other projects. Quality and efficiency of production can be assured because of the long-term relationships.

Development chain: The collection of activities and processes are associated with the introduction of a new product. It includes decisions about product architecture, make or buy decisions, selection of suppliers, early supplier involvement, and strategic partnership.

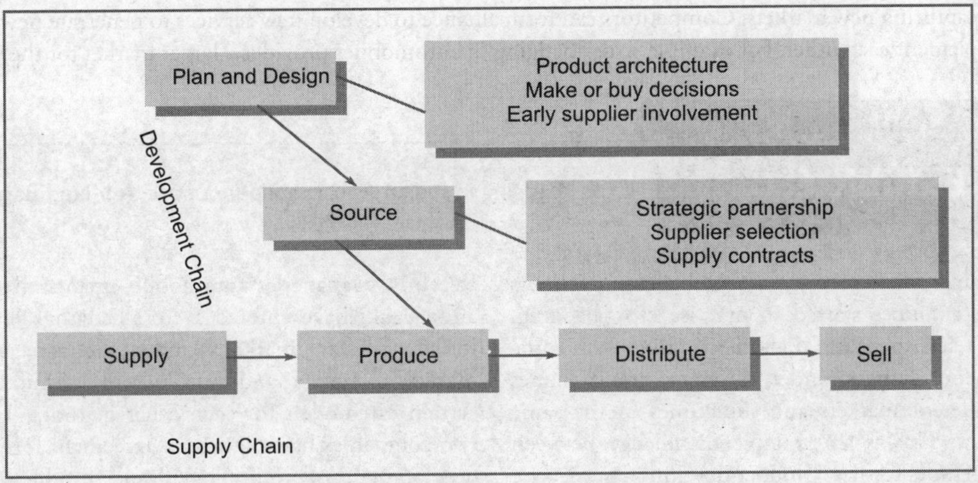

FIGURE 6.4 Development chain and supply chain in development process

Strategic Alliance with Other Partners for Development Capacity

In a market where changes are slow and long-term, investing in talents and building in-house capability for product development is recommended. It is a form of vertical integration for development process in strategic management terms. For example, GM India Science Lab is created in Bangalore as global research and development centre which supports new product design for GM. But in a dynamic market, risk in investing its own capabilities is high and hence, it is recommended to have strategic alliance with external partners for development. Several criteria can be used to select right time for alliances:

- The market is risky
- Powerful competition
- Organisation do not have technology
- Development time is predicted to be long and uncertain

Strategic alliance can be formed with design studios, professional designers, key customers, industry peers, and sometimes with competitors. Alliance with key customers provides an opportunity for the organisation to expand its market after its successful product launch. Deep understanding of customer requirements and strong commitment from development team can be expected if a customer also collaborates in design team. For example, while designing many medical diagnostic equipment, partnership with health centres and hospitals is critical. Similarly, in software services, a strong collaboration is required with customer to provide customised software for him. Sometimes an organisation may collaborate with customer to develop products and jointly market them in other local and international markets. Customers might also be interested in partnering with small firm or a start-up organisation to create competition for their larger and powerful suppliers which increases the negotiation power for the customer.

Peers that complement an organisation's capabilities in product content, assembly, service support, and system integrator are important for commercial success of the product. The alliance with these organisations could provide critical customer access, access to capacity and access to expertise which are non-core. Organisation must choose partners carefully to ensure a shared vision, strategy compatibility and win-win results. Complimentary capabilities of partners will drive alliances.

Partnership with competitors can also result in win-win situation in terms of developing variants of products and also capturing new markets. Competitors can form alliance to develop new services to penetrate new markets and complement each other. For example, cross-badging in automobiles provides a larger market for the partners.

Exhibit 6.1 Cross-badging in Indian Automobile Industry: A Mixed Bag

To reduce the time to market, global manufacturers of automobiles started to practise cross-badging. This refers to selling the same product with some cosmetic changes under different brand names in different markets and sometimes in the same market. This is an example of alliance between competitors for new product development.

In India, rather than working out as a win-win proposition, cross-badging is resulting in cannibalisation, with one brand eating into the share of the other. Renault and Nissan, which have a global alliance, share compact cars Micra and Pulse, respectively; it's the same car with the same specifications, features, dimensions and petrol and diesel engines but with different outlook. But unfortunately instead of a pick-up in sales, the badge-sharing automakers have witnessed cannibalisation to the tune of 30–40 per cent that year.

Recently, Japanese automobile giants Toyota and Suzuki have entered a cross-badging alliance for the Indian market. Under the agreement, by 2019, Toyota and Suzuki will manufacture certain car models for each other in India. These two companies have signed an agreement for joint development of technologies and products. As a part of the agreement, Suzuki will supply the Brezza and Baleno models to Toyota and in return Suzuki will get the Corolla model.

Under cross-badging, these cars will be converted mutually with change in interiors and exteriors and will be marketed under the name of the company selling them, i.e. say Suzuki Baleno with changes and a new name, selling under a Toyota badge. This cross-badging will help Suzuki to experiment in mid-size sedan and Toyota will benefit with entering small car segment market. Will it succeed?

Collaboration with Customer for Development

It is well-known that in software services and related IT services, early involvement of customers is essential for developing customised software services. The customer here is another typical organisation, who wants to improve their internal processes and automate them. The contract with IT service provider provides scope for collaboration. Similarly, logistics services are designed after deep understanding of customer requirements. For example, TVS Logistics Services, a third party logistics service company in India, provides a comprehensive in-bound logistics support for Ford India plant at Chennai. As Ford follows vendor managed inventory system and just-in-time inbound delivery of supplies, a strong co-ordination is essential. So, the logistics service provider initially involves the client in designing the service process and also sets the metrics of performance. These examples shows that in many service designs, the customer is an automatic alliance partner. So the entire life of the product should be observed in terms of its relationship with customers. These inputs along with tolls like quality functional deployment (QFD) will help development teams to bring out new products successfully.

In the case of product development, customer inputs and feedback form major contributions of customers. The various forms of inputs that can be used for product development are:

(a) The new emerging needs and wants of customers
(b) Where and how do customers buy the products? (in terms of SKUs, retail outlet or online buying)
(c) How do customers store the product? (difficulty in storing, space constraints)
(d) How do customers use the product? (right usage or wrong usage or used for different applications which are not intended)
(e) How do customers dispose the product?

Exhibit 6.2 Threadless Fashions

Some firms have begun to involve customers into the product development process, for example, by soliciting new product concepts from them and pursuing the most popular of those ideas. Threadless, a young Chicago-based fashion company was started in 2000 by designers Jake Nickell and Jacob DeHart. It focusses on hot fashion items, T-shirts with colorful graphics. This type of product is typically either runaway success or miserable failures. Despite such challenges, none of Threadless' hundreds of products have ever flopped.

What's the reason behind this success? Interestingly, Threadless has no hi-tech market research or forecasting system and the company does not adopt a complex, flexible manufacturing system. Rather, it relies on a community of customers, users including hobbyists as well as professional graphic designers, who submit, inspect and approve all designs. This means Threadless can leverage a pool of talent which is external and ideas that are much larger than the company could possibly afford if it relied instead on an internal process. Moreover, the company will manufacture only those designs that have gained the necessary number of preorders from interested customers, thereby ensuring each product's success.

Each week on the Threadless' website, customers can evaluate between 400 and 600 new design submissions on a scale from zero to five. On an average, each design is rated by 1,500 people. On the website itself, customers can express their desire to purchase a submission. Threadless uses that information to determine which products should be developed and manufactured. It currently produces between four and six new designs each week, and the creators of those submissions receive a $1,000 reward each. Also, the name of each winner is printed on the label of his or her particular t-shirt. At last count, more than 400 designs have been chosen for manufacturing from among more than 35,000 submissions, and the Threadless community was thriving with more than 120,000 people signed up to submit, evaluate and purchase new designs.

(Adopted from 'Susumu Ogawa and Frank T. Piller, Reducing the Risks of New Product Development, *MIT Sloan Management Review*, Winter 2006.)

Product and Service Development Technology

Many different and emerging technologies are used as a part of product development process today. The knowledge of product technology and service technology is important for development of products but technology in process has undergone a lot of changes. Many of us who know about manufacturing systems definitely know about the software, Computer Aided Design (CAD). A powerful CAD system helps in designing products ranging from small motor to large aircraft. Similarly, simulation software is also used in product design as well as service design. It provides a lot of insights into product design and helps in visualising how the product will perform in real life. The simulation helps in the following ways:

1. It helps in designing a complex service system containing some waiting lines and inter-connected service sub-systems. (For examples, hospitals, airport, theme park and so on)
2. It also helps in studying product/services robustness and resiliency with what-if analysis and scenario development.
3. It also helps in prediction of failures of products.
4. It also helps in developing a service system virtually with many replications so that one can study its performance to enable improvement in service systems.

Apart from CAD and simulation, a lot of knowledge management software tools are available to support information management in product development. Product lifecycle management (PLM) is a famous supporting tool for new product development and it assists in coordinating new product development across a network of design partners including suppliers.

Product Lifecycle Management

The product lifecycle management is increasingly gaining importance, especially for organisations in manufacturing, technology, telecom and other related industries. It was formerly known as product data management (PDM). The product lifecycle is shrinking for current generation products and pressure to launch new products is at peak now. Today's products are complex and require collaboration of specialists of various disciplines. Due to global competition, organisation must introduce new products more frequently, watch these products throughout their lifecycle in terms of their performance, take corrective actions and poor performing products must be removed from the market.

This situation leads to formation of networks called design networks and development networks where each player is an expert and jointly designs, develops, and manufactures the product. To manage this network, it is required to have a network where product data like drawings, bill of materials and probable materials are developed, shared, modified, with high level information security. PLM does not refer to any software or method. It is a concept with a collection of systematic, organised method of creating, collecting, distributing, tracking, and recording product design and development data and information.

> *PLM is an integrated, information driven approach comprised of people, processes/practices, and technology to all aspects of a product's life, from its design through manufacture, deployment and maintenance-culminating in the product's removal from service and final disposal. By trading product information for wasted time, energy and material across the entire organisation and into the supply chain, PLM drives the next generation of lean thinking.* (Grieves, 2006)

It can be also be described as the quick, concurrent, coordinated and highly interactive development of the product through the collaboration of design teams from the manufacturer, the marketing department, the supplier base, the external design experts and customers. PLM seeks to leverage modelling and simulation tools along with cross-functional communication, decision making and purposeful action to continuously shrink the design and development times necessary to successfully bring new products to market. It uses PDM and CAD through web-enabled design tools and it needs support and participation of supply chain partners. PLM also uses quality functional deployment and built-in quality assurance system. The major drivers of PLM are networked economy, cross-enterprise collaboration, time to market pressure, product data security, warranty and service cost and supply chain transparency.

3D Printing and Product Development

3D printing, or additive manufacturing, is having a large impact on product design and manufacturing. The technology is not only transforming how products are manufactured, but also how they are designed, and how quickly they are launched. As the technology continues improving, the availability of suitable raw materials is improving, and the cost of producing with this technology is going down.

Within the next decade, every commercial airliner may not hold parts inventory but use 3D printing to produce parts on demand. 3D printed parts are now used in medical industry, healthcare industry, manufacturing and even food industry for developing prototypes. The increased efficiencies of additive techniques are having a transformative effect on the product design workflow. 3D printing is not the sole driver of this trend, but the ability to produce more complex designs, the dramatically improved lead times, and the increased efficiencies of the technology are supporting the development process.

One of the most significant impacts that additive manufacturing is making on product development is in the prototyping phase. With normal manufacturing, a functional prototype of the end-use product would have to be tooled. In the case of offshore manufacturers, the prototypes would then have to be shipped back to the designers. Any changes to the design result in increase in transportation and co-ordination costs. 3D printing changes all that. Design teams can now have prototypes produced locally and immediately without any tooling. Prototypes can be easily iterated, allowing designers to make mistakes, learn from them and improve designs early in the design process without incurring heavy costs or long delays in production. This new tool also allows designers to get feedback from customers early on. By the time the product is ready for full production, all issues would have been sorted out and ready for launch.

Risks in New Product Development

Developments of new products involves a knowledge generation process that bring out outcomes like product patents, process patents and hence new knowledge. The development team is often facing a lot of uncertainties during the development process. These uncertainties give rise to risks and loss for the organisation. The development team has to take multiple decisions pertaining to areas of technology strategies, design strategies, sourcing strategies, marketing and commercialisation strategies. Many times, organisations face risk in product development process due to safety issues, environmental issues and regulatory issues. Before commercialising a complete product, it is better to audit the product concept and prototype with some external agency in all the above issues and certificate should be provided.

Risk taking involves taking decisions under some uncertainties with respect to both internal and external business environment. The uncertainty is due to lack of perfect knowledge about future. Risk can be reduced by collecting more information on technology development, market development, market trends, competitor's actions, government policies and other micro and macro factors. Risk management generally involves the following steps:

(a) Identifying risk factors in the process

(b) Evaluation and measurement of these risks
(c) Prioritisation of these risks based on impact and loss
(d) Development of mitigation strategies and action plan
(e) Follow-up with corrective actions

The various tools available for identification of risks in the process are:

- Personal knowledge
- 5 Why's
- Cause and effect diagram
- Pareto chart
- Checklist

Many tools are available for evaluation of risks:

- Failure modes and effect analysis
- Scenario analysis
- Simulation
- Decision tree analysis
- Stochastic modelling
- Bayesian belief networks

The probability of success of new product development depends on many types of risks, namely technology risk factors which include technology newness, threat of substitutes, and probability of obsolescence, commercial risk factors and execution risks.

Sometimes, risks emerge with time, especially from market conditions. Big pickup trucks have always been big fuel guzzlers and Ford USA wants to redesign big F-series pickup truck to reduce its fuel consumption. Ford spent $3 billion and took nearly five years to develop an innovative truck. It was made with all-aluminium body. The new vehicle weighed 700 pounds which was less than prior model and had 20 per cent better fuel economy. Just as Ford released its new F-150 in late 2014, crude oil process slumped, falling from $115 a barrel in June 2014 to $69 in December of that year. The gasoline prices dropped and consumers were less worried about fuel economy. For Ford, the market has fundamentally changed from when the product was first planned.

Some risk issues emerge after launching the product.

- Product failure/Product risk –recalls etc., (Product recalls involve logistic at a larger scale and hence more cost)
- Warranty issues
- New product introduction leads to cannibalisation and deviation in forecast estimation
- Product safety issues

Flexible development process that allows faster on-going corrective adjustments in product development decisions through continuous and real time data collection, knowledge and feedback will assist in mitigation strategies.

New Trends in Product/Service Development

Reverse Innovation

The traditional approach of developing new product designs in developed economies and then launch inferior versions in developing economies is undergoing some changes. Reverse innovation is the strategy of innovating in emerging (or developing) markets and then distributing/marketing these innovations in developed markets. Many companies are developing products in emerging countries like China and India and then distributing them globally. Vijay Govindarajan introduced the 'reverse innovation' concept. He is the Earl C. Daum 1924 Professor of International Business at the Tuck School of Business and founding director of Tuck's Center for Global Leadership.

Some examples of reverse innovation:

P&G's honey-based cold remedy (Vicks Honey Cough) developed in Mexico found success in European and the United States market.

Nestle's Maggi brand – Low-cost, low-fat dried noodles developed for rural India and Pakistan found a market in Australia and New Zealand as a healthy and budget-friendly alternative.

In 2010, GE's Indian arm collaborated with Triveni Engineering and Industries Ltd to manufacture steam turbines in the 30-100MW range. The company plans to then take advantage of lower input costs incurred in manufacturing and export these products to markets in West Asia, Indonesia, Europe and Latin America.

Product Design and Sustainability

The Cradle to Cradle design paradigm offers a positive approach for the environmental challenges that we are facing today. The sustainability approach has proven that it is possible to produce products that do not harm the people and the planet, but support their health while generating profit at the same time. Mother Earth has limited resources and nothing comes from moon or other planets. Even the air and water are scarce today. It is better to design our products so that they are environmentally friendly. The following hints should be considered in designing products:

(a) Product must consume less materials while production
(b) Design must consider the issue of remanufacturing and recycling (Easy to dismantle, design for redesign and for recycling)
(c) Production process should not consume more energy
(d) Product must be designed for self-destruction without damaging environment after its use
(e) Product design must consider water consumption during production
(f) Carbon footprint must be considered while designing the products
(g) Products must be designed to consume less energy
(h) Products must be designed to release less pollution gases

SUMMARY

New products and services are important drivers of revenue for any organisation as old products and services may become obsolete with time. Whether it is a consumer product company or a services company, new product and service development process is important for the survival and growth of the company. However, this process is a complex one. Three important developments recently put a lot of pressure on product and service innovation. Time to market has reduced tremendously which means new product development time should be compressed. Product lifecycle is shrinking which means new innovative products should be introduced more frequently. Finally, product technology is continuously changing and hence process also needs to be changed.

The resources and market conditions perspective describes the importance of product and service development strategically for an organisation. A number of strategic factors influence the operation resources required to develop new products and services. From market perspective, competition is intense from both international and local players. Customers are empowered with information and PLC is shrinking. More customised offerings are expected in the market and time to market is coming down drastically.

The production or service delivery process is highly related to product and service design. Integrated approach of developing product by considering existing processes increases the success rate. The operations and supply chain perspectives on product design are important for long-term survival of product in the market because supply chain and production cost depend on the design. The level of product/service change should be considered for proper resource allocation. The different steps involved in product development process should be considered to find opportunities to reduce time for developing the product. Concurrent engineering, also called simultaneous engineering, is a process for designing and developing products in which different phases of new product development overlap with each other rather than a sequential process.

The market dynamics also affect product development process. To succeed in the market, competitive priorities in operations, namely cost, quality, flexibility, time and responsiveness should also be used for product development process. These dynamics affect product/service development in several ways. The internal resources also affect product development processes in terms of its capacity to develop new products as well as technology requirements. The development chains, supplier collaboration and customer collaboration provide capacity build-up for organisation. The technologies like PLM provide new competitiveness to development processes.

The development process faces several risks both internal and external due to technology forces, market forces and other organisational and external factors. New trends in product development like 3D printing, reverse innovation and green products make new product development process both more challenging and more interesting.

Key Terms

1. Time to market: Time gap between new product concept development and launch of the new product.
2. Product lifecycle: The different phases of product life after the launch in terms of its sales performance.
3. Internet of things: A network of connected devices through Internet and communication is possible within this network
4. Concurrent engineering: Concurrent engineering, also called simultaneous engineering, is a process for designing and developing products in which different phases of new product development overlap with each other rather than a sequential process.
5. Development chain: The collection of activities and processes that are associated with the introduction of a new product. It includes decisions about product architecture, make or buy decisions, selection of suppliers, early supplier involvement, and strategic partnership.
6. Production keiretsu: It is a web of interlocking relationships between a big manufacturer (Toyota) and its suppliers.
7. Cross-badging: This refers to selling the same product with some cosmetic changes under different brand names in different markets and sometimes in the same market.
8. PLM: It can also be described as the quick, concurrent, coordinated and highly interactive development of the product through the collaboration of design teams from the manufacturer, the marketing department, the supplier base, the external design experts and customers.
9. Reverse innovation is the strategy of innovating in emerging (or developing) markets and then distributing/marketing these innovations in developed markets.

CONCEPT REVIEW QUESTIONS

1. Explain the strategic importance of product/service development process from the perspective of organisation's resources.
2. Explain the strategic importance of product/service development process from the marketing dynamics perspective.
3. Why is there a need for integrating product development with process development?
4. Explain different factors to be considered in product design process with respect to operations and supply chain requirements.
5. Relate level of product change and resource requirements.
6. Explain the new product development process.
7. What is concurrent engineering? How does it help new product development process?
8. How speed and flexibility can be incorporated in development process?
9. How collaboration with customers helps service development process?
10. How strategic alliance with suppliers enhances the product development process?
11. How alliance with other partners helps development process?
12. What is cross-badging? How collaboration with competitors can be a competitive advantage for product development?
13. What are the risk factors in new product/service development?
14. What is product lifecycle management? What is its contribution to development process?
15. How does 3D printing play a role in product development?

CRITICAL THINKING QUESTIONS

1. Due to increase in air-pollution, people suffer from many breathing related problems. Suppose your company wants to introduce a portable product which can generate oxygen and absorb carbon-di-oxide like trees and plants for our houses and which can be attached to our nose and which can be fixed at our houses like air-conditioners. Strategically develop a plan to introduce this product in the market. What kind of analysis would you make and what internal and external factors determine your strategy?
2. Visit a modern retail outlet and collect information about new products introduced in the recent period. Prepare a report on their performance and success rate.

PROJECT ASSIGNMENTS

1. Summarise your experience as a customer and as a manager with respect to test marketing of some consumer products.
2. Many consumer durables claim that they are designed with environment friendliness and provide many factors. Analyse their claims with actual perception in the market. Collect the factors that they touch on like energy consumption, disposal, etc.
3. In which industry do you see more frequent launches of new products? Why? What factors drive them to do it this way?

REFERENCES

1. https://www.newsbytesapp.com/timeline/Business/.../suzuki-toyota-to-share-cars-in-ind
2. Sethi, Rajesh. "New Product Quality and Product Development Teams", *Journal of Marketing*, Vol. 64, No. 2 (Apr., 2000), pp. 1-14.
3. Luchs, Michael G., Swan, K. Scott, and Griffin, Abbie (2018). *Design Thinking-New Product Development Essentials from the PDMA*, Wiley.
4. Grieves, Michael (2006). *Product Lifecycle Management*, Tata McGraw Hill.
5. Saaksvuori, Antti and Immonen, Anselmi (2002). *Product Lifecycle Management*, Springer.
6. https://www.newsbytesapp.com/timeline/Business/19253/92117/suzuki-toyota-to-share-cars-in-india.
7. https://economictimes.indiatimes.com/cross-badging-same-car-different-brand-has-few-takers-in-india/articleshow/17484830.cms.
8. Ogawa, Susumu and Piller, Frank T. "Reducing the Risks of New Product Development", *MIT Sloan Management Review*, Winter 2006.
9. Sheffi, Yossi (2015). *The Power of Resilience*, MIT Press.

CHAPTER

7

Operations Strategy and Sustainability

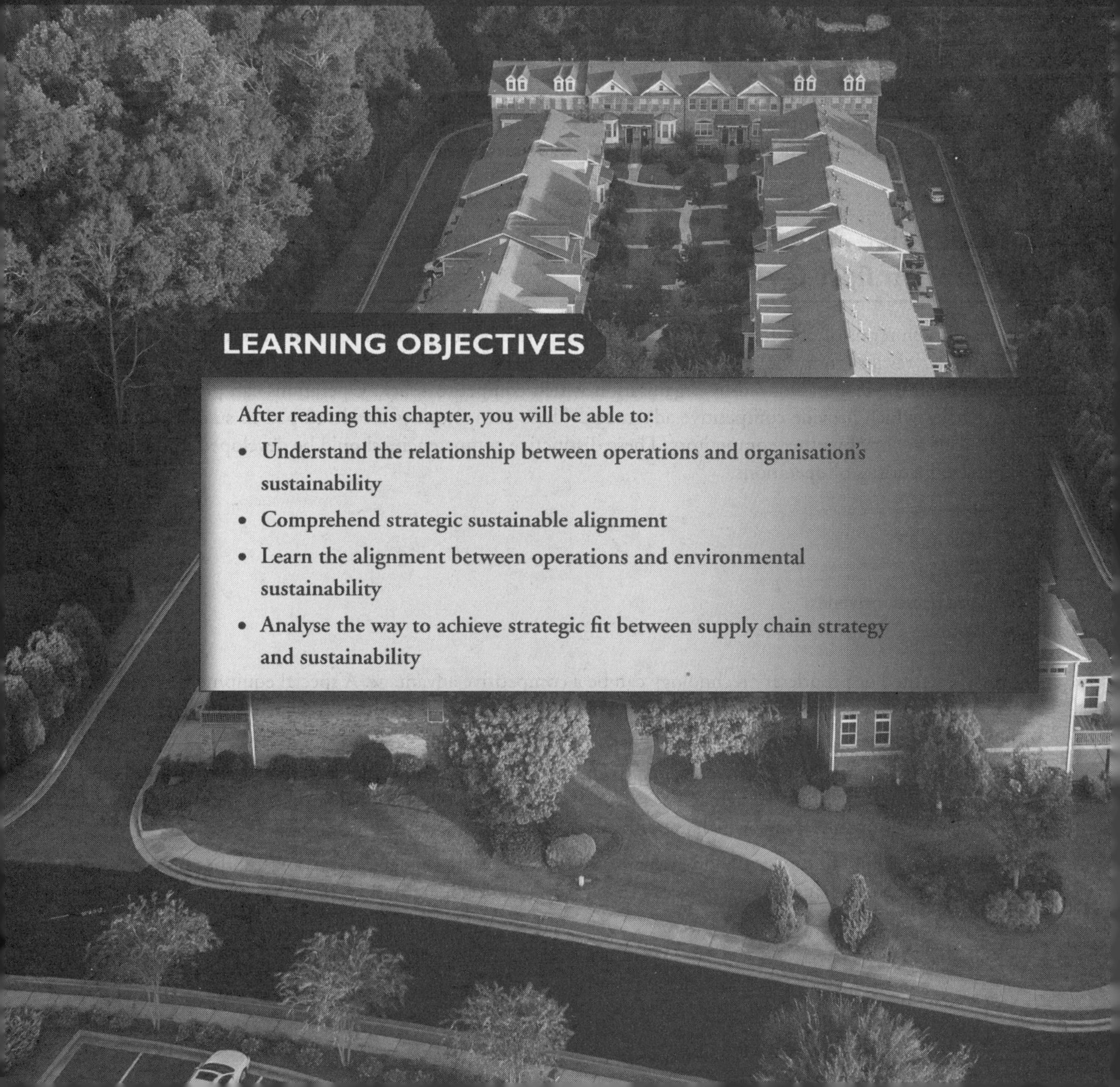

LEARNING OBJECTIVES

After reading this chapter, you will be able to:

- Understand the relationship between operations and organisation's sustainability
- Comprehend strategic sustainable alignment
- Learn the alignment between operations and environmental sustainability
- Analyse the way to achieve strategic fit between supply chain strategy and sustainability

Introduction

The word 'sustainability' became a buzz word in an environmental context for all businesses. This word appeared in a United Nations report (WCED, 1987) by former Norwegian Prime Minister, Gro Harlem Brundtland in 1987. Brundtland defined sustainable development as, "Meeting the needs of the present without compromising the ability of future generations to meet their own needs". This relates to sustainability of environment, resources of all kinds, social and cultural systems as well as economic development.

Before this, the word 'sustainability' in business context means steady growth of a company in terms of profit, market share, and shareholders value. Sustainability means consistent performance and survival of organisation in the long run. To sustain continuous growth, the organisation and its components must be flexible, agile, responsive and must keep sustainable supply of resources so that the market demand and challenges can be met.

Sustainability is also frequently used to describe corporate social responsibility works related to protection of environment. This includes planting of trees, restoration of lakes and ponds and initiatives to reduce carbon footprint.

For this book, sustainability will be addressed at two levels. First, at organisation level, how operations strategy can contribute to organisation strategy on sustainability of business in the long run. At second stage, how operations strategy can contribute to sustainability of environment, resources of all kinds, social and cultural systems as well as economic development. This is highly related to the definition given by Brundtland.

Competitive Advantage Through Operations (A view on first level)

Sustainability in terms of profit, market share and shareholders value is called economic sustainability. Economic sustainability results from creating sustainable competencies. Competitive advantage means sustainable competency in the market enjoyed by organisation which competitors lack. Operations can provide a variety of competencies which provide competitive advantage. These competencies are developed in such a way that it is very difficult to copy by other competitors. These distinctive competencies should be developed in the following competitive priorities of operations.

- Cost
- Quality
- Flexibility
- Speed/responsiveness
- Process

Process: Patented or proprietary technology can be a competitive advantage. A special equipment in the process system can also bring competencies. Sometimes organisation culture results in higher productivity and lower turnover of employees.

Quality: Better and highly innovative quality practices form better competencies. Winning a Baldridge National Quality award, implementing six-sigma in-depth and getting many international business orders due to its quality can create competitive advantage which are difficult to copy.

Flexibility: Flexibility in capacity and batch size, ability to quickly change production to other products, quick changeovers and cross-training of employees in the case of service operations.

Speed: Faster delivery, on-time delivery, high responsiveness, minimum lead time can improve time to market.

Cost: Lowest production cost due to economy of scale, cost reduction through innovation, methods improvement and better practices.

To compete in a sustainable manner through operations, the resources' sustainability becomes important. The resources include

(a) Natural resources like minerals, water, air, etc.
(b) Human resources
(c) New processes and technologies

Aligning these resources and related capabilities become more important so that competitive products and services can be delivered to the market in a sustainable manner. Capabilities on these resources should be monitored continuously and strategic actions should be taken accordingly.

Operations Strategy and External Sustainability (A view on second level)

The other view is also important as to how operations strategy makes organisations more sustainable in terms of environment, society, and economic front. Sustainability is bigger than a public relations initiative, a green product line, and corporate social responsibility (CSR). For our understanding, sustainable operations strategy has three broad areas of focus:

Social: Decisions and actions that affect all members of society (e.g., violence, education, public health, human rights, child labour, poverty, etc.)

Economic: Strategies related to economic needs of people and business. Securing food, water, shelter and comforts. Business need to make profit continuously.

Environmental: Protecting and restoring the living eco-system. Decisions and conditions that affect earth's ecology.

This sustainability can be termed as sustainability of social, economic and environmental development. The economic viability of an organisation may be in danger if the issue of sustainability is not factored into the organisation. In an organisation, promoting sustainability as a key strategic goal, design efforts must focus on reducing the full lifecycle impact on environment in terms of pollution during usage and disposal.

Operations Strategy and Organisation Sustainability

Market challenges faced by Indian Organisations recently

Scanning of Indian market and world market in the last ten years reveals the importance of operations strategy for success in the marketplace. Markets are becoming more mature, and time lag in terms of products, product life, and trends in different countries are becoming less and markets demand more in terms of varieties, latest technology and less lead time for new products. Growth of ecommerce in different categories of market also put operations under tremendous pressure to perform. The following are major observations in the market.

Indian companies face competition from the companies in China, Korea, Europe and USA due to globalisation. So, the Indian companies should also become multi-national organisations and compete against the best in the market. When more competitors are present in a market, it will result in reduction in prices, pressure on lead times, delivering best quality and differentiation become more and more difficult.

The following factors are important dimensions of a market:

a. Customers' expectations are always changing
b. Technology grows at a break-neck speed
c. Infrastructure grows with better connectivity
d. The demographic profile of customers keep on changing
e. More choices for customers due to competition and entry of foreign companies

Customer expectations and competitive priorities that an organisation needs to implement could be best understood using the concepts, order qualifiers and order winners. These concepts adopt the competitive priorities according to market situation and accordingly, operations strategy is formulated.

Order Qualifiers: These are set of attributes that customers and users expect in a product or service. If any of these are missing, customers will not consider it for buying. These are minimum requirements for a service or a product to be considered.

Order Winners: These are attributes above the order qualifiers which motivate the customers to buy the product. These attributes help brands and companies to differentiate their offerings from competitors.

What constitutes order-winning and order-qualifying attributes might change continuously from time to time. For example, during 1990s, Indian organisations tried to compete on quality and projected quality as order winning attributes. But in 2000s, it was JIT and Theory of Constraints that helped organisations to cut costs and become efficient. In 2010 and beyond, organisations wanted to compete on time to market, flexibility and technology. Now companies look beyond their organisation and look at supply chain for competitiveness. So, attributes move between order winners and order qualifiers. May be we also get some more new attributes of competitiveness from operations and supply chain in near future.

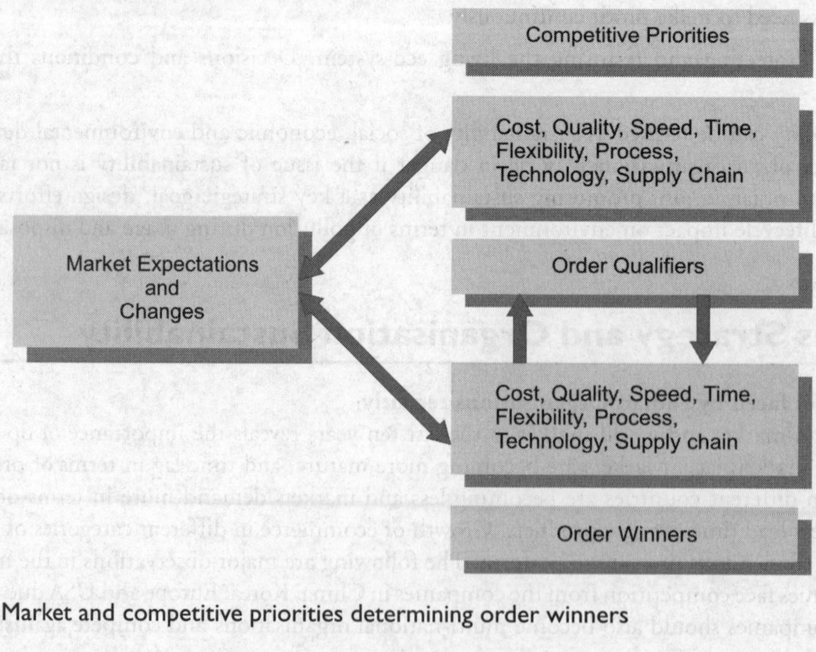

FIGURE 7.1 Market and competitive priorities determining order winners

Sustainable Alignment

The process of continually reconciling operational resources with market dynamic requirements is called sustainable alignment. Uncertainties as well as availability of resources exist in markets. So, the process of attaining alignment between the market and resources is even difficult due to uncertainty. Different parts of a firm control different forms of resources and co-ordination of these departments is required for achieving alignment. Based on market situations, the competitive priorities change and to compete based on certain competitiveness like cost, quality, etc., the organisation must deploy the right kind of resources on time to succeed in the market. The competitive strategic process decides on mix of competitive priorities to be deployed in the market. To match this, the resources deployment also fine-tunes with strategy formulation.

Some of the dimensions of market requirements resulting due to either intrinsic and extrinsic needs of customers or organisation's marketing strategy are:

- Brand strength and reputation
- Level of differentiation
- Level of distribution

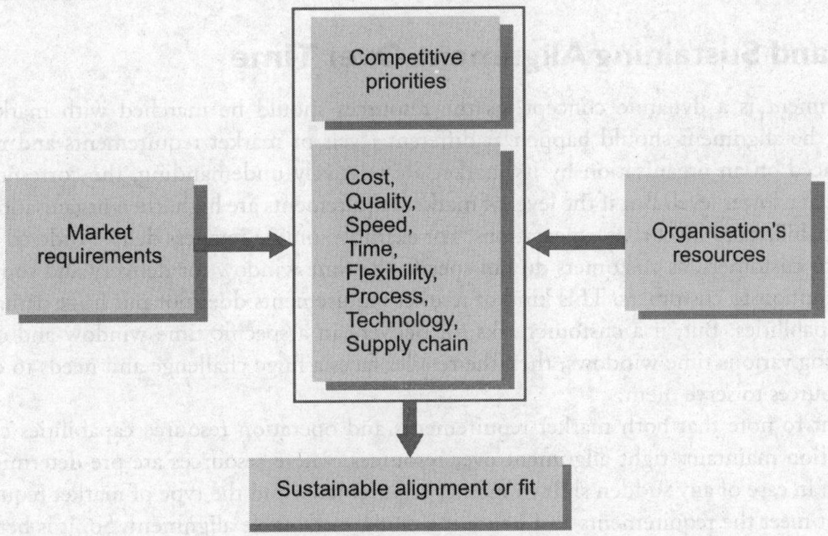

FIGURE 7.2 Sustainable alignment

The organisation resources and capabilities include the following:

- Productivity
- Process competitiveness
- Time to mobilise a specific resource
- Research and development resources

Table 7.1 provides some more ideas on matching the competitive priorities with resource capabilities.

TABLE 7.1 Competitive priorities and matching resources

Competitive Priority	Resources/Capabilities in Demand
Cost	Low cost labour, low cost country production, large scale production system, economical transportation, control over raw materials, technology capability
Quality	Best processes, human resources, continuous improvement culture, technology, investment in process improvements, quality certifications
Flexibility	Lean practices, quick changeovers, total quality management (TQM), total productive maintenance (TPM), technology, excess capacity, flexible capacity, dedicated and flexible facilities
Time/Speed	Alternative mode of transportation, methods, innovation in process, order co-ordination, technology
Process	Patented process/technologies, innovation,
Supply Chain	Supply chain capabilities, network of factories, supply chain visibility, analytics, technology in supply chain

Achieving and Sustaining Alignment Over Time

Sustainable alignment is a dynamic concept, as the resources should be matched with market requirement with time. Also the alignment should happen at different levels of market requirements and resources. If the requirements placed on an organisation by its market are relatively undemanding, the corresponding resource capability will be at a lower level. But if the level of market requirements are high, then organisation must develop resources and capabilities to meet that expectations. For example, online retailers deliver ordered products at any time of the day to customers, as customers do not specify the time window for delivery and sometimes retailers do not give that option to customers. This kind of market requirements does not put huge demand on retailer's resources and capabilities. But, if a customer asks for delivery in a specific time window and other customers are also demanding various time windows, then the retailer faces a huge challenge and needs to deploy complex software and resources to serve them.

It is important to note that both market requirements and operation resource capabilities can change over time. If organisation maintains tight alignment over resources, where resources are pre-determined, then there will be a problem in case of any sudden shift in market requirements and the type of market requirements. Tight alignment cannot meet the requirements and hence it is not a sustainable alignment. So, it is better to maintain loose alignment with flexibility in resources and broader capabilities which can provide some protection against unexpected changes in the market.

Many organisations, once started, fail to exist even for one year. The obvious explanation is that organisations fail to reconcile market requirements and operation resources because of either misinterpretation of either market or operation capabilities and sometimes both. At the same time, business history recorded many incidents, where the organisations had their moment of market success and competitive glory but then failed, never to comeback. They might have effectively reconciled resources and requirements at some point of time but failed to sustain that position. Many macro-economic factors influence these market shifts and have huge influence on the survival and success of the organisation. This means that strategies will be formulated again and again over time to maintain sustainable alignment over time.

New Approaches to Operations Strategy

Operations strategy with support from operational resources can also get support from new management approaches, such as total quality management (TQM), lean Management, and theory of constraints and so on. Many organisations have benefitted from these initiatives and gained significant competitive advantage through them. These approaches sometimes are considered as substitutes for operations strategy. Many organisations have implemented Six Sigma principles, and some are using enterprise resource planning. Whether these tools and approaches are strategic in nature or not, they have provided competitive advantage to organisations. So it is important to understand how these approaches can complement and support operations strategy in the long run.

Total Quality Management

Total quality management, a buzzword phrase of the 1980's, has been killed and resurrected on a number of occasions. The concept and principles, though simple, seem to be creeping back into existence by "bits and pieces" through the evolution of the ISO9001 Management Quality System standard. Companies who have implemented TQM include Ford Motor Company, Phillips Semiconductor, SGL Carbon, Motorola and Toyota Motor Company. TQM is the concept that quality can be managed and that it is a process. The following information is provided to give an understanding of the key elements of this process.

Total Quality Management (TQM)

Total = Quality involves everyone and all activities in the company

Quality = Conformance to requirements (meeting customer requirements)

Management = Quality can and must be managed.

TQM = A process for managing quality; it must be a continuous way of life; a philosophy of perpetual improvement in everything we do.

TQM is the foundation for activities which include:

- Meeting Customer Requirements
- Reducing Development Cycle Times
- Just In Time/Demand Flow Manufacturing
- Improvement Teams
- Reducing Product and Service Costs
- Improving Administrative Systems Training

The ten steps to TQM are as follows:

1. Pursue New Strategic Thinking
2. Know your Customers
3. Set True Customer Requirements
4. Concentrate on Prevention, Not Correction
5. Reduce Chronic Waste
6. Pursue a Continuous Improvement Strategy
7. Use Structured Methodology for Process Improvement
8. Reduce Variation
9. Use a Balanced Approach
10. Apply to All Functions

Principles of TQM

The principles of TQM are as follows:

1. Quality can and must be managed
2. Everyone has a customer and is a supplier
3. Processes, not people are the problem
4. Every employee is responsible for quality
5. Problems must be prevented, not just fixed
6. Quality must be measured
7. Quality improvements must be continuous
8. The quality standard is defect free
9. Goals are based on requirements, not negotiated
10. Lifecycle costs, not front end costs
11. Management must be involved and led
12. Plan and organise for quality improvement

Processes must be Managed and Improved

Processes must be managed and improved! This involves:

- Defining the process
- Measuring process performance (metrics)
- Reviewing process performance
- Identifying process shortcomings
- Analysing process problems
- Making a process change
- Measuring the effects of the process change
- Communicating both ways between supervisor and user

Key to Quality

The key to improving quality is to improve processes that define, produce and support our products. All people work in processes.

People

- Get processes "in control"
- Work with other employees and managers to identify process problems and eliminate them

Managers and/or Supervisors Work

- On processes, provide training and tool resources
- Measure and review process performance (metrics)
- Improve process performance with the help of those who use the process

TQM Process Improvement and Problem Solving Sequence					
Plan (Plan a Change)			**Do (Implement the Change)**	**Check (Observe the Effects)**	**Action (Embed the Fix Into the Process for Good)**
Define the Problem	**Identify Possible Causes**	**Evaluate Possible Causes**	**Make a Change**	**Test the Change**	**Take Permanent Action**
1. Recognise that what you are doing is a "PROCESS" 2. Identify the commodity being processed. -Process Inference 3. Define some measurable characteristics of value to the commodity. 4. Describe the "process" Process Flow Analysis's Flow charts List of steps 5. Identify the "Big" problem Brainstorming Checklists Pareto analysis	"BRAINSTORM" what is causing the problem. Determine what past data show • Frequency distribution • Pareto charts • Control charts sampling	Determine the relationship between cause and effect, • Scatter diagrams • Regression analysis • Determine what the process is doing now • Control charts sampling	Determine what change would help Your knowledge of the process • Scatter diagrams • Control Charts - sampling • Pareto analysis ****Then make the change	Determine what change worked (confirmation). Histograms • Control charts - sampling • Scatter diagrams	Ensure the fix is embedded in the process and that the resulting process is used. Continue to monitor the process to ensure: A. The problem is fixed for good. and B. The process is good enough • Control charts - sampling ****To ensure continuous improvement, return to step 5.

Lean Systems and Just-in-Time Systems

The just-in-time approach attempts to minimise inventories. It accomplishes this by ordering and producing in small batches. Ideally, as each order of raw material arrives from a vendor, it goes directly into production, and as each batch is finished at one work centre, it is moved to the following work centre where the previous order has just been completed and work has begun on the new order. Hence, inventories of raw materials and purchased parts are purposely kept as small as possible, as are inventories of partially completed goods between operations.

Naturally, this means that a disruption anywhere in the system can easily cause the entire system to come to a halt since there is little slack between operations. However, the Japanese see this as an opportunity to learn where the weak points are in the system and to correct those problems so they do not occur again. By way of contrast, most U.S. manufacturers carry safety stock "just in case…". According to the JIT philosophy, buffers of inventory tend to cover up or hide problems that keep recurring and are never resolved, partly because they are not always obvious and partly because the presence of inventory seems to make the problems less serious. Needless to say, the additional inventory carries a burden in terms of holding costs.

Factors that enable JIT system:

1. In order to maintain a JIT system with little inventory and small run sizes, it is necessary to have quick, low-cost changeovers and setups.
2. In-process inventories are kept small by running small run sizes. The ability to quickly change over equipment and relatively low-cost setups permit them to do this and keep inventories low in the process.
3. The willingness to commit the time, effort and money to correct problems at the source is essential to the success of the system.

The Japanese have had a national goal of full employment through industrialisation since World War II. The strategy for obtaining market dominance has been targeted to specific product areas in particular, automotive assembly and consumer electronics. They directed their best engineering talent to the shop floor, not to product design activities. They also worked to improve product quality and reliability above what competitors could supply. Central to this effort were two philosophies:

1. Elimination of waste
2. Respect for people

Elimination of Waste

Toyota's Fujio Cho identifies seven prominent types of waste to be eliminated.

1. Waste from over production
2. Waste of waiting time
3. Transportation waste
4. Inventory waste
5. Processing waste
6. Waste of motion
7. Waste from product defects

This definition of JIT leaves no room for surplus or safety stock. No safety stocks are allowed because if you cannot use it now, you do not need to make it now; that would be waste. Hidden inventory in storage areas, transit systems, carousels, and conveyors is a key target for inventory reduction.

The seven elements that address elimination of waste are

1. Focussed factory
2. Group technology
3. Quality at source
4. JIT production
5. Uniform plant loading
6. Kanban production control system
7. Minimised setup time

Focussed Factory Networks

The Japanese build small-specialised plants rather than large vertically integrated manufacturing facilities. Plants designed for one purpose can be constructed and operated more economically.

Group Technology

This is a philosophy in which similar parts are grouped into families, and the processes required to make the parts are arranged in a specialised work cell. Instead of transferring jobs from one department to another to specialised workers, the Japanese considers all operations required to make a part and group those machines together. The Group Technology (GT) removes movements and queue time between operations, reduces inventory and the number of employees required. Workers, however, must be flexible to run several machines and processes. Due to their advanced skill level, these workers have increased job security.

Quality at the Source

It means do it right the first time and when something goes wrong, stop the process or assembly line immediately. Factory workers become their own inspectors, personally responsible for the quality of their output.

JIT Production

JIT means producing what is needed and no more. Anything over the minimum amount necessary is viewed as waste, because effort and material expended for something not needed now cannot be utilised. This is in contrast to relying on extra material just in case something goes wrong.
JIT is typically applied to repetitive manufacturing, which is when the same or similar items are made one after another. It does not require large volumes and can be applied to any repetitive segments of a business regardless of where they appear. Under JIT, the ideal lot size is one.

Uniform Plant Loading

Smoothing the production flow to dampen the reaction waves that normally occur in response to schedule variations is called uniform plant loading. When a change is made in a final assembly, the changes are magnified throughout the line and the supply chain. The only way to eliminate the problem is to make adjustments as small as possible by setting a firm monthly production plan for which the output rate is frozen.

Kanban Production Control System

A kanban control system uses a signaling device to regulate JIT flows. Kanban means "sign" or "instruction card" in Japanese. In a paperless control system, containers can be used instead of cards. This kanban pull system tries to co-ordinate between departments or work centres by means of signaling when the next lot should be produced.

Concept of Pull and Push Production System

The concept of pull in lean production means to respond to the pull, or demand, of the customer. Lean manufacturers design their operations to respond to the ever-changing requirements of customers. Organisations that are able to produce to the pull of customers do not need to manufacture goods in a way that traditional batch-and-queue manufacturers must rely on. The planning for delivery of product to customers is less troublesome, and demand becomes more stable if customers have confidence in knowing that they can get what they want when they want it.

Kanbans are manual pull devices that allow an efficient means to transfer parts from one department to another and automatically reorder products using minimum/maximum inventory levels. They are a signal, such as an empty container returned to the start of the assembly line, that signals the need for replenishment of materials to a user.

- Kanbans are used in "pull" manufacturing systems, where product is manufactured to the pull of market-driven demand.
- Kanban systems must be convenient and easy to use .
- Pull systems react to needs, they don't anticipate them.
- Successfully deployed kanbans deliver the right amount of material to the right place exactly when it is needed.
- Several pull techniques can be used for different products at the same worksite.
- Great speed can be achieved in manufacturing, and product is not manufactured when a need does not exist.
- A kanban or pull system means providing the workers with what they need when they need it—tools, software, capital equipment, access, feedback, or the opportunity to participate.
- Kanbans or cards are used when the move time and distance between producing and consuming departments are significant.
  - o Each card controls a specific quantity of parts
  - o Cards are returned to the producing department after parts are consumed, triggering production of the next batch
  - o Single card systems are used when the products are able to be resupplied prior to running out
  - o Multiple card systems are used if several products are manufactured by the producing worksite or if the lot size is different from the move size
- Physical kanbans, kanban squares, or shelf reserves are used when the producing and consuming worksites are physically adjacent.
  - o Must have relatively close proximity
  - o Used when major queue of parts is maintained in the producing department. Maximum and minimum queue size can coordinate production between worksites with different capacities
  - o Physical area holds enough space to cover variations in rates
  - o Goal of the producing department is to fill the space reserved for the part

Goal and TOC Philosophy

The Theory of Constraints (or TOC as it is called) is a relatively recent development in the practical aspect of making organisational decisions in situations in which constraints exist. Dr. Eliyahu M. Goldratt first described the theory in his novel, *The Goal.* In many organisations, TOC logic forms major portions of that organisation's philosophy of continuous improvement.

TOC has been used at three different levels, Production Management—TOC was initially applied here to solve problems of bottlenecks, scheduling, and inventory reduction.

Throughput Analysis—application of TOC has caused a shift from cost-based decision making to decision-making based on continuous improvement of processes in which system throughput, system constraints, and statistically determined protective capacities at critical points are key elements.

Theory of Constraints Logical Processes—this third level is the general application of TOC reasoning to attack a variety of process problems within organisations. TOC logic is applied to identify what factors are limiting an organisation from achieving its goals, developing a solution to the problem, and getting the individuals in the process to invent the requisite changes for themselves.

A constraint is anything in an organisation that limits it from moving toward or achieving its goal. Of course, this assumes that an appropriate goal has been defined. For most business organisations, the goal is to make money now as well as in the future. There are two basic types of constraints— physical constraints and non-physical constraints. A physical constraint is something like the physical capacity of a machine. A non-physical constraint might be something like demand for a product, a corporate procedure, or an individual's paradigm for looking at the world.

The steps in applying TOC are as follows:

1. Identify the system's constraints. Of necessity, this included prioritisation so that just the ones that really limit system progress towards the goal.
2. Decide how to exploit the system's constraints. Once we have decided how to manage the constraints within the system, how about the majority of the resources that are not constraints? The answer is that we manage them so that they just provide what is needed to match the output of the constrained resources. We never let them supply more output than is needed because doing so moves us no closer to the goal.
3. Subordinate everything else to the above decision in Step 2. Since the constraints are keeping us from moving towards our goal, we apply all of the resources that we can to assist in breaking them. Constraints are not acts of God. Practically, in all cases their limiting impact can be reduced or eliminated.
4. Elevate the system's constraints. If we continue to work towards breaking a constraint (also called elevating a constraint) at some point, the constraint will no longer be a issue. It will be broken.
5. If the constraint is broken, return to Step 1. When that happens, there will be another constraint, somewhere else in the system that is limiting progress to the goal.

The process must be reapplied, perhaps many times. It is important not to let inertia become a constraint. Most constraints in organisations are of their own making. They are the entrenched rules, policies, and procedures that have developed over time. Many times, when we finally break a constraint, we do not go back and review and change the rules and policies that caused the constraint initially. Most constraints in organisations today are policy constraints rather than physical constraints.

For a manufacturing organisation, with the goal being to make money now as well as in the future, TOC defines three operational measurements that measure whether operations are working towards that goal. They are:

- Throughput: The rate at which the system generates money through sales. This is considered to be the same as contribution margin (selling price — cost of raw materials). Labour costs are considered to be a part of operating expense rather than throughput.
- Inventory: This is all the money the system invests in things it intends to (or could) sell. This is the total system investment, which includes not only conventional inventory, but also buildings, land, vehicles, plant, and equipment. It does not include the value of labour added to work-in-process inventory.
- Operating Expense: All the money the system spends in turning inventory into throughput. This includes all the money constantly poured into a system to keep it operating, such as heat, light, scrap materials, depreciation, etc.

The following four measurements are used to identify results for the overall organisation:

Net Profit = Throughput – Operating Expense

Return on Investment (ROI)= (Throughput – Operating Expense)/Inventory

Productivity = Throughput/Operating Expense

Turnover = Throughput/Inventory

Given the measurements as described, employees can make local decisions by examining the effect of those decisions on the organisation's overall throughput, inventory, and operating expense. A decision that results in increasing overall throughput, decreasing the overall inventory, or decreasing the overall operating expense for the firm will generally be a good decision for the business.

The Theory of Constraints does away with much of cost accounting. It is clear that application of cost accounting principles (primarily, the allocation of costs in order to make decisions at the local level) leads to poor management decisions at the department as well as in upper levels of the organisation. In fact, TOC virtually eliminates the use of economic order quantities (EOQ), production lot sizes, deriving product costs, setting prices, determining productivity measures, and the use of performance incentives.

Most individuals will readily see the use for the Theory of Constraints in the improvement of production scheduling or in improving manufacturing. This is simply incorrect. Although it is true that the Theory of Constraints provides us with simple examples in the manufacturing environment, TOC is truly applicable to any process in any organisation. This includes universities, hospitals, service providers of all varieties, government and, of course, manufacturing.

Operations Strategy and Sustainability

Today, organisations face challenges of unprecedented scope and magnitude. The resources which were plenty in the past are becoming scarcer and costlier. The supply chains have become global, vulnerable to risk and more complex. The competitive advantages are disappearing fast and competition is intense. Government policies are uncertain and frequent policy changes affect supply chains and trade across globe. Successful strategies followed in the past are not successful today. A transformational change is required in strategy and it will provide sustainable competitive advantage.

External challenges are as follows:

(a) The markets in developed world have reached mature status in many categories and only in innovative product categories, some growth is experienced.

(b) Majority of market growth originates from emerging markets. These markets force companies to follow new and different business models.

(c) Financial investors and institutions are demanding full disclosure related to impact of climate change, impact on society and other social and environmental sustainability issues on business performance.

(d) Governments and non-governmental organisations are putting huge pressure on organisations to reduce greenhouse gas emissions.

(e) Supply chains are now more vulnerable to environmental and weather related incidents like floods, rains, etc.,

(f) Customers demand more transparency and accountability from organisations in the area of supply chains, fair labour standards, material sourcing and product lifecycle management. They are willing to pay more for sustainable products.

(g) Planet's resources are finite and hence they are under stress. This stress will increase further with growing demand from emerging and developing markets.

The operational definition of sustainability consists of three broader areas as given by WCED, social, environmental and economic.

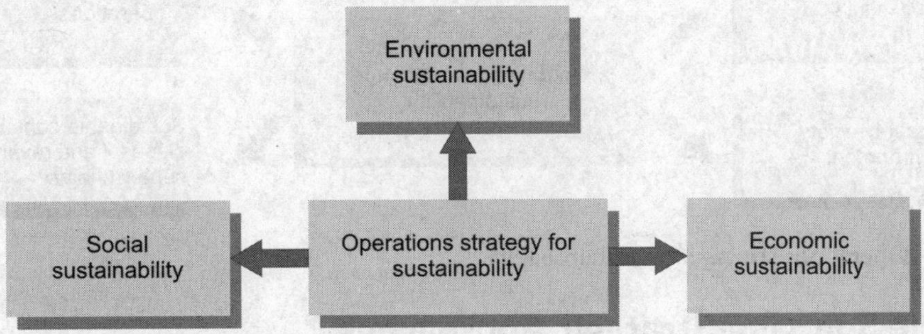

FIGURE 7.3 Sustainability framework

Economic sustainability: Sustainability in terms of profit, market share and shareholders value is called economic sustainability. Economic sustainability results from creating sustainable competencies. Operations management practices are at the core of these competencies. Resource alternatives, productivity improvements, quality practices, process technologies and methods can give competitive advantage to organisations and they can grow continuously.

Environmental sustainability: It refers to the capability of organisation to produce products and services without compromising the natural systems and living beings. Both operation practices and supply chain practices need to adopt to environmental sustainability. Earth provides a lot of resources which we indiscriminately use and waste. These resources cannot be sustained for long time, if we practise only economic sustainability and ignore environmental sustainability. The existence of an organisation itself will be a question mark if we do not protect and nurture our environment.

Social sustainability: It deals with choices made by organisations that will affect current and future generations to live a healthy life. This means that organisation should operate in a responsible manner to take care of its customers, employees, immediate community and society in general. It should consider health, safety and quality of life of its employees, community and society. Operations employ more people and is responsible for them and their extended families.

To address all these dimensions from operations perspective, the following strategic operations dimensions are considered.

(a) Sustainable sourcing
(b) Sustainable internal operations
(c) Sustainable consumption, disposal and reverse supply chains
(d) Sustainable society and environment
(e) Sustainable supply chains

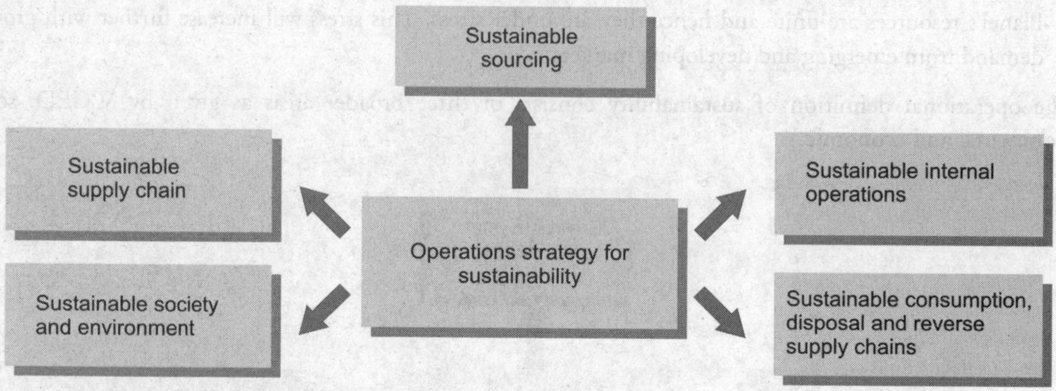

FIGURE 7.4 Operations strategy for sustainability

Sustainable Sourcing-Strategic Approaches

Business does not exist in isolation and is connected to a network of its supply chain partners. Consumers see the activities of its supply chain and transparency of the supply chain becomes compulsory. They also hold companies accountable for their wider supply chain irrespective of length and breadth of supply chain. If any activities by supply side partners, even if they are at periphery of the supply chain, affects environment and society, then its supply chain sustainability is questioned. Making procurement function more responsible, ethical and green is required at this moment. Also making the entire upstream supply chain more sustainable in terms of social impact and environmental impacts with economic survival is key important strategic issue.

Drivers of Sustainable Procurement

Regulations: Organisation's effort on sustainable procurement is initiated mostly by compliance to government regulations on environment and social dimensions. Regulation is a motivator in finding new solutions to environmental and social problems. It also can lead to new ways of reducing waste, reducing pollution and developing environmental and social friendly policies.

Customers: The pressure to be environmentally friendly can come from customers. Consumer facing companies face protests and resistance from pressure groups and environment related non-governmental organisations (NGOs). Organisations with global visibility are driven towards sustainability sourcing due to customer pressure and transparency issues.

Competitors: Big competitors may lead the industry towards sustainable sourcing. When a competitor gains a competitive advantage due to green supply chain and sustainable practices, other organisations have to respond to this challenge and result in industry wide sustainable practices. Small players gain from large competitors due to the fact that when large competitors force suppliers to practice sustainability, small players also buy from same suppliers and hence sustainability becomes easy.

Suppliers: Sometimes, suppliers themselves may drive sustainability practices in the supply chain. Big suppliers catering to many different supply chains may be forced to follow sustainability or on their own take initiatives to gain more market share. This results in better sustainability practices in the supply chains.

Many supply chains are successful and able to sustain their success due to the factor 'trust' between the supplier and the buyer. It determines the price and profitability of the buying company. The atmosphere of trust creates an open, transparent ecosystem where both parties come together, collaborate, face challenges and come out with feasible, sustainable solutions. Organisations attempting to implement sustainability practices among supply partners through enforcement, monitoring policies and compliance are lacking success. Only authentic collaboration towards agreed goals on sustainability practices in procurement with trust-based relationship will ensure long-term sustainability. The true value is created by engaging and collaborating with suppliers as part of a larger sustainable procurement strategy. For example, an OEM may intervene and help a supplier to improve its operations, enhance its capacity and practice sustainable operations.

Some of the issues related to our definition of sustainability in sourcing are:

(a) Supplier indiscriminately polluting air, water bodies and land
(b) Employment of child labour in their production
(c) Poor labour standards at supplier facility
(d) Poor safety standards at supplier facilities
(e) Poor wage rate and working conditions
(f) Poor relationship with immediate community of the facilities
(g) Effect on rights of tribes, community and socially disadvantaged people
(h) Environmental issues like destruction of forests, flora and fauna and water bodies
(i) Ethical issues is sourcing

Creating a Sustainable Sourcing Organisation

Companies must work towards a strategic approach aimed at advancing agreed goals and generating much more value through collaboration. The following steps can be useful for this approach.

Align sustainable procurement and core business strategies: There should be fit between corporate strategies and procurement strategies. Embedded sustainability must be a part of strategy. Operation level sustainability initiatives should be aligned with strategic approaches.

Institute sustainable procurement policies: Sustainable procurement procedures and policies will help institutionalising the ideas and put them to practice. These policies should be supported by board of directors so that it works best. Some examples of policies and procedures are supplier sustainability code of conduct, zero-tolerance list, supplier diversity policies and so on.

Create a sustainable supplier roadmap: Organisation can categorise suppliers based on their sustainability performance and initiatives and provide them the road map to improve. Before going forward, the sustainability plan should be tested with few suppliers and the fine-tuned plan should be applied to all suppliers.

Engage supplier management in goal setting: While developing sustainability goals, organisations can engage supplier management for joint goal setting and strategy formulation.

Document baseline performance: Current performance on sustainability should be documented for each supplier on each dimensions like water footprint, carbon footprint and so on. This will help in target setting and formulation of road map.

Training and capacity building: It may be possible to build supplier capacity by leveraging organisation's resources for supplier training and support. Suppliers can advance fast and become more sustainable with the help of organisation. Organisations can also learn from supplier's specific sustainability competencies.

Monitor and measure supplier performance: After establishing baseline, companies can formulate measurement and monitoring system for suppliers.

Sustainable Internal Operations

Companies need to look inward at their own internal operations and their impact on all dimensions of sustainability, before requesting supply chain partners and other partners to practice and implement sustainable operations. To improve sustainable internal operations, major strategies are focussed on the following areas:

- Sustainable product design
- Sustainable processes and activities
- Lean and green operations
- Community development
- Employee health and safety
- Ethical practices in operations

Sustainable Product Design

The focus of product and service design has shifted to environmental sustainability. The design of product must address the following important sustainable enabling product characteristics.

(a) Ease of disposal without pollution
(b) Ease of recycling and reuse
(c) Ease of remanufacturing
(d) Minimum material use in products
(e) Ease of tracing and tracking of its location, use and performance

Sustainable Processes

The focus must be on process improvement related to sustainability, such as employee involvement, waste reduction, energy conservation and emission control. Internal operations also should concentrate on investing in capabilities to recover pollution-causing chemicals during manufacturing, to develop substitutes for non-renewable inputs and setting up waste treatment plants. Sustainable internal operations should adopt lean practices and set up small teams to concentrate on bringing energy savings, reducing pollution, improving working conditions and making internal resources sustainable.

Case Study on L&T Company

All 24 L&T campuses across India have achieved water positive status in 2016. To effectively manage its water footprint, L&T undertook many initiatives like zero waste water discharge campuses, water conservation, recharging groundwater through rain water harvesting and community watershed programmes. Treated waste water is used for gardening, toilet flushing and cooling tower applications thereby reducing fresh water consumption. Water storage initiatives like check dams, ponds and other structures are built by the company for the community. Resources like water are used for many manufacturing operations but was treated as free resource, and today it became a valuable resource.

Lean Operations

Lean production system reduces all forms of waste and hence there is a saving of resources. Good layout system reduces movement of materials and hence savings on energy and equipment. All practices related to TQM like TPM, Kaizen, and quality circles lead to reduction in waste and savings in resources.

Community Development

Manufacturing plants are mostly located near some resources like mines and waterbodies and sometimes near transportation facility like rail line. The exploitation of resources without sustainable practices leads to local destruction of ecosystem and the plant also loses its competency. The sustainable way of renewal of resources is important for the organisation as well as the community living near the plant. The manufacturing plant should use its corporate social responsibility (CSR) funds in the following areas:

a. Local community development by facilitating education, healthcare and basic amenities
b. Developing local environment with objective of water positive by constructing water saving structures
c. Developing more trees and making it environmentally less polluted place
d. Providing local employment

Employee Health and Safety

This is one of the important initiatives required in internal operations for achieving sustainable operations. By providing world class health and safety environment inside the factory, which is mandatory in developed nations, organisations can enhance their sustainable operations. It should be followed even in offshore facilities. Some issues related to this internal operations are:

1. Child labour should not be used
2. Proper working time should be maintained
3. Labour standards should be followed
4. Proper working conditions should be provided to employees
5. Wages should be at par with industry

Ethical Practices in Operations

Operations should follow ethical standards in all sub-areas of operations and supply chain management. The following areas should be given importance in terms of ethical practices:

- Understanding and compliance of all government rules and regulations in operations
- Following ethical standards in sourcing and supply management
- Following standard practices inside factory in procedures and processes
- Implementing all safety standards and precautions for employees and labour
- Implementing of standard policies for labour and providing good work environment for labour and employees
- No child labour and poor wages
- Following safety standards in materials and components.

Sustainable Consumption, Disposal and Reverse Supply Chains

Sustainability issues are extended to consumption and also beyond that with reverse supply chain and recycling. Organisations develop, produce and market many products and services. While consuming the product or service, the organisation must ensure sustainability with respect to consumer behaviour in terms of how they use the product and how they dispose the product after use. Organisations should take responsibility to educate the consumers properly in terms of use and disposal.

Reverse Supply Chain Management

The reverse supply chain is one of the emerging areas of interest in the field of supply chain management. It consists of list of activities involved in recovering used products for the purpose of recycling, remanufacturing and proper disposal by a manufacturer. Reverse supply chain or reverse logistics is the series of activities required to retrieve a used product from a customer and dispose of it properly or reuse after processing. The chain connects end users with manufacturer in reverse direction. Reuse and remanufacturing of products and materials are not new in the industry. Wastepaper recycling, metal scrap brokers and soft drink industry are all examples that have been around for a long time. In these cases, recovery of the used products is economically more attractive than disposal. But, in the recent past, there is a growing interest in reuse and remanufacturing among industries and that leads to more studies in the area of reverse logistics. The major forces behind this development are:

1. Environmental legislation related to disposal
2. Opportunity to recover some of the value from old products, e.g. computer components
3. Opportunity to remanufacture old products and to serve secondary markets
4. Opportunity to become an environmentally friendly organisation

The retail returns and returns from customers also come under reverse logistics with the objective to minimise overall returns. These supply chains are loosely linked and totally controlled by unorganised sectors. In Europe and U.S.A., companies use reverse logistic network to get back products like refrigerators, cameras, televisions, cars, cellular phones and industrial equipment. In India, not much initiative has been taken by industries. The environmental legislation will also come into force in India, and Indian companies should be proactive in implementing reverse logistics in their industries. Not only these companies do less damage to environment but they also gain competitive advantage by means of remanufacturing and recycling.

There are many issues related to management of the reverse supply chain. They are forecasting returns, design of reverse logistics network, inventory management of returns, role of outsourcing, integration using information technology and role of customers in returns. The reverse supply chain process is complicated further by the following unique dimensions.

- The reverse flow is supply driven and not demand driven. The end user must be willing to return the used products.
- The timing of return is unpredictable.
- The nature of products returned differs widely and hence, the type of network also differs.

Design of Reverse Logistics Network

The design of reverse logistics network deals with issues related to location of various activities of supply chain. It also deals with how to design the corresponding transportation links. The companies need to consider the following points, while designing reverse supply network:

(a) How to collect recoverable products from the former user?
(b) Where to inspect and grade collected products?
(c) Where to locate re-processing facility?
(d) Whether to use existing facility or acquire new facility?
(e) Whether to outsource re-processing or do itself?

Product Acquisition

The collection of used products potentially accounts for a significant part of the total cost, which can be compared with the last mile issue in distribution of products in the forward supply chain. The collection may occur through door to door, service centre, sales centre and sometimes through customers. In the case of paper and plastic, people go to individual houses and collect paper products. In the case of batteries, the point of purchase acts as collection centre (retailers). In the case of tyre re-treading, customer brings old tyres to re-treading centres.

Canon used to collect empty cartridges used in their printer through collection boxes kept at different places. Customers can deposit their used cartridges in these boxes and a courier company can send this to refilling. Dupont operates several facilities for recycling nylon from using carpeting material. Carpet dealers collect the carpet waste.

Testing/Grading

The location of the test and grade operation should be near collection centres. Early testing might save transportation of useless products. On the other hand, sophisticated testing might involve expensive equipment, which can only be afforded at a few locations. The economy of operating a test centre also should be considered while designing the network.

Companies like Bosch, which produces power tools, used to fix sensors so that it will give an idea that whether the motors inside the tool are worth remanufacturing or not. This idea definitely helps the company to reduce costs.

Reprocessing and Recycling

Often, the reprocessing stage requires the highest investments within reverse logistics network. The process involves disassembly, repair work, reuse in new products and re-assembly. The critical issues involved are how to reduce the uncertainty in the supply of products to be manufactured, how to ensure a sustainable volume of products to be manufactured and whether to outsource remanufacturing (open-loop system) (Figure 7.6) or to integrate with existing operation (closed-loop system) (Figure 7.5).

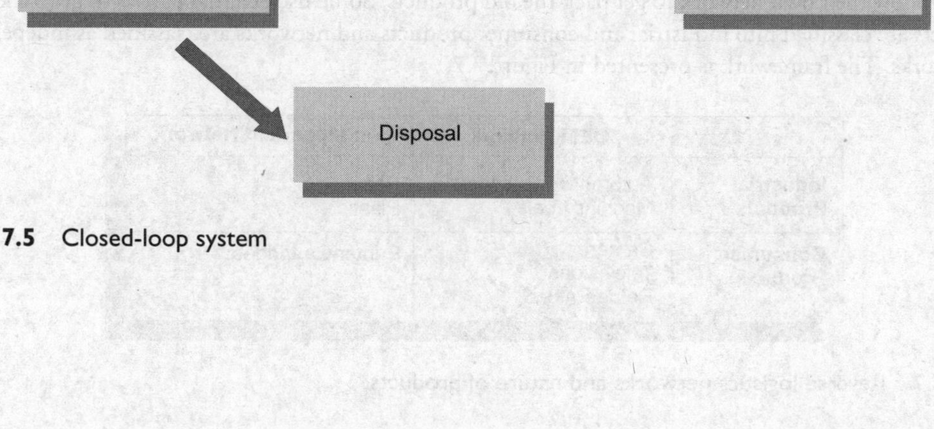

FIGURE 7.5 Closed-loop system

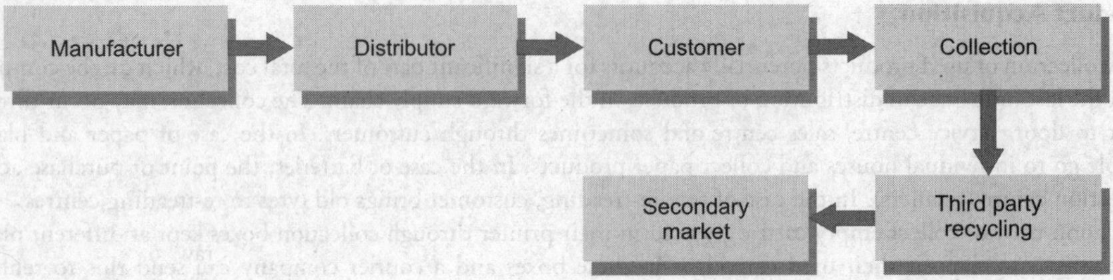

FIGURE 7.6 Open-loop system

Role of Forward Supply Chain in Collection

Recycling can often be described as an open-loop system, i.e. the products do not return to the original manufacturer but will be used in other industries. In this case, possibility of integration of forward and reverse networks is scant as the actors differ in both channels (e.g. paper recycling). Remanufacturing and reuse often leads to a closed-loop system. Here the used products are returned to original producers. The remanufacturing or recycling operation is completed and components and products are again reused. (e.g. Kodak single use cameras).

Reverse logistics may take place either through the original network directly using traditional middleman or through specialised logistical providers. Even if the same actors are involved, integration of forward and reverse distribution may be difficult; at the routing level, since collection and delivery may require different handling.

There is a high degree of uncertainty in supply in terms of both quality and quantity of used products, returned by consumers. High quality products may justify higher transportation costs and thus more centralised network structure, whereas extensive transportation of low value products is uneconomical.

Some researchers in this field addressed the issue of procurement of new components for recyclable products in the context of Kodak's single use cameras. Customers take the used cameras to a photo-finishing laboratory, where the film is taken out and processed. The laboratories receive a rebate for each used camera they subsequently return to Kodak. The reusable parts (the circuit board, plastic body and lens aperture) of the returned cameras are put back into production after inspection. Since, there is an uncertainty involved in return of cameras, the researchers developed a closed loop queuing network to find an ordering policy for the procurement of new components that minimises the total expected procurement, inventory holding and lost sales cost.

A Framework for Networks and Products

Based on case studies and comparing network ownership and type of products, a framework was developed. Some companies follow their own network to get back the old products. Some use external parties to get back products. The products are classified into industrial and consumer products and networks are classified as independent and OEM networks. The framework is presented in Figure 7.7.

	OEM Network	**Independent Network**
Industrial Products	Automotive Batteries Machine Tools	Paper Plastic
Consumer Products	Cameras Televisions Refrigerators	Printer Cartridges

FIGURE 7.7 Reverse logistics networks and nature of products

Reverse Supply Chain Networks

The reverse logistics or reverse supply chain is an issue that has received growing attention in the last decades, due to occurrence and simultaneity of several situations. On one hand, there is a concern about environmental matters, sustainable development and increasing level of state legislation with respect to environment. On the other hand, business opportunities are emerging out resulting from recycling, remanufacturing and reuse of components. Many organisations save money on usage of remanufactured and recycled products.

The reverse logistics is a process of planning, implementing and controlling flows of raw materials, in process inventory and finished goods from a manufacturing, distribution or use point to a point of recovery or point of proper disposal. Reverse supply chain or reverse logistics is the series of activities required to retrieve a used product from a customer and dispose of it properly or reuse it. And for a growing number of manufacturers, in industries ranging from carpets to computers, reverse supply chain networks are becoming an essential part of business.

In reverse supply chain networks, the major facilities considered are collection centres, warehouses, remanufacturing or recycling plants and proper disposal places. There are many research papers, related to design of independent reverse supply chain networks and researchers have used a variety of mathematical tools for analysis and design of networks. Basically, these networks are independent of forward networks and are operated separately to handle old product collection and remanufacturing. Copiers, electronic scrap, sand for recycling, refrigerators and cameras are some of the cases, where products are handled through independent reverse supply chain networks.

Integrated Supply Chain Networks

A major issue in reverse logistics system is the question of how forward and reverse channels or networks should be integrated. The role of existing forward system and its facilities in collection and logistics process of old products is to be explored. The network configuration may be requiring some changes due to reverse collection and logistics process. The redesign of existing network by considering the reverse flow and the location of new facilities is to be researched further. A few literatures were available dealing with this problem of integration and these networks are called closed-loop supply chains. A careful study of literature reveals that most of the studies on **closed-loop supply chains** deal with networks where the returned products are reaching the manufacturer. Moreover, these studies pertain to cases where the organisation concerned is also involved in remanufacturing and redistribution of refurbished products.

Even though various alternatives are given in the literature to handle reverse flow of products, the comparison analysis of different network configurations for both forward and reverse logistics is lacking in the literature. A special category of supply chain networks emerges out of the investigation. In this, forward supply chain network facilities are used for collection and storage of old products but the collected old products are not reaching the original manufacturers. Instead, these are routed to third party remanufactures, which buy the old products from the organisations. It means the reverse flow products partially use the existing network before reaching the third party facility. This type of network is referred to as **bi-directional open-loop supply chain networks (BDOLSCN)**. In such situations, given the potential location of external recycling plants, it may not be always economical to operate reverse collection process with the existing forward distribution network of facilities.

Sustainable Society and Environment

In 1970s and 1980s, when an Indian public sector company was able to set up a plant somewhere, before starting the work of the plant, they completed the community facilities required for its employees like residential colony, hospitals, schools, etc. These facilities were also extended to immediate community near the plant. This improves overall well-being of the society and hence conducive environment for the plant as well as for people.

The above was also true with respect to some private organisations like Tata Group in India. With the growth of globalsation, products are now produced piece by piece in several countries to be shipped to their final market, people need to commute long distances for work. Healthy communities depend on healthy business and vice versa.

The social and community sustainability can be enhanced through corporate social responsibility (CSR) activities. This can be multi-fold and make the organisation water positive, emission neutral, energy neutral and cultural and society positive. These activities make the organisation more sustainable and also create synergy and harmony between the organisation and its environment, the immediate community and nature.

Sustainable Supply Chain

A supply chain is a network of individual enterprises and facilities functioning continuously to facilitate the transformation and movement of products and services of different forms from suppliers to customers. It exists and operates to satisfy the demand of customers. A supply chain comprises a set of suppliers, a manufacturing plant or a set of plants, distributors, retailers and customers. These entities are mostly separate enterprises with or without their own facilities like storage, service and manufacturing. These entities are connected by three flows of goods, money and information. Product flows are facilitated by third parties like transporters and warehouse operators who are indirectly involved in a supply chain process.

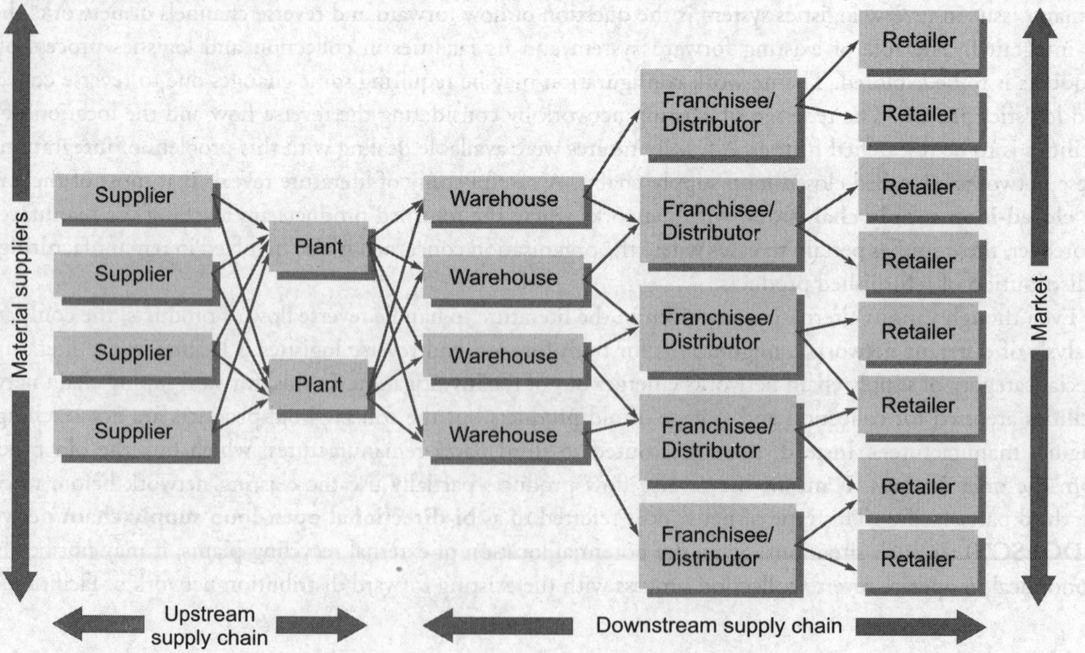

FIGURE 7.8 Supply chain network

When movement of goods takes place in a supply chain, the role of transportation and storage cannot be ruled out. The different modes of transportation are used across a supply chain. The pollution generated by cargo transport vehicles like ships, trucks, trains and airplanes is enormous and hence, there is a need to reduce this pollution. To make it a more sustainable supply chain, the activities of transportation and warehousing are to be made more sustainable.

Transportation and Sustainability

With supply chains becoming increasingly global, freight transport disproportionately outgrew economic development over the last decade. This can be related to offshoring production and services and further specialisation in supply chains leading to increase in international trade. It is important to remember that transportation is the largest energy consumer and also a major polluter of air in the supply chain.

The impact of transportation of cargo on land, rail or air has some externalities other than air and water pollution and greenhouse gas emission.

(i) *Noise*: The traffic noise measured in decibel levels is causing a lot of health problems to people. The social cost from traffic noise pollution is estimated at 40 billion euros in Europe alone. A reduction in noise can be achieved through better design of tyres, roads and engines. A strong regulation is required to reduce noise pollution in transportation.

(ii) *Accidents*: Road freight transport vehicles share roads and highways with other road traffic, cyclists and pedestrians and are therefore, more at risk of being involved in accidents than rail or water transport. Due to heavy weight of transport vehicles, the fatal rate is very high. The casualty rate varies from country to country due to road safety and vehicle maintenance standards, age of vehicles, etc. When electric vehicles replace ordinary fuel based vehicles, a new dimension on safety emerges due to low noise of these electric vehicles and hence, many road users may not notice these vehicles due to low noise.

Strategies to Reduce Environmental Impact of Freight Transport

The selection of transport mode and resulting emission can vary significantly between different circumstances. Depending on the location of different supply chain facilities like supplier plant, manufacturing plant, sea ports and distribution centres, the strategies for sustainability in the case of freight transportation vary widely. In the following paragraphs, we introduce the strategic approach to reduce emissions in supply chains.

Change of transport mode: In India, freight are transported predominantly by road transport irrespective of distance. Inland waterways are limited and under developed. Indian railways does not equip itself to handle large volume. But in future, it possibly changes for good. The Government of India plans to have freight corridors in Indian Railways so that separate lines can be dedicated for freight transportation. It is also motivating organisations to use sea routes for transporting bulk goods and cargo within countries, from Chennai to Mumbai and Cochin. In that case, organisations should look for alternatives to reduce emission and cost. Containerised transportation and multi-modal transportation will bring more uniform standards in freight transportation which will reduce cost and polluting emission.

Reduction freight transportation: Much of the increase in emission from freight transport is caused by globalisation and international trade. Local manufacturing and de-centralised manufacturing will reduce transportation of freight to a large extent and emission can happen only from manufacturing while less emission will occur from transportation. This means production should be closer to consumption or market and freight transportation can be minimised with local sourcing. Labour may be costlier in some locations but this can be more than compensated by reduction in transportation, lead time, inventory, uncertainty and risk in the supply chains.

Reduction in emission from current mode of transportation: Better maintenance of vehicles leads to better fuel efficiency and it results in reduced emission. Similarly, right load on the vehicle improves performance of the vehicle and reduces emission.

Alternative fuels: Some of the alternative fuels available with less emissions are compressed natural gas (CNG), bio-fuels, and liquified natural gas (LNG). The engines need to be modified accordingly and today truck manufacturers already brought out new vehicles with modified engines. Electric vehicles are going to be the future and hence, carbon emission may come down in cities drastically. But emission might occur somewhere else due to generation of electricity.

Information technology and emission reduction in freight transportation: Information technology can be deployed in freight transportation to reduce emission. Optimisation software helps in developing better routing and scheduling of vehicles in a logistics network system. Vehicle tracking system (VTS) connects the vehicles with the centralised offices which helps in tracking vehicle, online warnings of motorway congestion and suggesting alternative routes. It also helps in monitoring drivers and controlling them. Online platforms help freight companies and truck owners to get return loads so that vehicle utilisation improves dramatically.

Sustainable Warehousing

The World Economic Forum (2009) estimates that about 13 per cent of all supply chain emissions stem from logistics buildings. Despite management initiatives like 'just-in-time' and other inventory reductions in modern supply chain, warehouses are found everywhere in the supply chain. The environmental effect of warehousing consists of two levels, the emission from the construction of warehouse and the operational emission.

The most widely practised popular standards for assessing the sustainability of warehouse design are LEED, the Leadership in Energy and Environmental Design framework from the US green building council and BREEAM, the Building Research Establishment Environmental Assessment Method from the Building Research Establishment (BRE) based in the UK. Both schemes rate warehouses on sustainability by awarding points in several weighted categories. For example, LEED categorises warehouses sustainability from 'certified' to 'platinum'. It suggests the following weighted factors for warehouse sustainability:

- Water efficiency
- Material and resources
- Indoor environmental quality
- Sustainable sites
- Energy and atmosphere

Sustainable activities as prescribed by any certification assessors can be implemented by warehouses to reduce emission and become more sustainable.

SUMMARY

The link between operations and sustainability is addressed at two levels. First at organisation level, how operations strategy can contribute to organisation strategy on sustainability of business in the long run. At second stage, how operations strategy can contribute to sustainability of environment, resources of all kinds, social and cultural systems as well as economic development. This is highly related to definition given by Brundtland. In the first level, the competitive priorities of operations are linked to competitive advantage. The process involved in sustainable alignment where the resources are matched with market dynamic requirements is explained by connecting to competitive priorities of operations. The new approaches of competitiveness like TQM, JIT and TOC are also explained. In the second level, the link between operations and three types of sustainability, namely environmental, social and economic sustainability, is addressed in detail. The sustainability dimensions are discussed in association with operations functions—sourcing, internal operations, consumption, disposal and reverse supply chains, society and supply chains.

Key Terms

Sustainability: Brundtland defined sustainable development as, "Meeting the needs of the present without compromising the ability of future generations to meet their own needs". This relates to sustainability of environment, resources of all kinds, social and cultural systems as well as economic development.

Competitive advantage: Competitive advantage means sustainable competency in the market enjoyed by organisation which competitors lack.

Order qualifiers: These are set of attributes that customers and users expect in a product or service. If any of these are missing, customers will not consider the product for buying. These are minimum requirements for a service or a product to be considered.

Order winners: These are attributes above the order qualifiers which motivate the customers to buy the product. These attributes help brands and companies to differentiate their offerings from competitors.

Sustainable alignment: The process of continually reconciling operational resources with market dynamic requirements is called sustainable alignment.

TQM: A process for managing quality; it must be a continuous way of life; a philosophy of perpetual improvement in everything we do.

Theory of constraints: The management philosophy where production is scheduled based on bottleneck capacity.

Economic sustainability: Sustainability in terms of profit, market share and shareholders value is called economic sustainability.

Environmental sustainability: It refers to the capability of the organisation to produce products and services without compromising the natural systems and living beings.

Social sustainability: It deals with choices made by organisations that will affect current and future generations to live a healthy life.

CONCEPT REVIEW QUESTIONS

1. What are the two levels of sustainability?
2. Explain the competitive priorities of operations.
3. Give an account of market challenges faced by Indian organisations.
4. Explain sustainable alignment in the context of operations strategy.
5. Explain how to achieve sustainable alignment over time.
6. Explain the role of TQM in operations strategy.
7. Explain the role of JIT and lean practices in operations strategy.
8. Explain the role of theory of constraints (TOC) in operations strategy.
9. How are sustainable initiatives challenged by external factors?
10. What are the drivers of sustainable procurement?
11. Explain the procedure in creating a sustainable procurement.
12. List and explain strategies involved in sustainable internal operations.
13. Explain the role of reverse supply chain in sustainability road path.
14. Enumerate the steps involved in reverse logistics network.
15. What are the major strategies in reverse supply chain?
16. Relate sustainability with freight transportation and how sustainability can be practised in warehousing?

CRITICAL THINKING QUESTIONS

1. As an individual, how do you practise sustainability at household level?
2. Consider a service organisation like a hospital. Evaluate a hospital on sustainable factors by

developing a suitable scaling and evaluation method.

3. Take one common waste product like PET bottles, plastics, paper or metal parts. Study the reverse logistics network involved in recycling of these products. Map the reverse supply chain with partners and stakeholders.
4. Collect five different sustainability reports of five different companies and compare their performance.

PROJECT ASSIGNMENTS

1. Do you know any organisations that practise reverse supply chain? Select one of them, study its operation, map its reverse supply chain and explain how the company's strategy helps it in terms of resources and competitive advantage.
2. With slowdown in globalisation and increase in localisation, how do operations perform against environmental sustainability? By moving production closer to market (from China to USA or Mexico), what implications will it have on sustainability? Critically examine with examples.

REFERENCES

1. Barros, A. I., Dekker, R. and Scholten, V. (1996), "A two level network for recycling sand: A case study"- Econometric Institute Report Series 9673/A. Erasmus University Rotterdam, The Netherlands.
2. Beamon, B. M. and Fernandes, C. (2004), "Supply-chain network configuration for product recovery", *Production Planning and Control*, Vol. 15, No. 3, pp. 270-281.
3. http://sustainabilityreport.larsentoubro.com/CS-WaterPositiveCampuses.asp.
4. Bernon, M. and Cullen, J. (2007), "An integrated approach to managing reverse logistics", *International Journal of Logistics: Research and Applications*, Vol. 10, No. 1, pp. 41-56.
5. De Britto, M. P., Dekker, R. and Flapper, S. D. P. (2003), "Reverse logistics-a review of case studies", ERIM report series-ERS-2003-012-LIS.
6. Dupont (2001), Press Release, June 6.
7. Fleischmann, M. (2003), "Reverse logistics network structures and design- a chapter" in Guide, V. D .R., Jr and Van Wassenhove, L. N (2003) "Business aspects of closed-loop supply chains", Carnegie Mellon Univ Press.
8. L. N. (1997), "Quantitative models for Reverse Logistics: A review", *European Journal of Operational Research*, Vol. 103, pp. 1-17.
9. Flesichmann, M., Beullens, P., Bloemhaf-Ruwaard, J. M. and Van Wassenhove, L. N. (2001), "The impact of product recovery on Logistics network design", *Production and Operations Management*, Vol. 10, pp. 156-173.
10. Guide, V. D. R. Jr. and Van Wassenhove, L. N. (2000), "Closed-loop supply chains", *INSEAD Working paper*, 2000/75/TM/CIMSO/15.
11. Guide, V. D. R. Jr. and Van Wassenhove, L. N. (2002), "The reverse supply chain", *Harvard Business Review*, Vol. 80, Feb. 2002, pp. 25-26.
12. Spengler, T., Ploog, M. and Schroter, M. (2003), "Integrated planning of acquisition, disassembly and bulk recycling: A case study on electronic scrap recovery", OR Spectrum, Vol. 25, pp. 413-442.
13. Spengler, T., Puchert, H., Penkuhn, T. and Rentz, O. (1997) "Environmental integrated production and recycling management", *European Journal of Operational Research*, Vol. 97, pp. 308-326.
14. Grant, David B., Trautrins , Alexander and Wong, Chee Yew (2013). "Sustainable Logistics and Supply Chain Management", Kogan Page.
15. Apte, Suhas and Sheth, Jagadish N. (2016). "The Sustainability Edge", University of Toronto Press.

CHAPTER

8

Strategic Resource Management

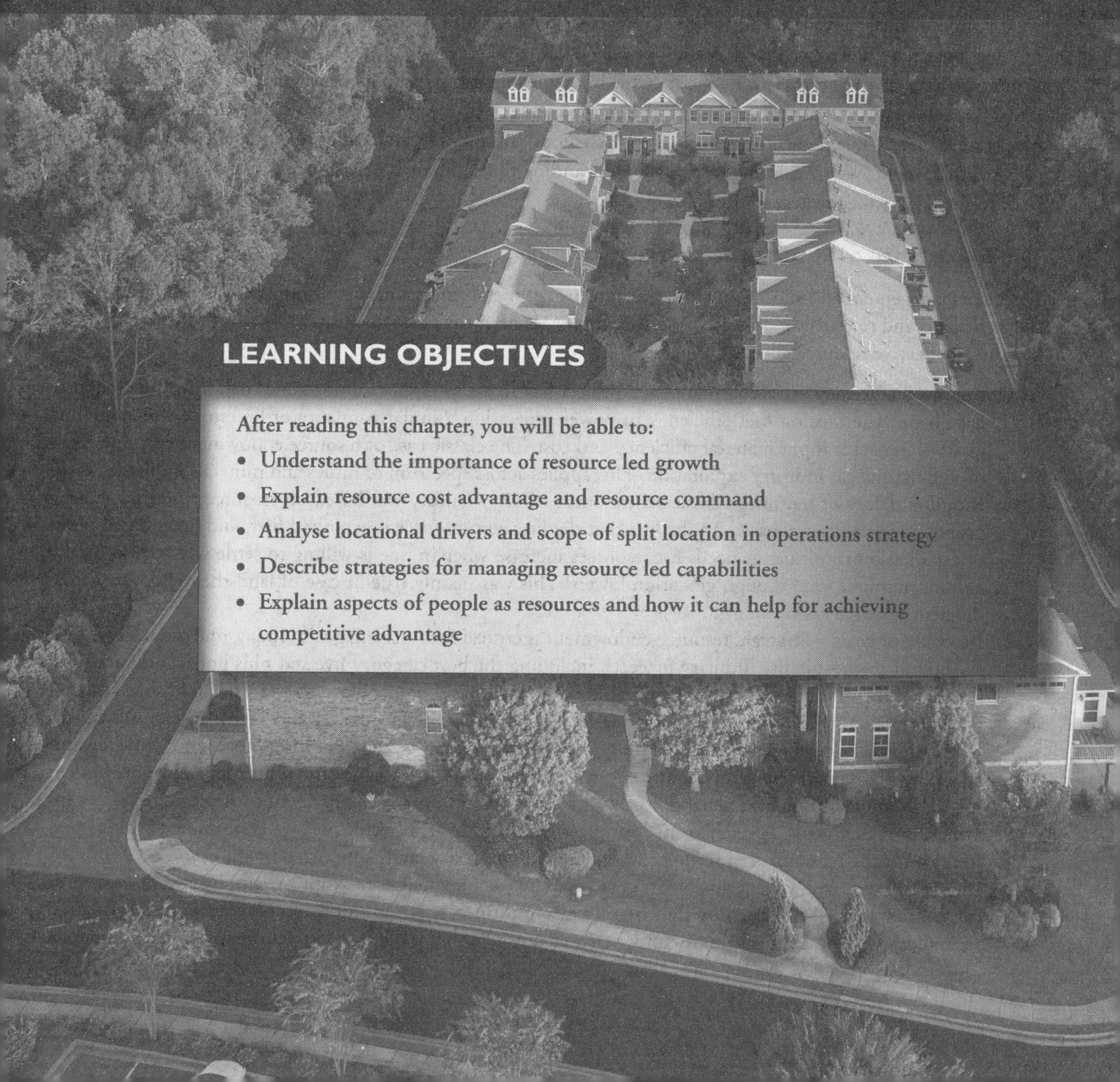

LEARNING OBJECTIVES

After reading this chapter, you will be able to:

- Understand the importance of resource led growth
- Explain resource cost advantage and resource command
- Analyse locational drivers and scope of split location in operations strategy
- Describe strategies for managing resource led capabilities
- Explain aspects of people as resources and how it can help for achieving competitive advantage

INTRODUCTION

Strategy is concerned with inter-connecting an organisation's resources and capabilities to the market and external opportunities that arise from the external to the organisation. The interface between strategy and internal resources become more advantageous for organisations while focus is on external market forces. As it is known that external market and industry environment have become more unstable, internal resources and capabilities become the source of competitive advantage.

Resource based theory argues that the possession of strategic resources gives an organisation a huge opportunity to gain competitive advantage (CA) over its competitors. These competitive advantages result in more profits and better enhancement of shareholders' value. A strategic resource is an asset that is valuable, rare, difficult to imitate and non-substitutable. These resources can provide capabilities to the organisations. Resources refer to what organisation owns, whereas capabilities refer to what it can do with resources.

An equal strategic exercise for success is not only owning these resources but how to allocate and utilise them. When it comes to the organisation, the focus is on achieving goals, primarily growth goals. But as a business leader, the main focus must be on having the right resources to support these goals. Allocating resources is a strategic exercise. While there is no control over the amount of resources to be allocated, there is control over how to best utilise them. When working towards understanding the company's needs, it can be pinpointed where the resources will have the greatest impact.

The Importance of Strategic Resource Allocation

Resource management and allocation is a strategic aspect of the business with major impact. The business requires the right tools and resources to succeed, and the employees need the same to effectively perform their jobs. Some benefits of effective resource allocation include:

1. Improved efficiency – If a thermal power project has access to higher caloric value coal, it would obviously have better combustion fuel efficiency in power generation. Similarly, quality of limestone from the lime quarry can decide input material efficiency and cost. The classic case of resource endowment efficiency is in oil and natural gas industry exploration. This applies across spectrum of mines and minerals industry. David Ricardo's theory of rent, the Classical Economist of 18th Century was based on resource efficiency and he propounded the theory based on the fact that the first best resource is exploited first, and down rated order of exploitation continues as needs for resources increase wherein one is willing to settle with economically efficient resource even though gradation lowers! This was mainly true in case of land then and now across different resource endowments.
2. Reaching of goals – Strategic resource endowment is critical for reaching goals. Today, one can observe that the best of the hospitality industry projects, including the best category five star plus hotels, are successful because of their location. It may be accessible easily from travel points like airports, central business district wherein business meetings are held or delegates to hotel are being invited and many others. Obviously, when a property developer has such a plot, one can nurture reasonably ambitious goals and work towards achieving the same. The same is true for any other service like healthcare, education and government service. Manufacturing also benefits reaching goals with appropriate deployment of strategic resources for achieving higher goals. A sugar plant in India which is located in fertile and water abundant regions performs much better compared to those which are located in dry lands supported by monsoon.
3. Improved employee satisfaction – Strategic resource deployment can improve employee satisfaction as capabilities are well-nurtured by right resource commitments. For example, employees in an information technology development centre will find increased satisfaction if it is located in a cluster of similar companies

and knowledge institutions wherein employees can cross learn and improve their efficiency. It naturally helps them to contribute better.

Such kind of opportunities provide scope for better employee retention. It is commonly believed that cluster location which is rather strategically developed by corporate and policy makers ensures long tenures of employees. They also find it comfortable if other auxiliary requirements like community living, healthcare and education institutions are available. This leads to next advantage of reduced stress to employees. One can see this not only in the service sector but also in manufacturing.

4. Less time spent on projects – This is another significant advantage on strategic resource allocation especially for project management. Most successful projects require appropriate and timely allocation of resources. Typically, under project conditions, resource competitiveness is high. Some of the resources are likely to be in high demand. This is especially true of critical manpower and equipment. It may be useful at times even to create redundancy of such critical resources in a project mode. For example, we can look at a situation wherein a company makes a strategic move of buying out a manufacturing plant away from domestic country. In such case, integration of the plant operations can happen on project mode wherein key managerial resources are deputed for integration of business. Many times, senior management resources are provided with redundant time and cost provisions so that the delay is avoided. Similarly, things happen in scientific research, new product development, especially in auto, pharmaceuticals and high technology areas like robotics. As these projects are sensitive to time to reach market, one needs to be sensitive to resource allocation.

However, properly allocating resources is often easier said than done. Every day, CEOs are faced with the same dilemma— How should resources be used within the company?

Ongoing Resource Allocation as a Best Practice

When you take the time to understand your company and its resource needs, you become well-positioned to support growth. However, don't get too comfortable. While you may have the right resources in place presently, you most likely will need to reassess them later as you move towards your goals and set ones. A study by McKinsey found that the organisations that allocated resources and reallocated resources gained 30 per cent higher total returns to its shareholders yearly.

Early Stage Resource Allocation—When you're just starting out, your resources are likely more focussed on proper allocation of funding, talent acquisition to fill key roles, and functions like research and development.

Growth Stage Resource Allocation—Over time, your company will achieve its growth goals and you'll set new ones. At this stage, your resource needs will shift to things, such as additional employees, training tools, implementations of processes and procedures, and production facilities and equipment.

End Stage Resource Allocation—Whether you're preparing to take your company public, sell your business, or take part in a merger or acquisition, you will – once again – need to re-evaluate your resources. This time, your resource needs may include advisors to guide you through the process, or new or additional technology and tools to manage investor relations.

No matter the stage of your business you're likely to be faced with requests from department leaders for new software, improved equipment or additional staff members. How do you determine where your resources (whether capital or people) should be used to maximise efficiency and maintain employee "happiness"?

This chapter deals with the resources, their classifications and related capabilities in detail. It will also provide frameworks on how these resources should be deployed and re-deployed overtime to have a sustainable competitive advantage.

RESOURCE LED GROWTH

In most of the organisations, some kind of resources drive growth apart from market dynamics. Resources determine cost as well as competitive advantage. They are tangible and intangible assets of a firm. The tangible resources include factories, products and intangible include reputation, brand and intellectual property rights and people and leadership skills, so on.

Capabilities: It is a subset of resources that enables a firm to take full advantage of other resources. Resources are not productive on their own. A brain surgeon is close to useless without a radiologist, anaesthetist, nurses, surgical instruments, imaging equipment, and a host of other resources. Capability results from combination of resources and its proportionate deployment wherever required. To perform a task, a team of resources must work together. An organisational capability is a "firm's capacity to deploy resources for a desired end result." A cement manufacturer acquired a major limestone mine and made investment in a conveyor system to move minerals to the plant without any break, leading to competitive advantage for the company. Surprisingly, the conveyor was built across a rough terrain. The terms, capability and competence, are used interchangeably which are the application of resources.

The organisation's resources are classified as follows:

TANGIBLE

(a) Financial (cash, securities, borrowing capacity)
(b) Physical (plant, equipment, land, mineral reserves)

INTANGIBLE

(a) Technology (patents, copyrights, trade secrets)
(b) Reputation (brands, relationships)
(c) Culture

HUMAN

(a) Skills/knowhow,
(b) Capacity for communication and collaboration
(c) Motivation

TANGIBLE RESOURCES: These are physical assets owned by an organisation and provide some advantages. These include buildings, warehouses and their locations, mines, ports and their locations. The primary purpose of resource analysis is not to value a company's assets, but to understand their potential for creating competitive advantage. Information that an airline possesses tangible fixed assets with a book value of $8 billion is of little use in assessing their strategic value. To assess an airline's ability to compete effectively in the world airline industry, we need to know about the composition of these assets, the location of land and buildings, the types of plane and their age, and so on. The extent of achieving return on capital employed will determine how effectively the assets are utilised as well as how good they are to attract further resources. Tangible resources are more relevant for manufacturing operations and service operations. These resources drive most of the cost and hence need to be utilised and allocated properly.

INTANGIBLE RESOURCES: For most organisations, intangible resources are more valuable than tangible resources. It includes intellectual, technological and reputation resources. Brand names and other trademarks are a form of reputational asset, their value is in the confidence they instil in customers. For example, the brand TATA is a reputed one in India and spread across different categories of products and services. This value is indirectly reflected in the premium price that customers are willing to pay for the branded product over that for an unbranded and the trust shown by customers on brand. Brand value (or "brand equity") can be estimated by taking the price premium attributable to a brand, multiplying it by the brand's annual sales volume, then calculating the present value of this revenue stream.

The value of a company's brands can be enhanced by extending the product/market scope over which the company markets those brands. For example, the company ITC in India slowly moved away from tobacco products to consumer products but it extended the ITC brand to all categories and enjoys customer trust.

Like reputation, technology is an intangible resource whose value is not evident from most companies' balance sheets. Intellectual property includes patents, copyrights, trademarks, etc. Over the past 25 years, companies have become more attentive to the value of their intellectual property. For some companies, their ownership of intellectual property is a key source of their market value. Process technology, customer focussed technology and service technologies help many organisations to compete in the market. In information technology area, many retailers and manufacturers developed their own IT systems and solutions which make them more competitive.

Human Resources

The human resources of the firm are the talent, strengths, skill set and effort offered by its employees. These are not appearing on corporate balance sheets for the reason that people are not assets owned by organisations but they offer their services under employment contracts. Identifying and motivating human talents within an organisation is complex and hard. Human resource has various dimensions and organisation must understand and appreciate this diversity of dimensions. It needs to be appraised on various dimensions like attitude, motivation level, learning capacity and potential for collaboration apart from formal education, experience and training. The tools like competency mapping identifies an individual's strengths and weaknesses. The aim is to enable the person to better understand himself or herself and to point out where career development efforts need to be directed. Emotional intelligence also plays an important role in human resources.

Culture: Culture is the values and behaviours that contribute to the unique social and psychological environment of an organisation. It relates to an organisation's values, traditions and social norms. Organisational culture includes an organisation's expectations, experiences, philosophy, and values that hold it together, and is expressed in its self-image, inner workings, interactions with the outside world, and future expectations. It is based on shared attitudes, beliefs, customs, and written and unwritten rules that have been developed over time and are considered valid. Culture is identified as one of the key resources for organisation as it is related to performance of human resources. It also means the following.

(1) The ways in which the organisation conducts its business, treats its employees, customers, and the wider community,
(2) The extent to which freedom is allowed in decision making, developing new ideas, and personal expression,
(3) How power and information flow through its hierarchy, and
(4) How committed the employees are towards collective objectives.

It affects the organisation's productivity and performance, and provides guidelines on customer care and service, product quality and safety, attendance and punctuality, and concern for the environment.

In operations, tangible resources provide a lot of cost advantage for the organisation, while intangible resources like technology and human resources also play a major role in gaining competitive advantage.

Thus, resources led growth for competitive advantage is a desirable and sought after competitive phenomenon. Tiruppur is a leading hosieries and apparel exporter and domestic market supplier in India. It forms a cluster of large number of small and medium scale industries that are into conversion of cloth to apparel for international brands. The resource advantage for this cluster includes entrepreneurial skills of locals; access to knowledge and techniques towards cotton industries from nearby city, namely Coimbatore; labour availability and cluster initiative created by trade agencies and Government of India for nurturing growth.

Such resources have led for growth of firms giving advantage in operations like setting up value chain linkages and synchronising operations strategic perspectives and market requirements.

RESOURCE COST ADVANTAGE AND RESOURCE COMMAND

According to Porter, cost advantage is one of the three types of competitive advantage that a firm may possess. Cost is also equally important to vitalise differentiation strategy. The cost behaviour is complex to understand and individual process has linkages that affect the cost.

The value chain provides the basic approach to cost analysis. Each activity in the value chain involves both operating costs and assets in the form of fixed assets and working capital. Raw materials and purchased inputs make up a part of the cost of every value added process. The need to assign fixed assets to value chain activities reflects on the fact that the quantum of assets in an activity and utilisation of assets add to the activity's cost.

Organisation's assets like factories, warehouses, inventory, and transportation facilities are related to tangible operations related resources. These resources command competitive advantage for the firm in many ways, especially through cost benefits. According to Porter, ten major cost drivers determine the cost behaviour of value chain activities—economies of scale, learning, the pattern of capacity utilisation, linkages, interrelationships, integration, timing, discretionary policies, location and institutional factors. These cost drivers are mostly under the control of the organisation and produce long-term advantages for organisation.

These cost drivers which are connected to internal resources need to be understood for gaining competitive advantage and command over resources. Most of the tangible resources are related to operations and supply chain activities. These resources need to be analysed in terms of cost drivers to understand how each resource can be used strategically for gaining competitive advantage. We will analyse the relevant cost drivers with respect to all physical resources.

Economies of Scale

Economies of scale arise from the ability to perform activities differently and more efficiently at a larger volume. Scale of operation of plants, warehouses, and ports determine the economies of scale benefits. The mining cost in an alumina mine decreases with the scale of operation. This means that per tonne processing cost for alumina for a large plant is less than that for a smaller plant as economies scale arises out of reduction in fixed cost over a large output which is created by capacity design.

This is different from capacity utilisation advantage which also gives similar result. Increasing capacity utilisation distributes the fixed cost of facilities over larger volume, while economy of scale implies that an activity operating at full capacity is more efficient at larger scale. Full capacity utilisation in a smaller plant is less economical than full capacity utilisation in a larger plant. Scale due to size is an important aspect and has natural influence on capacity utilisation. Linkage between economies of scale and capacity utilisation drive industry normal capacity of a plant or production or service unit. At the normal capacity of the plant, average cost production reaches the bottom of U shaped cost curve meaning that it achieves lowest cost of production for the given factor units. It is important to note here that the normal capacity of a plant in an industry changes mostly over time and mostly evolves for better. This could be because of technological advancement in production or operations. Typical example is of a cement industry in India which was less than 300,000 tonnes per annum in 70s and is now around 1.5 to 2 million tonnes per annum as of 2018. This shows that scale economies have moved almost five times in less than four decades. This was possible with standardisation of dry process of clinker manufacturing in Indian cement industry.

Economies of scale are not all equivalent. The relevant measure of scale varies among value processes and industry. For a global market, world wide scale is the relevant cost driver and for local market, national level scale is enough. Economies of scale in transportation depend on regional or local scale or sometimes on scale of the buyer. A transport operator achieves economies of scale and offers a discount to customer, if he also promises return load. The cost of a delivery to a given buyer often remains fixed irrespective of the volume making large buyers less costly to serve. Understanding how economies of scale affects cost requires an understanding of specific mechanisms and the measure of scale that is in alignment with the mechanisms.

A firm can influence not only the extent of economies of scale but also the type of scale that decides the cost. Acquiring large mines extracting minerals will improve economy of scale for an organisation in the aluminium and copper extracting sectors. But, some mineral deposits deplete rapidly in some mines and hence appropriate scale is required.

Learning

The cost of a process which is a value activity can decline with time due to learning and knowledge accumulation. Earlier, learning effect was more pronounced in labour intensive business. In contemporary business, learning is effective in knowledge based businesses and services. The cost can be reduced in the areas like scheduling, layout design, product design modifications, labour efficiency and better methods due to learning over time. Learning will also reduce cost of projects, construction of facilities, and warehouses. It can also be passed on to partner industry, which results in spill over effect and reduces cost. Through supply chain learnings, the best practices can be adopted by other supply chain partners across the supply network which will improve supply chain competitiveness. For example, Toyota learnings were implemented by its suppliers and hence resulted in a highly effective supply chain for Toyota.

Capacity Utilisation of Assets

When a process has substantial fixed cost associated with it, the cost of the process will be affected by capacity utilisation. Fixed costs create a penalty for underutilisation. Capacity utilisation of resources like factory, warehouses and service facilities, depends on seasonal, cyclical and other demand and supply fluctuations. So, the pattern of utilisation over the entire period in reference is the correct cost driver instead of utilisation at one point of time. Frequent changes in utilisation will increase cost rather than constant utilisation, though they both have the same average utilisation. Marketing policy choices of products, stock keeping units, marketing and distribution will determine utilisation.

Strategic operating decision in design, especially in certain process industry and assembly need to be sensitive towards the same. In a sugar factory, capacity variability can be handled up to 30 per cent and upwards by adjusting milling, clarification and condensation through vacuum pans as some of them can be by-passed during low requirement and augmented during peak by putting all the available facility into action. When it comes to automotive line, challenge will be there where they vary by increasing or decreasing working hours and number of shifts. One has to carefully design while setting a facility as it may have key impact on operating cost. Imagine a hotel which has variability in occupancy to be as wide as 60 per cent between peak and off demand. Cost management by adjusting capacity and saving some of the overheads will be critical for their viability.

Linkages with internal processes and supply chain activities

The resources used internally which drives cost are also influenced by other resource based processes internally and also external supply chain activities. Inbound logistics and operations are related and utilisation of trucks and vehicles inbound depends on scale of operation in the plant. The linkage between different resources should be studied and resource deployment should be done accordingly. Linkages with suppliers and downstream supply chain partners also determine the resource effectiveness. If a supplier follows vendor managed inventory (VMI) policy, and stocks inventory closer to plant, the deployment of resources in terms of warehouses and transportation will get reduced drastically.

Location of downstream partner like distributor's warehouse will determine outbound and packaging cost. The synergy effect in sharing of resources within the company and leveraging supply chain collaboration will greatly drive down resource cost.

Operating strategy has an immense role in enabling supply chain linkages. For example, a car manufacturing company has the benefit of Tier I companies supplying on VMI or milk run JIT basis around its factory, such as manufacturer will have a greater competitive advantage. Locational cluster helps such industry. There are certain firms who focus engaging third party and fourth party logistics service providers and also Importer on Record (IOR) service providers to enable synchronised supply chain activities.

Integration of value activities of resources

Each resource is used in some value adding processes. The level of vertical integration by putting different resources together drives cost. The company Ford used to have a complete vertically integrated complex plant to produce cars in the nineteenth century in Detroit. All value adding processes are highly integrated. In fashion retailing, Zara closely deploys all its resources and production is highly integrated. But, other fashion retailers mostly outsource production and deploy more resource on marketing and distribution. Perdue Foods is another example of integrated supply chain system.

Cement plants in India is another example for integrated value activities. The resources of mines, minerals, plants, grinding units and packaging all deployed at one place to leverage cost advantage.

Location of Facility Resources

The geographic location of resource facility can affect its cost as its location is relative to other value adding processes like assembly, mining, distribution centres and so on. Location determines the following costs.

- Inbound and outbound costs
- Material handling costs
- Customer service costs
- Labour costs
- Energy costs

The location also decides the mode of transport and customer service level in many industries. Right location of tangible resources and network of facilities improve the cost performance and increase customer service better.

LOCATION OF RESOURCES: FACILITIES AND SPLIT LOCATION

The number of production facilities as a part of resources is influenced by many factors like in-bound logistics and out-bound logistics cost, capital available but two simple metrics help managers to decide the optimal number of plants. Market-to-plant ratio and value density.

Market-to-plant ratio (MPR): This metrics gives economic viability of multiple production facilities and it is calculated as

MPR = (Global market demand for a product)/(Minimum efficient size of a production facility)

For example, if the market size for a company's product is two million units and minimum size of the plant is 500,000 units, then the MPR is four. An MPR close to one means that market demand is insufficient to support multiple facilities. MPR tends to be higher in stable, high demand, mature markets allowing multiple plants. For companies in high technology industry and growth oriented industries, it is closer to one.

Exhibit 8.1 Split locations in Indian Cement Industry

Traditionally, cement industry was close to lime query. Availability and allocation of mining rights were the deciding factor. This led to the traditional 'hub-and-spoke' model of manufacture of cement and sell on a radius of 600–700 kms depending upon rail and road connectivity. There is certain grinding mix material like fly ash or pozzolanic material that needs to be brought in for grinding along with clinker.

There are two kind of split locations for cement industry that became possible. First, companies decided to set up grinding units near the market, especially where cement demand is higher than supply. The objective is to be close to customer. Ramco Cements has the following grinding units:

1. Chengalpet - This grinding unit with a capacity of 0.5 MTPA is located in Kanchipuram district and was commissioned in May 2009. The plant is in close proximity to the Tamil Nadu customers, especially Chennai, which is well connected by road through NH-45 and by rail through main Chennai-to-Trichy broad gauge line.
2. Salem: This Grinding unit has an installed capacity of 1.6 MTPA. The unit was set-up and commissioned in 2009 with the objective of serving the markets of Salem and its surrounding areas.
3. Kolaghat, West Bengal: This unit, which commenced production in February 2010, has adopted the latest technology with sophisticated control equipment to ensure consistent quality of cement. It has a capacity of 0.95 MTPA. The plant is located in Kolaghat in the district of Purba Medinapur and is in close proximity to the customers of West Bengal, Assam and Orissa. The facility is well connected by road through NH-41 and NH-6 and by rail through the main Howrah-Kharagpur broad gauge line.

Second, companies choose to set up near power plant or any other material which may be required and its transportation to clinker plant can be avoided. Ramco has one such in Vizag. This grinding unit with a capacity of 0.95 MTPA is located near Visakhapatnam and was commissioned in March 2015. This plant is located just on NH 5 located between Yellamanchilli and Anakapally. The plant has close proximity to Vizag Steel Plant, Vizag Port, Gangavaram port and NTPC Simhadri Super Thermal Power Plant.

The reasons for opting split grinding units depend on the lesser transport cost, availability of manpower, and market demands. The advantage of split grinding unit is its adoptability for grinding special cements and supply to the customer whenever the need arises, by procuring suitable raw material.'

According to an industry source which sums up locational factor of cement, "In the last few years, we have seen the rise of separate grinding units. These require less space and lower investments. Hence, such projects are chosen by new entrants into the cement market who want to start making a presence quickly and with less risk. Grinding units are also put up near power plants where fly ash is available or near steel plants where slag is available. This reduces the cost of transporting raw material which can constitute 35-45 per cent of the PPC or PSC product. Split locations are expected to be on the rise near the consumption location. On the other hand, integrated units will find favour close to the limestone mines."

Thus, cement industry, like other mineral processing industries, is resource-oriented with limestone being its key ingredient (approximately 85 per cent). Hence, cemenet factories are located around limestone-rich belt. Logistics expense to cater to the diverse market from centralised source brings pressure on cost competitiveness. Splitting grinding closer to the market seems like an option.

Source: www.ramcocements.in accessed on 22 August 2019
http://www.indiancementreview.com/News.aspx?nId=ZpYTs-r3kAub88pDJroUatw==, accessed on 22 August 2019.

Value density: It means the relationship between a product's value and logistical costs associated with distribution. When a product is value dense, organisations have an incentive to centralise manufacturing, even MPR suggests otherwise. Alternatively, low value-density products offer incentives to de-centralise production with more plants. Low value-density products to be produced are closer to market to reduce the distribution and out-bound costs. Electronic and high-tech products are value dense and they are of high value. They are compact and easy to ship through distribution channels. Sometimes sensitive supply chains are shipped by air transportation.

Bulky or heavy products, such as cements and furniture are low value dense products. The transportation and warehousing costs are very high as they occupy large space in trucks as well as in warehouses. So, there is an incentive to locate production closer to market to reduce logistics cost.

Many resource based industry like cement, aluminium, coal based power plants, and iron and steel basically locate their integrated processing facility near natural resources like mines. This is due to high in-bound logistics cost and also due to nature of materials. But at the same time, products like cement have low value density and hence, the industry faces high cost of both in-bound and out-bound or distribution costs.

Split Location: In the case of cement industry in India, the total costs of in-bound and out-bound logistics are estimated to be around 25–35 per cent of price. To reduce costs of logistics, cement companies have followed a split location strategy in recent times. In cement business, clinker is manufactured near limestone quarries and is transported to distant grinding units, which are near customers' location. The concept of grinding unit is to source raw material for grinding locally with reduced logistic cost. This also reduces the cost due to economies of scale in transporting a large amount of clinkers to grinding units instead of cement bags to markets. This means that a part of the production takes place closer to market and this kind of locating one plant process at two places is called split location. This strategy saves a lot of money for production and also helps saving packaging costs. This also saves transport cost by transporting clinkers by rail which is cheaper than road transport in India.

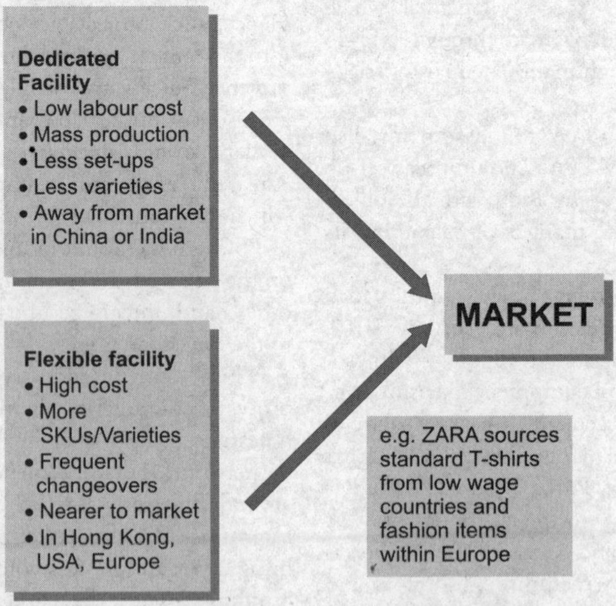

FIGURE 8.1 Dedicated facility vs flexible facility

FLEXIBLE FACILITY RESOURCES: The deployment of facility resources often helps many supply chains compete in the market. Many companies want to balance responsiveness to market with cost efficiency in operation and supply chains. Companies segment their products according to competency requirement and accordingly these products are produced. The products which are fashion oriented with short life cycle need to be produced closer to market with flexible production system. These flexible facilities feature quick changeover time and less lead time. Though cost-wise higher, these facilities can improve responsiveness of the supply chain and meet the demands of customers quickly. For stable demand items, a larger dedicated facility, may be away from market, is used by many organisations (Figure 8.1).

Thus, one may observe that there are different aspects like demand, resource endowments and technology impacting firms resources led growth.

STRATEGIES TO MANAGE RESOURCE LED CAPABILITIES

An organisation's capability is a firm's capacity to deploy resources for a desired outcome and resulting in a competitive advantage. Capability is synonymous with competence. A certain combination of various resources create distinct capabilities. For example, a dedicated production facility at offshore and a flexible facility near market give highly responsive competency for the company like ZARA. Another example may be a situation where R&D centre is close to production facility resulting in flexibility in new product development and hence time to market can be reduced.

To identify a firm's capabilities, functional analysis and value chain analysis should be conducted. A functional analysis brings out various capabilities in each function relative to other functions. A value chain analysis identifies distinct capabilities which add value to product or service which is the result of certain combination of resources.

Functional analysis reveals certain operations related capabilities like low cost production, speed and flexibility in operations, quick changeovers, quality practices, JIT, product design, lower inventory and so on. Value chain analysis results in certain competences in inbound and outbound logistics, scheduling of vehicles, routing and optimisation, and economies in transportation and distribution.

Capabilities can be categorised under different groups. Here, we have put two relevant groups for this discussion, namely operations capabilities and supply chain capabilities.

TABLE 8.1 Capabilities in operations and SCM

Operations Capabilities	Supply Chain Capabilities
Quick changeover	Close collaboration with suppliers
Just in time	Common components
Less lead time	Postponement capability
Economy of scale	Inbound cost
Split facility	Distribution network
Quality practices	Routing/Optimisation
TQM/Six Sigma	Co-location

There are two ways in which an organisation evolves capabilities.

Evolvement of capabilities by action: In many organisations, there are certain basic capabilities evolved over time by trial and error method . The integration of different resources like people coordinating with equipment, materials, technology and other resources in a production system evolved over time by practice. These kind of routine capabilities form basis of many organisations. Routinisation helps in translating directions and operating practices into capabilities.

Development of capabilities by resource integration: Some of the capabilities will be developed by integrating effort of various resources through learning and practice. Ikea, a Sweden based furniture retailer, uses modular design of furniture along with component level inventory to sell finished products with good service level. It also resulted in reduction in transportation cost and inventory cost.

APPRAISAL OF RESOURCES AND CAPABILITIES

The competitive advantage of a firm and its sustainability over a long period depends mostly on its resources and capabilities. Identifying and appraising resources and capabilities for competitive advantage is an important part of resource based strategy formulation. The appraisal process is based on three stage processes:

1. Establishing competitive advantage to resources and capabilities
2. Sustainability of competitive advantage with resources and capabilities
3. Allocation of returns to resources/capabilities

Establishment of Competitive Advantage

Resources and capabilities provide competitive advantage under certain conditions, namely scarcity and relevance. If a resource or capability is widely available in the industry, it may not bring competitive advantage of any form. For example, e-commerce companies are now promising same day delivery to compete in the market. But competitors also promise the same. So, the resources deployed for same day delivery do not provide long term competitive advantage. For example, a cement integrated plant located in coastal area of India, and near to a port, will enjoy sustainable competitive advantage for some period as transportation through sea is now allowed for in-land cement distribution. Competitors will find it difficult to copy and start a new plant in coastal areas in a short period of time. The resource or the capability must be unique and scarce so that it provides competitive advantage for the firm.

A capability must be relevant to modern market conditions. The direct to customer model of Dell with its customisation capability and supply chain capabilities was relevant during the period from 2002 to 2015. But, with change in market conditions, their capabilities have become threshold requirement where competition is also catching up, denying unique competency advantage for Dell. A resource or capability must be relevant to emerging market situations.

It may be useful to relate with hierarchy of competency that firms may have. A firm may have a core competency wherein its capability or competency gives advantage in reducing cost and is best among all its resources. For example, talent recruitment and retention at the shop floor may be a unique capability giving the firm a competitive advantage. However, other players in the industry may still possess such core competency and match competitive intensity. Distinctive competency is one which gives edge over competitors over a short duration as the firm has acquired a unique resource or capability and firms will take time to match the same. Third, unique competency is about ability of the firm to create an IP or trademark and protect it for a substantial period. This normally happens in knowledge industries and in case of products-based manufacturing like pharmaceuticals; high tech machinery and so on. Finally, strategic assets are those competencies which are confidential and difficult to reverse engineer. Later, they become intangible like KFC or beverage brands like Coke and Pepsi.

Sustainability of Competitive Advantage with Resources and Capabilities

The establishment of competitive advantage will not result in profits for long run. The competitive advantage need to sustain for longer period of time to make long term profit. Sustainable competitive advantage depends on durability, transferability and replicability of resources or capabilities.

Durability: Some resources are more durable and hence sustainable. Patents of technologies and processes give sustainable competitive advantage. Some resources like a capital equipment usage will be shortened due to technology change. Large capacity in a stable market provides sustainable competitive advantage.

Transferability: Many firms buy resources and capabilities if they want to imitate competitor's strategy. The ability to buy a resource or capability depends on its transferability—mobility of resources between firms. Some resources like raw materials, finance, and standard services are transferable and can be bought and sold with ease. Some resources not easily transferable either due to firm specific or their value declines on transfer.

Sources of immobility are:

- Resources with immobility: Natural resources like mines, large capital equipment, and some type of people may make it difficult for firms to acquire these resources without relocating themselves.
- Risk due to imperfect information on capability and resources: Imperfect information about quality and productivity of resources develops risk for buyers. This is true especially for human resources, where prospective employer do not have complete information about potential employee.
- Inter-Dependability of Resources: Some resources work better with home team and when it is bought by another company, it may not perform well due to change in team and its incompatibility.

Replicability: Capabilities sometimes can be copied easily by competitors. Processes, methods and technologies can be easily copied and hence, one needs to patent these to avoid losing competitive advantage. Complex processes, culture of an organisation and management style are most difficult to replicate. For example, Toyota Production System featuring some of the best practices of management was being adopted by many western companies but success rate is low.

Allocation of Returns to Competitive Advantages

Superior capabilities generate returns for the organisation. Normally credit should go to owner of that capability. But this is not always clear due to involvement of human resources in developing capabilities along with other resources of the organisation. Human capital intensive firm faces problems in mobility of this resource. The degree of dependency on human resources in developing operations capabilities and supply chain capabilities is relatively less and hence competitive advantage also remains with organisation for long time.

FORMULATION OF STRATEGY BASED ON RESOURCES AND CAPABILITIES

The following steps can be used for strategy formulation based on resources and capabilities:

1. Identify the strategic resources and capabilities
   The value chain analysis and functional analysis dealt in the previous section will provide the key resources and capabilities inside the organisation. These include manufacturing capabilities, new product development capabilities, lean supply chain management, a strong brand and so on.

2. Evaluation of resources and capabilities on its importance and strengths

   The criteria used in appraisal of resources and capabilities mentioned in the previous section can be used to find its importance. Some capabilities are common and fully diffused in the industry like car assembly techniques. Some capabilities are not available and totally outsourced like information technology and it does not pose any threat in terms of competition. Some resources are difficult to copy that are inbuilt in the organisation like organisation culture, global scale and less time to market.

   Further to grade one's strengths in capabilities, we need to look internally as well as externally assessing relative strengths. Internal focus should bring out profile of resources and capabilities along with their evidences on success and performance, consistency and also where it is not performing well. Benchmarking is a powerful and quantitative tool to assess the performance relative to competitors. It provides a systemic framework where one can compare any functions and processes with global competitors.

3. Developing strategy implications

   Strategic implications are twofold, How to leverage strengths, resources and capabilities to formulate competitive advantage in the market? and How to improve weaknesses and reduce its effect and how to convert weaknesses into strengths in some markets? One should work on strengths to differentiate one's brand, services and company by leveraging these resources and capabilities. The Indian company, ITC was strong in distribution of tobacco products in India over four decades. Later, when market for tobacco products started declining, the company made a smart move by entering into consumer goods market including agro based products and started leveraging the traditional distribution network and became successful.

Different companies within an industry have different unique capabilities resulting in differentiation of strategies within industry.

DEVELOPMENT OF RESOURCES AND CAPABILITIES

Resources are required to develop capabilities. Operations resources are expensive like factories and technologies and hence acquiring or developing resources needs to be done with precautions. Resources can be developed over a period of time and the most important example is human resources. With proper training and motivation, human resources can acquire skills and knowledge which transform into capabilities. Resources can also be acquired by merger and acquisition of other organisation. Cement companies acquire another company to get more resources of plants, mines and markets.

The relationship between resources and capabilities is complex and non-linear. More resources do not mean more capabilities. The organisation's ability to leverage its resources determines capabilities. Resources can be leveraged in the following ways.

- Concentrating resources: Converging most of the resources on a few clearly defined objectives; focussing efforts on few functions so that competency is developed in that area. A port can invest in better material handling system and other infrastructure so that competency is developed in terms of better turnaround time for vessels.
- Complimenting resources: Zara uses its resources effectively to compete in fashion market. Its factories are complimented by sewing contractors who are closely knitted with Zara. It takes care of procurement, cutting, pressing, tagging and final inspection and sewing by contractors who are located close-by.

- Conserving resources: Utilising resources to the core and recycling them for different products, markets and collaborating with other partners in resource application.

Replicating Capabilities

Capabilities can be fine-tuned and improved if the organisation replicates internally in various capacities. The replication can take place in different departments, markets, and across geographical areas. Replication attracts less costs and hence provides competitive advantage. Service process replication by many restaurant chains made them successful and one of the best example is McDonald's.

Development of New Capabilities

Developing new resources is a time consuming process but this can be accomplished with planning and execution. New resources can also be acquired by buying them. But developing capabilities poses a high level of difficulty. Capability is a result of collaboration of certain resources and their own capabilities. There is no fixed formula available so that one can deploy a mix of some proportions of different resources to gain certain capability. Capability normally evolves over a period of time and it is like Toyota Production System (TPS), which is unique and difficult to replicate.

Some approaches to develop new capabilities:

- Acquiring Capabilities Through Mergers and Acquisitions - If new capabilities can only be developed over long periods, then taking over a company that already possesses that capabilities can avoid the process of development. Many technology firms used this route to acquire new technology capabilities. But not all acquisitions are successful. Due to culture mismatch and people mismatch, many acquisitions do not result in desired capabilities. The acquiring company must find a way to integrate both the companies and their capabilities.
- Accessing Capabilities Using Strategic Alliances: Alliance with other companies is more cost effective compared to acquiring a company. A strategic alliance involves relationship between firms in terms of sharing some resources for common goals. In 1993, Proctor and Gamble, USA entered into a joint venture with Godrej Soaps in India to leverage Godrej's scale and distribution network in the soap category. Many corporates collaborate with Education and Research Institute for mutual sharing of academic, research and practical knowledge and skills.
- Creating Capabilities: It is a long process in which the firm needs to get necessary resources and then integrate them to derive capabilities. Creating capabilities involves complex interaction of physical resources, financial resources and human resources. Organisation's culture, values and norms play a major role in creating capabilities. Hewlett-Packard developed a new capability (Procurement Risk Management-PRM) in risk management in 2005. It has developed and implemented a model, business process and software to measure and manage supply chain risks on the procurement side. It gave a competitive advantage in risk management and a savings of $425 million in six years.

A systematic step-by-step incremental approach helps in capability development. Sometimes, the present organisational structure, systems and culture may not support development of new capabilities. To resolve it, companies need to develop new organisational unit that are geographically separated from the existing units. Knowledge management is another tool which supports development of new capabilities.

PEOPLE AS RESOURCES

Organisations are by default, people-centric. But how people, process, assets and technology are connected truly determines the extent of the capability and competitive advantage. When we analyse our resources and capabilities holistically, our organisational strategy becomes infallible over time.

To look at it holistically, collective capabilities are built on the premise of the resource pool's experience, skills and knowledge. For example, scientists use their research skills when making medical discoveries. The end-user, however, would only be interested in quick pain relief and not the inventor behind it. The firm would focus on ensuring such competencies exist in the right quantities so that new discoveries are achieved and hit the market consistently to achieve competitive advantage.

Similarly, let us look at the premier technology and management institutions in India which came up in the early stage of independence along with international tie up. These institutions have created a culture and vision to keep the edge and tradition to be premier education service providers in technology and management contextual for India through excellent people management practices. They have been able to recruit and retain at least two generations of faculty over last fifty years plus. Faculty has shown exemplary skills and competency in teaching, research and consulting and been at International conferences and forums. Though there could be many who may say that India is not among top 200, we have to reckon to the fact as an initiative it is still recent compared to many other international institutes of excellence. Our achievement was due to ability of nurturing talent.

Another entity which one would be proud of is ISRO and recent launch of Chandrayaan-II. The Chandrayaan-II was launched from Satish Dhawan Space Centre at Sriharikota, Andhra Pradesh on-board GSLV (Geosynchronous Satellite Launch Vehicle) Mark-III to head to the Moon's South Polar Region. For the first time in India's space mission history, the ISRO expedition was spearheaded by two women. While Muthayya Vanitha is the project director, Ritu Karidhal is the mission director. It may be noted that 30% of the team working on it comprised of women and it is India's first space mission to be led by women scientists. (https://www.indiatoday.in/trending-news/story/twitter-hails-m-vanitha-and-ritu-karidhal-women-behind-chandrayaan-2-great-role-models-for-girls-1572471-2019-07-23). This brings out importance of gender parity in work, especially in operations and how firms can strategise the same.

Thus, people and resources determine competitive advantage. Besides interpersonal and soft skills, capabilities include the relevant technical software and systems which the resources regularly use to capture market demands. The resources and capabilities tend to have the following tendencies:

- Irreplaceable attributes
- They are not overshadowed by other teams and capabilities
- The competitors cannot easily acquire the same staff elsewhere
- Firm can appropriate profits upon their utilisation

An absence or shortage of the requisite staff and capabilities corresponds to a lack in competitive advantage, which is why it is critical to ensure these resources and capabilities exist in the right numbers beforehand. Human resources are most flexible and at the same time most complex to understand the kind of resources.

There are certain industries in India which have performed well because people resources have been the edge. IT development, deployment and support because of engineering capabilities, healthcare, life sciences and pharmaceutical's because of people capabilities in nursing, medical practice, pharmacology and chemistry and so on. India's tiny, small and medium sectors contribute nearly 40 per cent of business because of entrepreneurial spirits and capabilities spread wide across. Thus, people resources are a strategic operational aspect which could give competitive advantage.

SUMMARY

Possession of strategic resources gives an organisation with a huge opportunity to gain competitive advantage (CA) over its competitors. These competitive advantages result in more profits and better enhancement of shareholders' value. These resources can provide capabilities to the organisations. Resources refer to what organisation owns, whereas capabilities refer to what it can do with resources. Innumerable firms achieved resources led growth by pursuing appropriate operating strategies. Resources could have been tangible resources like technology and plant giving advantage of scale economies or intangibles like brand value or intellectual property rights or patent which the firm could achieve. Some companies used specialised resources like material sourcing advantage especially in case of natural resources-based industries like paper, power (using coal), agro based products and oil and gas and so on. There are others who used people related resources and capabilities which could be entrepreneurial skills, specialisation of labour and competencies like in chemistry and engineering. Firms also used natural resource advantage for locational benefits like using water resources, infrastructure like being close to ports and railroad for managing logistics cost. Firms are then able to deploy operations strategy like split locations to exploit market reach and/or use material for savings on logistics cost. This has happened largely in cement industry in India and in some aspects in case of engineering, especially heavy engineering where sizeable component is close to site configuration. Thus, availability of strategic resources and its effective deployment for achieving competitive advantage differentiates successful firms from other players in an industry.

Key Terms

1. **Tangible resource:** Tangible resources are physical items, including cash, inventory, machinery, land or buildings. These items can be liquidated and have a set value. They are critical in understanding where a company stands in terms of financial position and ability to certain volume of business.
2. **Intangible resource:** An intangible resource is an asset that is goodwill, brand recognition and intellectual property, such as patents, trademarks, and copyrights. They are not in physical form, necessarily.
3. **Economies of scale:** Economies of scale are cost advantages enjoyed by firms when production becomes efficient. Firms can achieve economies of scale by increasing production and lowering costs. The size of the plant generally matters when it comes to economies of scale. The larger the plant, the more the cost savings.
4. **Split location:** Split location refers to a situation wherein process of manufacturing or assembling a product, certain processes especially close to customisation can be taken close to customer by setting up that process alone in a different location. There is a possibility of splitting process being close to material for transport cost advantages.
5. **Core competency:** A core competency results from a specific set of skills or production techniques that deliver additional value to the customer. These enable an organisation to access a wide variety of markets.
6. **Distinctive competency:** A distinctive competency is a competency unique to a business organisation, a competency superior in some aspect than the competencies of other organisations, which enables the production of a unique value proposition in the function of the business.
7. **Unique competency:** A unique ability that a firm acquires or develops and that cannot be easily imitated. Mostly, it is protected through IPR and copyrights.

8. **Strategic asset:** Strategic asset is that competency or capability that a firm commands which gives competitive edge in a secular or very long period and competition could not imitate.
9. **People resources:** People and their capabilities that form key to success of a firm in certain industries especially of knowledge sector. It can also be relevant for large worker related industries wherein people resources in terms of high productivity leads to competitive advantage.
10. **Capability:** A capability is the ability to do things and to choose for a way of life according to one's personal values. As it applies to human capital, capability represents performing or achieving certain actions/outcomes in terms of the intersection of capacity and ability.
11. **Competence:** Capabilities can develop into competence. "Competence" is the state or quality of an individual's work. A person and their work can be evaluated as competent if the performance is considered in relation to a job requirement and performance.
12. **Culture:** Culture refers to the set of shared attitudes, values, goals, and practices that characterises an organisation.
13. **Capacity utilisation:** Capacity utilisation is the extent to which a firm uses its installed productive capacity. It is the relationship between output that is produced with the installed equipment, and the potential output which could be produced with it, if capacity was fully used.
14. **Value creation:** A firm where goods and services are produced or assembled or processed, wherein at every stage of production, value is being enhanced by material, labour, capital or any other resource so that customer pays for the value of the services as product price.
15. **Supply chain management (SCM):** SCM is the integration of key business processes of a focal organisation on one side with downstream players to customer and customer's customer and on the other side, upstream players, including supplier and supplier's supplier. It also includes managing three flows, namely products/services, information and finance.

CONCEPT REVIEW QUESTIONS

1. Explain importance of strategic resource allocation and relate with examples.
2. Discuss about "resource led growth" and different categories of growth drivers with illustrations.
3. Elucidate the following:
   a. Economies of scale
   b. Learning and advantage for a firm. Is it limited to labour intensive operations? How is it different from specialisation of labour?
   c. Capacity utilisation of assets
4. Discuss linkages with internal processes and supply chain activities and relate with an example.
5. Explain the importance of location of resources as competitive edge for operations strategy.
6. Discuss the difference between integrated location and split location and their relevance for operations strategy.
7. What are the strategies that manage resources led capabilities?
8. Discuss sustainable competitive strategy based on resources and capabilities and its formulation and implementation.
9. Explain "human resources as an operations strategy differentiator in knowledge and people-based industries". Discuss with examples.

CRITICAL THINKING QUESTIONS

1. Imagine that you are supply chain manager of an auto major who wants to make his plant competitive which is located at Chennai. You have Tier I companies who supply components. How would you strategise operations of line feed to the plant from Tier I vendors who are in three different clusters? Further, these are critical and strategic components and you have two players for certain components. How would you distribute orders among them?
2. Assume that you are in charge of operations of a retail chain's big store. How would you approach planning and managing procurement, receipts and stock of:
   a. FMCG of branded goods (Daily twice)
   b. FMCG of store label goods (Daily twice)
   c. Perishables like vegetables, fruits, dairy and others
3. Consider a fertilizer plant which serves demand for a radius of 800 kms. You are the operations strategist advising the company in designing setting up outbound distribution by road, combination rail and road and use of coastal shipping for domestic movement. What are the factors you would consider in the design?
4. "Speciality hospital competitive differentiator is people resources". Elucidate.
5. "Service companies will have challenge in creating unique competencies as they cannot protect their design. However, some of them have been successful in creating through brand recall strategic assets." Elucidate.
6. Discuss on "Environment concerns and replantation are key as an operations strategy for plantation industry".

PROJECT ASSIGNMENTS

1. Visit a popular restaurant and map locational features as an operations strategic differentiator. Draw learning to turnaround a comparably less popular restaurant in the same area with similar customer profile.
2. Go through web research and analyse growth of a firm in pulp manufacturing industry by relating with resource endowments and its strategy towards sustainability.
3. Analyse growth of dairy industry in India, especially under cooperative framework and how resource endowment became a key operations strategy for achieving success.

REFERENCES

1. Porter, Michael E. (1985). "*Competitive Advantage.*" Free Press. ISBN 978-0-684-84146-5.
2. Prahalad, C. K. and Hamel, Gary (1990). "The Core Competence of the Corporation", *Harvard Business Review*, Vol. 68, Issue 3, p. 79-91 1990. Available at SSRN: https://ssrn.com/abstract=1505251.
3. Findlay, Ronald and Lundahl, Mats (1999). "Resource-Led Growth – A Long-Term Perspective, The Relevance of the 1870-1914 Experience for Today's Developing Economies", WP No.162, UNU World Institute for Development Economics Research (UNU-WIDER).

Operations Strategy and Performance Management

CHAPTER 9

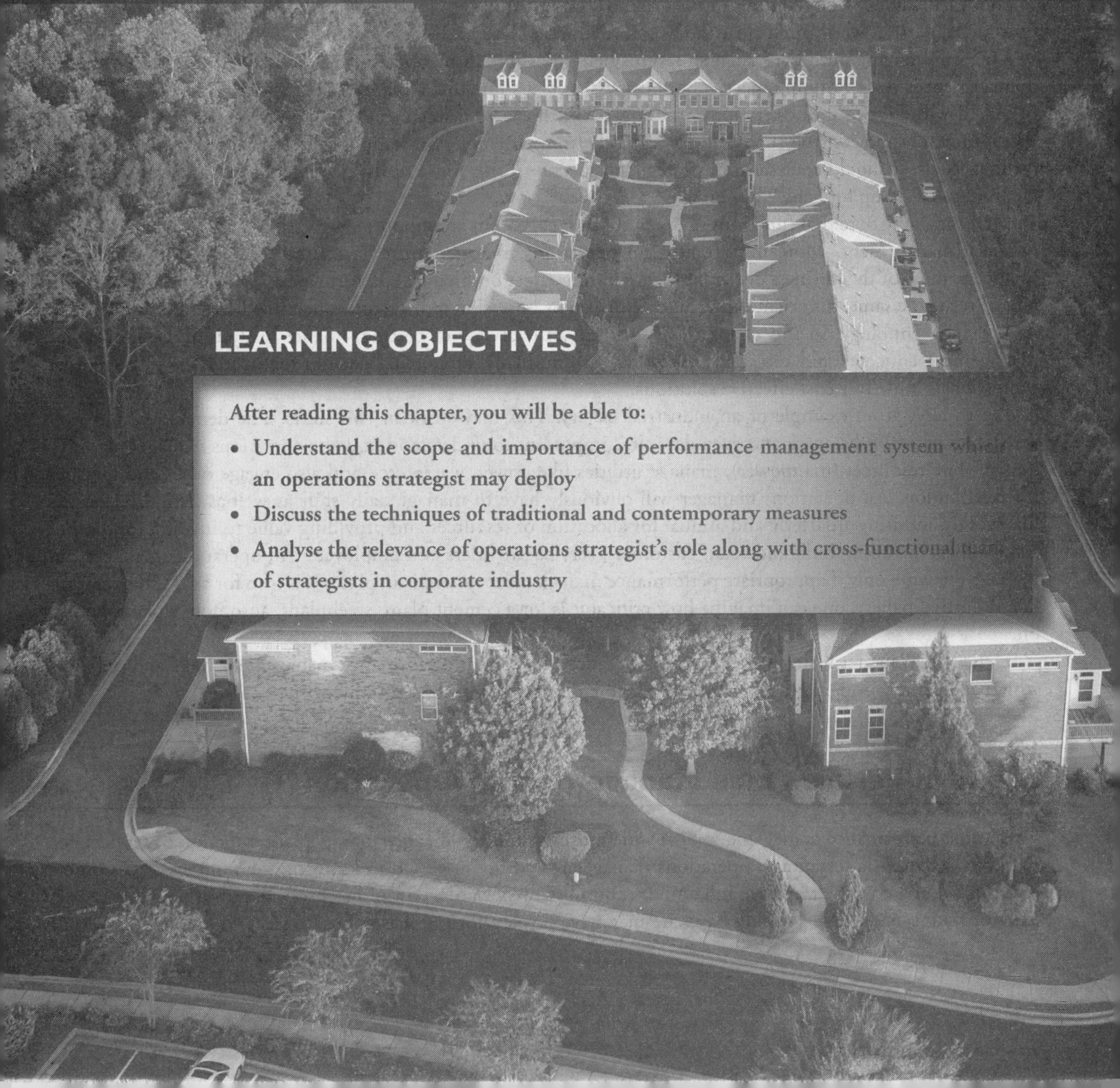

LEARNING OBJECTIVES

After reading this chapter, you will be able to:

- Understand the scope and importance of performance management system which an operations strategist may deploy
- Discuss the techniques of traditional and contemporary measures
- Analyse the relevance of operations strategist's role along with cross-functional team of strategists in corporate industry

Introduction

Performance management is a key aspect of any managerial function. In case of operations strategy, it is more critical as many aspects of operations are instantaneous and capable of impacting the satisfaction of stakeholders, including the customers. There are two aspects when it comes to managing operations performance, first, tactical adjustments that may be required for any occurrence of deviation and second, strategic adjustment that may be required, if the deviations are too frequent and substantial.

Let us take a simple situation of a long destination intercontinental flight where passengers hop for multiple destinations from a hub. A flight is delayed for ground reasons. It will badly affect operations and likely lead to a chaos, especially when reasons are not justifiable because of explicit slip in planning or execution of an operation like cargo loading. This could be due to a random failure of loading conveyer and peak traffic time leading to delay or replacement. In this case, it was an operational failure. However, if the same problem was repetitive due to poor maintenance or operations of the ground staff, it requires to look at replacement decision or engaging an outsourced partner who would treat this as a core function and improve reliability.

One can imagine numerous such situations being possible in manufacturing industry. Further performance management is basic to fulfil objectives of business. Lets assume that a plant has capacity to produce 1500 units of car a day under two shift operations. If it targets to achieve 90 per cent capacity utilisation, then it must ensure that it monitors and controls such delivery regularly from different workstations so that it can fulfil marketing and business goals. It should analyse from strategic perspective if this was a realisable target or what are the balancing facilities to be set up for achieving the same.

Here, one may note that functions of operations management are supported by various sub-systems, including financial management. More importantly, an operations manager must have fundamental understanding of finance as most of the business decisions have a lasting effect on financial performance. If an operations manager fails to relate the same, his orientation could be driven by obsession to overcome operating challenges and looking inward for technology. In this chapter, we shall see an overview of costing, finance analysis and performance management concepts and tools and how these are mutually supporting entities for operations management professionals to deliver cost effective solutions.

Let us look at an example of an industrial bakery. This may work in two shifts. The demand would vary across seasons, months, week and even days. It is important to understand how the operations manager plans his budget, hire resources (manpower), manage utilities like power, water, etc., and also engage outbound logistics for distribution. An operations manager will obviously have to manage daily shift as well as periodical targets like weekly, monthly, quarterly and annual for allocation of resources and providing value to investors and other stakeholders including bulk and retail customers, service providers and employees. An operations manager can manage the same only if appropriate performance management system is in place. If it is so for an SME operation like industrial bakery, one can imagine how critical it is for a cement plant, steel plant, automotive plant, and so on.

Hence, this chapter fosusses on uses and relevance of different performance management tools and practices which an operations manager can familiarise before deploying any chosen framework.

Scope of Performance Management in Operations

Operations performance management has a wide meaning and significance for any plant, function or service. For example, if there is a restaurant, operations manager would be interested in knowing the number of customers that dinned in a day, their average bill amount, number of stewards, cost of food served and so on. This is on a daily operating basis. On a weekly basis, he may have to plan for purchase of materials and scheduling of staff and so on. On a monthly plan, a much larger budget is drawn, and he needs to map performance to adjust plan and deployment of resources. In case of response consistently varying from the budget, then strategic focus like capacity, layout and supply network need to be evaluated. Thus, monitoring operating performance becomes critical.

Similarly, in a continuous plant like cement, limestone is crushed and prepared for kiln heating along with other binding material for formation of clinkers. Then clinkers are crushed and sent to packing stations for various lots like jumbo packs, regular size bags, even large size packs for bulk movement or from clinker to offsite crushers for local use in different geography and so on. A complex logistics operation and in-plant movement from lime quarry to plant and within the plant to different work stations demands stringent control mechanism to ensure smooth operations on a regular basis. The plant needs to ensure machine and men at all work stations are adequate and well-equipped for consistent desired output at shift level. Thus, monitoring of performance and managing performance through preventive and planned actions are vital for success of a cement plant. Further, apart from operational daily or weekly plan, plant needs to manage on medium and long term running of the plant to achieve business goals for which sustained efforts on performance management is a must. For example, when the plant produces different kinds or grades of cement it must have appropriate aggregate plan, approach to available resource utilisation like that of manpower, material and machines. From here, performance management also looks at some strategic issues like product lifecycle management strategy, new product development, automation and capturing with contemporary development in business in general and technology. A dedicated team of performance managers focusses to ensure efficiency and effectiveness of resources and look at every opportunity to serve the stakeholders. Further, a traditional strategic management process, budgeting process and leadership management look at performance management of operations as key aspect of ensuring a firm's or strategic business unit's sustainability and growth.

Scope of performance management in operations horizon clearly brings out the importance for an organisation. It is important to note that measuring and managing performance is culture and not just a policy. This has been proven by firms which have achieved excellence in business and have been emulated by many players, for example, Toyota Production System. Lean and continuous improvement hinges on measuring and constantly improving operating performance. Simple case would be that of Dabbawalas of Mumbai who deliver lunch boxes to working people across length and breadth of city. They succeed by managing their operations with an efficient performance management system and that of public transport, namely railway links which connects different nodes and whose operations are critical for delivery lunch boxes.

Thus, significance of operations performance management is clearly established in all business and horizon like long term, medium term and short term across the spectrum of stakeholders.

Traditional Operations Performance Management Metrics

There are number of traditional metrics used for managing operations performance by professionals. In fact, each industry has certain specific formats and guidelines based on its nature, characteristics, and level of regulatory needs. For example, in industries like food processing and hospitality, a detailed metrics is required to manage day-to-day activities. This measurement of performance in certain cases was a mandatory requirement while in others, it is more from internal management perspective. The ratios can be grouped under operational efficiency, responsiveness and financial performance metrics. These involved identifying a suitable numerator and a denominator which is important to be a meaningful controllable factor for effectiveness. Some of these are listed here to give an understanding of approach to operations performance management. These are not exhaustive but indicative.

Three groups of ratios are discussed here. These are ratios that capture operating efficiency, responsiveness and financial ratios. All these have complete relevance and significance for an operations manager to perform tasks and achieve operating goals of a firm or entity.

Operating Efficiency

These set of ratios reflect on operating efficiency at strategic business unit (SBU) or plant or even at machine level.

Throughput ratio: It measures how much product is being produced on a machine, line, unit, or plant over a specified period. For example, how much of cane is processed in a sugar factory in a day/week/ month/ season/ year. A plant may crush 5000 tonnes per day or 150000 per month or 9,00,000 in a season of six months or 12,00,000 in a year over two seasons (including a special season) in a year.

Yield ratio: This indicates a percentage of products that are manufactured to the inputs and to specifications. For example, if 5000 tonnes of cane is crushed a day (tcd), yield gives sugar recovery per cent, bagasse per cent, molasses and even press mud. These could be related to imbibition level (water used), steam ratio and power consumption.

Capacity utilisation: This indicates how much of the total manufacturing output capacity is being utilised at a given point in time. Suppose, if a 5000 tcd sugar cane processing plant crushes 4500 tcd in a day, then capacity utilisation is 90 per cent. It is important to have an appropriate window of time period to make a meaningful analysis.

Downtime in proportion to operating time: This ratio of downtime to operating time is a direct indicator of asset availability for production. For example, if a production line is down for 36 hours out of the available 720 hours in a month on a continuous production of three shifts, down time is 5 per cent. However, if for the year downtime is 48 hours out of the available 8640 hours, then downtime is only 0.6 per cent. It requires then analysis of downtime in a specific month.

Percentage planned vs. emergency maintenance work orders: This ratio metric is an indicator of how often scheduled maintenance takes place, versus more disruptive/un-planned maintenance. This is another critical operations performance metric. This is highly relevant in continuous process industries. For example, in sugar industry because acetic nature of material is being processed, there would be planned maintenance even during crushing season and plant goes through major planned maintenance during non-season with a complete overhaul. However, during crushing there are times when motors and drivers fail leading to unplanned maintenance and stoppage of processing. This is possible in many other products or service businesses.

Inventory turnover ratio: Inventory turnover ratio is measured by dividing the net revenue by the average inventory used to produce those goods. If the ratio is low like 2 or 3, it means that inventory is high compared to the ratio of 8 or 10. For operations function, raw material turns and work in progress (WIP) turns, which is cost of goods sold to raw materials and cost of goods sold to WIP, are also important.

Cash-to-cash cycle time: This measures the duration measured in days between the purchase of a manufacturing plant or business unit's inventory, and the collection of payments/accounts receivable for the sale of products that utilise that inventory. It is an important metrics which would require quick cash to cash cycle times for a business.

Customer rejects/return material authorisations/returns: This measures how many times customers reject products or request returns of products based on receipt of a bad or out of specification product or for a functional failure. This is a key quality related parameter.

Supplier's quality (inbound material): One of the metrics would be the self-certified vendors to total especially for Category A and B items. Also, one would look at number of ISO or any leading quality institutional certified vendors to total as a metrics for Category A and B items. Further, a measure of the percentage of good quality materials coming into the manufacturing process from a given supplier is used for rating supplier.

Responsiveness

On-Time Delivery to Commit: This metric is the percentage of time in which manufacturing delivers a completed product on the schedule that was committed to customers. There is a variant of this metrics which is delivering the product on customer request. This mainly occurs when customer wants a different schedule from what is committed.

Manufacturing Cycle Time: It measures the time it takes for manufacturing to produce a given product from the time the order is released to production to finished goods.

Time to Make Changeovers: It measures the time it takes to switch a manufacturing line or plant from making one product over to making a different product. This is an important measure for a multi-product line.

Engineering Change Order Cycle Time: It is a measure of how rapidly design changes or modifications to existing products can be implemented all the way through documentation processes and actual production. This is an important measure for capital equipment manufacturer and for design to engineering product.

Operations Financial Performance Analysis

Manufacturing Cost as a Percentage of Revenue: A ratio of total manufacturing costs to the overall revenues produced by a manufacturing plant or business unit. This is a key control measure for a plant especially when it works on target cost and target price.

Average Unit Contribution Margin: This metric is calculated as a ratio of the gross profit (revenue minus variable cost) that is generated by a product/pant/SBU, divided into a given unit or volume of production.

EBITDA: It measures earnings before interest taxes, depreciation and amortisation. EBITDA is current operational profitability of a business and gives an idea of funds available towards servicing capital both debt and equity and statutory payments.

Net Operating Profit: This measures the financial profitability for all investors/shareholders/debt holders, either before or after taxes, for a manufacturing plant or business unit. This considers profit either before tax or after tax, though profit after tax is a better indicator. This removes all non-operating incomes like profit from sale of assets.

Return on Assets/Return on Net Assets: This is a measure of financial performance calculated by dividing the net income from a manufacturing plant or business unit by the value of fixed assets and working capital deployed. Fixed assets plus net working capital is equal to capital employed.

Productivity in Revenue per Employee: This is a measure of how much revenue is generated by a plant, business unit or company, divided by the number of employees.

It may be noted here that most of these are lagging indicators meaning ex-post following an event. Examples of lag indicators include cash conversion cycle, operating profit ratio, revenue growth and so on. There are some important leading indicators which would help to predict future event or performance. Examples of lead indicators include number of innovations, number of patents, brand recognition and so on.

Thus, the combination of the group of three, namely operating efficiency, responsiveness and financial performance focussed with operating parameters, helps an operations strategist to analyse if the unit of comparison is functioning efficiently and effectively. If not, one may look at appropriate corrective actions depending upon if it is internal or external factor or whether the factor affecting is a key improvement area or a strategic disadvantage. For example, a power plant in India using domestic coal with low calorific value will have comparatively lower operating efficiency to one which uses imported coal with high calorific value. Though conclusion could be obvious to substitute with better quality coal, it may not be possible. This could be due to a simple clause that the plant using local coal has been given permission subject to utilisation of local resource and creating employment.

Hence a strategist must be able to link multiple parameters and arrive at appropriate decision. It is important to understand and still use these ratios and drive efficiency wherever possible.

In the following section, relationship between operating and financial risk and importance of cross-functional approach towards operations performance management are explained.

Operational Risk and Need to Improve Performance

Typically, operational leadership is responsible for product design, setting up and managing the production system to produce output; then for managing material requirement and ensuring material quantity and price and so on. These are all under the ambit of operations to fulfil sales and operations plan and budget. There is a volume to cost relationship linked with capacity utilisation factor which operations need to manage. Such a tactful management would allow production system to operate efficiently without incurring loss.

Though sales revenue targets are owned by sales and marketing team, it is important that the operations team provides the right kind of product and at the right price. Predominantly, sales target is set by the business development and marketing team in consultation with operations team. Operations team gets a target cost working along with finance which arrives at a target price.

The key operations responsibilities include achieving:

1. Volume of output
2. Desired output quality and within limits of reduction
3. Product performance efficiency

All these would take care of production quantity efficiency. If sales can convert every item produced (according to its sales and operations plan) as revenue, operations can be understood to have performed efficiently. The efficiency can be affected by factors like poor maintenance, poor quality management and improper equipment, support system, poor shop floor employee relationship, inadequate direct floor management, improper automation and control mechanism and so on.

Even if all these are operating as per plan and adequately, there could be negative variances. The other aspects that are to be managed by operations management team would include:

1. Material purchase price efficiency. Material to be procured at estimated/budgeted cost to avoid variance.
2. Material volume in purchase and use of strategies like JIT or volume base reduction and strategic alliances to ensure quantity and quality of input materials.
3. Use of preapproved quality vendors and reducing cost of inbound material quality, rejections and thereby, providing certainty of flow rate and time.
4. Efficient inbound material logistics cost including that of warehousing, yard management, transportation and material handling.

The above four heads along with a few others would impact the cost. Though most of the above is direct costs, there can be some additional indirect overheads like managerial salary which can also be considered as a part of operations budget or at least jointly with marketing and distribution budget. For example, if operations identify opportunities for postponement of product configuration, such product distribution network will be comparatively of low cost.

Thus, operations management and strategy would be responsible for performance of the sales and cost up to operating costs and arriving at operating margin. Variability in operating margin measured by Earnings before interest, depreciation and taxes is appropriate measure of operating risk.

There are certain businesses which by nature, product type and business cycle have a tendency for high operating risk compared to certain other businesses which could have a flow of steady state margin. High risk businesses could be like edible oil processing; manufacture of sugar; cotton textiles; some products like fertilizers;

manufacture of hybrid seeds and some seasonal services like hotels in vacation locations; etc. These businesses will have high EBITDA and vary across locations as well.

There are businesses which have low variability as many times income and expenses are estimated with reasonable degree of certainty. This would include essential services like private transportation; healthcare; insurance; fashions, apparel; leather shoes; automotive; jewelry and financial services and so on. These businesses have the ability to transfer cost escalations to customers by way of higher prices as a part of natural hedging.

There is a relationship which operations strategists and performance managers must understand. If an operations product or service business has a high operating risk by sheer nature of business like mentioned above, such companies should have a low financial risk measured by debt to equity as a neutralising strategy. Figure 9.1 on relationship between financial risk and operating risk shows the inverse relationship and ability of operations and finance strategists to align both.

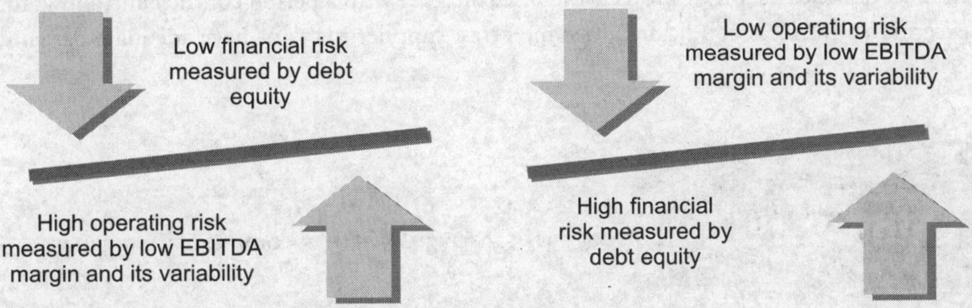

FIGURE 9.1 Relationship between operating and financial risk

This is easier said than done! When the input price rises, the firm must find working capital matching cash to cash cycle to pay for the receivables. This increases working capital and outflow of interest and thereby financial risk increases. The operating risk would also increase when the firm finds it difficult to pass on input price increase proportionately to the customers. Thus, operating risk and financial risk increasing simultaneously increase the business risk. Operations manager must understand this phenomenon clearly and manage input prices accordingly.

This must be worked as a cross-functional team effort and articulated well by the corporate planning team and senior management including the board of the firm. There are companies who have failed to manage the risk relationship and have been swayed by business cycle and financial system. With increasing financial surveillance, transparency in reporting system and ability of all stakeholders to communicate freely among their own groups, severe self-restraint are enforced against any discrete operational or financial initiatives that may disturb balance between operating and financial risks.

There are cases of sugar companies, airline operators, edible oil firms, real estate promoters, hospitality firms, fertilizers and few others in metal business who have faced such volatility and succumbed to pressure and failed. Hence it is important that operations strategists are conscious in risk evaluation and try to innovate products, process and operating systems to reduce risk of variability in EBITDA. Good supplier relationship management and treating suppliers and logistics service providers as long-term partners in business are vital for operations.

Two approaches in long term on strategic performance management can be pursued by operations strategists who are part of "thinktank" in corporate. An introduction is given here, and detailing is out of the scope of this book.

First, linking operations strategy to budget and policy. If a firm pursues a strategic initiative like reducing cost through targeted initiative like supplier rationalisation, then it takes a long time, say about three years to achieve the reduction. The cost reduction implication starts reflecting in improving operating margin and thereby, reducing operating risk either in the fourth year or fourth year onwards. During this process, operating budget must envision transitioning this period and allow for cost management approach through budgetary support. The finance professionals may understand the cost head and impact of cost saving measures. However, they may assign comparatively low priority to relate with technical aspects of strategic cost management project. It is the responsibility of operations strategists to team up with finance to ensure fund flow for operations as well as for strategic initiative which may include few years of sustained fund allocation. This is where linkages between operations strategy and operations budget must be established.

Second, operations may be affected by material price variance which could affect cost of goods sold as a firm produces output using those inputs. Some of the material prices could be volatile as discussed earlier in this subsection. To cite few, metal, minerals, agriculture-based products and so on follow such pattern. Normally, as a part of natural hedge, the supplier tries to pass on the price increase to the buyer. This may not be possible in all conditions. In most of the cases, buyer protects the price increase with a period contract and allows for negotiation only under exceptional business conditions. In some cases, supplier may not have adequate bargaining power to pass on material price increase.

Exhibit 9.1

Hedge risk through overseas commodity exchanges

To hedge risks involving the volatility in commodity prices, Dabur India Ltd and Emami, two homegrown consumer product companies, started trading on international commodity exchanges, way back in 2007–2009.

Dabur India Ltd started trading on the National Commodity and Derivatives Exchange Ltd (NCDEX) around 2007. Later, it went on to trading on five international commodity exchanges including the Chicago Board of Trade (CBOT), the Chicago Mercantile Exchange (CME), the London International Financial Futures Exchange (LIFFE), the Kuala Lumpur Commodity Exchange (KLCE), and London Metal Exchange (LME).

Dabur makes products, such as hair oil, shampoos, toothpastes and health supplements among others. "Given the high rate of volatility in the domestic and international market, it (the trading on international exchanges) is a key initiative in terms of sourcing primarily for our international operations", mentioned by its executive vice-president, supply management at Dabur India.

In 2009, the company was trading around 12 products on these exchanges. Its representatives had quoted that they managed to save 25 per cent of the total sourcing costs on commodities, such as spices, sugar and jowar. These savings helped in reining in the costs, and when other firms increased the prices of their products by up to 20 per cent, because of the steep increase in commodity prices, Dabur raised prices by only 5 per cent.

The cost of raw materials, such as crude, palm oil, wheat, and packaging costs rose up to 50 per cent in the previous year because of an extreme volatility in the markets, globally. These raw materials account for substantial costs for most consumer product companies.

Like Dabur, Emami Ltd, which manufactures a range of personal care products, also began hedging on KLCE. Hedging, however, seemed to be a new trend then in the consumer products sector while many companies did not trade on the exchanges.

Source: Article: To hedge risk, Dabur, Emami tap overseas commodity exchanges, Vijaya Rathore , https://www.livemint.com/Companies/1liIgbKXlinLFJRxWQKhrI/To-hedge-risk-Dabur-Emami-tap-overseas-commodity-exchanges.html.

Exhibit 9.2 Regulator advises banks to encourage hedging of agriproducts

To promote the commodity derivatives market with involvement of banks, the Reserve Bank of India asked during the last week of May 2015 to encourage borrowers of agricultural products to hedge their risk on commodity derivative exchanges. The circular asked banks to encourage "large agricultural borrowers such as commodity processors, traders, millers, aggregations, etc." to do this on recognised exchanges.

It was reported then that some banks had tied up with National Commodity and Derivatives Exchange (NCDEX) or its subsidiary for trading in spot markets for lending against stocks deposited in recognised warehouses and hedged on the exchange's platform. Borrowers who have taken loans for processing can buy the raw material from futures exchange to manage input material cost if they feel its price would rise in time or sell a processed commodity on the futures platform to ensure realisations if they see prices falling in future.

"Generally, this risk is more pronounced in cases where agri borrowers do not hedge the underlying commodity price risk. Hedging of this risk is beneficial to both borrowers and banks and, hence, it is desirable that a risk management culture is fostered among the stakeholders, including agri-borrowers and banks," said the circular mentions.

This shows that RBI recognised the importance of hedging commodity price risk and showed confidence in the commodity derivative system.

It is important for the processers to educate themselves about hedging the price risk of agri commodities. The ultimate impact depends upon scale of operation; requirements of hedging frequency and sophistication of market operations which must be in sync with the availability and use of these instruments.

Source: https://www.business-standard.com/article/finance/rbi-asks-banks-to-encourage-hedging-of-agri-products-115052801307_1.html

https://www.rbi.org.in/scripts/BS_CircularIndexDisplay.aspx?Id=9748.

Buyer or nodal firm in the supply network who is owning the brand/product in the market may also be constrained with a need to absorb material price increases and adverse material price variance because of demand by customers could be highly elastic. Typically, a large corporate with a sizeable balance sheet hedges price risk directly in the commodity market if the input material is traded. Otherwise, it may use a surrogate. Even in such a firm, the operating strategists have no role. Chief financial officer who handles treasury decides the same as a speculative risk and uses specialised commodity hedge services or if the business volume affords, they have their own hedging team in treasury which operates a corpus. The net of transactions in a year reflects as other income or losses from trade.

In reality, managing material price variance and risk must be a part of operations strategy as well. Hedging risk must be a part of operations budget. However, only few evolved companies could do this. Hedging for material price management is not possible for small and medium size companies because of the risk involved in commodity markets. Skill and sophistication required are high. Even some large firms do not consider taking market hedging route. But they do natural hedging process by passing on the burden to the customers. Alternatively, they balance financial and operating risks and thereby absorb in their business. Some companies have in their portfolio have businesses which can counter balance price risk without hedging and overall risk is averaged out.

Exhibit 9.1 shows how a firm managed purchase price risk through commodity hedging.

Let us look at an opportunity for agriculture-based processor like a health beverage manufacturer who uses sugar, malt and other material. Typically, corporate strategy of these companies is to spend heavily on brand building and ensure customers' stickiness to the brand as customer feels comfortable with the product. Hence, powerful brands have natural hedge by which they transfer increases in input prices to final customer, as product price increases. However, those who do not enjoy such brand power suffer because of drop in margin. These firms rely on procurement managers' ability to predict and advise during operations budgetary process like trends in input price and expected variance so that financials can be planned accordingly. If such small players have bandwidth to use commodity hedging through shared service, there is adequate cushion available for them.

In India, regulator, namely the Reserve Bank of India issued a circular in May 2015 encouraging banks to advise their customers to hedge price risks through commodity markets. Exhibit 9.2 gives excerpts from the circular.

Thus, in this subsection, the importance of operations strategists' role in managing performance through strategic initiatives and linking operations budget, strategy and policy towards involving cross-functions like operations, finance and marketing is discussed.

It may be useful to understand the importance of strategic cost focus in operations management. The following section gives basic approach towards the same.

Operations Perspective of Strategic Cost Management

Total cost of a product is the summation of material cost, inward logistics cost, production cost, outward logistics cost, other marketing variable cost, and other marketing fixed cost. The costs incurred right from the time of material sourcing to delivery of the finished product or service to the ultimate customer are measured in total cost management. While analysing the composition of total cost, it has been observed that the material cost accounts for 50 – 80 per cent of the total cost. While in the case of services, material cost can be substituted for information cost. Total cost approach for a business strategy includes the following strategic costs:

- Rationalisation of vendors
- Integration of vendors
- Reducing complexity
- World class manufacturing practices
- Strategic sourcing
- Cost of quality
- Network consolidation and customer insight

Rationalisation of Vendors

Companies have been purchasing their raw material from an array of vendors and have been trying to reduce the cost of purchases by putting one vendor against the other and ordering with least cost vendor subject to satisfactory quality of raw materials/components. This traditional approach stems from the assumption that the vendor always tries to display one-upmanship and it is always better to play one vendor against the other to identify the best vendor who offers raw materials/components and required quantity at the least cost. However, this exercise has two drawbacks.

1. Procedurally, the cost of purchase is higher as several vendors will have to be approached for an enquiry, floating of tender forms, tender scrutiny, negotiations, etc. Thus, it involves significant cost and time.
2. The approach that the vendor is an adversary and must be tested for integrity and price suffers from such attitude.

As a first step to minimise the purchase cost, a study of the performance of the vendors over a timeframe, say 3 to 5 years, would reveal that a significant percentage of the vendors had failed to satisfy the requirements of the company either because of quality, or price. Only about 30 – 40 per cent really engage themselves in the submission of tenders as well as negotiations. From those vendors who had responded to enquiry, only about 50 per cent have really delivered the goods and performed to the satisfaction of the company. Thus, it transpires that only about 25 per cent of the total vendors on the records of the company are active. So, it will surface if active vendors are kept on the records and the remaining can be deleted. This rationalisation brought about significant reduction in the cost of purchasing for a company.

Integration of Vendors

Attitudinal aspect of the company towards the vendor needs to change from the position of the adversary to that of a partner in progress. This would mean that a vendor is an important stakeholder in business and so associating the vendor in the crux of business is fast becoming relevant, the following steps are essential.

a. An analysis of the list of rationalised vendors would reveal the strengths and weaknesses of the vendors.
b. Based on the analysis, the company would be in a position to determine the factor which requires to be addressed in developing the vendor to satisfactorily supply raw materials/components at required price, quantity and quality.
c. Vendor development may involve assistance in finance or upgradation of technology or increase in the capacity of the vendor production to match futuristic requirements of the company.
d. The developed vendors may be few in number, whose performance over a time period would be monitored by the company to select the best of the vendors.
e. Thus, the selected vendor can be integrated with business process of the company, information like production plan, order book, etc., can be shared so that the supply of raw materials/components would match exactly to the requirements of the company and 'just in time' concept can be fully instituted. When this integration takes place, the vendor is assured of a much bigger quantum of supplies and better utilisation of the capacity leading to economies of scale.

The vendor and the company can share the benefits of the economies of scale and inventory cost saving in the right proportion and thus develop a win-win situation. In this process of integration, the vendor has turned from the adversary to a partner in progress (Exhibit 9.3).

Exhibit 9.3

Mahindra and Mahindra vendor rationalisation

Mahindra and Mahindra (M&M) manufacturing a variety of utility vehicles and tractors implements a vendor rationalisation strategy. They purchase raw materials/components from a host of vendors. The list of vendor rationalisation led to a reduction in the number of vendors from 650 to 450.

The reduction in vendors helped the company to achieve better efficiencies apart from being able to monitor the production closely. Mahindra and Mahindra felt that, "A smaller vendor base means we can manage the work better than before". Reduction in number of vendors resulted in higher volume to the revised group of vendors. With this advantage, Mahindra and Mahindra could negotiate for better prices with the vendors on the basis of higher volume of work to them.

M&M has centralised purchasing parts across two wheelers, commercial vehicles, passenger vehicles and tractors. The one sourcing strategy the firm adopted will help to reduce at least 2-3% cost of purchasing from component makers who supply parts to models across the segments and make the supply chain more efficient.

Source: http://www.livemint.com/Companies/1FOq6BpomN-LkmJLIsPLRSK/Mahindra-to-reduce-supplier-base-as-part-of-new-sourcing-str.html?utm_source=copy.

Reducing Complexity

Many companies rebel in adopting complex procedures in sourcing, procuring, transporting, inspecting and storing raw material components. These procedures need to be simplified. It is important to note here that complexity unnecessarily increases processes, activities and hence associated costs, delays and inefficiencies. At times, it leads to hidden costs as well. Hence rationalisation becomes important.

New tools and technologies have come up like optimisation of transport of insurance third party inspection, cargo consolidation, containerisation, MRP, JIT, etc., introduction of electronic data interchange and paperless communication coupled with Electronic Clearance Services (ECS) for fund transfer. Hence it is appropriate to use advancement in business processes and technology to achieve reduction in complexity of processes, activities and hierarchy of decision making. Such an approach not only brings operating efficiency and financial prudence through cost reduction, it also makes operation processes contemporary and responsive.

World Class Manufacturing Practices

To meet the specifications of International Standard Organisation (ISO) would require production facilities of uniform character and practices conforming to world class manufacturing practices. Not only the facilities but also the practices have a universal character acceptable to the stakeholders like vendors, producers and customers. With outsourcing of facilities becoming important, contract production has assumed enormous significance. Producing a product for another company under the brand in the company's facilities can be possible only when both the facilities and practices are of world class.

Another important feature of world class manufacturing facility is the accepted practice for treatment of solid, liquid and gaseous effluents of the statutory pollution control authority. world class manufacturing facility (WMF) also addressed concerns like global warming, emission of greenhouse gases and the necessity to develop a social commitment of being environmentally conscious and working towards sustainable development. World class practices equally apply to services, especially in the context of increasing transfer of business processes, call centre work and knowledge processes across the borders. The infrastructural requirements of these centres need to be of a world class quality and conform to such practices which are universal and are applicable to most countries which are outsourcing the business processing.

World class manufacturing (WCM) involves total quality management (TQM) and total plant management (TPM) and it's only befitting that these two are integrated with total cost management. For total quality management and total plant management embrace the entire organisation and lay down specific parameters for controls. The physical and abstract parameters need to be explicit to the relevant stakeholders in terms of values so that the impact on the top and bottom lines are fully understood. This is possible only if strategic cost management approach is integrated with total plant management and total quality management.

Strategic Sourcing

The scale of operation, be it manufacturing or services, reveals its size of being large or small. The necessity to continuously perform has added a new dimension like strategic sourcing, raw material sourcing, business process outsourcing (BPO), knowledge process outsourcing (KPO), etc. to integrate business processes/manufacturing processes across the borders which is resorted to improve both quality and quantity to reduce cost. More detailed discussion on strategic sourcing has been done in a chapter on "Supply Network and Supply Chain Strategies".

Many Indian companies like TATA, Sundaram Groups have sourced raw materials/components from across the seas. Many power plants have identified the sourcing partners in other countries to supply quality fuel at effective cost. The power plants in South India who are far from the coal and gas belt within the country have chosen the fuel requirements from abroad as part of a strategy. The IT sector in India has thrived in the last decade based on strategic outsourcing of business process, knowledge process and call centre works by companies from developed countries.

Cost of Quality

Professor Taguchi declared that "Quality is for Free". Any commercial product when offered for sale must satisfy quality standard as a part of production itself. In short, a product is marketable only if quality is built. So, no additional costs are incurred for introducing quality. Cost of quality incurred by a company is due to non-conformance of quality and for correction of defects. Such cost can be classified under four heads, namely prevention cost, appraisal cost, internal failure cost and external failure cost. However, these costs are not always explicit in books of account but must be identified culled out and accumulated. Some of the cost may have to be computed as they are intangible and are not reflected.

Indicative cost items are as follows:

1. Prevention cost which may include quality assurance; administration and system planning; quality planning, training, information and documentation.
2. Appraisal cost includes testing; inspection; quality audits; inspection of incoming raw materials/components; laboratory test of raw materials/components; online control for process; stage inspection; outgoing finished products; outside endorsement and depreciation of quality control equipment.
3. Internal failure cost includes scrap; rework; quality control investigation of internal failures; seconds; repair and trouble shooting and assignable variable.
4. External failure cost includes customer complaints for repairs; customer complaints for replacement; warranty cost; after sales services cost; returned material; product litigations; loss of goodwill and product recall.

These are indicative and not exhaustive.

Experience has shown that an increase in appraisal cost tends to reduce internal failure cost to the extent of 10 to 15 per cent. However, increase and intense prevention costs reduce internal and external failure costs to the extent of 30 to 40 per cent. It is important that by applying Pareto analysis, external failures are addressed immediately as the impact of the external failure cost is enormous. A finished product with a minor fault reaching the customer may end up with the replacement. An instrument costing ₹1 lakh had to be replaced due to faulty resistor costing of ₹1000 only. Again, if a facial cream supposed to improve the texture of the skin fails to satisfy the customer and to the discomfiture of the customer develops rashes, the company may face litigations not just replacement but loss of goodwill and market share. So quality assurance cost forms a part of total cost management and the integration of total quality management yield rich results.

Network Consolidation and Customer Insight

Efforts to reach a customer either with a product or service require proper networking. The network can be for proper warehousing and distribution. Selection of differentials of marketing, namely C&F agents, wholesale agents, stockiest, distributors, retailers, etc., forms a part of business strategy impacting operations strategy and such a choice can be done only through proper evaluation of alternative cost and benefits. This forms a part of the total cost management as this analysis cannot be a standalone computation but may have to be a part of continued strategic exercise evaluation and control. Changes in cost compared to the benefits will have to be monitored. This has to be compared to competitors; and value adding activities to the customer.

There have been companies like Amway who deal with fast moving consumer goods and who skips all tiers to reach the customer directly. It offers substantial reduction in cost by disengaging layers for a win-win situation. May not be comfortable for intermediaries but since they are not adding value, they are forced to accept rationalisation. Rationalisation of outbound logistics warehousing and distribution have yielded substantial reduction in marketing cost and these have been possible only through the evaluation of alternative in terms of cost and benefits as a part of total cost management. After sales service, as a part of marketing cost, was introduced based on annual maintenance contracts (AMC).

However, over the years after sales service cost has been built into total cost. It has been found that after sales service has led to substantial reduction in external failures, as it finds out any defects in the delivered products as matter of routine and repair immediately. Pre-empting any complaint from the customer after sales service cost have also increased the goodwill of the company as the customer is made fully aware of the product as well as its operational activity. Thus, incurring after sales cost entails positive cost benefit ratio.

Customer Insight

In a shift in paradigm relating to technologies, demand driven to competition driven, "pull technology" has come into its own. To effectively practise pull technology concept, a company needs to have its finger on the pulse of the customer—customer aspirations, customer needs (articulated and unarticulated), customer preferences and customer delight. For all this, customer insight and behaviour need to be fully understood.

Any customer would like to gauge the consumer surplus in every transaction, which in other words can be measured by the perceived surplus values over the price paid by the customer. Towards this, the total cost management has two pronged approaches.

1. Incur cost periodically to conduct surveys of customer behaviour towards actual transactions with the company and the perceptions of the customer towards the improvement they would like to see in the future.
2. To incur a cost like customer responsiveness cost through regular feedback from the customer as an item of cost forming part after sales services cost. The cost analysis of the customer response sheet on a regular basis can be done through a Pareto analysis of customer compliance, customer preferences and customer perceptions. This cost analysis can be the base for R&D programmes for innovations and identifing projects for investigation and development. These are strategic costs, which form a part of total cost management.
   Customer insight also helps a company to comprehend the emphasis laid by a group of customers on certain cost aspects. This can be traced even to cultural mindset of the customer.
   In India, it has been found that the customer insight is also towards minimising operational and maintenance cost of any durable equipment of machinery. Indian customers hold fuel efficiency of a two-wheeler or four wheelers more important. Again, energy efficiency about the electrical goods like air conditioner, refrigerators, etc., have been accorded the primary place. Thus, customer insight analysis identifies the area for cost reduction. Strategic cost management approach helps in developing the approach to achieve significant and sustainable improvement in the total cost.

Cost Reduction Programme

Total cost management could be rationalising the total cost system based on optimisation of the whole. It has been recognised that the optimisation of a part does not bring about the optimisation of whole, as sectional optimisation does not develop a "win-win" situation. Totality is more important and a wholesome approach is essential. In the same manner, the cost reduction exercises are not just cost cutting exercises. At best, cost cutting exercises are spasmodic short-term decisions which in the long run may prove detrimental. The company, for instance, in times of crisis, resorts to promotional advertisement, voluntary retirement schemes, etc. At times, these initiatives will be done in desperation.

Reduction in advertising and promotional campaign cost may reduce the company's visibility in the long term and its competitive advantage. Besides voluntary retirement schemes are known to drain the best of experiences and talents and the deadwood continues. So, the enterprise cost system as a part of total cost management develops a strategic approach towards cost reduction programmes towards building sustainability. The various techniques that were adopted to realise the necessary strategic cost savings can be identified as follows:

1. Reengineering business processes
2. Effective management of demand
3. Reducing commercial value leakage
4. Improvement of service effectiveness
5. Efficient tax planning, especially of indirect taxes and use of subsidies
6. Judicious outsourcing
7. Redesign and rescheduling of operations

As these are strategic cost initiatives, priorities should be kept stable at least over a medium term. "Enterprise cost reduction programme focusses on initiatives as a part of corporate strategy rather than entertaining occasional initiatives of cost cut measures". The strategic approach considers the following areas.

a. Aim of cost reduction programme should be all prevalent including every activity.
b. The long term major fixed cost becomes flexible and continuing focus on those costs will help greater control.
c. Continuously watch out for the sops offered by governments with respect to the specific industry as well as general economic scenario.
d. Look for judicious outsourcing as a long-term strategy taking into consideration distinctive competencies of the company rather than short term exigencies.
e. Another important area is the continuous monitoring of cost vis-a-vis prices to maintain and improve margins.
f. Post production cost including warehousing and distribution and after sales cost need to be appraised effectively for modifying tier management and discounts.

To effectively establish optimal relationship between physical programmes with time, it has become necessary to develop/design programmes with face value and sustainability as the main thrust.

Balanced Scorecard and Operations Metrics

Developed at the Harvard Business School, the balanced scorecard is a comprehensive, top-down view of organisational performance with a strong focus on vision and strategy. The balanced scorecard is founded upon the idea that financial measurements, while an important indicator of corporate performance, tend to be somewhat retrospective. Financial metrics typically tell how an enterprise has performed but give little indication as to how it will perform. A true balanced scorecard must include metrics that provide both historical and future insights. Thus, a scorecard must be comprised of both leading and lagging indicators. Leading indicators drive performance, whereas lagging indicators are showing results of past performance.

For example, in an operations analysis system, 'customer complaints' is a lagging indicator, while 'on-time delivery' is a leading indicator. To achieve 'balance', the methodology prescribes the strategic assessment of four perspectives, financial, customer, internal, innovation and growth.

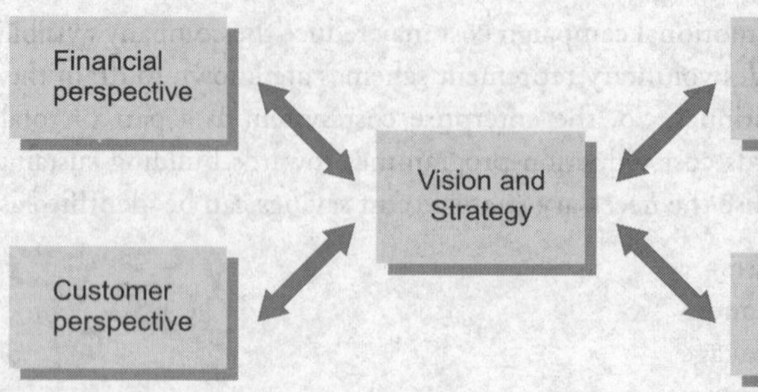

FIGURE 9.2 Balanced scorecard approach

Source: Adapted from Robert S. Kaplan and David P. Norton, Using balanced scorecard as a strategic management system, *Harvard Business Review*, July 2007, https://hbr.org/2007/07/using-the-balanced-scorecard-as-a-strategic-management-system, accessed on 25 February 2015.

The balanced scorecard forces operations chain managers to abandon the belief that traditional financial and operational measures are enough for strategic operations management analysis. To develop an effective scorecard, management defines the organisation's vision and goals. Next, while keeping organisational structure in mind, they must decide which operations strategies will lead to successful goal attainment. These strategies are then translated into specific tactical performance driving activities. Finally, metrics are established for each activity. Once a vision and subsequent strategy have been developed, the individual metrics or vital signs are integrated at relevant places.

The four main key elements in operations management are operational efficiency, optimisation of operating cost, customer satisfaction and continuous improvement of processes. The four key perspectives in balanced scorecard are internal business perspective, financial perspective, customer perspective and learning and growth perspective.

The four key elements of operations management may be measured through the four perspectives of balanced scorecard, thus establishing linkage between both. This tool provides framework approach, process orientation and linkages. For example, the operational efficiency can be assessed via the measures that equate with internal business perspective. Linking of balanced scorecard and operations management can be seen in Table 9.1 where operations strategy and operations parameters are presented.

Table 9.2 indicates the specific metrics that can be used for each of the above goals and objectives.

Advantages of application of balanced scorecard approach to operational performance management system are as follows:

1. It emphasises on the inter-functional and inter-firm nature of supply chains and recognises the need to ascertain the extent to which firms effectively work together and the extent to which functions are coordinated and integrated.
2. The framework will increase the chance that a "balanced" management approach is indeed practised within firms and among the internal departments and supply chain partners.
3. Measures relating to operations perspectives and four balanced scorecard perspectives provide across functions and process linkages. The cited measures in the table are suggestions that may stimulate management to create more appropriate measures to their unique circumstances.
4. The use of this approach should help operations managers focus attention on achieving goals that are beyond the typical measures of performances used within firms.

Thus, operational managers must be able to manage performance using balanced scorecard technique. This needs to be synchronised with firm level scorecard and drilled down from there. Then it can be further rolled down to different process centres/product centres and even to individuals at executive and managerial level for tracking their performance.

TABLE 9.1 Balanced scorecard goals for an operations management function

The Vision – To be a low-cost leader in selected product range

Operations strategy – Low cost manufacture – Effective vendor management

BSS Matrix and Perspectives	Customer Satisfaction	Operational Efficiency	Financial Efficiency
Financial	To be competitive in product price	Optimise operational cost	To increase productivity
Customer	Increase satisfaction	Ensure product availability on demand	Increase revenue from current customers
Internal Business Process	To improve vendor partnership	To increase vendor engagement	To increase investment on vendor development
Learning and Growth	To develop an efficient supplier relationship management	Integrated information system on real/near real time	To develop an efficient and effective financial process

TABLE 9.2 Operations performance parameters relating to balanced scorecard goals

BSS Matrix and Perspectives	Customer Satisfaction	Operational Efficiency	Financial Efficiency
Financial	% price lower than nearest competitor	Total operating cost in ₹ (gross and unit)	Profit margin %
Customer	Delivery performance in %	Fill rate in %	% of revenue increase
Internal Business Process	Number of self-certified vendors	Vendor responsiveness	Cash-to-cash cycle time in days
Learning and Growth	Number of vendor suggestions on improvements	Technology integration and visibility	Working capital management efficiency in purchasing

Triple Bottom Line and Operations Strategy

John Elkington in his book, *Cannibals with Forks: The Triple Bottom Line of 21st Century Business,* in 1997, introduced "the triple bottom line". This was first coined by him in 1994. This could be related to balanced scorecard in some sense. Like balance scorecard, triple bottom line emphasises on performance measurement beyond profits and profitability. Here a brief mention about its relevance to operations strategists and performance management is done. Figure 9.3 depicts triple bottom line.

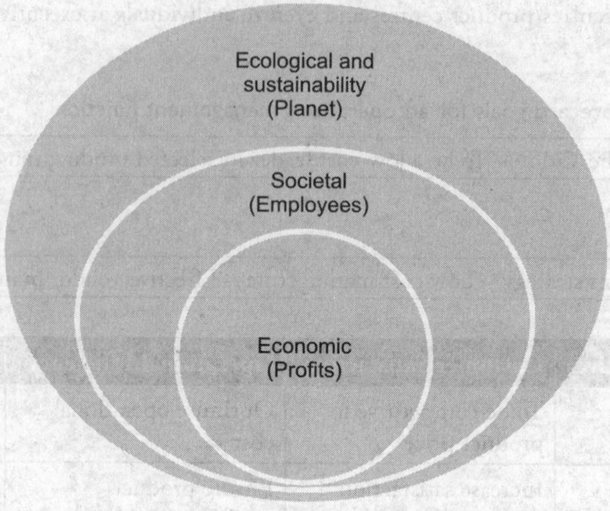

FIGURE 9.3 Triple bottom line

First measure is about profitability. It makes economic sense of entity to be in business. Customers pay for a product based on its value created from design to delivery. Earning profits for key stakeholders, namely investors or capital providers is important. It is also important for few other stakeholders like employees, government who benefits from taxes out of profits and suppliers. It is important for the operations strategy to conceive a product and run the production system efficiently and effectively.

Second, the bottom line of a company's "people account" is a measure in some shape or form of how socially responsible an organisation has been throughout its operations. This includes aspects like employees are paid fair remuneration, treated with respect and given equal opportunity across diversity conditions, adhering to statutory conditions as per labour standards and employment standards and so on. Operations strategy must also focus on suppliers, especially with whom there is a strategic alliance and a part of pre-approved vendor scheme to adhere to all these standards. Such ethical and responsible procurement standards are a part of international procurement policy. Triple bottom line recommends proactive practice of demonstrating societal values as a part of performance reporting.

Third, the bottom line of the company's "planet" account is a measure of how environmentally responsible it has been. Contemporary business is all about sustainability of resources in the planet for the future generation. The question is straight forward, How much of the resources do current customers and stakeholders use just because there is an economic sense? What would be the value one could demonstrate towards sustainability of resources in the planet? Certainly, global warming, depleting natural resources like water and pollution of air and water and so on. Firms have started focussing on deploying concept of reuse, reduce and recycle from product design to final delivery. We have discussed this in greater detail in a chapter on the same. Operations strategist must be sensitive to triple bottom line measures and manage strategies accordingly.

Operations Excellence Approach

There are number of business excellence models, awards and forums which promote excellence as a culture. Most of these are focussed on overall business performance with emphasis on quality.

Exhibit 9.4 ITC strategy towards sustainability

ITC Ltd. has implemented an afforestation programme of nearly 7 lakh acres that supports a large paper mill and possibly supplies to others too; a watershed initiative spread over 8,70,000 acres across 14 states, and nearly 43 per cent of energy met through renewable energy.

The company is into several segments, including FMCG, hotels, paperboards and packaging, agri-business and information technology. The company's operations have been about ensuring shareholders' profit, taking along its stakeholders, and fulfiling a responsibility towards people and the planet.

It had a sales turnover of ₹67,000 crore and profit after tax of ₹11,200 crore in the financial year 2017-18. In its annual report for that year, it had traced its more than 15-year journey in sustainability and benchmarks itself in accordance with Global Reporting Initiative standards. ITC has reported to be carbon-positive for 13 years in a row, water-positive for 16 consecutive years and solid waste recycling positive for the last 11 years.

In the company's sustainability report for 2018, it has pointed out that total shareholder returns are growing at a CAGR of over 22 per cent, "reflecting benchmark efficiency in serving financial capital". It has also claimed to have brought transformational change by making societal value creation a conscious strategic decision.

According to the company's top official, "This belief has spurred ITC to craft innovative strategies that orchestrate a symphony of efforts aimed at enriching the environment, creating sustainable livelihoods, empowering local communities and addressing the challenge of climate change."

The company had initiated setting up 23 platinum-certified green buildings and creating 6 million livelihood opportunities through its businesses and value chain. Its rural retail segment, e-choupal, has been widely acclaimed for its fair treatment of farmers who are their main suppliers.

Being engaged in paper production, which is both energy, water-intensive, and considered a polluting industry, ITC has taken up largescale afforestation. The company also does intensive watershed development in 42 districts.

The company has done extensive savings in energy consumption. Fuel oil consumption has been brought down by 50 per cent in biscuit production while water use in the paper plant at Bhadrachalam has been brought down from 60 cubic metres per tonne to 37 cubic metres per tonne. About 25 MW of power is also generated from bio-waste. These are relating to FY 2017-18.

Thus, the company has become carbon, water and solid waste recycling positive and triple bottom line reporting sets an aggressive competitive advantage.

Source: https://www.thehindubusinessline.com/specials/clean-tech/addressing-the-universe-with-a-triple-bottom-line-delivery/article24445176.ece.

The Malcolm Baldrige National Quality Award is administered by the Baldrige Performance Excellence Program, which is based at and managed by the National Institute of Standards and Technology (NIST). The award recognises U.S. organisations in the business, healthcare, education, and nonprofit sectors for performance excellence.

The framework considers eleven core values and relates to seven aspects of organisation performance management. Table 9.3 shows core values and appropriate aspect of performance management.

TABLE 9.3 Core values and aspects of performance management

Core values	Aspects of performance management
Systems perspective	
Visionary leadership	Leadership
Focus on success	Strategy
Ethics and transparency	Customers
Customer-focussed excellence	Workforce
Valuing people	Measurement, analysis, and knowledge management
Organisational learning and agility	Operations
Management by fact	Results
Managing for innovation	
Societal responsibility	
Delivering value and results	

It may be noted here that the core values and aspects linkages are not just linear but inter-woven. Among other aspects, operations also play a key role in performance of a firm linked to multiple core values like leadership, managing innovation, societal responsibility, customer value and valuing people.

Another important and well recognised award is that of The Deming Prize on TQM (Total Quality Management) in the world. It was established in 1951 to honour W. Edwards Deming who contributed greatly to Japan's proliferation of statistical quality control after World War II. Prof. Deming helped Japan build its foundation by which the level of Japan's product quality has been recognised as the highest in the world. Statistical quality control was promoted widely by him to be implemented in Japanese companies which saw advancement through quality improvement. Over the years, it has grown under the guidance of the Japanese Union of Scientists and Engineers (JUSE).

There is no standard framework for this award. Individuals and companies are expected to set their own objectives and demonstrate implementation of TQM as an exemplary effort yielding tangible results. There are a number of Indian companies who have won this award.

Another popular framework in Europe is European Foundation for Quality Management (EFQM) framework, which is non-prescriptive business excellence framework award. EFQM uses three components to analyse cause and effects of organisation performance. Table 9.4 depicts the same.

Though the framework largely defines business excellence framework, there is substantial focus which needs to be brought by operations strategist. Thus, the above models lead to operations excellence model which operations strategist can make as basic framework for operations performance management and synchronise the same with overall business model and excellence framework.

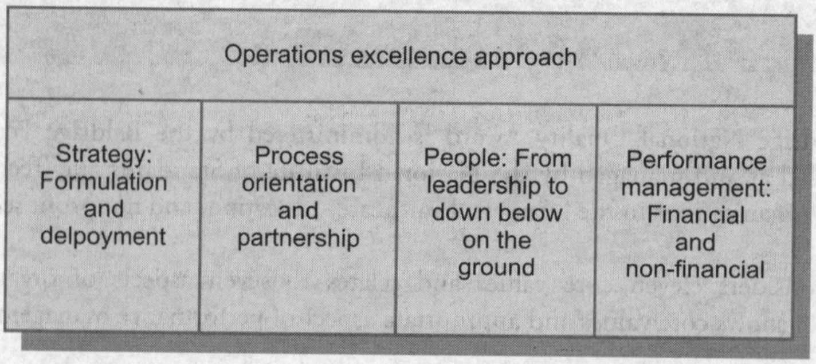

TABLE 9.4 EFQM framework

Core values	Criteria	RADAR logic
➢ Adding value for customers ➢ Creating a sustainable future ➢ Developing organisational capability ➢ Harnessing creativity and innovation ➢ Leading with vision, inspiration and integrity ➢ Managing with agility ➢ Succeeding through the talent of people ➢ Sustaining outstanding results	Enablers: ➢ Leadership ➢ Strategy and policy ➢ People ➢ Partnership and resources ➢ Processes Results: ➢ People ➢ Customer ➢ Societal ➢ Financial	➢ Results aimed ➢ Set of approaches ➢ Deploy approaches ➢ Assess ➢ Refine

This subsection can be concluded with a view that operations strategist could be a part of corporate strategy group and work with operations team for seamless integration of operations, finance and other functions for achieving excellence.

SUMMARY

Performance management in operations is a key responsibility of the operations manager. There are physical performance parameters in operating function to be achieved like capacity utilisation, throughout efficiency, input–output ratios to standards, quality and so on. Technical performance is defined by machinery set up and operating conditions. Tracking of such performance is critical to achieve desired financial results and ability to budget operations. This again has impact on resource management which includes people and financial resources. There are also statutory requirements in certain industries as per the Act to maintain performance report from perspective of various acts like Essential Commodities Act, Labour Regulation and so on.

Apart from these, an operations manager must be familiar with finance fundamental tools and techniques in performance management. Operations team would be involved in budgeting of plant or SBU and at times, even at product or cost centre level. Further operations team need to constantly evaluate purchase of new equipment and replacement of old equipment. Such proposals need understanding of capital budgeting techniques even before they involve finance team for a deeper evaluation.

Visioning and implementing operations strategy is one of the key responsibilities of the operations manager. Apart from strategy envisioning skills and constantly mapping competitive horizon to be an aggressive or even for risk neutral player, at SBU, operations level need to have an approach towards bottom up planning and implementation management. Here apart from managing performance using financial and physical parameter monitoring tools, it may be useful to deploy a balance scorecard approach where financial, customer, internal business process and learning and growth perspectives approach are part of the same. Each of the perspective would be around a vision and strategy and would have defined metric, unit of measure, target and proposed action.

It may be noted here that the above discussed performance management approach is based on need to be running a firm in a competitive environment and where the objective of the firm is to constantly strive to improve competitiveness, especially through operations function. Hence there is a need for benchmarking and competitive mapping exercise which needs to be deployed. Operation managers must have their own peer level network to solicit competitive intelligence and strength performance of their respective SBU or product or cost centre.

Key Terms

Balanced scorecard: It is a framework to align business activities to the vision and strategy of the organisation, improve internal and external communications, and monitor organisation performance against strategic goals. It was originated by Robert Kaplan and David Norton as a performance measurement framework that added strategic non-financial performance measures to traditional financial metrics to give managers and executives a more 'balanced' view of organisational performance.

Capacity utilisation: Capacity utilisation is the extent to which an enterprise or SBU or a line uses its installed productive capacity. It is the relationship between actual output that 'is' actually produced with the installed equipment, and the potential output which 'could' be produced with it, if capacity was fully used.

Direct cost: Direct costs refer to materials, labour and expenses related to the production of a product. It is an expense that can be traced directly to (or identified with) a specific cost centre or cost object, such as a department, process or product.

Fixed cost: It is a periodic cost that remains more or less unchanged irrespective of the output level or sales revenue, such as depreciation, insurance, interest, rent, salaries and wages.

Indirect cost: It is an expense (such as for advertising especially corporate brand building campaigns, IT, security, supervision) incurred commonly and therefore, difficult to assign to or identify with a specific cost object or cost centre.

Net profit margin: The ratio of net profits to revenues for a company or business segment expressed as a percentage. It shows how much of each unit of currency earned is translated into profits.

Operating ratio: It is a ratio that shows the efficiency of a company's management by comparing operating expense to net sales.

Operating budget: An operating budget is the annual budget of an activity stated in terms of SBU/ division/functions or cost centre. It contains estimates of the total value of resources required for the performance and estimated value or revenue.

Throughput ratio: Throughput ratio is the rate at which a plant or service centre is able to produce a product or service for a given unit of time. Those with high throughput (output) levels are able to be more competitive than lower throughput firms because they are able to produce a given product or service more efficiently.

Total cost management: It is an approach for effective management of a business through specific focus on various processes along the value chain and customer driven practices. It encompasses all stages of a product lifecycle.

Variable cost: Variable costs are the costs that vary depending on a company's production volume. They rise as production increases and fall as production decreases. Variable costs can include direct material costs or direct labor costs necessary to complete a certain project.

CONCEPT REVIEW QUESTIONS

1. Explain the importance of performance management approach in operations management and its relevance based on your understanding on any of operations business.
2. What are the key aspects of operational budget and how should an operations manager use techniques explained here in this chapter?
3. Describe traditional methods of managing operations in a plant and role of a manager in monitoring the same.
4. Explain the following:
   a. Baldrige Award
   b. Deming Prize
   c. EFQM Framework

d. Operations Excellence model
5. Describe the concept of strategic cost management and various steps to be followed in implementing the same.
6. What are the different traditional operating performance metrics used by an operations manager? Critically analyse the importance and limitations of each of these metrics.
7. What are the different traditional operating financial performance metrics used by an operations manager? Critically analyse the importance and limitations of each of these metrics.
8. Explain the concept of vendor rationalisation using an example and how it can be implemented?
9. Analyse the importance of strategic sourcing for managing operating costs and quality.
10. Explain the framework of balance scorecard and its relevance for performance management.

CRITICAL THINKING QUESTIONS

1. Describe with an example the application of balance scorecard framework for an operation management department like a bank branch.
2. A hotel named "Comfort Chennai" in the heart of the city has the following operating parameters compared to its peers in the same city.

For the year April – March	2014-15	2015-16	2016-17	2017-18
Number of rooms	360	360	360	360
Available rooms (On average)	350	340	352	346
Occupancy	85%	70%	62%	65%
Occupancy – Industry average in Chennai	75%	75%	68%	70%
Average room rent (ARR)	8000	9000	9000	8000
ARR – Industry average in Chennai	5500	6400	6700	5600
Revenue per available room (RevPAR)	5500	6000	5000	4500
RevPAR industry average in Chennai	4000	4600	4200	3500
Actual average discount	8%	9%	12%	9%
Revenues				
Room rents realised	To be arrived from above data			
F & B	3162	3603	3194	2874
Banquet sales	1405	1533	1278	1150
Other operating incomes	1054	1150	958	862
Total income	To be arrived from above data			
Gross margin	47	45	49	45
Operating margin	28	27	30	29
F & B and Banquet utilisation	68	72	60	58
F & B and Banquet margin	40	42	36	32

As an operations analyst, critically analyse the performance of the hotel and prepare a report for action. You may take comparative hotel information from web and use peer analysis as well.

3. As an operations manager, critically evaluate the need for preparing different types of operations report, namely daily, weekly, monthly, quarterly and annual for managing SBU for an industry with which you are familiar. You may relate the same for budgeting process and explain the importance of operating performance management for budgeting and achieving strategic alignment for growth of SBU.
5. "Operations manager are expected to be technocrats or experts in delivering production and output and controlled environment management is the scope. Beyond this, top management must direct operations head for effectiveness." Elucidate.

PROJECT ASSIGNMENTS

1. Visit the nearest retail store and discuss with the operations manager of the store about various operating performance measurement tools and techniques used by him. Prepare a report critically analysing the same and suggest areas of improvement.
2. Discuss with Dean (Academics) about operating challenges of a management education institution on resources like infrastructure, faculty finance, and evaluate operations performance management system used.

REFERENCES

Ananthanarayanan, P. S. (2014). *Management Accounting*, Oxford University Press of India, New Delhi.

Chandrasekaran, N. and Ananthanarayanan, P. S. (2014). *Strategic Management*, Oxford University of India, New Delhi.

Modarress, B., Ansari, A. and Lockwood, D. L., "Kaizen costing for lean manufacturing: a case study", *International Journal of Production Research*. Vol 43, No: 9, 1 May 2005, 1751–1760.

Tanaka, T. (1993). "Target costing at Toyota". *Journal of Cost Management*, Spring, pp. 4–11.

http://www.livemint.com/Companies/1FOq6BpomNLkmJLIsPLRSK/Mahindra-to-reduce-supplier-base-as-part-of-new-sourcing-str.html?utm_source=copy, accessed on 25 February 2015.

Kaplan, Robert S. and Norton, David P., "Using balanced scorecard as a strategic management system", *Harvard Business Review*, July 2007, https://hbr.org/2007/07/using-the-balanced-scorecard-as-a-strategic-management-system, accessed on 25 February 2015.

https://sustain.wisconsin.edu/sustainability/triple-bottom-line/.

CHAPTER 10

Global Operations Strategy

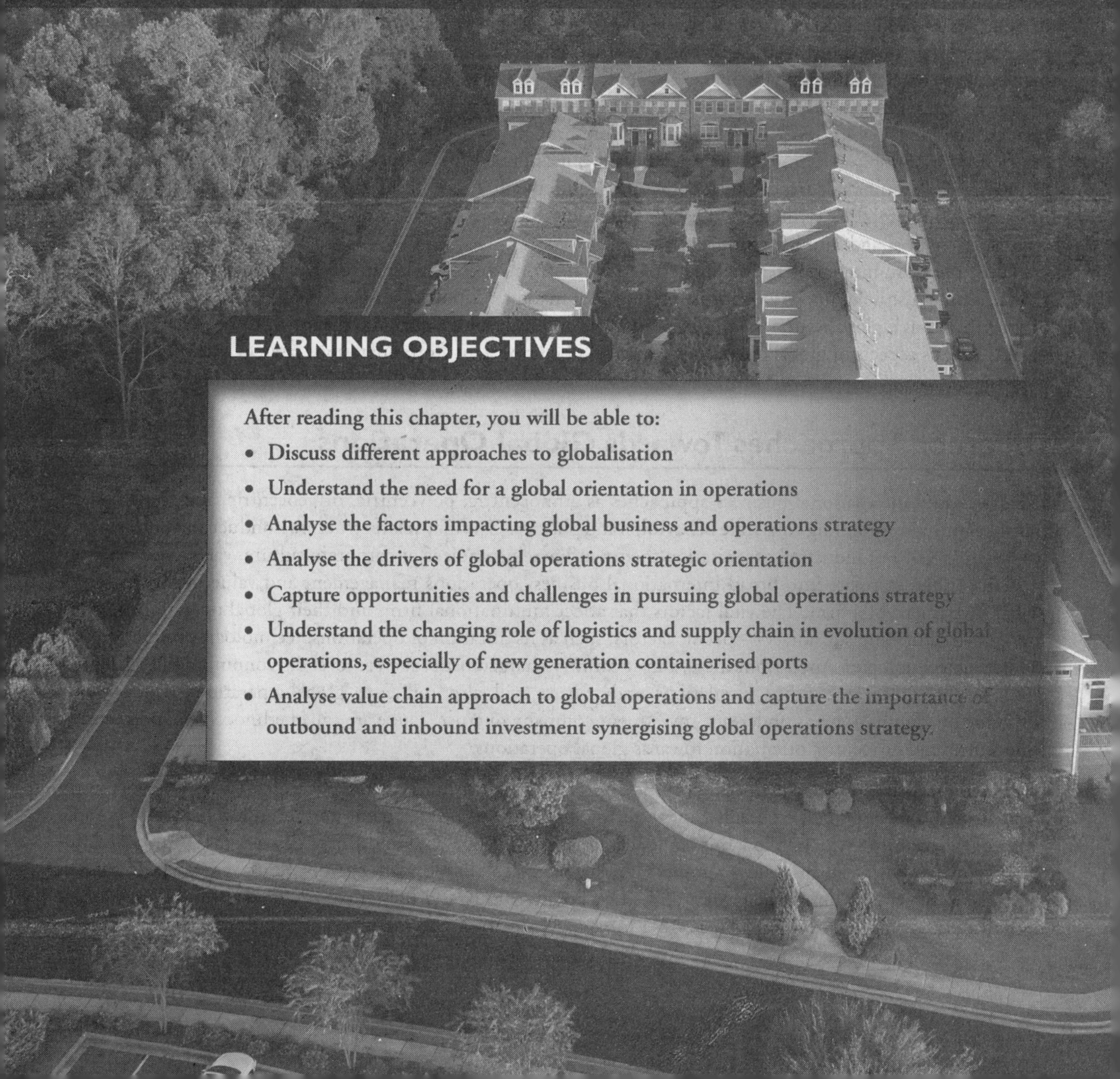

LEARNING OBJECTIVES

After reading this chapter, you will be able to:

- Discuss different approaches to globalisation
- Understand the need for a global orientation in operations
- Analyse the factors impacting global business and operations strategy
- Analyse the drivers of global operations strategic orientation
- Capture opportunities and challenges in pursuing global operations strategy
- Understand the changing role of logistics and supply chain in evolution of global operations, especially of new generation containerised ports
- Analyse value chain approach to global operations and capture the importance of outbound and inbound investment synergising global operations strategy.

Introduction

Global business strategy and its success is key for many large multinational corporations (MNCs). MNCs spread across globally as trading partners from a base country; set up their own subsidiaries or joint ventures for spreading their business across globe. They may standardise operations to globalise or set up localised operations or a combination of both. We have a number of companies like Unilever, Johnson & Johnson, Ford, Citibank, Bank of America, Samsung, Apple, HP, Hindalco, Toyota and many others operating in different parts of the globe. They have seen a market opportunity and have identified an operations strategy to pursue and implemented the same successfully to progress in their vision.

There are companies which pursue international business opportunities to strike gold through opportunity of resource advantage or market requirements in a target country or as a gateway to a large geography. This will be more bilateral or in few selected countries. Singapore, Dubai or Hong Kong played as a host country to reach out to new markets. On the other hand, Australia and Guinea who are rich in minerals have been operating at global scales with their own investment or through international joint ventures in copper, bauxite and other precious metals. Many of such international operations could be by and large by corporate or through government entities. In case of some international business operations involving companies from China or Guinea, the government may be investing in business either individually or through local promoters along with international players. Apart from ownership structure, it has clearly laid out approach towards operational strategy which could be influenced by dominant partner philosophy and requirement. Prima facie, there is nothing like what is right or otherwise! Bilateral investment in capacity and facility is more driven by need basis rather than standardised approach to global and multi-locational operations.

Thus, there are numerous reasons for going global. Companies are a part of evolution and want to garner growth through scale of operations for being in global market. Countries also encourage firms to reach pinnacle of growth through globalisation. Maturity of markets and technology facilitate the same. In this chapter, we will discuss various aspects of global operations which will be important from operations strategy perspective.

Different Approaches Towards Global Operations

Experts classify international business approaches as ethnocentric, polycentric, or geocentric, and these choices translate into corresponding corporate behaviours and policies. One may relate structure-conduct and performance paradigm (S-C-P) of industrial organisation theory influencing choices of corporate culture, values and beliefs.

These values translate into broad international business operations management and value maximisation of global investment of a firm. The vital factors that affect multinational firms and their global operations include strategy, structure and subsidiary—specific factors, such as its duration of operations, technology, production and marketing technologies. Apart from these, a host country characteristic, such as level of economic and technology development, political stability, regulations and culture will also influence global operations strategy of a corporate or a group of firms under one investment company or trust. These are called ethnocentric, polycentric, regiocentric and geocentric orientation towards global operations.

1. **Ethnocentric approach:** In ethnocentric approach, parent country company which enters a new country brings in its resources, especially capital, technology and key management jobs regardless of location. Some of the countries which follow this approach are Japan, Europe, U.S and Korea based firms. With an ethnocentric policy, the firm deploys resources like key management jobs with parent country nationals. Resources from the parent country help for a unified corporate culture and tighter control, and the desire to transfer the parent firm's core competencies to a foreign subsidiary in a structured and controlled pace. In case of

technology and capital deployment, it retains much tighter control on operations. Whenever there is, if any, proprietary process or technology involved, this approach is the most preferred one.

2. **Polycentric approach:** In the polycentric approach, international business operations are driven using host country resources for the subsidiaries of home country as and when a firm enters an international geography. However, the parent country keeps control of most of the strategic decisions, especially relating to investment, technology, appointment of key management resources and branding policy and so on.
   The polycentric approach has both merits and demerits. Use of resources from host country makes it self-sufficient and independently manageable. It thrusts financial and operating viability as an independent entity. Parent entity through their corporate thinktank do handholding till it reaches some stage. When management team is hired from host country nationals, it then eliminates language barriers and cross-cultural adjustment problems of managers and their families. The disadvantages of the polycentric approach are equally strong. Local managers may have difficulty in bridging the gap between the subsidiary and the parent company because the experience and exposure they possess may not have prepared them to work as part of global enterprises. Hence, they travel through a learning curve both on understanding culture, technology and successful transformation of ideas into action through operations. Language barriers, national loyalties, and a range of cultural differences may isolate the corporate headquarters staff from the various foreign subsidiaries. Despite the advantages and disadvantages, firms opt for such an approach when market in host country is substantial or there is any other resource advantage for operations like availability of raw material or labour.

3. **Regiocentric approach:** With regiocentric approach, a firm's choice of its international operation is driven on a regional basis and the resource deployment are based on 'the best in the region'. This must provide an opportunity of shared operations of services and support across firms in the region. This could be, for example, centralised procurement of key resources for all plants in South Asia or using a common third-party logistics service provider or an IT system and support for a unified IT strategy.
   Regiocentric approach takes a somewhat larger operational view than that of polycentric approach. It is possible to develop a new product or service for firms in a region and share the development cost among subsidiaries. For example, Europe, South America or South East Asia provide such opportunities. In this approach, a mix of parent-country resources, host-country resources and third-country resources can be used depending on the specific needs of a subsidiary through a common planning and implementation group whose focus is to optimise such investment.
   This approach has become more popular as many multinational companies are choosing to organise on regional basis. One of the main advantages of this approach is that it reduces the need for costly duplication of support services like sourcing, logistics, HR managers and IT. Most multinational companies prefer regiocentric because the sales and operations are concentrated on the region. When it comes to the corporate level, the regiocentric approach may be limiting as ethnocentric approach and multinational companies may fail to understand the features of the regions outside of their home region. The difference is only between a host country and a region.
   This model is more popular in cases where product and services can be rationalised across a region instead of a country and brand recognition goes well with the region than in any one of the host countries.

4. **Geocentric approach:** This approach seeks the best resources for key deployment throughout the group firms by the parent investment firm. It is agnostic to nationality or belongingness of resources like management team, material, processes and even capital. It seeks the best for each subsidiary for their global operations. It focusses on investment in a host country and optimises by seeking the best across. Seeking the best resource for deployment, irrespective of the resource base is the most consistent with the underline philosophy of a global corporation towards its international operations.

A geocentric policy is based on assumptions that high quality resources are available not only at home country, but also in the subsidiaries across host nations where the firm will like to set up its global operations. Resource availability and transferability from one country to another are key for this model. Under current conditions of trade and capital movement, such an assumption is valid and works well.
The geocentric approach has merits and demerits. Among its advantages is the possibility of making the best use of its resources across nations. It builds a corporate culture of resource deployment at home working with several cross breed of resources. This helps in functions like finance and human resources as well as in operations. Technology adoption and transfer are easier in such an approach.

The four global operations approaches are somewhat mutually exclusive. They were originally discussed for management structure and mainly for deploying senior managers who were controllers of resources. However, here we have extended the concept of resource deployment across management functions as it is fit for the same.

A firm chooses international operations strategy based on investment firm's philosophy on control and intent on financial security and top management attitude. It requires host country's external environment being congenial for growth. Choice of approach will be determining the type of global operations from trading to subsidiary plant or service operation. It also determines its international investment on development of new products and services; choice of technology and design of supply network. Further, it addresses more specifically, on location of plants for global demand or for fulfiling any specific host country demand. Each of these approaches present different and unique operations management challenges as well as opportunities. More specifically, when an organisation uses different countries for its production and service business, different tax laws and other significant operations related factors like environment, health and safety (EHS) laws, restrictions on raw material usage, especially if it is natural resource based or tariff laws limiting to production and trade and so on, may apply. Therefore, it is highly recommended that operations professionals need to be knowledgeable about the laws and customs of each country in which the firm operates or intends to enter as it orchestrates its global operations strategy.

Further, the above can be presented as given in Figure 10.1 especially for a service business, though it works for product manufacture, assembly and processing.

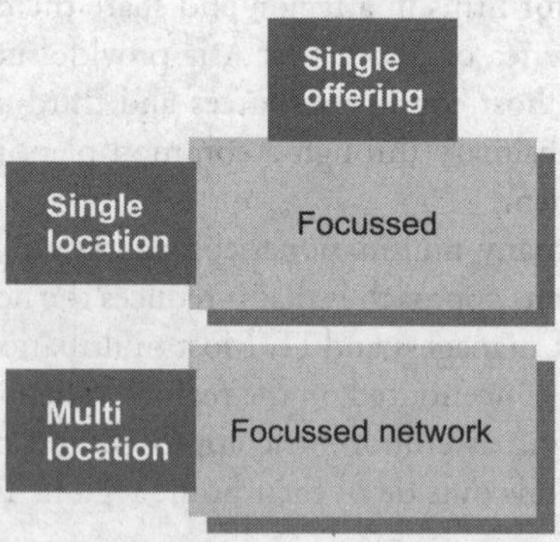

FIGURE 10.1 Growth strategies across location and offering

It may be noted that few firms choose to be single location and single offering which could be a service or a product. Typically, this would be a niche and market specific offering. Second, possibly, such a firm specialising on a product/service adds on to portfolio of products/service by getting more into customer value or spend as opportunity in related business arises. This would be more of a related diversification in a specific geography. Example of a focus business where a firm is in single location and single product or service would include large private hospitals, education institutions or in product like agricultural equipment like pumps and motors for the Indian market. Clustered service, namely more services for domestic market includes when the hospital enters into pharmacy business, especially into online pharmacy for domestic market or an education institute sets up online learning portal and job portals.

There is another choice which firms have towards their operations strategy. A firm may opt for focus network wherein a single offering is provided in multiple locations. One of the classic examples is that of hotel chain management company like Choice Hotels which enter into agreement with property owners across countries and geography where a traveller can choose from Choice Hotel Group network. Business which the firm focusses on is management of properties for leisure and business. Similar example of Focus network is Disney across geographies other than USA. Another option for firms is multi offering at multiple locations. For example, Hindalco of Aditya Birla Group globalizing through a transformational merger is a typical example of the company growing across geographies on metal business of copper and aluminium and their upstream and downstream products.

The above analysis can be linked to the degree of global integration and the extent of local responsiveness. These are called generic international strategies and closely link to what was discussed about as Ethnocentric, Polycentric and Geocentric. Regiocentrism is not relevant here as it is a mid-point on an option of fully global versus being the best at a regional or limited geography. Operations strategy in each of these makes strategic decisions with respect to product development, technology, supply network, location decisions and that of organisation development process in operations like quality management and so on, as shown in Figure 10.2.

		Degree of global integration	
		Low	High
Extent of local responsiveness	Low	Domestic firm	Global firm
	High	Multi domestic firm	Transnational firm

FIGURE 10.2 Generic internationalisation strategies

A firm or its investment arm decides on deployment of any of these approaches or a combination to determine how operational effectiveness can be used to achieve a sustainable competitive advantage of a firm or group of firms through a common investment management firm.

Need for Global Orientation in Operations

Certain changes impact businesses across the globe. Today, we experience technology developments impacting production, demand, customer aspirations and flow of capital. Knowledge and information flow are at the speed of light! Customers are swayed by international brand disposition and willing to experience international brands. Otherwise, how could one justify proliferation of automotive brands especially of two wheelers and four wheelers in India. Four-wheeler markets are dominated by Suzuki, Hyundai, Ford, Volkswagen and so on. Similarly, in two-wheeler market, we have Honda, Suzuki and others are directly competing with Indian brands or with joint venture brands. Hence, it is important to have inbound global operations by firms to capture aspirational customers.

On the other hand, we have Indian firms going for outbound investment in international markets. Such moves are necessitated by market forces towards input material or components or technology and at times, market opportunity as well. Apart from such competitive drive, global operations are driven by capital availability and proprietary technology leading to exploitation of market opportunities and increasing customer base. Thus, global operations are driven by market forces relating to demand of increasing customer base, large size sales revenue potential, increasing profitability, effective deployment of capital, resources availability and technology and processes.

Factors Impacting Global Business Conditions and Operations Strategy

Numerous factors influence global operations. From time immemorial, international operations have taken place through trade, licensing and franchising. What is more exciting now is opening of economies, investible opportunities, advances in technology and logistics! Global operations have been a reality with an ability to locate in a low-cost geography and be responsive to serve across globe at a reasonable total cost of transactions and fulfilment rate.

Global Competition Being a Reality:

Global competition is fully evolved in most of the industries including that of manufacturing and services. These could include consumer electronics; computer and related hardware; software; industrial electronics; home equipment; fast moving consumer goods; automobiles; paints; pharmaceuticals and services like banking, insurance and financial services, so on. The changing nature of world business; emergence of desire to be international by companies; strategic alliances and product sharing and scope provided by financial markets have an impact on global operations strategy.

A. Changing nature of world business

Changing nature of world business is driven by many other developments in international business and trade. First, technology, especially in information, communication and electronics have made the globe into a village. Communication is swift, and lot of data and information could be easily shared. This creates easy workflows to coordinate deliverables. The opportunities in service aspect of manufacturing or in pure play service businesses are extremely high. For example, in contemporary new product development practice, an automobile, car, can be developed in less than 20 months with sharing of design and component developments through virtual involvement of designers, developers and component manufacturers. This was not that easily possible about two decades ago. This has led to global operations of new product development. Similarly, in service business, one can see innumerable operations across geography to deliver value to customer. Simplest value chain activity delivered across boundaries is that of information technology software development, implementation and value add by way of near and offshore support from a host country. It has been interesting to see how after rapid changes in health insurance requirement in United States like necessity for sign in by patient and medical professional on their interaction which developed opportunities for live capture of such interaction and sharing instantaneously wherein both parties agree to capture their discussion and way forward. Three-dimensional printing and smart manufacturing are again further developments which demonstrate advancement of technology for global operations.

The other important development that has changed the world business is advancement in trade practices by WTO. The WTO agreements cover goods, services and intellectual property. Scope of agreements include individual countries' commitments to lower customs tariffs and other trade barriers. These clauses provide an opportunity to service new markets. There are defined procedures for settling disputes. These agreements are not static and are changing from time to time. Many are now being negotiated under the Doha Development Agenda, launched by WTO trade ministers in Doha, Qatar, in November 2001. It is interesting to note that how some of the countries like India, Brazil, China, South Africa and Russia have looked at these developments positively. A country like India despite small share of trade to global volume of trade stood firm on certain clauses to ensure fair and inclusive trade practices. Such developments built political and economic environment that enabled cross border investment for mobility of capital, technology and processes for wide reach of market.

Another significant contributing factor for reality of global competition is the enablement of movement of goods with growth of logistics sector like container movement from number of new generation ports. Since 1980s, China's investment in manufacturing resulted in phenomenal increase of production and exports. New generation of ports facilitated such export led growth. Further many other new generation ports in Asia like Tanjung Pelepas in Malaysia, Port of Salalah and Aden Port in Yamen, to name a few, facilitated movements of goods to some of the developing countries. Guinea in West Africa opened investment which increased competition, especially for mineral based industries.

Thus, advancement in technology, ease of trade and efficiency in supply network through effective logistics made global competition a reality.

B. International companies:

Companies are becoming international in terms of their outlook and operating size. This is natural corollary of the above conditions. When the market opportunities are aplenty, companies gear up operating capability to charter growth plans. Operating perspective that they may have to investigate would include new product/service development or existing products in a new market. In such cases, focus of an operations strategist is into facility decision relating to location and capacity planning; deployment of appropriate technology and production process (It is not mandatory to set up uniform level of technology across nations and markets!); designing of supply network and plug the value chain for appropriate value creation and finally, operating organisational processes like quality system and methods.

International companies follow the models based on type of management they will like to have which include ethnocentric; geocentric; regiocentric and polycentric. This has been generally used for categorisation of management structure and style. This might also relate to which part of value network a firm's operation is into. It could be mere supply of raw material or component to full scale production and distribution in host country market and exports from there to other countries. Today aspirations of companies lead towards the same. We can see many international companies spread across different parts of the globe, operating successfully on a well-designed model.

Here, we have taken up the growth of Saint Gobain in India from the open source information available.

This firm's growth shows how a firm can expand international operations with the support of domestic policy environment and efficient demand management. There are numerous such companies across the globe who achieved similar traction towards global operations.

C. Strategic alliances and production sharing:

Strategic alliances are an agreement between two or more companies to work together to develop or manufacture or assemble and sell and service a product or service. It becomes a part of global operations when companies across geography attempt to do this. Strategic alliances are done based on technology, cost advantage, reliability of supplies and so on. It is further driven by operations perspective and/or on marketing perspective.

In technology space, few open source software developers allow their platform to be available for different application developers so that the benefit of development can be shared on success basis. Such kind of strategic alliance is the level I basic alliance model. This can truly allow global IT applications development professionals to participate and is a "win-win" strategy for both. This happens not only in technology space but also in manufacturing or services business. For example, US based professional body of medical professionals may select virtual scribes in India, Vietnam or Ireland to complete live capture of interaction between patient and medical doctor for record wherein both confirm capture of interaction. Though a firm from India, Vietnam or Ireland may approach and individually sell such a service to a doctor, it is also possible for a group of doctors through a forum to reach out to a firm for a strategic alliance to evaluate such an opportunity. As a group, they buy such a service at a target cost. Such operations strategy is more for a medium term, say 12 to 24 months before getting into long term tie up. In such cases, basic driver of operating relationship is minimising cost for an agreed service level.

Exhibit 10.1

Growth of glass manufacturing major Saint Gobain in India

Saint-Gobain is a group of companies with its origin in France. The companies are into design, manufacture and distribution of materials and solutions which are key ingredients in the well-being of all. They are into glasses in buildings, transportation, infrastructure and in many industrial applications. They provide comfort, performance and safety while addressing the challenges of sustainable construction, resource efficiency and climate change. Saint-Gobain Group operates in advanced countries and benefits from sustained growth in emerging markets. With 2018 sales of €41.8 billion, Saint-Gobain operates in 68 countries and has more than 180,000 employees. The group offers its expertise through leading European and international brands, and research centres.

In 2019, the company inaugurated a third float glass manufacturing plant in Chennai with an overall investment of ₹1,200 crore. It has already two such plants in Chennai. According to the company's sources, the facilities would meet the growing demand of both the domestic and international glass markets. The other facilities which are set up include, apart from the firm's third float glass manufacturing plant, an advanced magnetron coater and glass solutions line and a 72 million litre capacity rainwater harvesting reservoir.

The initiatives at the company's World Glass Complex, completed at an estimated ₹1,200 crore, have taken its cumulative investment at Chennai to over ₹3,000 crore.

Saint-Gobain is a French company which has more than two decades of experience after their first entry into India. According to the company sources, "As one of the fastest growing economies in the world, India was an important market and investment destination for Saint-Gobain".

During the past two decades, the company has invested in developing new markets, new world-class manufacturing facilities and technology and human capital. It may be noted here that earlier the parent company had set up Saint-Gobain Research India which was aimed at developing innovative solutions in building material industry. This helps not only markets such as India, but also the world.

It may be noted here that the company has developed the market in India by bringing the best technologies and building world-class manufacturing facilities in line with the government's 'Make in India' mission. According to the company, the third float glass plant will be the 'largest' in India and the region and was equipped to manufacture a range of complex products that cater to the needs of sustainable habitats and affordable luxury.

The company's India growth is an interesting phase of high growth track record starting from 1996. The company has expanded substantially with its investment in many related areas and deep in few areas like float glass plant with about five plants across India. It has also focussed growth in Southern and Western parts of India. Its main location is Chennai, holding a substantial size of capacity and investment. This may explain advantages of logistics infrastructure like location of ports. Figure 10.3a and b on Saint-Gobain India growth (chronological) from 1996 to 2018 and Table 10.1 on investment in business and locations help to draw the above inference.

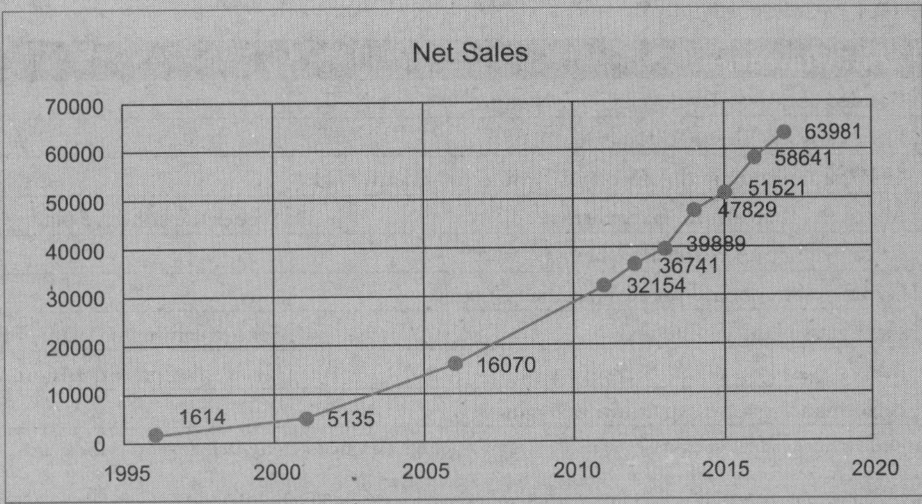

FIGURE 10.3a Saint-Gobain India growth from 1996 to 2018

Year	1996	2001	2006	2011	2012	2013	2014	2015	2016	2017
Net Sales	1614	5135	16070	32154	36741	39889	47829	51521	58641	63981
5-year CAGR		26%	26%	15%					13%	

FIGURE 10.3b Saint-Gobain India growth from 1996 to 2018

TABLE 10.1 Investment in business and locations

Year	Activity/Investment	
1996	Delegation established in India	Bicron (now crystals) plant, Bengaluru
1997	Abrasive plant, Nagpur	
1998	Sekurit, Chakan (Pune)	
2000	Float glass I Chennai	
2002	Acquires AZS plant, Palakkad	Glass mirror plant, Chennai
2004	Weber plant, Wada (Near Mumbai)	
2005	Float glass II Chennai	Sekurit laminated plant, Chennai
	Crystals Expansion, Bengaluru	
2006	India gypsum Acquisition	Glass: magnetron coater I, Chennai
	Plaster boards plants, Wada (Near Mumbai)	Sekurit tempered plant, Chennai
2008	Abrasive plant, Himachal Pradesh	Gyproc plastic boards plant, Bengaluru
	Performance plastics plant, Bengaluru	
2009	Silicon carbide plant, Bhutan	Expansion of Palakkad plant
2011	Glass float III Jhagodia (Gujarat) Acquisition	Glass solutions Plant, Chennai
	SEPR sintered plant, Palakkad	
2012	High performance refraction plant, Halol (Gujarat)	Non-woven abrasive plant, Bengaluru
	Vetrotech Plant, Chennai	

TABLE 10.1 (Continued)

Year	Activity/Investment	
2013	Bonded abrasive plant expansion, Nagpur	
2014	Float glass IV, Bhiwadi (Rajasthan)	
2015	SEPR aluminium and AZS plant, Perundurai, Tamil Nadu	
2016	Abrasives - Expansion, Bengaluru	Weber tile adhesive plant, Chennai
2017	Glass magnetron coater II, Chennai	
	Gyproc plaster board plant, Hagadia (Gujarat)	
2018	Float glass plant V, Chennai	Sekurit laminated plant, Bhiwadi
	Adfors' glass grid plant, Bengaluru	Glass solutions expansion, Chennai
	Performance plastic expansion Bengaluru	

Source: https://www.thehindubusinessline.com/companies/saint-gobain-inaugurates-3-key-facilities-near-chennai/article26112755.ece ; Accessed on 30 July 2019
https://www.saint-gobain.co.in/saint-gobain-india/ourjourneysofar, Accessed on 30 July 2019.

Most often quoted example in service operations is that of logistics sector with people and cargo movement. Airlines operate under a number of major alliances. The top three alliances are mentioned in Exhibit 10.2.

Exhibit 10.2 Major Airline Alliances across the Globe

Star Alliance was founded in 1997 which is based in Frankfurt. It was started with five-member airlines, namely Lufthansa; Air Canada; Scandinavian Airlines; Thai Airways and United Airways. By April 2018, the alliance has grown to a total of 21-member alliances across the globe. By 2018, the alliance operated over 18500 departures in a day which was achieved with a combined fleet of over 4500 aircrafts. It was reported to have handled an annual traffic of 728 million passengers in a year by then.

OneWorld, the next airline alliance was set up in 1999. It is head quartered at New York. The alliance was founded by British Airways, American Airline, Cathy Pacific and Quantas. By 2017, it had 13-member airlines. Then, it had a combined fleet of 3500 aircrafts which facilitated 13,000 daily departures and handled a passenger traffic of 527.9 million.

SkyTeam is another big alliance founded in June 2000. The alliance was originally founded by four members, namely Aeromexico; Air France; Delta Airlines and Korean Air. As of March 2018, SkyTeam has 20 members with a combined fleet of 1400 plus and handling an annual passenger traffic of 730 million.

Advantages of alliance include:

1. Pooled capacity and availability across routes through network and optimisation load factor.
2. Code share flights among alliance partners with high density and code share are available outside alliance partners as well.
3. Better customer (passenger) engagements through affinity programmes, including frequent flyer benefits and lounge access.

Hence, strategic alliance among airline brings advantage to different stakeholders.

Source: https://simpleflying.com/the-3-major-airline-alliances-star-alliance-oneworld-and-skyteam-why-are-they-good/. Accessed on 19 August 2019.

Similarly, a Shipping Alliance is also operational for cargo movement through ocean. It is also known as Ocean Alliance. It is a group of ocean carriers joining forces to create a cooperative agreement forming a strategic alliance covering various trade routes through cooperation between its members on a global level. Like airlines alliance, shipping alliance helps consolidation of assets for revenue deployment. It further helps in reducing operating costs as bunker costs and port charges form nearly 60 per cent of shipping lines operating cost which are variable. Consolidation efficiency helps them to manage their resources and business better. This happens because of the usage of common resources, such as ships, port terminals and networks around particular routes. However, it may be noted here that the alliance does not lead to sharing of cargo details, rates and customer information. Further, it does not entail share benefits with individual liners. (https://freighthub.com/en/blog/shipping-alliances-mean/#)

It is not that we see such global operations in large infrastructure and asset-based sectors. It happens across industries depending upon the operating positioning that may be required for a given market. As explained earlier on spectrum of relationship among supplier and a firm, strategic alliance could vary from simple share of a guaranteed volume of share of business in supplies to sharing of technology and preparedness through concurrent engineering and so on. One can imagine a company like Dell which operates in India may have components vendor from India and global markets. Typically, Dell is expected to operate under Just in Time as it is configuring a product to customer request. Aggregation of such order request is served at the line of assembly. Typically, there will be a third party logistics service provider who aggregates supplies from vendors and fulfils production schedule requirement. Such a third-party logistics service provider could also Import on Record for some of the foreign suppliers and operating on alliance mode. There would be a couple of engagements that would happen like between foreign suppliers and Dell; Dell and third-party logistics service provider; and foreign supplier and third-party logistics service provider. Such operations are undertaken by clear establishment of service standards, standard operating procedures and rewards and penalties for achieving or otherwise desired performance levels.

Apart from above, one can think of several strategic alliances among many businesses and partners across industries and geography. Generally, firms form a cluster and operate for optimising resources and profitability at the cluster level so that globalisation benefits are aplenty.

It may be noted here that alliances are motivated by international operations to access product or production technology; augment production capability; improve market access and for pooling of capital. Japanese companies have long practised Keiretsu, the linking of companies into industrial groups. There can be two types of such alliances, namely financial keiretsu and production keiretsu. A financial keiretsu links companies together with cross holding of shares, sales and purchases within the group and consultation. This comes useful not only in domestic growth of operations but also across borders wherein they can set up large production plants and set up suppliers' ecosystem through this. A production keiretsu is a web of interlocking relationship between a big manufacturer like Toyota and its suppliers.

Production sharing means that a product might be designed and financed in one country, its materials produced in other countries and sold in yet other countries. The country that is the highest quality, lowest cost producer for an activity would perform that portion of the production of the product. Such strategic choices for operations depend upon the acumen and risk assumption capability of top management in globalisation of operations. The advantages may include increase in productivity; exposure to global competition and thereby new learning and ability to look at low cost operations strategy; international operations facilitating cross pollination of ideas and development of new products and services and finally, many more new jobs in domestic/host market. Only possible disadvantage in spreading global operations could be that local labour market may be affected by new wage trends and inability of local labour to catch up with production requirement leading to inbound migration of workforce. Thus, strategic alliances have likely impact on global operations strategy and are more likely to be favourable and growth driven rather than inhibiting growth.

d. International financial conditions:

International financial conditions would influence global operations. When we depict financial conditions, it naturally captures stock of capital at different countries which includes availability of investible funds, inflationary trend, foreign currency rate, interest rate for savings, volatility of stock market, national public finance and policy impacting its debt and thereby quality of macro economy.

Impact of all above factors may be observed at multiple levels of global operations management. We have listed some of the key areas of focus:

1. Trends in production and cost of material may turn adverse because of inflation and change in foreign exchange rate. Ultimately, focus on operations is to manage impact on net cost of material for conversion.
2. Cost of plant and machinery and thereby, set up and expansion cost of plant and creation of new and additional capacities. This will also encourage many new entries into a country or region and intensify competition. Hence, an operations strategist must actively evaluate the entry of competition, intensity of rivalry among firms and increase normal capacity of operations for achieving economies of scale and make it an entry barrier. This can be done easily by dominant firms in an industry.
3. Another area of operations linked to international financial conditions is development of new products, innovation, technological collaborations and investment in sophisticated production technology when capital is cheaper. Automating processes to reduce the amount of labour needed, particularly processes that are labour intensive can be attempted under such favourable financial conditions.

   Once capital becomes dearer, operations strategist would find it difficult to evaluate such options and invest for moving up the value chain.
4. Another area of global operations being influenced by international financial conditions includes that of setting up an extensive supply network. Especially when industries spend substantial amount of money in distribution of goods and services or in case of inbound material, favourable financial condition is one wherein an evaluation of the available network for designing optimal supply network with plants, regional distribution centres, inventory level and transport arrangement. Thus, firms exploit global financial conditions to optimise total landed cost and final cost of goods produced.
5. During conditions of increasing cost, firms look at global operations strategy towards setting up plants in low cost countries especially to take advantage of resources including that of labour. Now with advancement in trade through containerised cargo and setting up of new cargo terminals across strategic ports have facilitated exercising such locational options for optimising cost and maximising profit at consolidated level of operations.

The above conditions have appeared earlier in business. Due to the fall in the value of dollar between 1975 and 1995, the prices of US products/services abroad fell, and demand increased. This facilitated firms from Japan and other countries to build factories in US. They captured reasonable size of the market. This mainly happened in auto sector and consumer goods sector, especially in consumer electronics. Japanese manufacturers moved upscale towards higher priced products. This was possible because companies were ready to move quickly to shift strategies as world financial conditions changed. It took some time for leading US players to respond as their local economic conditions wherein not so favourable and in any case, it being a liberal and capitalist economy, there was not too much of reactions to start with. However, domestic firms started reacting only after they were hurt deeply.

It may be noted that opportunities are usually available to reduce risk through properly deploying global operations strategies. One can build smaller, more flexible factories across key regions and serve demand in those regions and trade to others based on economic conditions. This will suit especially those who are looking at exploiting domestic resources and optimise distribution costs. Typically, products of low value and standardised are easily amenable for such split location and addressing of global demand.

Second, one may look at the opportunity of using foreign suppliers for materials, parts or products. Whenever there is an adoption of fair-trade practices and international trade agreements through WTO enabling trade without protectionism, firms are likely to compare procuring material from international sources as well as domestically. For example, in India still certain quantity of steel is imported from Korea, especially steel that is used in auto and auto ancillary manufacture. There are two reasons—one reason is to match demand and supply for a quality and at a time window and second, according to some manufacturers imported steel is of matching quality or shade better in terms of quality. Further, landed cost at the factory gate is lower than domestic purchase price as of 2019. Manufacturers apply pressure by procuring from international sources so that the domestic firms would improve on efficiency and achieve cost advantage. One can think many other such products, services and even commodities. This is also true in case of import of coal by power plants in India.

Finally, operations strategist while deploying global orientation must be involved in carefull planning and forecasting of demand and supply conditions. This is required because operating risks through global trade can be higher because of increased lead time and at times, need to buy at certain volume. The latter is especially true of bulk items. Hence, a firm must track changing conditions of business and imbibe the best practices in manufacturing at a global scale. It may be needed necessarily to be competitive in local market as global firms can come up with inbound investment in plants.

All the above connotes balancing of operating, financial and portfolio risk at global level.

Customer obsession with quality and service

Contemporary society customers are more informed. Proliferation of use of smartphones, increased accessibility of world wide web through Wi-Fi availability and active presence in social media make a customer simply powerful! Awareness of quality in terms of reliability and performance is high. Customers are conscious of the warranty terms and cost built on purchase price for providing warranty which was earlier present only in developed world. Third party support services of warranty have been an advantage to customers as well as manufacturers. There is a tendency to compare among geography on such parameters and expectations have been universally common. Hence, global operations strategists are under challenge to achieve the highest possible level of quality and the best of customer service. If one looks at this positively, globalisation of operations leads to increased customer awareness due to demonstration effect across geography.

Scarcity of operational resources

Operational resources like materials, manpower, money and managerial capability are required for production or process or assembly of goods and delivery of services. Though all these are important, in operations management focus is mainly given for materials and manpower. Raw material is naturally endowed and need not necessarily be available across geography. Similarly, labour endowment in terms of number, ability and productivity could vary. Both resources are also closely linked to geopolitical conditions influencing operations.

Raw materials like titanium, nickel, coal, natural gas, water and petroleum products are periodically unavailable or in short supply across regions. Most of these are traded and value added across regions for local consumption and trade. For example, India imports coal, bauxite, alumina, silica, steel and raw skin for processing of leather, and so on. Naturally, industries dependent on such trade need to have well-structured global perspective in their operations strategy.

A shortage of any necessary input to convert into output through processes including skilled manpower, can be a challenge for an operations manager. India has abundant availability of skilled manpower. One may have to see if the quality of such skilled manpower is the best or we need to supplement. For example, though India has a long history of being in textile industry and labour has been trained over decades of experience, Bangladesh and Sri Lanka workforce have higher productivity as well as Chinese and Vietnamese workforce! In tea industry, India had an edge which was again lost to Sri Lanka and Nigeria. On positive note, Indian workforce has been good in business process outsourcing, knowledge process outsourcing, software solutions development and implementation, pharmaceutical bulk drug manufacture because of a large number of chemists in India and so on. Inbound investments in BPOs, KPOs, IT and pharmaceuticals will substantiate as proof of competitive skills of our workforce. This has attracted global operations strategists from different countries to consider locating back office operations in India.

Advanced technologies impacting global operations

Firms can use advanced technologies for favouring global operations strategy as it helps in increasing economies of scale; reduced cost and take a broad focus of taking enhanced product or service across geography with minimal customisation to cater to local demand. Location decision using advanced technologies helps to serve global demand with minimal number of plants yet establish leadership in the industry. Some of the examples of those firms who have followed this operations strategy include Apple, Dell and IT service firms locating in India and Ireland but catering to global demand.

The other advantage of advanced technologies is increased product and service quality. As we have seen over a period, new technologies have taken up quality of product and service. Some of the examples include automotive parts for four wheelers, two wheelers and so on; smartphone technology; laptops and financial services. Global operations naturally help for adoption of such technologies. Further, such advanced technologies help for reduced scrap in manufacture. Such reduction naturally brings down material costs and helps a firm to achieve cost reduction. For example, a firm developed cold forging technology for turning machine parts looking at cold forging technology used elsewhere. This has helped the firm to be leader in developing cold forged components and subcomponents for auto sector. It is a leading global player wherein 60 per cent of its production being sold in USA and Europe. The firm's sale in USA and domestic market are almost same. Keeping global operations in mind, the firm invested on such technological advancement. One can list a number of such cases wherein advanced technologies have improved product and/or service performance level.

Faster responses to customer needs

Global operations strategy may also focus on faster responses to customer needs by effectively managing their network of nodes and flows, namely plants, regional distribution centres, inventory and transport management for distribution towards primary, secondary and last mile movement. As mentioned earlier, Importer on Record by third logistics service providers help line feed for a quick turnaround of assembly so that the firm can respond to customer needs quickly. Global operations strategists in high tech products like medical equipment, capital equipment and in case of some consumer electronics work on the faster response time to customer requirement. With development of logistics services across the globe and rationalisation of trade practices, this has been a reality and not a constraint for setting up global operations.

Faster introduction of new products and services

Firms are aggressively expanding their products and services from all over the globe. Product innovation and launch of new products is critical for sustainability of a firm. If one looks at auto sector, new brand launch which will be a variant of an existing product is an annual feature. Product launch takes a lot of time as components are manufactured at different parts of globe. From design to test market, number of iterations take place. Unless, global operations orientation is in place, product launch cannot happen at such a pace. Even in case of pharmaceuticals, one would understand despite confidentiality and secrecy involved in new product development, process requires ability to work across geography to quickly launch the same. Firms use global operations for idea development, product refinement and test marketing before commercialisation which is more relevant when launches are at global scale. Hence, global operations strategy facilitates new product development faster and that of services as well. In case of service, a high amount of customisation to a region or country may be required. When it comes to a country like India, service customisations challenges are aplenty because of market heterogeneity. However, globalisation of operations facilitates new product development and reduces time to market.

Social responsibility issues

Social responsibility issues are getting attention across the globe. Be it domestic market or international market, social responsibility issues and ethics will continue to play an important role. First, a firm has a legal commitment to do what is right. A product and/or service needs to be marketed following statutory norms of production and delivery to a customer. Every country has its own laws which directs welfare of citizens as customers and various stakeholders. Not only for customers, related aspects have legal binding which are high but also for employees, creditors and Board of Directors, and so on. A company must abide by the laws of land wherever it is located and transact its business with. For example, an IT company having its development centres in India will follow rules of our land. However, its near shore office or onsite office will follow rules of the respective country. It must fulfil statutory requirements including social benefits that it may have to provide. But this is more threshold requirement of business.

Similarly, one can look at the impact business would have on environment and mandatory requirement of pollution control and addressing of issues relating to Environment, Health and Safety (EHS). Firms have been following ISO 14001 & ISO 45001 and other certification process to establish that required standards are being followed. When a firm participates in global operations, some of these are mandatory. For example, importers of apparel from Tiruppur through sourcing agents, buyers and direct procurement require proactive mandatory self-declaration that responsible procurement practices are being followed and ethical standards are fulfiled. This covers aspects like landfill, waste reduction, recycling, energy conservation, avoidance of chemical spills, appropriate water disposal, etc. In textiles as well as other industries, international supply network decisions thrust on social issues are being addressed. Product safety for customers and for those who handle at various stages of movement across supply network is important. Similarly, employee safety and likely impact of manufacture by assembly, processing or any method of state changes do not cause injury and endanger life of employees and immediate society where people live nearby. Global companies audit these parameters on a regular basis. Such practices have helped for betterment and evolution of standards of operations across countries.

Global trade and trends in operations

Global trade and production base across countries who participate in trading of goods and services over the years are analysed here. Statistics shared by World Trade Statistics Review 2019 by WTO helps reasonable understanding of global operations.

Table 10.2 depicts growth of world merchandise trade volume and real GDP at market exchange rates. It can be observed that as and when world merchandise exports grew, real GDP also grew. It is here that these discussions are focussed on importance of global operations. Data show significant increase in indexed value over the ten years showing importance of trade.

TABLE 10.2A World merchandise trade volume and real GDP at market exchange rates, growth

	2008	2009	2010	2011	2012	2013	2014	2015	2016	2017	2018
World merchandise trade volume	2.1	–12.6	13.9	5.2	2.2	2.5	2.7	2.3	1.6	4.6	3.0
World real GDP at market exchange rates	1.5	–2.0	4.1	2.9	2.3	2.4	2.8	2.8	2.4	3.0	2.9

TABLE 10.2B World merchandise trade volume and real GDP at market exchange rates, index

	2008	2009	2010	2011	2012	2013	2014	2015	2016	2017	2018
World merchandise trade volume	100.0	87.4	99.6	104.8	107.1	109.8	112.7	115.3	117.2	122.7	126.3
World real GDP at market exchange rates	100.0	98.0	101.9	104.9	107.3	109.9	112.9	116.1	118.8	122.4	125.9

Most common way of trade in goods and services is that of intermediate products. Such intermediate products are exchanged within global value chains (GVCs). Such GVCs can be connected through worldwide networks to produce goods and services. For example, a tennis ball may be used in London at Wimbledon court. Modern tennis balls are made of a hollow rubber core, covered in a wool or nylon shell which is known as the nap. Pressurised air inside the rubber core makes the ball bounce. For the first Wimbledon tournament in 1902, balls were hand stitched, which meant no two balls ever bounced the same way. These days, a heated press is used to bind the cloth to the core. This is how the seam (the white markings on the ball) is created. There are other materials like adhesive and equipment which are used in the process of manufacture. Though USA and Europe lead manufacture of tennis balls, Eastern countries are also building capacities. It is important to note here that a tennis ball has GVCs across nations before it is manufactured at USA or Europe.

Becoming a part of production chains is an opportunity for developing countries to boost their economic growth by taking advantage of their natural resources, productive capacities, workforce or specialised skills.

TABLE 10.3 World merchandise exports by product group and annual growth, 2008-2018 (US$ billion and average annual percentage change)

	2007	2008	2009	2010	2011	2012	2013	2014	2015	2016	2017	2018	CAGR
Agricultural products	1132	1343	1177	1354	1649	1655	1732	1753	1569	1589	1736	1820	4%
Fuels and mining products	2675	3554	2300	3074	4122	4164	4051	3782	2442	2079	2634	3250	2%
Manufactures	9533	10476	8380	9989	11519	11503	11859	12287	11419	11240	12161	13167	3%
Total	13340	15373	11857	14418	17291	17322	17642	17822	15430	14908	16531	18237	3%

Source: WTO estimates

It can be observed from Table 10.3 that though exports of agricultural products grew at a higher annualised compound annual growth, absolute growth of manufacturing is staggering. It may be noted that this has been possible because of GCVs across nations. We analyse few more datasets to understand proliferation of global operations.

TABLE 10.4 World's leading traders of goods and services

	(rank)			(rank)	
Country	**2008**	**2018**	**Country**	**2008**	**2018**
United States of America	1	1	India	16	11
China	3	2	Singapore	13	12
Germany	2	3	Canada	10	13
Japan	4	4	Mexico	17	14
France	5	5	Spain	11	15
United Kingdom	6	6	Belgium	14	16
Netherlands	7	7	Russian Federation	12	17
Hong Kong, China	15	8	Switzerland	18	18
Korea, Republic of	9	9	Ireland	26	19
Italy	8	10	Chinese Taipei	19	20

Source: WTO-UNCTAD-ITC estimates

It may be noted from Table 10.4 that all the countries continued to be in top 20 and most of the ranking in first 10 remained almost very close. Countries like India, China, Mexico and Canada improved their ranks.

The analysis could be more relevant when we look at GCVs from forward and backward participation. Economies participate in GVCs in two ways. First, they import inputs to produce the goods and services they export. This is known as backward GVC participation. Second, they export domestically produced inputs to partners involved in the later stages of production which is known as forward GVC participation. For example, Saudi Arabia and Brunei Darussalam show high rates of forward GVC participation, reflecting their roles as core oil suppliers to GVCs. Other exporters of primary products, such as Peru and Chile, participate at the start of supply chains and therefore have high rates of forward GVC participation. All these economies require few inputs for their production processes. China's role within GVCs has evolved considerably. The economy has advanced its domestic capacity to produce industrial goods, thus reducing its level of backward GVC participation. At the same time, it has increased its exports of industrial goods to South-East Asia partners, boosting its forward GVC participation.

Table 10.5 shows growth of some of the selected economies in performance in merchandise exports which is manufactured goods and service exports. Most of these are Asian countries and performance of countries like Vietnam, India and Bangladesh are interesting to note.

TABLE 10.5 Growth of selected developing countries in merchandised exports, 2008-2018

Average percentage change over previous year	
Nigeria	–3.5%
South Africa	1.5%
Brazil	1.9%
Turkey	2.4%
United Arab Emirates	3.7%
Mexico	4.5%
India	5.3%
China	5.7%
Bangladesh	9.8%
Vietnam	14.6%

Growth of selected developing countries in commercial service exports, 2008-2018

Average percentage change over previous year	
India	8.6
Singapore	9.4
Viet Nam	10.0
Chinese Taipei	10.1
Thailand	12.4
Panama	13.0
Philippines	14.1
Macao, China	14.5
Qatar	29.3
Myanmar	40.9

Source: WTO - UNCTAD - ITC estimates

Thus, gross value-added index across network of nations in products and services traded highlights the importance of global operations.

Change in containerised movement of goods and importance of logistics:

It may be observed from the table on World Top 20 Ports in terms of containerised cargo handling the following:

1. There has been a substantial increase in containerised cargo movement, especially from Asia.
2. Among the top 20 ports, 10 ports are from China, 16 (including Chinese Ports) are from Asia, three from Western Europe from a cluster and only one from USA west coast.
3. This shows importance of Asia in global trade and operations and how some of these countries have been influencing global operations. As mentioned earlier, China has a substantial share of forward as well as backward movement of GVCs in supply network.

4. Though it may be interesting to look into distribution of movement within a region versus across region, it is important for this discussion that increasing global operations and need of firms to be sensitised about the same to stay competitive.

World Top 20 Ports, 2008–2017 (in 1000 TEUs)												
Rank	Port	2008	2009	2010	2011	2012	2013	2014	2015	2016	2017	CAGR
1	Shanghai, China	27980	25002	29069	31739	32529	33617	35304	36537	37133	40233	4.1%
2	Singapore	29918	25866	28431	29937	31649	32240	33869	30922	30903	33666	1.3%
3	Shenzhen, China	21414	18250	22509	22570	22940	23278	24037	24204	23979	25208	1.8%
4	Ninsho-Zhoushan, China	11226	10502	13144	14510	15670	16774	19430	20620	21560	24607	9.1%
5	Hong Kong, China	24494	21040	23699	24384	23117	22367	22283	20073	19813	20770	-1.8%
6	Busan, Korea	13452	11980	14194	16184	17046	17686	18683	19469	19456	20493	4.8%
7	Guanzhou, China	11001	11190	12550	14260	14743	15309	16626	17625	18857	20370	7.1%
8	Qingdao, China	10320	10260	12012	13020	14503	15520	16624	17510	18010	18262	6.5%
9	Dubai, UAE	11827	11100	11600	13000	13270	13641	15249	15592	14772	15368	3.0%
10	Tianjin, China	8500	8700	10080	11580	12300	13010	14050	14090	14490	15040	6.5%
11	Rotterdam, Netherlands	10800	9743	11145	11876	11865	11621	12297	12235	12385	13734	2.7%
12	Port Klang, Malaysia	7970	7309	8870	9603	10000	10350	10946	11887	13169	11978	4.6%
13	Antwerp, Belgium	8664	7309	8468	8664	8633	8578	8978	9654	10037	10450	2.1%
14	Xiamen, China	5034	4680	5820	6450	7201	8008	8572	9183	9613	10380	8.4%
15	Kaohsiung, China (Taiwan)	9677	8581	9181	9636	9781	9938	10593	10264	10464	10271	0.7%
16	Dallan, China	4503	4552	5242	6400	8060	9912	10128	9450	9583	9707	8.9%
17	Los Angeles, USA	7850	7261	7831	7940	8078	7869	8340	8161	8856	9343	2.0%
18	Hamburg, Germany	9737	7007	7900	9014	8863	9302	9729	8821	8910	8860	-1.0%

World Top 20 Ports, 2008–2017 (in 1000 TEUs)												
Rank	Port	2008	2009	2010	2011	2012	2013	2014	2015	2016	2017	CAGR
19	Tanjun Pelepas, Malaysia	5600	6016	6530	7520	7700	7628	8524	9120	8028	8260	4.4%
20	Leamcha-bang, Thailand	5134	4537	5068	5731	5830	6041	6583	6780	7227	7670	4.6%
	Total of Top 20 Ports	245101	220885	253343	274018	283778	292689	310845	312197	317245	334670	
	Total World	433253	484361	509440	472273	540816	587484	624480	651201	N/A	N/A	
	Share of World	56.6%	45.6%	49.7%	58.0%	52.5%	49.8%	49.8%	47.9%	N/A	N/A	

Note: N/A-Not available

Source: http://www.iaphworldports.org/iaph/wp-content/uploads/WorldPortTraffic-Data-for-IAPH-using-LL-container_2018_final.pdf

Inbound and outbound flow of global operations

Firms adopt global operations strategy for market expansion using base resources and production to reach to market. They may set up distribution network for extending base. In such cases, domestic production provides scale economies which could be because of material or technology expertise. Market potential is exploited by designing supply network of regional distribution centres and serving customers. For example, a subcomponent or assembly component manufacturer from India can supply to USA and Europe using this model.

Second, a firm can move up in value chain either by backward linkages of source materials or by converting intermediate products in forward/downstream linkages. Exhibit 10.12 on Hindalco depicts how a firm can successfully create value by adopting both strategies.

Exhibit 10.3

Hindalco Growth through one of the Biggest Outbound Operations through Acquisition

In 2007, Hindalco acquired Novelis Inc, a firm based in USA in aluminium industry. The cost of acquisition was US $6 billion which was the second largest acquisition by an Indian firm through an outbound investment strategy. Hindalco revenue turnover was US $16 billion, in 2007. This investment in downstream aluminium industry where Hindalco had no capability was then intriguing because of possible challenges in integration and achieving synergy. One interesting advantage Hindalco had was that it was used to handing complex global operations. It had owned then 46 manufacturing facilities across 13 countries.

Novelis Inc was aluminium rolling, then producing about 19 per cent of the world's flat rolled aluminium products. Firm's strength was technology for recycling used aluminium beverage cans. By 2007, it used about 38 billion cans annually for producing recycled aluminium. Apart from its capability in rolled products, Hindalco had advantage of Novelis Inc's presence in Europe, Asia and South America apart from USA.

The questions that arise from operations perspective are as follows:

1. How will the operations perspectives like product development, spread, innovation; facility location; supply chain network and operating organisation capability and processes help Hindalco?
2. How will market requirements like cost, dependability, flexibility, quality and speed be fulfiled by this merger?
3. What are the possible synergies across value chain that Hindalco can achieve? Will it be scale economies through plant operations or balance sheet advantage by adding up individual performance and reducing portfolio risk?
4. Will the company be able to naturally hedge movement of raw material and finished products, alumina prices in commodity market with this acquisition?

Some of these questions are more ex-post analysis and sound academic. The aluminium industry value chain is depicted in Figure 10.4.

The world aluminium industry can be categorised along value chains as follows considering the three main steps, namely bauxite mining; aluminium production and manufacture of customer identifiable aluminium products which may be an end product or an intermediary. There are four groups of firms on these three categories.

a. Upstream focussed companies which concentrate primarily on bauxite mining and conversion into alumina.
b. Production companies which make aluminium products leveraging cost effective resource like power.
c. Value added downstream producers which buy aluminium and then convert into customer products.
d. Integrated giants which combine the benefit from scale and integrated operations with dominant presence across value chain.

Hindalco has moved up the value chain and has presence in upstream segment, middle segment and downstream segment. It is typically a global operations company with integrated facilities running independently in some parts and together in a few instances. When we say integrated, our understanding is that from alumina to product, it goes through own facilities. This is where physical integration of value chain happens. Novelis Inc is this way an independent subsidiary operation. According to the published information, there are two sources of input material for Novelis Inc plants: (1) recycled aluminium, produced by remelting post-industrial and post-consumer scraps; and (2) primary aluminium, produced from alumina (extracted from bauxite), processed in a smelter. Primary aluminium and sheet ingot can generally be purchased at prices set on the London Metal Exchange (LME), plus a local market premium that varies by geographic region of delivery, alloying material, form (ingot or molten metal) and purity. Recycled aluminium is generally purchased at a discount compared to the price of primary aluminium depending on type and quality of the scrap, geographic region, and other market factors (http://www.hindalco.com/upload/pdf/hindalco-AR-subsidiary-accounts-2-2017-18.pdf). Hindalco benefits through this merger as most of the downstream advantages are from Novelis Inc.

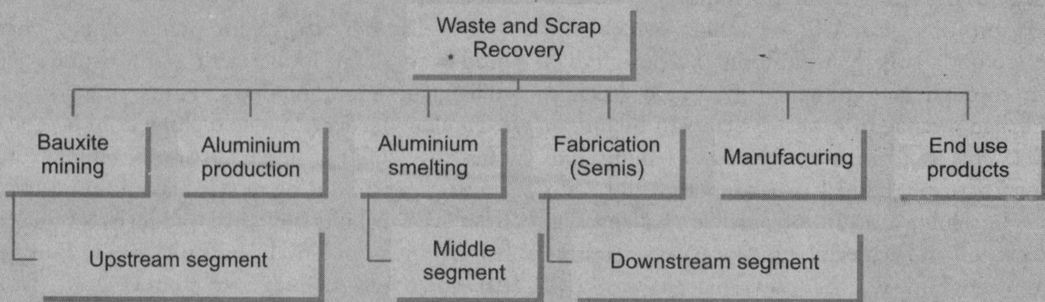

FIGURE 10.4 Aluminium production chain: stages of processing

From Table 10.6, it can be observed that Hindalco is among top 10 producers of alumina in the world.

TABLE 10.6 Top 10 producers of alumina, by capacity

Rank	Firm Name	Annual capacity (Kt)	Parent country
1	Aluminium Corporation of China (Chalco)	15 944	China
2	Alcoa	14 370	USA
3	China Hongqiao Group	12 500	China
4	Rip Tinto	10 930	Great Britain
5	UC Rusal	9 733	Russia
6	Norsk Hydro	5 712	Norway
7	South 32	5 216	Australia
8	East Hope Group	5 216	China
9	Hangzhou Jinjiang Group	3 840	China
10	Hindalco	3 145	India

Source: OECD (2019), Measuring distortions in international markets: the aluminium value chain, OECD Trade Policy papers, No 218, OECD Publishing Paris. http://dx.doi.org/10.1787/c82911ab-en

In Table 10.7 consisting of top 20 producers of primary aluminium by capacity, Hindalco figures as the 18th.

TABLE 10.7 Top 20 producers of primary aluminium, by capacity

Rank	Firm Name	Annual capacity (Kt)	Parent country
1	China Hongqiao Group	7 802	China
2	UC Rusal	4 402	Russia
3	Xinfra Group	4 322	China
4	Aluminium Corporation of China (Chalco)	3 987	China
5	Alcoa	3 402	USA
6	Rio Tinto	3 389	Great Britain
7	State Power Investment Corporation (SPIC)	3 103	China
8	Emirates Global Aluminium	2 600	United Arab Emirates
9	Henan Shenhuo Group	2 402	China
10	Yunnan Aluminium Co Ltd	2 216	China
11	East Hope Group	2 079	China
12	Norsk Hydro	2 060	Norway
13	Hangzhou Jinjiang Group	2 037	China
14	Vedanta Resources	1 570	India
15	Jiuquan Iron and Steel Co Ltd (JISCO)	1 555	China
16	Hunan Zengshi Group	1 506	China
17	Qinghai Provincial Investment Group Co. Ltd	1 374	China
18	Hindalco	1 343	India
19	Shaanxi Youser Group	1 220	China
20	Vimetco N V	1 178	Netherlands

Source: OECD (2019), Measuring distortions in international markets: the aluminium value chain, OECD Trade Policy papers, No 218, OECD Publishing Paris. http://dx.doi.org/10.1787/c82911ab-en.

The above two tables show dominance of China in production of aluminium and its products in downstream. To illustrate with one category, world aluminium semis production moved from 26 million metric tonnes in 2001 to 58 million metric tonnes in 2015. In the same period, China's production of semis moved from 3 million metric tonnes to 26 million metric tonnes.

Large contribution of aluminium industry growth is from contribution from Extrusions, followed by flat-rolled products and smaller amount by wire—cables. It may also be helpful to see product usage share across the world, North America and China.

TABLE 10.8 Product usage share across world, North America and China

Product Usage in	World Share %	North America %	China %
Building and construction	26	12	27
Transport	26	35	18
Power	14	7	12
Container and packaging	7	18	8
Consumer durable	5	6	17
Machinery and Equipment	9	6	9
Others	13	16	9

It may be clear from above industry analysis that Hindalco acquisition of Novelis Inc is more promoted by downstream growth and rest of world, other than China. Novelis Inc operational performance reflected by overall shipment in FY 18 was 3188 KT and in FY 19 was 3274 KT.

The shipment mix was 63 per cent towards can, 20 per cent automotive and 17 per cent specialities as of FY 19. Revenues were at US $22.3 billion in FY 19 compared to US $11.5 billion in FY 18. Adjusted EBITDA in FY 19 was US $1368 million compared to US $1215 million in FY 18.

Table 10.9 highlights Hindalco Ltd operating performance which also substantiates its strong performance over the years.

TABLE 10.9 Operating performance of Hindalco Industries Ltd

	FY 18	FY 19
Alumina (KT)	2881	2893
Aluminium metal KT	1291	1295
Aluminium value-added products (excluding wire rods) KT	307	321
Revenue in ₹ crores	21090	23775
EBITDA in ₹ crores	4790	5202

Thus, outbound investment integrating value chain has supported Hindalco to achieve its vision on global aluminium operations and continue to be a leading global player in a competitive market.

Source:

1. Hindalco Industries Ltd Q4 & F19 Earnings presentation 16 May 2019.
2. Hindalco: Globalizing through transformational merger; Excerpted from India's global power houses: How they are taking in the world; by Nirmalya Kumar, Pradipta K Mohapatra and Suj Chandrasekhar.
3. (http://www.hindalco.com/upload/pdf/hindalco-AR-subsidiary-accounts-2-2017-18.pdf).

As we have noticed how outbound investment facilitates global operations strategy and implementation, there are a number of cases of inbound strategic investments into India by international firms.

The motive could have been:

1. Leveraging technology to reach new markets as in the case of automotive companies, construction industry and machinery and equipment, and so on.
2. To exploit resource base like cost advantage through labour or workmen efficiency or natural resource like in case textiles, agricultural products like coffee, tea and other plantations and consumer electronics including manufacture of mobile phones by Apple and Samsung in India.
3. To benefit locational advantage on longitude and use cost arbitrage in case of services industry like banking and financial services; information technology and number of other BPOs and KPOs.
4. To serve large market requirements by creating and sustaining demand by marketing products where the firm has matured in terms of technology and cost leadership been able to serve a large market in India. We had discussed in this chapter how Saint Gobain Ltd, France based glass company achieved competitive advantage in India. There are numerous such companies in different segments like consumer electronics (Samsung, LG and others), elevators and escalators (Schindler success), insurance through JVs and FMCG like shaving razors (Gillette), etc.
5. Combination of above.

This, inbound and outbound investment to achieve linkages in value chain and exploit market potential is possible through execution of appropriately designed and implemented global operations strategy.

SUMMARY

Large firms must reach out to global market through right choice of strategy towards achieving competitive advantage. Changes in global business environment with liberalisation of policies by most of the countries have become a competitive challenge for players in a developing economy like India. It opened international players with vast experience, better technology and deeper pockets to venture into India. Inbound investment gave opportunity to enter JVs and technology transfer. Further such a large opportunity gave confidence to venture into global operations through setting up plants in abroad and/or grow through inorganic choices like mergers and acquisitions. The kind of opportunities exploited include automotive, auto components; metals and minerals; agricultural processed products including food and beverages and pharmaceuticals. There were a lot of such engagements which happened in services industry like information technology, logistics infrastructure, banking and financial services, hospitality and healthcare. Over the decades, one can see how firms have matured in deploying global operations strategy and one can expect this to intensify further.

Key Terms

1. **Ethnocentric:** It is evaluating other cultures according to preconceptions originating in the standards and customs of one's own culture.
2. **Polycentric:** Polycentric approach is a type of global business orientation in which firms attempt to spread out the appeal of their products or services among multiple countries. It occurs when a business decides to broaden its operations and focus on sales outside of its home country.

3. **Regiocentric:** Regiocentric approach is an international business approach wherein the business is oriented towards different countries lying within the geographic region of business.
4. **Geocentric:** The geocentric approach is a method of international business where the MNC's approach with the most suitable model for the firm irrespective of their nationality.
5. **Global company:** A global company has a foothold in multiple countries, but the offerings and processes are consistent in each country. The company uses the same ingredients and manufacturing processes, regardless of local culture. In a global model, the business does not adapt to local norms, but rather, it imposes its existing business model on the country.
6. **Transnational company:** Transnational companies operate in multiple countries across the globe. This strategy differs, however, in the way the firm operates in each country. A transnational product keeps its same characteristics, regardless of the country in which it is sold. The product does not change according to local customs or preferences.
7. **Multi-domestic firm:** A company that follows a multi-domestic strategy fits its products to each country in which it does business. Its product features are tailored to the local domestic environment, considering different food preferences, religious customs and other characteristics that define the locality.
8. **Outbound investment:** An outward/outbound direct investment (ODI) is a business strategy in which a domestic firm expands its operations to a foreign country.
9. **Inbound investment:** An inward investment involves an external or foreign entity either investing in or purchasing the goods of a local economy.
10. **Value chain:** A value chain is a set of activities that a firm operating in a specific industry performs to deliver a valuable product for the market.
11. **Supply chain network:** A supply network is a pattern of temporal and spatial processes carried out at facility nodes and over distribution links, which adds value for customers through the manufacturing and delivery of products.
12. **Importer of record:** Importer of record is a term used in customs law. It refers to an importer, whether an entity or individual, who is responsible for ensuring that legal goods are imported in accordance with the law of the place.

CONCEPT REVIEW QUESTIONS

1. Discuss different culture and value-based approaches to global operations, merits and demerits of each of them and possibly give some examples.
2. Analyse global operations towards service business using the framework of offering and location preference. Give some examples you are familiar with.
3. Discuss the different approach to internationalisation strategies. Relate local responsiveness and global integration; and relate with culture and value-based approaches.
4. Elucidate the need for global operations orientation a firm may have to take to stay competitive.
5. Discuss the changing nature of business and how it helps in global operations.
6. Analyse trend in internationalisation of a firm with an example like Saint Gobain as discussed in the text.
7. Explain strategic alliance spectrum and production sharing in the context of global operations strategy to be pursued by a firm.
8. Discuss the importance of advanced technologies in global operations strategy. Give some examples.
9. Analyse the importance of social issues and responsible procurement in global operations. Give some examples you are familiar with.

CRITICAL THINKING QUESTIONS

1. Analyse inward investment in operations of a company like Gillette or Hyundai or any other company of your choice and see how it integrates. Use operations strategy framework of operations strategy focus areas and market requirements.
2. Discuss a firm's inward investment and setting up of operations which had to exit the market. Try to rationalise entry and exit of the same firm. You may choose Lafarge Cement or Nokia Plant at Chennai.
3. Describe the growth of Chennai based ports and those around Chennai like Krishnapatnam in handling containerised cargo.
4. Analyse recent policy changes of government under trade facilitation to have introduced direct port delivery and direct export of cargo to facilitate global operations. You may take perspective from a company of your choice.

PROJECT ASSIGNMENTS

1. Using open source information, analyse the growth of one of the Indian global companies describing its growth strategy and how operations function has helped in achieving synergy through value chain integration.
2. Discuss with an IT major senior management team member or from open source and prepare a note on IT company's global operations opportunities and challenges over the years.
3. Using open source information, analyse policies adopted by Chinese policy makers and corporates to build competitive edge in aluminium industry.
4. Discuss the growth of new generation container ports (top 20) and their primary and secondary hinterland. How could have corporates established competitive edge in global operations?
5. Choose a Special Economic Zone (SEZ) and discuss possible global operations strategy integration that can be pursued by a firm.

REFERENCES

1. http://news.bbc.co.uk/sportacademy/hi/sa/tennis/features/newsid_2997000/2997504.stm.
2. https://www.wto.org/english/res_e/statis_e/wts2019_e/wts2019chapter04_e.pdf.
3. https://www.wto.org/english/res_e/statis_e/wts2019_e/wts19_toc_e.htm Accessed on 20 September 2019.
4. https://www.iaphworldports.org/statistics.
5. https://simpleflying.com/the-3-major-airline-alliances-star-alliance-oneworld-and-skyteam-why-are-they-good/ Accessed on 19 August 2019.
6. https://freighthub.com/en/blog/shipping-alliances-mean/#.

Cases

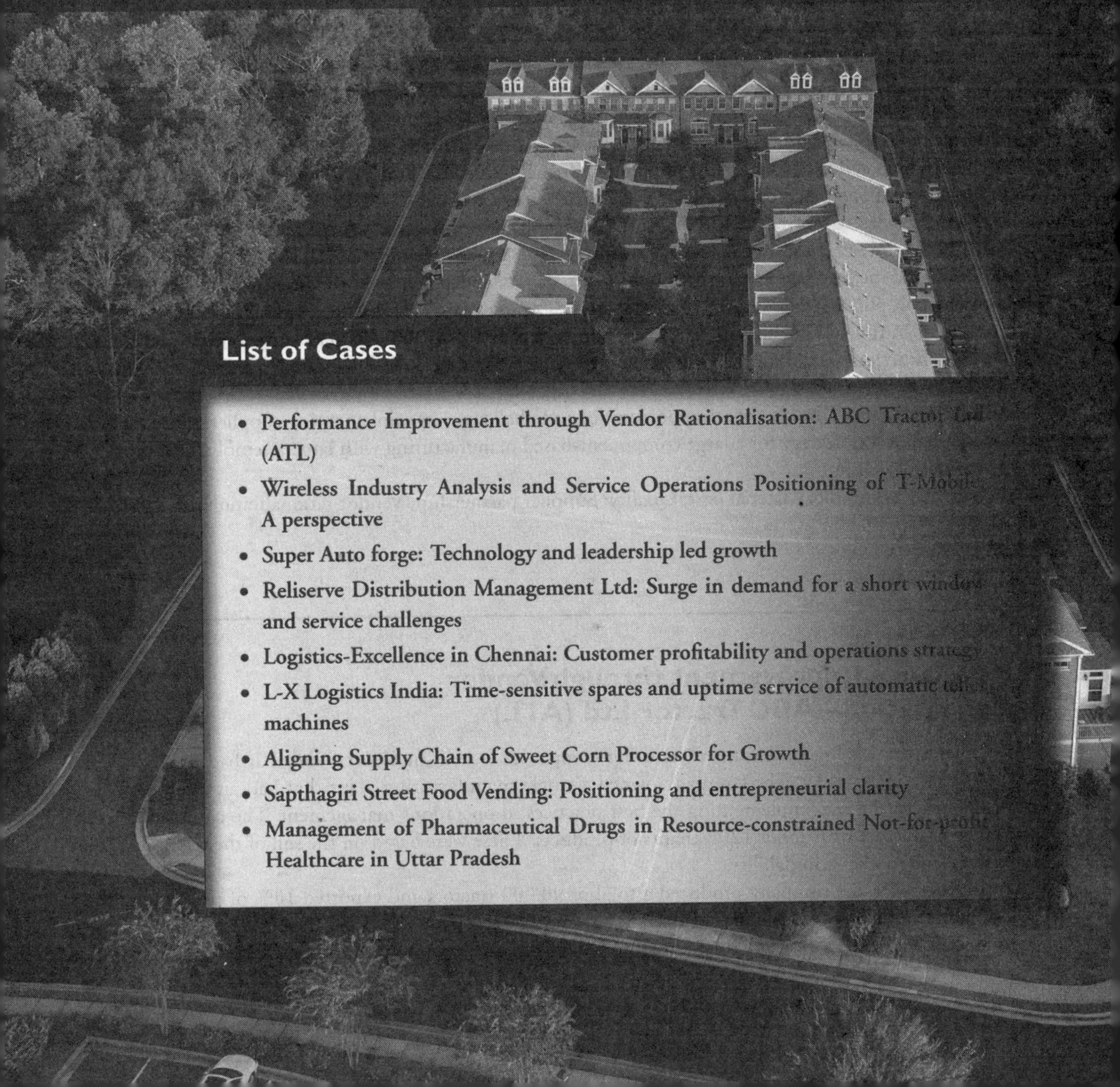

List of Cases

- Performance Improvement through Vendor Rationalisation: ABC Tractor Ltd (ATL)
- Wireless Industry Analysis and Service Operations Positioning of T-Mobile: A perspective
- Super Auto forge: Technology and leadership led growth
- Reliserve Distribution Management Ltd: Surge in demand for a short window and service challenges
- Logistics-Excellence in Chennai: Customer profitability and operations strategy
- L-X Logistics India: Time-sensitive spares and uptime service of automatic teller machines
- Aligning Supply Chain of Sweet Corn Processor for Growth
- Sapthagiri Street Food Vending: Positioning and entrepreneurial clarity
- Management of Pharmaceutical Drugs in Resource-constrained Not-for-profit Healthcare in Uttar Pradesh

Performance Improvement through Vendor Rationalisation: ABC Tractor Ltd (ATL)

(**Disclaimer:** The case is based on authors' experience in the Operations and Supply Chain area and it is not reflective of any company in India which is into the manufacture of tractors. The case is meant for academic discussions and facilitates decision making in operations and supply chain management. This is not reflecting the operating issue of any real-time tractor company in India.)

Abstract

ABC Tractors Ltd (ATL) is one of the leading tractor manufacturing companies located in Central India with a sales turnover of ₹6,000 crore in 2018-19. It is a single manufacturing company and has an international tie-up for manufacturing. The company has implemented best practices in operations management. It offered a wide range of tractors. There were about 120 variants of products that were available based on the soil of the region, customer preferences, and other market characteristics. The company was facing the huge task of integrating its entire supply chain and at the same time, it had to reduce its costs, inventory, and improve customer satisfaction. Material and components cost was a serious concern for the company and had been increasing steadily. The project 'Synchronize to Power' (S2P) was initiated to optimise its supply chain and rationalise its inbound movement of mainly material and component sourced, and costs were initiated. Tiering of suppliers and cluster formation were critical decision area which required to be planned. There were 470 items, 1740 vendors and the value of materials purchased amounted to ₹2560 crore. This was the focus area analysed for rationalisation. Issues relating to just in time (JIT) and supplier relationships were to be discussed as ATL envisioned at improving its supply chain function. Quality initiatives and cost managements were to follow in such a rationalisation project.

Learning Objective: To understand opportunities and challenges in implementing supplier partnerships and vendor rationalisation strategy for a large component-based manufacturing with large assembly operations.

Key Words: Just in time; Material cost; Quality; Supplier partnership; Vendor rationalisation.

Case

Performance Improvement through Vendor Rationalisation – ABC Tractor Ltd (ATL)

ATL is one of the leading tractor manufacturing companies located in Central India. It had a sales turnover of ₹6,000 crore in 2018-19. The company owned a single manufacturing plant that had an international tie-up for manufacturing and implementing the best practices in operations management. The company offered a wide range of tractors with about 120 variants of products. These were based on the soil of the region, customer preferences, and market affordability.

During 2018-19, the company produced a total of 90,000 tractors and exported 10% of the same to South Asian countries. The rest were sold in the domestic market. The company was facing the huge task of integrating its entire supply chain and at the same time, it had to reduce its costs, inventory, and improve customer satisfaction.

The corporate goal was being cost-focussed, effective inventory management, and improved customer satisfaction. The top management wanted Mr. Rajendra Agarwal (Raj), Vice President – Supply Chain, to come out with an action plan. Raj is a mechanical engineering graduate from IIT Delhi and has a management degree from IIM Ahmedabad. He has worked in the operations department of large auto manufacturers throughout his career and his last assignment was a similar experience in a truck manufacturing company in Chennai.

Raj observed that material and components cost was a serious concern for the company and increased steadily. There had been a steep rise in steel prices and other metal prices used in component manufacture. Material cost accounted for nearly 52 per cent of the cost of production at the operating level. The operating margin was 18 per cent. Labour cost was a significant portion of the cost of production accounting for nearly 9 per cent.

He called his team members, Steve and Sania, to work on a rationalisation plan. He wanted to make a presentation to management for approval. Steve and Sania worked on streamlining the company's supply chain process. They named the project as 'Synchronize to Power' (S2P) to optimise its supply chain and rationalise its inbound which was mainly material and component sourcing and costs related to the same.

The project 'S2P' included:

Supplier partnership and vendor base rationalisation was one of the focus areas of the project. There were then 1740 vendors. Steve suggested that in four years, number of vendors must reduced to 870. The rate of reduction must be by dropping off 5%, 10%, 15% and 20% of suppliers each year for four years. Sania felt the targets were steep and the company was well-respected for developing vendors and ancillaries. She felt that such a move would hit the corporate image. Steve suggested that such a drive would be appreciated because it could become cost-competitive and reduce planning and coordination costs. He also viewed that there was enough scope of rationalisation through the tiering of vendors. Further, more componentisation was possible if they worked with the product engineering team. Sania altered him stating that every managerial decision involved a penalty cost and they might have to judge the same. However, she agreed for the target and put a number to penalty cost that it could not be more than 15% of the savings under this head. Steve argued that rationalisation could be looked at with two options. One, reduce class C vendors from the first years and in the last year, reduce Class A and B along with Class C. The other option is to reduce class C from Year I and gradually reduce class A and B from year 2. He was of the view that instead of a penalty, it would give an advantage in price negotiation. Sania felt that when vendors per item were reduced, price negotiation was not a reality! Steve was of the view that dropping vendors was the right time to push cost savings across the supplier network and not necessarily margin, as vendors could use this to improve their efficiency!

This strategy makes tiering of suppliers and cluster formation a critical aspect which had to be planned in detail. This, as mentioned earlier, required working with a product engineering team. Further supplier relationship managers had to be involved who would implement this plan for four years. Six supplier relationship managers were handling accounts as shown below:

Material/Item category	Value in ₹crores	No of items	No of vendors	Supplier relationship manager
Class A	2100	20	80	2
Class B	300	90	360	2
Class C Vendors	100	260	1300	1
Class C Open market	60	100		1
Total	2560	470	1740	

Sania was wondering how to propose the rationalisation of the same. She mentioned to Steve that JIT was implemented for component supply and supplier relationship managers (SRMs) were shown to be a part of the vendor relationship. Steve said that in his understanding, not all category A items had the potential to be in JIT and which should ideally be so. But SRMs mentioned that though items might be supplied under JIT, still vendor relationship was important as these were critical and strategic items.

Steve was of the view that in four years, JIT from the current level of 50% should move up to 80% which means that most Category A must be there. Sania was mentioning that it could be difficult as some component vendors were located as far as Chennai and Vadodara. Steve was clear that they might look at some transit or near plant supply alternatives to achieve the same. Sania then felt that they might have to look at 3 or 4 PL operators who could be expensive and work against the strategy. Steve said that detailing would be better as they could be shared users realising pooled scale advantage.

Sania mentioned that another area of rationalisation was quality systems and self-certification. The performance tracking had to be on ISO/QS certified suppliers and those who could do self-certifying their supplies. Then, there were only 180 suppliers who are ISO/QS certified and out of which, 80% work on self-certification. Steve and Sania believed that in four years, ISO/QS certification must be for both categories A and B and another 10% of category C. All ISO/QS certified suppliers must supply on self-certification. The current cost of quality is about 1.5% of total material cost and of which 80% or 1.2% of total material costs were costs due to rejections. This must be reduced to 0.2% of the total material costs. Sania recommended that 50% of this savings year on year for four years should be used for vendor rationalisation and adjusted against future supplies after four years from the vendors.

Sania also observed that non-JIT supplies carried an inventory of 45 days. She was of the view that it could be reduced to 20 days. The minimum amount of savings would be 15% at the cost of capital of money in working capital. She also felt that JIT supplies use unsophisticated operators. These operators were supplied from a warehouse about 30 km away from the plant. Such inefficient operations resulted in adding up to 0.7% of the cost of those materials and could potentially be rationalised by 60% efficiency.

Steve proposed that cost management approach could potentially result in savings of 0.5% to 1% in total material cost. This would include some of the above-discussed savings as well. Sania mentioned that she would depict the savings through cost management initiatives for an easy understanding of the management. She also mentioned that knowing Raj, they must be ready on the difference between target costing and TCM and share complete details of the report.

Steve said, "We need to prepare an evaluation of each of the proposals, quantify, provide strength and challenges including that of soft issues, implementation plan and review mechanism. Sania was nurturing a dream of becoming a key responsible person for this project so that she could move on a fast track growth in supply chain function.

QUESTIONS

1. Prepare a detailed report recommending the advantages of vendor rationalisation and how the same can be achieved. Evaluate other opportunities like JIT and tiering of vendors.
2. Describe and detail quality improvements and advantages of the same.
3. What are all components that go into the cost management approach and relate to the savings of material costs by adopting this strategy?

Wireless Industry Analysis and Service Operations Positioning of T-Mobile: A perspective

(Disclaimer: The case is based on authors experience in Operations and Supply Chain area based on open source information. It is not reflective of pecuniary aspects or investments in the industry or any company operating in this industry. The case is meant for academic discussions to understand the importance of industry structural analysis and relating with a company for operations area strategic decision.)

Abstract

This write up is focussed on how an industry structure would influence strategic decisions in operations management like service offering and service product mix, innovation, technology, service supply network (both backward and forward linkages) and performance. Industry competition forces business strategists to pursue organic and inorganic growth initiatives and it is imperative that functional strategists, especially that of operations, ensure synergy. If one has to develop such a perspective, this write up is likely to show contour of such an analysis. This write up gives a high-level orientation of such analysis and management professionals in a firm within an industry need to build nitty-gritty of operations strategic issues. Using open source information of the industry in USA market, the write-up discusses how T-Mobile has been managing competition through its product service offering.

Learning Objective: To understand industry structural analysis, market share and various product offerings, and how a company can manage its operations strategy to stay competitive.

Key Words: Business model; Competition analysis; Strategy; Organic growth; Inorganic growth.

Case

Introduction

According to the New York Times, "The Wireless Telecommunications Services industry consists of companies engaged in providing wireless communication services, such as paging, cell phone, and other satellite telecommunication services. The industry excludes cable television services utilising satellite delivery. One of the most exciting phases of this industry would be with rollout of 5G wireless technology which would be a boom for the Internet of things (IoT), autonomous vehicles (especially cars) and mobile media. According to a Deloitte report, it is expected to provide US $150 billion to GDP and create 370,000 new jobs over the years.[(1)]

Opportunities for the Industry

The breakthrough technology by way of the 5G network would lead to an increase in mobile applications for connected cars. Already a huge investment is being made in this area to make connected autonomous cars a reality. Apart from connected cars, customers are looking at remote home monitoring and control systems, education, entertainment, wearables for health monitoring and vast banking and financial services applications including m-Payments. Beside business to consumer segment, business to business segments like predictive maintenance and employee training and development are possible areas where advancement in wireless technology would impact. The analytics industry visualises advancements in artificial intelligence and deep learning to positively impact value for money in most parts of the business. This would help in effective business planning and direct investment for growth.

Naturally, all these can impact the wireless industry positively with more smartphones being in use and widening the reach. Reach advancement would require investment for building a network of towers and taking the reach far and wide. One of the research reports mentions the industry in the US building small and powerful towers across rural places as well all over the geography in USA.

The industry revenue and market share based on service revenues for mobile wireless service is given in Table 1.

TABLE 1 Service revenue and market share based on service revenues for mobile wireless service providers ($/ million) 2013 - 2016

Service providers	2013		2014		2015		2016	
	Revenue	Market share %	Revenue	Market share %	Revenue	Market share %	Revenue	Market share %
Verizon wireless	69,033	36.50	72,630	38.70	70,396	38.10	66,580	36.80
AT & T	61,552	32.50	61,032	32.50	59,837	32.40	59,386	32.80
T-Mobile	20,535	10.90	22,375	11.90	24,821	13.50	27,844	15.40
Sprint	29,263	15.50	27,959	14.90	25,845	14	24,215	13.40
U.S Cellular	3,595	1.90	3,398	1.80	3,350	1.80	3,051	1.70

Source: https://www.thenetworkmediagroup.com/blog/is-the-us-mobile-industry-competitive[2]

It can be observed from Table 1 that there is an oligopoly in this market and the top four players are the dominating firms. With ongoing inorganic move of takeover of Sprint by T-Mobile, it is again the top three firms that dominate the industry.

About T-Mobile

T-Mobile is a wireless communication service provider, the major shareholder of which is a German telecommunications company, Deutsche Telekom. It is the third-largest wireless carrier in the US with a customer base of over 280 million people who are serviced through its multiple brands like T-Mobile, MetroPCS, and GoSmart. It has approximately 51,000 employees.[3]

1. Business Model

Market

The company provides wireless communication services to three categories of customers:

a. Branded postpaid customers, including customers that are qualified to pay after using wireless communication services;
b. Branded prepaid customers, including customers paying for wireless communication services in advance. The company's branded prepaid customers include customers of T-Mobile and MetroPCS; and

c. Wholesale customers, including machine-to-machine (M2M) and mobile virtual network operators (MVNOs) that operate on its network, but are managed by wholesale partners.

The company's service plan offerings allow customers to subscribe to wireless services separately from the purchase of a device. It offers T-Mobile ONE plan (T-Mobile ONE), which gives its customers calls, text and fourth-generation (4G) long-term evolution (LTE) data on their device. On T-Mobile ONE, video streams at digital video disc (DVD) (480 progressive (p)) quality and tethering is at third-generation (3G) speeds. Thus, the company's offering includes wireless communication services to three categories of customers — prepaid, postpaid and wholesale. Besides, it also offers wireless devices like handsets, tablets, etc., and accessories which are manufactured by various suppliers to these customers through retail outlets and third-party websites. Recently, it has started a television service through Layer^3 TV which focusses on providing television services on any device that has an internet connection.[(4)]

T-Mobiles value proposition is contract freedom which did not necessarily bind customers to the carrier. They launched the Uncarrier No Contract programme to provide simple, fair and straightforward pricing for customers. Over the period, the company has been launching different value propositions through this uncarrier programme, some of which include free international roaming, free music and video streaming services like Pandora and Netflix and unlimited data plan.[(5)].

Revenue Share Across Offering

The T-Mobile finances across different businesses are shown in Table 2.

TABLE 2 T-Mobile revenue and expense across segments

	Revenue	Expenses	% of TR
Postpaid plans and phones	26.4	18.5	61%
Prepaid	13.1	8.7	30%
Wholesale and other	2.3	1	5%
Mobile broadband	1.3		
Adjusted Depreciation and amortisation		7.1	
Other expenses		4.8	
Total	43.1	40.1	
EBITDA	14.9		
Non-GAAP net income	3		
Total free cash flows	5.65		

Source: T-Mobile product offerings, revenue and net income for 2017. Data from www.trefis.com (2018)[(6)]

The market capitalisation of T-Mobile was $47.7 billion, as of 16 May 2018.[(7)] It has a total revenue of $43.05 billion.[(8)]

Competition

T-Mobile's major competitors include AT&T, Verizon, and Sprint. They compete for their market share over a saturated customer base (see Table 3). The top four service providers — AT&T, Verizon, T-Mobile, and Sprint — represent 93 per cent of total subscribers.[(9)] Their competitive strategy includes low price and value-added services to attract customers. They also compete for providing better network coverage through network improvements.

TABLE 3 Top U.S. wireless carrier metrics Q1 2018 (ranking by subscribers, retail + wholesale)

		Subscribers (million)	Net Adds (million)	Postpaid Smartphone Net Adds (million)	Blended Churn (Avg. Monthly)	% Share of Total
1	Verizon Wireless	151.482	1.025	0.22	1.28%	35
2	AT&T	143.832	2.63	0.042	1.65%	34
3	T-Mobile	74.018	1.433	0.76	2.22%	17
4	Sprint	53.6	-0.019	0.185	2.33%	12
5	US Cellular	5.063	-0.033	-0.01	1.65%	1
6	C Spire*	n/a				
7	Shentel	1.025	0.009	0.038	2.44%	0.2
	Total	429.02				

Source: https://www.fiercewireless.com/wireless/how-verizon-at-t-t-mobile-sprint-and-more-stacked-up-q1-2018-top-7-carriers [9]

Operations

T-Mobile resources include a GSM network operating on a wide range of spectrum exclusively licensed for it. It modernises and expands its network through partnerships with various suppliers/vendors like Ericsson and Nokia Siemens.[10] For example, it is expected to launch the 5G network with equipment's supplied and maintained by Ericsson. In this model, the company and the vendor combine to deliver a network and its service to their customers.

T-Mobile delivers its services and products through multiple channels — online, customer care, direct and indirect corporate retail stores and business dealers.[11] This multi-channel approach gives them the capabilities to expand customer reach and convenience to customers.

Operations strategy covers technology, size and scale economies, processes, employees and managerial productivity, supply chain network and advantages because any specific factor could make it a competitive differentiator. However, when the top four are competing intensively, it may be difficult to achieve differentiators in this service industry. Dominant firms match in all competitive drivers to hold on to their market share or else they perish.

TABLE 4 Market share %

Category->	Postpaid subscription		Prepaid subscription	
Company	Q3 17	Q3 18	Q3 17	Q3 18
AT & T	29.6	28.8	27.1	29.3
Verizon	42.1	41.9	10	8.2
Sprint	12.2	12.1	15.7	15.7
T-Mobile	14.2	15.4	36.8	36.5
U.S. Cellular	2	1.9	10.3	10.3

Source: https://www.fiercewireless.com/wireless/how-verizon-at-t-t-mobile-sprint-and-more-stacked-up-q1-2018-top-7-carriers [9]

The following can be observed from Table 4:

- The top two players, namely AT&T and Verizon have a market share of 34 per cent and 35per cent, respectively, in combined postpaid and prepaid services. Both have a different approach to the markets. While

AT&T has equal footing in postpaid and prepaid markets in terms of market share, Verizon is predominantly in postpaid services and has fourth position in the prepaid service. This shows that with a differentiated approach, one can still be dominant and can have matching rivalry competitive behaviour.
- The next two players, who compete at the next strata of market share, have similar operations pattern. Sprint has a similar market share in both the segments while T-Mobile has positioned itself as a leader in prepaid service.
- It may be also noted that postpaid service has an average churn rate of 1.2 per cent. Sprint has a high churn rate of 1.6 per cent, while AT&T and Verizon have about 1 per cent churn rate. In the prepaid segment, the average churn rate is 5 per cent and T-Mobile was 4 per cent for the period 2018 Q3.

Thus, the companies have an appropriate operating strategic focus towards product/service offerings. Such focus helps in achieving performance parameters and hold on to competitive positioning in an intensely competitive market. Further, according to available report, Capex expenses by the top players in the USA wireless service industry are about US $30 billion on an average over a period of five years. It is estimated to go up to US $37 billion by 2023 at a CAGR of 5 per cent. Capital intensity as per cent of industry revenue is about 17 per cent. Thus, capital spend, especially on technology, holds the key to service development and holding on to market requirements to stay competitive in this business.

2. Competitive Forces and Challenges

Porter's five forces help one to assess the external environment of the organisation considering the competitors' activities. The five forces are,

1. Rivalry of Competitors
2. Threat of New Entrants
3. Threat of Substitutes
4. Bargaining Power of Buyers
5. Bargaining Power of Suppliers

Rivalry of Competitors

The rivalry is very intense among existing players of the wireless industry due to big/established players (AT&T and Verizon) and market saturation. Since a company's revenues are directly related to its subscriber base, they all try to outcompete each other for the market share leading to a price war. The wireless industry provides standardised services to customers making it a highly competitive market. This leads to low prices and possibly decreased profitability.

Threat of New Entrants

New entrants in an industry bring innovation and provide new value proposition to customers. This threat is less likely here, as this industry requires a large up-front investment and licensing making it difficult for new players to enter the market. Additionally, brand value is high among existing players and the new players would most likely enter through acquisitions.

Therefore, brand value and intangible assets act as entry barriers, and required capital and licenses are the other factors which make it a high entry cost. This industry has high entry and high exit barrier which should give high profitability. Instead, rivalry among firms leads to the opposite condition of low profitability.

Threat of Substitutes

Threat of substitutes exists as similar services are provided by competitors to meet customer needs. Additionally, a substitute to voice service in wireless is the emergence of voice over data technology. This can be said to be low as wireless companies are service providers for the data as well thereby balancing it.

Bargaining Power of Buyers

Wireless companies rely on their own and third-party retailer channels to deliver their products to end customers. The higher the customer base, the lower the bargaining power to service provider. This is because of the combined or group bargaining power! The churn rate, discussed earlier, indicates bargaining power. It is clearly in favour of customers, especially on prepaid services. Firms spend on brand loyalty and structure their service supply network to ensure that brand stickiness is high. The proportion of spend is high as there is a need to counter the bargaining power of buyers. The third-party /resellers are wholesale customers, have medium to high bargaining power as they provide deep discounts, or they could switch to a rival.

Bargaining Power of Suppliers

T-Mobile uses numerous suppliers for buying its equipment. Some suppliers could be in dominant positions due to their niche products and lack of substitutes leading to higher bargaining power to suppliers and reduced profitability to the company.

3. Competitive Strategies

The following section describes the strategies that T-Mobile could use or it already used to address the challenges described above.

Organic Growth Strategies

- T-Mobile could build differentiation as a concept company. In the past, it delivered its product and services on a concept differentiation,[13] such as no-contract plans, unlimited data, etc. Such actions in the past have helped T-Mobile gain subscriber base and retain existing ones giving them an edge over their competitors.
- The company can innovate new products and services. This again helps the company to stay ahead in the competition and against any new entrants.
- It can continuously provide improvised value-added services and customer satisfaction
- It can, also, understand and address customer needs. This would make it less likely for customers to switch to alternatives.
- It requires cost leadership – gain an advantage over competitors by minimising operational costs.

Inorganic Growth Strategies

Through mergers and acquisitions, T-Mobile could increase its market share/ customer base, thereby increasing its revenues. For example, the recent announcement of the merger with Sprint (if it goes through) would increase their market share, revenue and consolidate assets/system for optimising their operations. It is interesting that after the merger, T-Mobile would be like AT&T with an equal share in both the segments.

4. Business Model Evolution

It may be noted that revenue of T-Mobiles is from the following services:

- Postpaid customers – about 60 per cent of total revenue
- Prepaid customers – about 30 per cent of total revenue
- Wholesale – about 4 per cent of total revenue
- Mobile broadband – about 2 per cent of total revenue

Based on the above split up, gaining loyalty of postpaid customers is of utmost importance for the company's revenue. Considering this, enhancements in the following area would be the focus of the company,

- Ability to provide content
- Multi-device usage and support new technology
- Expand their network for better service. A new 5G network might give a first-mover advantage for T-Mobile. This would provide new market segments and growth opportunities.
- Integrate analytics capabilities that provide insights from network data — measure voice quality, LTE issues,[12] etc. Using this, the system would eventually evolve from a reactive to a proactive model.

5. Best IT - Supported Proposal

Increasing network bandwidth and maintaining higher quality networks are important to support a growing customer base and customer satisfaction. For this insight, it is important to integrate analytic capabilities to the existing CRM solution. This could further be enhanced to provide predictive analytics and automated actions.

Role of IT: The most essential way in which IT would be used to support this proposal is by information management and data storage. A few sub-activities are listed as follows,

- Develop and integrate the analytics application with the wireless network infrastructure
- Develop business rules and data models for analytics
- Provide application support and maintenance

Conclusion

In the highly competitive industry of the USA wireless service industry, T-Mobile holds fourth position in terms of market share and revenue. The first two players are in highly competitive intensity holding to their respective position. If T-Mobile were to be reckoned as a serious contender among the top four, which it is currently, it must ensure that its operating strategy is focussed on achieving the required rate of return which matches with the market rate of return and provides additional return to attract capital to hold on to the market share. It may be noted that T-Mobile is not only retaining its position in the market with better performance, but also intends to buy out the third player, namely Sprint so that it can consolidate its market share and investments. On completion of such a move, it could improve its position in both the markets.

Note: Author N. Chandrasekaran acknowledges support of Lakshminarayanan Ganesan, who is an IT professional living out of Philadelphia, USA and was a student of MS programme at Boston University, in developing this case.

QUESTIONS

1. Analyse industry competitive drivers of US wireless industry.
2. Discuss the competitive positioning of T-Mobile compared to the other leading players and how its service product offering compares with that of competitors.
3. "Being a leader in one product segment and follower in the other segment which cannibalises the first one can be an operational strategy and still be among dominant firms in an oligopolistic market!" Elucidate.
4. Map the dominant players across operations strategy decision areas like service offers, capacity measured by customer base/revenue earned, technology, supply network, organisation development across performance perspectives like quality, speed, and responsiveness in the US wireless industry.

REFERENCES

1. https://www2.deloitte.com/us/en/pages/technology-media-and-telecommunications/articles/telecommunications-industry-outlook.html
2. https://www.thenetworkmediagroup.com/blog/is-the-us-mobile-industry-competitive
3. https://csimarket.com/stocks/TMUS-Business-Description.html
4. https://www.reuters.com/article/us-layer3-m-a-tmobile/t-mobile-to-launch-tv-service-in-2018-buy-layer3-tv-idUSKBN1E722M
5. http://trentyockey.blogspot.com/2015/03/value-proposition.html
6. https://www.trefis.com/stock/tmus/model/trefis?easyAccessToken=PROVIDER_605d56c3251341036583c1d7c0b44cc24248e96e
7. https://ycharts.com/companies/TMUS/market_cap
8. http://www.vault.com/company-profiles/telecommunications/t-mobile-usa,-inc/company-overview
9. https://www.fiercewireless.com/wireless/how-verizon-at-t-t-mobile-sprint-and-more-stacked-up-q1-2018-top-7-carriers
10. https://www.fiercewireless.com/5g/t-mobile-to-build-but-not-necessarily-sell-5g-30-cities-year
11. http://whoseint-mosfaves.blogspot.com/2009/04/pricing-strategy-of-t-mo.html
12. https://www.fiercewireless.com/wireless/t-mobile-deploys-ericsson-data-analytics-to-measure-voice-quality-detect-volte-issues

Super Auto Forge: Technology and leadership led growth

(**Disclaimer:** This material was prepared by Chandrasekaran N. based on discussions with Mr. S. Seetharaman and Mr. M. Sundaram on 9 July 2019 and with other references on this material. This is purely meant for academic discussion and classroom learning only.)

Abstract

This case on Super Auto Forge Ltd (SAF) is focussed on the integration of operations perspective and market requirements of the company, and relates the same to its growth. Starting from nowhere S Seetharaman, Chairman of Super Auto Forge, had an ambition to be an entrepreneur in the space of production-driven business using traits like ability to learn and develop to become a leading player supplying to Tier I auto component vendor and directly to OEMs. In a matter of two decades, the company transformed by developing cold forging technology by using an indigenously developed technology process. Pursuing homegrown technology drives zeal, adoption of excellence in manufacturing and cost advantage for Tier II and Tier I parts assembly units. Such forces were the driving force of Super Auto Forge (SAF) and its promoter. During this phase, the company had focussed on the development of processes and managing implementation, which are the key drivers of its growth not only in India but across the globe, especially developed markets. Leadership of the company believed that locational advantage in facility decision can be exploited for the international growth of the firm provided the leadership is clear about operations strategy formulation and implementation.

SAF took some key strategic initiatives for achieving growth. This included implementation of quality management processes, continuous improvement through learning and operations people related HR practices. It also worked on seamlessly focussing its supply chain on domestic and international markets. Leadership played a critical role in the growth of the firm. The company is growing inorganically by acquiring a plant near Chennai in a neighbouring state. It is looking at various risks in terms of operations, finance and business portfolio SAF faced and how they can be handled.

Learning Objective: To understand the importance of leadership in developing home-grown technology and pursue operations strategies relevant for creating a competitive differentiation in the industry.

Key Words: Operations strategy, Choice of technology, Indigenous development, Technology process, Quality management, Leadership.

Case

Super Auto forge: Technology and Leadership Led Growth

Mr. S Seetharaman (SS), the visionary leader and promoter of SAF was thinking about the Strategic Core Committee meeting of his closely held private limited company which was to be held a day after. It has a couple of independent directors as a part of the committee. One of the main agendas includes emphasising on appropriate initiatives of the best operating practices at the plant level and living up to traditions of SAF in achieving operations excellence.

This is a project of fully finished and ready to assemble CV joint parts in Sri City. This is their second venture into a similar product with a higher level of technology interface. More importantly, for the first time, the company has started a plant operation outside Chennai, Tamil Nadu. SAF has international marketing offices and distribution centres in the USA and Europe. SS is convinced that the plant at Sri City provides an excellent opportunity, as the ecosystem there is appropriate for growth with automotive companies and well-established export processing zone. SAF has pursued an inorganic growth strategy by acquiring a unit that was in an early stage of operation and is about 90 km away from Chennai. Hence, coordination with top management in the initial set up and stabilisation process should not be difficult. SS was focussed on how to drive the communication of positivity, aggressive implementation of operations strategy and spirit of operational success among key role agents which include senior management, middle management, and employees in the new plant. Members of this committee were those who would carry such a spirit across the other stakeholders and hence, they had to be galvanised about the project.

SAF: Genesis and Early-stage Development

SS comes from a family of a conservative social background. However, his father, S. Sankaranarayanan was a brilliant entrepreneur who experimented with his innovative ideas in varied businesses like leather processing, tailóring of garments for defense during the war period, medicines from indigenous herbs, industrial packaging, civil works and so on. He took an early retirement to give back to society through social activities. He did not want his sons to be in business. However, his zeal had motivated SS who, by then, had become a qualified mechanical engineer. SS worked for three years with Larsen and Turbo before deciding to be on his own.

In 1974, SS had set up Micro Turns at Guindy in Chennai, a turning shop to produce turned components. This was a small initiative by him. He was confident of the market and his investment. His father encouraged him, and zeal was at its high. What worried him was the scarp that was generated while turning components!

Cold Forging – Breakthrough Idea to Implementation in India:

SS was a voracious reader of technical matters as well as general outlook. Wastages in turning and disposing of the same created an interest in SS to look for opportunities wherein more advanced techniques of production can be deployed. Review of a literature helped him to understand forging metals for forming parts that enabled process speed, efficiency, and precision. Savings in material, labour, and overheads while generating components were adequate to invest his time and energy on this self-learning and experimenting process. This was the key trait of entrepreneurship which was fine-tuned and imparted to SS by his father!

His pursuit of forging did not stop with traditional applications based on heat. He was more attracted by cold forging technology used elsewhere in India which eliminated the heating process for precision. He understood that MICO at Bengaluru was using cold forging in the manufacture of spark plugs. As one would know, it was using German technology. Upon observing the same, SS gained a lot of confidence to develop it indigenously. It must be noted here that it is a one-man effort. He lacked capital or bandwidth of any institutional backing or large business family experience and risk-taking ability to pursue this. His gut feeling led him to commit his time, money and effort to refine, redo and recreate and finally, achieve perfection in cold forging technology for machining metal (mostly steel) parts, in 1997. SS summarised it as follows:

"I boldly purchased, in 1974, a forge press from Ametep, Faridabad. It was ₹5 lakhs investment. My father was keen that I must pursue my belief and go ahead. It was a big decision then." He further adds, "When we forged apart in room temperature (rationale of cold forging!), the high vertical pressure applied caused a huge horizontal force and tools suffered frequent breakages. Then, we focussed on the metallurgy and the quality of tools and succeeded in making a ring design that could withstand the pressure."

SAF received major support from one of its automotive customers who was then leading in commercial vehicles segment, namely TELCO, in 1980. Rane Madras was also an SAF client since 1977. Some of these customer associations continued for four decades mainly because of SAF's ability to produce from the stage of designing to final production to customer requirements at an outstanding record of reliability and speed. There were not many cold forging companies in India that could do this.

It stands out to the customer by way of savings in the cost of material and other direct components. SAF was able to achieve productivity gains that were passed on to customers. Compared with the conventional method of cutting, cold forging gave more than ten times increase in turning of output for the same capital and labour ratio. In recognition of his contribution, International Forging Congress awarded the "Forge Master Award" to SS in 2011. It was a grand recognition for his contribution to technology and the industry.

Key to operations strategy, in the initial phase of growth, was to adopt relevant technology and being a pioneer with indigenous development; process development and focus on organisation development through quality initiative. After having finetuned the processes, SAF had market benefits like cost reduction; quality and speed of response. As of 2012, SAF was doing around 20 million pieces a year. According to Ravishankar, "We make disc brake piston for all the three major Indian manufacturers – Brakes India, Bosch, and Mando. We make a million such pistons a year. We also make critical components for CV joints. We produce 10 million pistons a year. All vehicles, right from the low-end Maruti 800 to the most sophisticated cars produced in India, have our caliper piston component. We are significant suppliers of drive shaft parts, brake parts, ball joints, suspension and assembly components".[1]

This is the market reach achieved by SAF while pursuing operations excellence and endorsement by clients. It may be relevant to discuss various efforts and areas of focus that were initiated over the years.

Next Stage of Growth Through Exports

In 1991 and 92, SAF added customers like Ashok Leyland, Bajaj and Escorts, to name a few. Each of these had requirements for varied SKUs, as the product is different. The confidence that SAF could create in customers helped them to stay focussed on supplying auto components to auto majors. Escorts was in the business of agricultural farm equipments. Given the conditions wherein the auto industry had opened in the early 1990s in India, SS realised that it was important to be a supplier to international players who were "who is who" in the industry. In 1995, there was an opportunity to supply to Bosch at a three months' notice. SS was convinced that it was not right to strike the opportunity as he felt SAF was still not ready with a differentiator, namely precision in quality and thereby managing cost. He used to invest time and money in finetuning technological expertise in cold forging for that kind of part forming.

Around that time, there was an opportunity with BOSCH, US. SS personally represented SAF in vendor selection meetings in the USA. He carried a sample of 287 kg to showcase fineness in finishing that SAF could achieve! About seven thousand parts in a product of three was the outcome of such an entrepreneurial streak! It was just beginning in making history for SAF. "Urge to do" was the underlying drive for operations excellence. SAF, led by SS, was pursuing a strategy of technical perfection. It was not concerned with immediate short-term wins.

SAF fully utilised the opening of the Indian automobile industry and the entry of multinational auto majors in India. These companies preferred cold forged parts. This required SAF to expand product lines and capacity. It assumed risk and invested in the same. In 2007, Chrysler Motors identified SAF as a sourcing partner for CV joint parts. SAF decided to set up a dedicated 100 per cent EOU at Madras Export Processing Zone (MPEZ) in Chennai, which was again within greater Chennai city limits. It was close to the airport and seaport.

After this breakthrough, SAF supplied to leading players in the USA and Europe. Exports grew significantly along with the domestic market. Both geographies complemented each other in growth. Exhibit 1 shows segment-wise growth and share in total revenue.

EXHIBIT 1 Revenue share between domestic and exports

Category	2013-14	2014-15	2015-16	2016-17	CAGR
Domestic	106	150	180	232	30%
Exports	225	226	269	308	11%
Total	331	376	449	540	18%
Share in % of total					
Domestic	32	40	40	43	
Exports	68	60	60	57	

In the year 2016-17, the USA contributed 40 per cent; Europe contributed 17 per cent and the domestic market contributed 43 per cent of the total revenue. It is interesting to observe that export revenue was higher than domestic sales. Sales from India and the USA were almost equal.

SS mentioned that, "It was reflection of our technical capability to be direct supplier to international OEs like American Axle & Manufacturing, ABB, Atlas Copco, Bosch, Chrysler, Comstar, GE, Hyundai, Iroquois Nationals, Mando, Nepco Inc, Nexteer Automotive, NTN Corporation, Saint Jean Industries; TVS; WABCO and TRW Automotive and so on. It was a matter of pride that we could focus our efforts and stay aggressive in a niche chosen area and moved from Tier II supplier to Tier I manufacturers to direct OE supplier as well. For us, being present in multiple nodes of the supply network was critical for sustained growth. I cherish this journey which we started in the 1990s by exporting to the USA in a period when a lapse in supply had penalty in dollars. It was a nightmare for a company of our size and tradition! But that fear instilled discipline and aggressive drive towards operations excellence! If I had chosen to be conservative by avoiding the risk of having international buyers, I would not have led SAF to this growth track. If you ask me, that decision was key to upward kink in our growth curve".

He continued that, "Objectivity of international buyers and referrals helped to grow our business. Our confidence also grew year after year. The company had got Star Export House status in 1998 as it was exporting since then. Till 2005, SAF did not have a marketing department. This spoke volumes about operations strategy and linkage to our market requirements! Even now, at the CXO level, we felt that the market was not a constraint as long as you were able to establish a competitive edge".

Overview of Operations of SAF

SAF is the largest manufacturer of cold and warm forged components in India. In the CV Joints components and Aluminum Braking components sector, SAF is one of the top three global players. Its main activities are categorised as cold forming; cold extrusion; precision warm forming; precision finish machining; heat treatment; finish treatment and sub-system assembly. Product are categorised as drive shaft parts (42%); brake parts (28%), suspension parts (20%), non–auto (6%) and others, including power transmission and steering (4%). SAF facilities are shown in Exhibit 2.

SAF production facilities have enabled it to become the largest manufacturer of cold-forged components in India. It has achieved leadership in aluminum forging technology. As mentioned earlier, it has an edge because of self-developed forging technology. Since it has been in a focussed segment, it could achieve a dominant market share for part families among domestic customers. It may be noted that SAF production capability helped to achieve a single-source vendor for many export customers.

SS mentioned that, "SAF production focus has always been to stay focussed on core strengths. Further, from the early stage, the product portfolio has been to create a niche positioning for the company in Tier II. Later, it could graduate to Tier I through the sub-assembly system. One can notice how the firm has continually climbed the value chain from turning machine parts to sub-assembly through the best of forging technology using the best of machine tools! One of our approaches has been product churning and vitality index. The vitality index had been improving by moving up towards high-value critical components over the years. This has helped us to benchmark among top performers in our category and stay ahead of competition in the chosen area of operation and product category."

EXHIBIT 2 SAF facilities

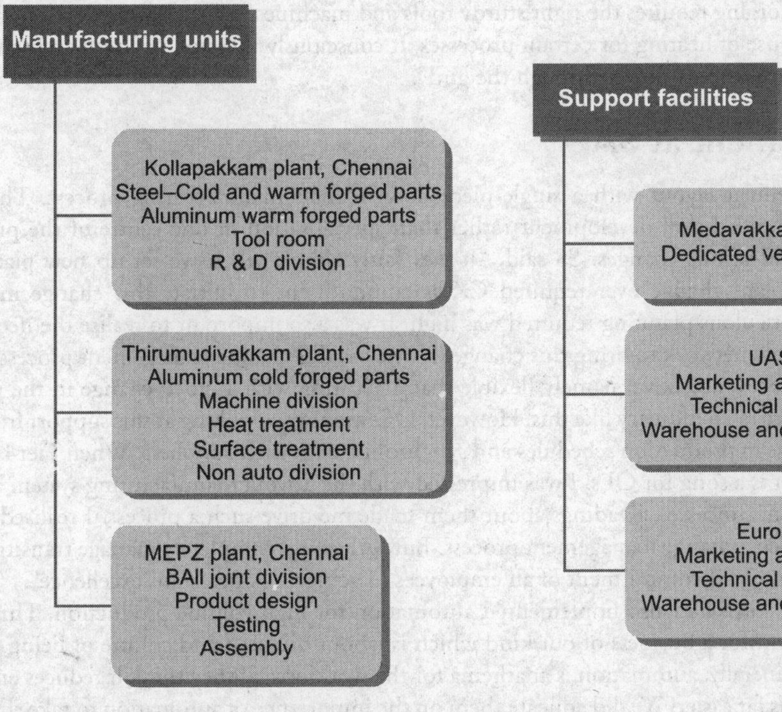

On technology and product development, SAF has been encouraging the R&D division to develop in-house cutting-edge technology. The company has continuous endeavour towards technology improvements by investing in R&D lab and personnel to develop tools, materials, and pilots for cost reduction and productivity improvement. A senior management professional was focussed full time on working for futuristic technology development. What SS started as an initiative, when he had set up the business, is today institutionalised as a culture in SAF. Murali Shankar, Managing Director of SAF and Ravi Shankar, Joint Managing Director who is a part of the core team with SS, ensure that the culture stays fit and healthy for sustained growth.

SS mentioned that, "A team works tirelessly on the same. The lab has extensive simulation capability to indulge in proper testing and corrections so that advances in research are meaningful. SAF business depends upon the ability to use the best of tools in forming, shaping and assembly of parts. Modern state of art tool room has been enabled. It is the key for the MEPZ export unit subassembly plant where CV joints are made. All these technology and product development initiatives are focussed on reducing development lead time. Reduced lead time helps to be "quick to market" which leads to achieve competitive advantage. Further, it helps for a reduction in product development cost and hence, cost leadership as well! Material saving through tool room advancement and technology adoption brings reduction in direct cost. These are key to our success. SAF has been working on concurrent and collaborative engineering with its customers. On its supplier side, there is a limited requirement for collaborative engineering compared with our alignment with customers. On the supply side, it is more to do with technical expertise, capital equipment and material usage where collaborative engineering is required."

He further added, "Expertise in product re-engineering had been successfully demonstrated by SAF. It recreated products which were turned parts into forgings. It also converted castings into forgings. In terms of material used, SAF led the replacement of steel as material used to aluminum parts. This reduced the part's weight and improved efficiency. We take pride in developing some of the high critical shaft products which are expected to crack while in case of an accident. Thus, it improves safety. Such innovations have been phenomenally successful giving credit to our engineering capability. Since our process involves a high amount of force to be used, precision force application in cold forging requires the right sturdy tools and machines. All such were developed internally. Since SAF continued the use of heating for certain processes, it consciously invested in alternate fuel energy like windmills and used to wheel/export power through the gird".

Process Development at SAF

SAF has implemented cellular layout with a single-piece flow in their manufacturing process. This required investing in employees rounded skill development rather than specialisation in one centre of the process unit. It also required design and layout changes. SS said, "It was fairly simple when we set up new plant in 2007 at MEPZ. The existing plant change over required CXOs commitment to initiate this change management process. The extent of meticulous planning required was high. It was also important to realise the need to adjust completely across the supply network to bring this change. However, this change management process helped for implementing another process objective, namely flexible manufacturing with a quick change in the production schedule. This is a challenge in an industry like this. However, OEs are always looking at this support from vendors as they can work on change in production schedules and synchronise with their suppliers. When Tier I and Tier II vendors implement this, it is a song for OEs! I was impressed with the Toyota manufacturing system and Toyota Supply Chain Management processes. Readings about them made me drive such a process. I realised challenges are aplenty when we do such a change management process. But SAF could completely manage transition because of its entrepreneurial culture and commitment of all employees in achieving operations excellence".

SS added further that, "SAF had also implemented automation for high volume production. This is again a critical process development for a business of our kind which is labour oriented and culture of being benevolent towards the workforce. Generally, automation is anathema for the workforce as they think it reduces employment growth; and fault finding is far easier! We did educate them on the importance of automation to take the company to the next stage of growth. We invested heavily in training and development. Those programmes were designed in such a way where workforce including supervisors and managers at the shop floor understand long-term growth opportunities while we embraced automation. Such a planned implementation of automation helped us to further drive our quality management process. We adopted lean practices and the elimination of non-value-added secondary operations. These were critical for controlling costs and improving customer satisfaction. Imagine that we are handling a large export order for ball joints parts on a short window. Such an order cannot afford rejections or rework where high precision is involved. If we miss the deadline, the penalty is going to be in foreign currency and loss of credibility with the customer.

In some cases, we are single-source vendor and the customer has a strategic relationship with us. SAF must rise to the level of customer operating efficiency at our local plant. I inculcated the spirit of trustee of customers' quality and ability to work as their extended arms in our location. This required investments in upgrading of machines and improvement in technology, apart from training. We did this to achieve improvement in throughput, quality, and productivity. We set new norms for measuring productivity and showcased significant improvements to employees. In certain areas, gains were as high as three times simply because of reduction in change over time, elimination of waste and automation. However, one must look at complete system productivity than in isolated areas. That way, I am convinced that our efforts paid off well as acknowledged by our customers whose order reflects in growth of revenue and profitability. We also implemented a significant process of preventive maintenance to meet overall equipment effectiveness targets".

Thus, process development in SAF helped to systematically build quality initiatives across operations in all plants and the R&D division. The company could choose robust and capable processes that helped in case of all stakeholders like suppliers, employees, and customers. The process development facilitated for understanding of assembly. The functional requirements helped staff at the floor to skill themselves appropriately for changing market requirements and to establish a competitive advantage for the firm in the market. The company used learning and development as a key management process, including learnings from internal job accomplishments by refining from mistakes and from external sources like material and equipment suppliers and customers.

Systems and Practices Enabling Manufacturing Process

SAF has been involved in daily review meetings (DRM) without fail on any single day over the last four decades. Its operating team at plant level reviews previous day production and relates to the current daily schedule. It ensures that the multi-disciplinary team resolved operating issues so that customer commitments were fulfiled on time. The focus of DRM was issue resolution with the customer in focus and not pinpointing failures.

SAF also had weekly review meetings and quality adherence review. The object of this review was to look at the causes of failure and corrective actions that were to be enabled. If DRM failed to resolve any customer related pain points, weekly review committee spent time in designing an approach to address customer order fulfilment. These reviews were discussed among senior management from corporate and plant level executives so that direction was clear. The idea of these meetings was to avoid last-minute pressure in handling customer accounts.

The monthly measurement review meeting was chaired by CXO of respective units and corporate as well. It happened strategic business unit (SBU) wise. Key performance index (KPI) and key results area (KPA) were addressed. KPI metrics gave a lot of causal factors and helped to probe into them. On the other hand, KPAs showed the impact of KPI in certain results like customer-facing, process efficiency and cost, and financial factors. This was extremely useful when SAF processed a large export order or implemented a change like complete automation of large-scale production. According to some of the senior management team members, these meetings had inculcated a lot of responsibility among the managers and helped them to use their authority with accountability. Along with this, there was another set of meetings chaired by CFO of the company over the years, as a routine, on monthly cost analysis of plants and corporate. SAF insisted on cost sheets being prepared at multiple levels like product group-wise, customer order wise and some of the major cost centres. Budget versus actual analysis helped them to understand how they were managing operations concerning operating profit for which cost management was the most critical activity.

As mentioned earlier, SAF had phenomenal quality focus and quality systems in place. The company followed Kaizen meticulously across plants and centres. Apart from this, quality circles were formed and frequently reviewed possible continuous improvements that could happen from the shop floor. All employees were encouraged to participate in quality circle meetings. There was a senior management team and a budget was provided for quality management. The quality process was key to the excellence of SAF's operations programme and growth with customers.

The company had implemented TS – 16949 Quality Management System across the company. SO/TS 16949 is an ISO technical specification aimed at the development of a quality management system that provides for continual improvement, emphasising defect prevention and the reduction of variation and waste in the automotive industry supply chain. Further, SAF had been certified for ISO 14001 which addresses environmental management. The company had high level of practices towards reducing pollution, water management and reducing and using heat energy through alternate systems like solar and windmill. SAF practiced OHSAS 18001 for occupational and safety management and provided the highest priority for workmen safety procedures and all employees are adequately trained on the same. The company had moved away from tradition and had employed women in shop floor handling jobs where they could compete along with men. The company had implemented "learn while you earn" programme for women and encouraged their employment showing their commitment towards parity in jobs. One can see how effectively employees, including women, were participating in Kaizen and quality circle initiatives. It may be noted here that Madras Management Association announced SAF as winner of the 15th MMA Award for Managerial Excellence for 2016 in the manufacturing category.[2] This is again a significant recognition for the excellence journey of the company.

Supply Chain as an Edge

SAF implemented Kanban and the supermarket system in the supply chain. Sundaram, Executive Director, Supply Chain, mentioned that, "SAF in early stages of deployment itself was focussed on reducing inventory and moved towards Vendor Managed Inventory methods. It introduced the Kanban system wherein vendors refill based on drawl and demand at the shop floor. We have created a supermarket system. In a supermarket (like the Toyota Production System - TPS), customers (processes) buy what they need when they need it. Since the system is self-service, the sales effort (materials management) is reduced. In this system, the shelves are refilled as products are parts withdrawn on the assumption that what has drawn will be drawn again, which makes it easy to see how much has been used and to avoid overstocking. The most important feature of a supermarket system is that stocking is triggered by actual demand. In the TPS, this signal triggers the 'pull' system of production. SAF has also provided technical and quality support to suppliers. The company realises the importance of the role of suppliers in their operations excellence journey and needs to have customer delight which is possible only with the support of all partners in the supply network. We treat some of them as our strategic partners, especially when critical components and strategic items buying are involved. Hence, we assist them in upgrading technology and facilities without directly investing capital. We have been involved in concurrent engineering for strategic items. There had been regular training and cluster group programmes for improving suppliers."

SS mentioned about a game-changer practice in vendor management. He said that, "We have initiated a practice of paying all vendors by fifth or sixth of the following month for all supplies received and taken to stock till the end of the previous month. This is practiced over three decades in all our plants. This is contradicting working capital and cash cycle practice recommended by financial consultants. Most of the companies will try to reduce inventory, improve receivables by reducing credit period and ensuring proper collections. Further, they try to have a long period for payables. Some companies even take pride in having negative working capital. On the contrary, we pay quickly to our vendors. Sixty percent of our vendors are dedicated suppliers and the balance is competitive who supply to many other large plants. The reason why we do the same is that vendors have two important commitments, namely payment of salary on time and certain statutory payments towards labour, duties, and tariff for power consumption. If we enjoy cost advantage by outsourcing some aspects forging to them, we must ensure that they are healthy and provide predictable service so that we could offer flexibility to our customers. Arbitrage overpayment cycle and cost help us to design appropriate cash management of us as well as for vendors. This has been a unique practice for a loyal vendor management system".

SS added that, "I have been particular that some of the employees become entrepreneurs by becoming suppliers to us. I did not see any conflict of interest if they are willing to assume risk and be competitive along with other vendors. We have created a vendor park in one of our plants mainly to encourage supplier development. One thing which we have made clear is that adherence to responsible procurement and ethical practices in supply management is a rule within and essential for our operational excellence journey. Such engagements reduce supply risk and avoid contingencies".

Human Resource Practices Facilitating Operations Excellence

SAF had a structured training-based skill matrix. This was especially helpful when it implemented changes to the cellular production system and deployed a quality management system. The latter had been a part of the operation process from the early stages of business. The company had genuinely encouraged suggestion schemes and implemented a merit award. Since several employees led initiatives like Kaizen and quality circles, HR practice and quality practices intertwined for the benefit of both the systems. The company had been practising monthly performance incentive schemes at the shop floor level. Half-yearly appraisal and feedback mechanisms were formally practiced across the organisation. There were counselling sessions organised for selected employees. Mentorship roles were assigned, and mentors and prodigies were also constantly evaluated in a structured way to map improvements.

The company encouraged the participation of employees in various events organised by industry forums and employees won laurels for their performance. It had structured and well-meaning employee welfare schemes. All employees were provided with fair and reasonable welfare schemes under normal and contingent conditions. There was a regular monthly review mechanism both on employee welfare and safety, especially at the workplace. With recruitment of women at the shop floor, the company ensured the utmost safety for them and fair treatment without any harassment from any person so far. As mentioned earlier, employees were encouraged to go in for higher studies and "earn while you learn" is being practiced.

SS mentioned that, "SAF pioneered with employee stock option equivalent bonus schemes for senior management employees who spent twenty-five years with the company. The bonus amount was very attractive and required a huge cash outflow. But I insisted that it is important to recognise people who have stayed with us and been a part of the journey. Despite all these, I have some concerns about people management practice. It is difficult for a company of our size to attract lateral and senior talent at the top level who could be committed for long-term growth. We have limited success in this area though we pay a very high market salary. Second, I feel that the quality and attitude of engineering graduates who want to take the shop floor job have changed from strategic engagement to transactional engagement. They leave quickly as they are value-added in our practice. Instead of preferring a stable and career-oriented job with us, they were lured by greener pastures for short term gains. We must survive in such a market practice. I would say these two are the major limiting factors for our growth despite the fact we are a zero-debt company and a highly profitable company compared to the peers in the segment. Our unused debt capacity is high. This is my only conservatism in our growth plans."

Customer Service, a Key Focus of Supply Chain Function

Some of the SAF customer service perspectives were interesting and comprehensive. They followed principles of service organisation in certain areas though it was a production unit by business. SAF believed in serving customers by locating distribution centres close to the plants of customers. Since plants were in Chennai, while customers were located across cities in India, the USA, and Europe. Managing distribution centres for customer order fulfilment was critical for success. With most of its customers, SAF had Just-in-Time (JIT) commitment which means that their management of distribution centres must be exceptional. Since they served a family of products and certain common parts were there in their product portfolio, the company could achieve a high level of order fulfilment. These were possible with constant and structured engagement with end-to-end players in the supply network which triggers customer demand management. The company provided customers end-to-end logistics support with professional, contractual and transparent dealing on value-added services.

Conclusion

SAF achieved growth driven by the technology it had deployed and a significant part of it is homegrown. It had achieved the status of a preferred global supplier for its international customers who provided a substantial share of total revenue. It had constantly enhanced its value to the customer by being responsive, proactive and quality-driven. The company had prioritised quality production over volume. Instead of achieving economies of production through volume, it had achieved a cost advantage by reducing rejection and eliminating waste. The company had been applying financial prudence and opted for a strategy of low operating risk and low financial risk through operations excellence programmes. People management practices led to the adoption of cellular manufacturing and enriched people with multi-skills. Its policy of energy conservation, use of alternative sources of energy and contribution towards society by fair and ethical practices contributed towards sustaining operations excellence over four decades.

SS and senior management are now confronted with the implementation of an operations excellence programme at a newly acquired plant at Sri City close to Chennai plants. There is going to be a new set of employees who come with some experience and middle management including the supervisory level and above. The plant manager will be retained. It requires an initial period of mentoring by senior managers from existing plants to do cultural fit for embarking on the operations excellence programme at this new plant. Further, there is a set of clients likely in Sri City as there is a presence of auto companies. Export from the plant is also possible as ports are located nearby, though little further by 40 km compared with Chennai MEPZ plant. SS is relying a lot on the experience of integrating this facility with overall business as this is company's first venture in four decades outside Chennai. They have never moved to other parts of Tamil Nadu as well. The confidence stems from the fact that Sri City has a locational advantage and it is near Chennai for senior management to oversee operations. The key success factor is the ability to go through employee processes in manufacturing like quality circle and kaizen along with safety, health, and environment. One another advantage SS could see is advanced manufacturing processes for sub-assembly similar and marginally better because of vintage to MEPZ plant. SS is convinced that if the team can deliver at MPEZ and win customer delight, it is natural he could infuse confidence among stakeholders, namely the Board of Directors and operating strategy team across plants and more specifically in Sri City.

QUESTIONS

1. Explain the integration of operations perspective and market requirements of Super Auto Forge and relate its growth.
2. "Pursuing homegrown technology drives zeal, adoption of excellence in manufacturing and cost advantage for Tier II and Tier I parts assembly units." Elucidate with experience of SAF.
3. "Development of processes and managing implementation are key drivers of growth for a company." Discuss with example of SAF.
4. "Locational advantage in facility decision can be exploited for the international growth of the firm provided the leadership is clear about operations strategy formulation and implementation." Elucidate with the example of SAF.
5. Analyse key strategic initiatives and their value for SAF growth. You may focus your discussion on HR practices and that of the supply chain for domestic and international markets.
6. "Leadership is critical for growth of a firm." Elucidate based on the role of SS in growth of SAF.
7. What do you think about the importance of Sri City plant integration? Please draft a note if you were to advise SS.
8. Explain various risks in terms of operations, finance and business portfolio that SAF faced and how they can be handled?

REFERENCES

1. Viswanathan, S. and Ragunathan, Jayanthi, The Super Forge Master, *Industrial Economist*, December 2012
2. https://www.thehindubusinessline.com/news/national/mma-awards-for-managerial-excellence/article8797891.ece Accessed on 12 September 2019
3. https://www.superautoforge.net Accessed on 12 September 2019

Reliserve Distribution Management Ltd: Surge in demand for a short window and service challenges

(**Disclaimer:** The case is for an academic purpose and not reflective of the business situation of any company with which the author is associated with now or in the past. Business problem is articulated for a desired learning for operations management students and not to create any opinion of any company or its customers.)

Abstract

Reliserve Distribution Management Ltd (Reliserve) is into third-party and fourth-party logistics service provider business. Their customers are manufacturers of consumer electronics and other durable goods segments around the same type of products. Apart from manufacturers, Reliserve also has e-commerce portals and other players who are into e-business as their customers. Reliserve mainly provides warehousing, transportation of primary, secondary, and last-mile movements. Order management is one of the critical tasks which it must do. More importantly, the market had been growing for retailers in consumer electronics and fashion goods for their principals. They were demanding Reliserve to keep growth in tandem with theirs. The challenge is that Reliserve has to improve resources base on short notices and serve for short windows. Such demand for service had applied pressure on sustaining growth to keep pace with the growth rate of customers. However, the risk of failure is passed on to Reliserve as customers pay for the time and extent they use the services of Reliserve. The case addresses how a Reliserve can face such a challenge!

Learning Objective: To understand the philosophy of traditional strategic planning versus deployment of emergent strategy and align facility decisions with that of aggregate planning methods.

Key Words: Emergent strategy; Aggregate planning; Facility decision; e-commerce.

Case

Dilemma

Reliserve Distribution Management Ltd is into offering warehousing, transportation, inventory management, and network design solutions. It is also into verticals like consumer electronics and other consumer durable products segment like watches, jewelry, home equipment, safety devices, medical equipment and so on. The senior management of the company has observed a key opportunity which Mr. Shyam Lal Yadav (Shyam), Vice President (Business Development), wants to pursue. It is an opportunity with the distribution of goods through alignment with e-commerce portals. However, Keshav Patel, Promoter and CEO of the company, was not keen and wanted to take a guarded step as an exponential growth in the e-commerce platform may require substantial capital, tremendous managerial time and operations challenge as space and people are to be added at a fast pace and on flexible terms.

Shyam was worried that if the opportunity is lost, Reliserve may be bulldozed by competition. He discussed this with Julie Johnson, Chief Strategy Officer, and wanted to make an informed decision. Julie also performed the role of Executive Assistant as Keshav trusts her objectivity and neutrality in decision making. She also chaired the ethics committee of the company. She advised Shyam to get this decision opportunity analysed through a third-party neutral strategy advisor. She was of strong view that Keshav may be open to listening to an expert from outside. This is mainly because he runs the company as a professionally managed one, despite being closely held. Thus, they roped in James Samuel, Partner of Vision Centric Strategy Consulting LLP (VCSC).

Upon listening to Shyam along with Julie and Keshav in a detailed briefing session, James mapped the business problem. He had another one-to-one meeting with Keshav to understand his vision and priorities.

James's dilemmas are—Should there be a traditional business call or an emergent strategy to be pursued and face the outcome? What are the possible advisory in operations strategy decision areas, namely facility choices and aggregate plan models to be pursued? He pondered over his next meeting with his client's key management professionals during the weekend at an off-site strategy session.

Introduction

James is a leading management strategy consultant based out of New Delhi. He has Ph.D. in Management and about two decades of experience in the corporate industry and a decade as an independent management consultant. After working with a leading MNC for about 15 years in South Asia, he decided to come back to India and settle down, as then it was the most happening place. He started VCSC with two other professionals, of which Sachin Iyer is a chartered accountant and Rashmi Kapur is an engineer and a management graduate. Rashmi is an alumnus of a leading technology and business school in India. She had been with an IT company for about 15 years. She had been part of its growth from inception to listing in the stock market till it reached a size of about a billion-dollar company. Though a partner leads client engagement, critical advisory decisions are consultative in practice. However, the process ensured that there was no other engagement with the client or any other conflicting engagement like with that of competitor advisory service engagement. In this situation, James decided to go all alone as e-commerce is the most growing sector and they have quite a few prospects at different stages. VCSC is clear on its ethical standards and the high moral standards are more important than the revenue they could generate.

Team and Perceptions

Reliserve is a distribution management company based out of New Delhi. Keshav has about twenty-five years of experience in leading an MNC FMCG company before starting Reliserve about seven years back. He was supported by friends and family in the first stage. After initial success, he got some venture capitalists interested in the company about three years back. He is a team player and believes in engaging with customers, prospects and asset providers continuingly. Keshav was keen to grow the company across verticals and set up a professional service-oriented distribution management company. He was of the view that the core of Reliserve must be distribution management. He avoided branding linkages to supply chain, as it connected in the market either as linefeed inbound material movers or transport management companies with select opportunities in storage. He wanted a clear focus on what his company should be known for and its core competency! He focussed on distribution management which is predominantly an outbound movement of goods with storage, movement and inventory management as a value-added service through the channel. He believed that because of his background in MNC, FMCG consumerism in India is bound to stay and requires distribution as a link between terminal points, namely manufacturers and consumers in channel movement.

Keshav mentioned in a meet with James that, "According to CSI market data, typically in transport and logistics industry, operating margin is between 7% and 9% and net margin is about 5% to 7.5%. What matters is the growth rate and being able to garner business in growth verticals! A company like ours should have a portfolio of stable and medium margin customers as well as premium customers. If e-commerce is growing exponentially, we need to be there with a sizeable share and must be reckoned as the key competitor among service providers. But Reliserve has received the first two tranches of investors. We must reckon that they have been provided with risk capital. A distribution management company cannot get debt capital easily as there are hardly any long-term asset-based financing opportunities. Even if we were to get funding for a warehouse, no one gives money for land which is a substantial component of the project cost. We do not own operating assets like trucks and warehouses, or any warehouse operating equipment. Our strength is client relationships and a deep understanding of the market. Clients believe that we are here to stay because of our conservative approach to risk management."

Shyam, who oversees business development, aims to take the company from its current size of ₹300 crores to ₹900 crores top line in five years at a compound annual growth rate (CAGR) of 25 per cent and slightly more! He has pressure of target but enjoys and feels healthy to run after the same. According to him, any business which gives a net margin, even marginal (which could be a trend at that time in that business!), but has a potential to average after industry profitability moves up, then that business must be garnered. This is a point of discontent with Keshav who is insistent on transaction wise margin. He discourages those which are at low margin at the start of the growth curve as early entrants. For him, many times, such low margins businesses are past growth phase and deep into maturity phase of the life cycle. Keshav steered the growth of the company because of his financial prudence and ability to raise capital with risk capital providers. He was of the view that financial and managerial resources cannot be stretched far and wide.

Julie got an international management degree after her graduation in Economics from a leading school. She went for an international programme on a sabbatical. She was handpicked for this position by venture capitalists who have invested in the company. She as a resource brings comfort to investors as she can demonstrate an overall perspective with her skills in industry analysis. She is more balanced and moderates between the time horizon of the short term and long term.

Growth of e-Commerce Industry in India

India's e-commerce industry is growing fast and is one of the most dynamic channels of transactions that customers seem to prefer. This could be because of increasing internet penetration. E-commerce is India's fastest-growing and most dynamic channel for commercial transactions. The Indian e-commerce market is expected to become the second-largest in the world. The market is expected to reach $64 billion by 2020 and $200 billion by 2026 from $38.5 billion as of 2017. (Source: https://www.ibef.org/industry/ecommerce.aspx).

Some of the noticeable changes in Indian customers are the growing appetite for international brands; better quality foreign products; increasing income levels; ability to spend on trending purchases and increased awareness. Categories like lifestyle products, consumer electronics, clothing, footwear, jewelry and accessories, health and beauty, household goods, art and collectibles, event tickets and online music have tremendous patronage for online sales. This has been mainly because of technology explosion which made many e-commerce platforms active and enabled in different devices, including handheld phones. The evolution of analytics-driven customer engagements, providing customers in numerous reviews, peer customer experience, and the ability to see product dimensions and virtually feel the product have all contributed to the growth. The maturity of hyper-local logistics has also phenomenally contributed to the growth of this segment. Government initiatives, such as Digital India, Skill India, Startup India and Make in India are policy level environmental changes contributing to the growth of the e-commerce industry.

According to the India Brand Equity Foundation (IBEF) presentation, some of the major developments in India's e-commerce sector are:

- Walmart's acquisition of Flipkart, an Indian e-commerce platform, for $16 billion;
- Launch of the Paytm Payment Bank, India's first bank with zero charges on online transactions, no minimum balance requirement and free virtual debit card
- 21 private equity and venture capital deals worth $2.1 billion in 2017 and six deals worth $226 million in January-April 2018 in the Indian e-commerce sector.

There are international players in India like Amazon, eBay (now being sold to homegrown Flipkart, which was recently acquired by Walmart), Alibaba and others, who are facing competition from the domestic players, such as Flipkart, Snapdeal, TataCliq as well as with inventory led e-tailers (electronic retailers). These players have intensified competition but have fueled growth as well.

With no major entry barriers and with few e-tailers, the Indian market for e-commerce has grown at a fast pace for the past three years. Omni-Channel retailers, such as Shoppers-Stop, Reliance, Croma, etc., have also embraced e-commerce as another sales channel to increase digital footprints. Currently, there are approximately 1.2 million transactions per day in e-commerce retailing.

According to IBEF, the share of sectors would be:

- Electronics: 47%
- Apparel: 31%
- Home and Furnishing: 8%
- Book: 7%
- Baby Products: 2%
- Beauty: 2%
- Other: 7%

The major business to customers (B2C) players are Flipkart, Myntra, Jabong, Amazon, Snapdeal, eBay, PayTM, Shopclues, Pepperfry, Zomato, BigBasket, Alibaba, etc.

India's internet economy is expected to double from US$125 billion as of April 2017 to US$250 billion by 2020, majorly backed by e-commerce. India's e-commerce revenue is expected to jump from US$39 billion in 2017 to US$120 billion in 2020, growing at an annual rate of 51 per cent, the highest in the world. (https://www.export.gov/article?id=India-e-Commerce). Further, mobile e-commerce (m-commerce) is growing rapidly as a secure supplement to the e-commerce industry. According to industry leaders, m-commerce could contribute up to 70 per cent of its total revenue. The number of smartphone users is expected to reach 650 million by 2019 which had an Internet user base of over 478 million in 2018.

Major Buying During Holidays Sale

The major buying during holidays, "Big sales", through e-commerce are during Diwali festival (October or November of the year); Dussehra (October); Rakhi festival (August) and Christmas (last week of December). According to a report, e-commerce shipments are expected to increase by 60-70 per cent during the first major sale in October with total sales of $2.5 - 3 billion on the back of heavy discounts on electronics. Competitive rivals are expected to engage in a discounting war to gain sales in categories like smartphones, televisions, and fashion, which together contribute almost 70 per cent of their sales. The marketplaces have increased order volume from brands by 50 – 80 per cent for this festive season over that in 2017.

Reliserve Opportunities and Challenges

Shyam presented that they must engage with e-commerce brands in a big way and pitch for the 2020 sale from January onwards. He was of the view that the companies develop their annual plan with a growth rate of above 80 percent and the majority, say about 30 percent of the sale coming in these four periods. Spread of sale during these periods would be Diwali contributing about 12 per cent; Dussehra about 10 per cent and balance two-holiday sale about 4 per cent each. Assuming that about 80 per cent growth in the sales happened in 2018, he was pitching for XYZ Ltd's (customer of Reliserve) internal growth in this segment at about 40 per cent. Currently out of the 140 warehouses the company operates across India, it may have for this operation earmarked vertical space of about 2.5 million square feet and fixed employee component of about 300 and recruited another 1800 on seasonal employment through contract service providers.

Keshav mentioned that the business requires hiring of warehouses additionally to equivalent amount or more, assuming 80 per cent capacity utilisation. This would mean about 1 million to 1.25 million square feet to be identified and contracted. Further, it would require the hiring of warehouse equipment and 100 full-time permanent employees. All these would require a minimum commitment of ₹100 million upfront. There are other costs like managerial time in marketing and identifying such locations; base commitment costs and other indirect overheads like insurance and so on. Considering the margin to be marginal as it is a competitive business, he was wondering if Reliserve must be aggressive.

Julie came up with two perspectives—she was of the view that e-commerce is going to be the future and being in that business is critical for Reliserve. Key success factors could be the ability to manage space, hire temporary staff through contract service providers, IT systems for order processing, quality standards, error rejections, and contract management. She felt operations strategy must focus on these areas and that future lies exactly here. Maybe this has to be balanced with more growth in high margin low volume project-centric businesses in the portfolio. Second, financial viability must be managed by better managing utilisation factors. However, Keshav mentioned that if we ramp up space and support services by July 2019, our customers would use the resources and services between August 2019 and January 2020. What would the company do with these resources between February 2020 and July 2020? Will operating for e-commerce business seem like running seasonal sugarcane crushing from November to May because of seasonality factors?

Julie threw back questions to Keshav on whether Reliserve can sustain 25 per cent year on year growth in business so that operations strategy synchronises with corporate strategy. There is a certain uniqueness of problems to operations strategy like which of the locations to grow for serving e-commerce so that e-commerce plan for growth syncs with their actual sale? If there are going to be variations, what level of flexibility should be built in Reliserve operations strategy? How is this to be covered in the master agreement with e-commerce players? Second, how to plan for managerial, supervisor level and operator level staffing on fixed rolls? What type of aggregate plan to be pursued? Third, Shyam's interest would be an overall growth rate of 25 per cent with a net profit margin of about 6 per cent. Currently, the bottom 30 per cent sale in the portfolio contributes 2.5 per cent which is where e-commerce comes in. The next 40 per cent is in 7 per cent and the last 30 per cent is in the rage of 10 per cent. Will investors bet further on these numbers?

Conclusion: Keshav wanted Julie to invite James to provide an operations strategy and link it with corporate strategy so that they can present the investors with risk, return and investment demand considering the questions mentioned above.

QUESTIONS

1. How can Reliserve synchronise operations strategy with corporate growth strategy, especially for the e-commerce segment?
2. What are the options of the aggregate plan they can consider for achieving this growth?
3. Justify your recommendation for pursuing growth with numerical calculations. Make necessary assumptions by referring to open source industry data for similar businesses.

REFERENCES

1. https://csimarket.com/Industry/industry_Profitability_Ratios.php?ind=1101
2. //economictimes.indiatimes.com/articleshow/65776866.cms?utm_source=contentofinterest&utm_medium=text&utm_campaign=cppst
3. https://www.ibef.org/download/Ecommerce-March-2018.pdf
4. https://www.ibef.org/industry/ecommerce-presentation

Logistics-Excellence in Chennai: Customer profitability and operations strategy

(**Disclaimer:** This case is based on common knowledge and discussions in forums about this business. The name of the company; and financial and business numbers are imaginary. The figures are illustrative and neither supported by factual records nor verified. The objective of this case is to discuss academic discussions to apply the concepts and framework for a similar business situation.)

Abstract

Quick2config Comp Ltd (QCL) was served by the L-X India subsidiary, L-X Chennai. It is in the business of manufacturing a computing device which is configured to order. L-X Chennai was Importer of Record (IOR) for QCL India. Such an arrangement would mean that L-X Chennai was the conduit for feeding inbound material to QCL India from its suppliers from abroad. QCL India identifies suppliers and shared the full operations plan. L-X Chennai received components from suppliers and supplied on a short window of less than two hours to in-plant assembly from its distribution centre. While QCL India was customer for line feed, suppliers to QCL India were also customers of L-X Chennai for stocking and keeping material on their record on behalf of them. Such an arrangement worked well during the steady-state business of QCL India. Whenever the market conditions were affected, the feed rate would change, impacting the revenue opportunities of L-X Chennai. Being a dedicated service provider to its customers, how would the firm align its strategy? One may note that as a service provider, this customer by design is a sole customer because of the Importer of Record. Revenue comes from the customer and customer's suppliers. The case addresses such a complicated decision environment.

Learning Objective: To understand the operations strategy of the global supply chain pursued by leading consumer durable computing company and its partners' role in fulfiling customer demands and their volatility.

Key Words: Vendor Managed inventory (VMI); Importer of Record (IOR); Supply chain management; Business to Business (B2B); Inbound movement; Just in Time (JIT).

Case

Deepak Sahu, Chief Financial Officer of Logistics-Excellence (L-X) India, was preparing for a meeting with Rajan Saxena, CEO of L-X, who has asked him to discuss the profitability of a leading hardware computing client business, namely Quick2config Comp Ltd (QCL). QCL was served by L-X Chennai, a subsidiary of L-X India. During the operations review, Rajan was informed by Ravi Vaidy, QCL Account Manager of L-X Chennai, about the reduced movement of stock from the warehouse (see Exhibit 1 in the Annexure). L-X Chennai was the sole operator of vendor managed inventory, which was an operations-focussed subsidiary of L-X India. R'avi was of the view that the demand for QCL is declining in India as the industry had matured and probably moved into the declining phase. He was worried as the number of deliveries was volatile and the average has been coming down in the last one year!

Deepak felt that the situation could be a temporary phase, as India has an aspiring population that was young and would buy hardware. Further, the small- and medium-scale segment was potentially huge and there was a replacement market as well. He was of the view that this industry could have had short business cycles but not decline or become a sunset industry.

Further, in any case as importer of record, L-X Chennai might not lose its relevance as it was a dedicated operation. Rajan's interest was more to see from overall account management and he wanted to understand whether in short to medium term, the cost of operations was covered. Second, success of L-X Chennai business was key to cover fixed overheads costs like corporate office expenses including the salary of the management of L-X India. Revenue of L-X India was 15 times more than L-X Chennai operation. But profitability in L-X Chennai business was reasonable and absorbed certain overheads of the parent company in India. In supply chain solutions, operations of L-X Chennai were more predictable than a warehouse or a pure-play transportation. Alternatively, technology and solution designing were more infrequent high margin business.

L-X Global

The company was founded with a focus on the cargo transportation business, which subsequently grew to include extended supply chain and logistics services, such as warehousing and freight management. L-X Global was a global supply chain solutions provider that mainly focussed on the East and South East side of the globe. It was the largest home-grown supply chain solutions company and leading regional supply chain management partner to many of the world's leading brands across Asia-Pacific region.

The company's strengths were the location of key hubs, deep-rooted understanding of local terrains, and in-depth presence. Such advantages helped in providing a wide range of specialised services, such as the strengths and ability to deliver customer value through its technology, processes, and people. Further, such services empowered its customers to achieve a comprehensive footprint and seamless global connectivity across the region.

The company had established regional connectivity by setting up greenfield operations in emerging markets. It also expanded its scope of services in the supply chain from the design of solutions to implementation for a client. It, thereby, expanded its scope of service and products from vendor managed inventory in the electronics and technology industry to temperature-controlled and cold storage solutions. It had increased its offering to sectors like electronics, chemicals and healthcare, consumers, the retail sector and e-commerce. The company had innovated supply chain solutions which was an app for vehicle efficiency and commuter ease of movement. This demonstrated its ability in offering an innovative solution in the supply chain domain.

The company had grown across geographies using its ability to develop, design and deliver solutions and business models in the space of supply chain whether it was cargo transportation, storage or inventory management for business to business segment or transportation in people movement segment.

L-X India

L-X first entered India in 2004 providing freight, customs clearance services, and finished goods distribution across India. Over a period, it delivered customised end-to-end supply chain solutions. It was operating as one of the largest service parts network of the country, across more than 81 forward serving locations and satellite hubs. Working closely with its last-mile partners, L-X India was also able to leverage on its pan-India network to achieve time-specific deliveries for its clients. L-X India constructed one of the first green warehouses in India.

QCL Chennai

QCL India was a part of the global operations of the parent company that had set up a plant in Chennai. QCL Global was a game-changer in its industry when it introduced a "made to order" computing device. It had a presence in developed nations and growth markets like BRICS countries. There were six plants across the globe, including one in China and India each. The objective was to derive a competitive advantage through operations.

Chennai plant was serving about 15 per cent market share of total domestic demand. It had another 40 per cent capacity to serve other countries apart from India. One of the reasons to be based out of India was to serve the export market as well. India's tier II and III cities were growing fast to fuel demand for QCL products. Hence QCL was focussed on such growth markets. However, there seemed to be seasonality in the purchase of their technology durable products, especially in the ultimate customer segment. Purchases happened during the beginning of the academic year which was typically between June and July of a year in India. Another spurt in demand happened during the festival season of October to January, as many gave high-value gifts during the festive time.

B2B segment also followed a similar pattern. In India, the financial year was between April of the current calendar year to March of the following calendar year. Typically, office equipment would be a capital decision and happened mostly around the end of the first quarter which was June or the beginning of the second quarter, July. Corporate spend during Deepavalli was also a common phenomenon, mainly as they were giving a gift to stakeholders including their employees. Hence, the demand for QCL will be skewed over five months in a year, namely between June and October and again between October and December.

Different stakeholders in India had been persuading QCL to increase capacity through additional investment. Though the company and its board were aware of the opportunities, they took a guarded approach. Interest of domestic stakeholders including that of policymakers was high because of the employment it generated!

QCL India's approach to go on measured production was mainly because it had reserved capacity for meeting out a surge in global demand or drop in production owing to environment changes in any of the other locations. The plant in India was the latest, they were comfortable in making its capacity as buffer capacity. It was to be noted that QCL India's Chennai plant capacity acted as a buffer for global demand to the extent of reserved capacity. Second, it had by then achieved the maximum allocated domestic capacity. Operations strategy was that this production facility would serve domestic demand and part of global demand.

L-X Chennai, and QCL Connect

L-X Chennai operated as a dedicated warehouse and line fulfilment service to QCL. It was the Indian customer centre and was introduced to 34 suppliers from nine countries as 'Importer of Record' (IOR).

"Importer of record is a term used in customs law. It refers to an importer, whether an entity or individual, who is responsible for ensuring that legal goods are imported under the law of the place. Importer is responsible for filing legally required documents. Payment of the assessed import duties and other taxes on the imported goods are to be given by the importer of record."[1]

Thus, IOR was a customs term for the entity responsible for ensuring that the imported goods comply with local laws and regulations, filing a completed duty entry and associated documents, paying the assessed import duties and other taxation for those goods. The importation of goods carried with it many legal obligations concerning duties, country of origin, and other regulatory matters which were enforced by the customs. There was a need for a license to import, thus an importer number must be established with the customs, and a bond provided in customs favour to import. The importer or (IOR) would be held liable for all customs-related aspects of the import transaction.

First, the value proposition of this arrangement for QCL was that it provided tremendous flexibility as it could decide on product mix in a short window like from a week to a shift. Second, duty was paid on the product as and when assembled. Stock holding and feeding to line at L-X Chennai was more of being a bonded warehouse operator. Hence, there was cost saving as well. Third, QCL or its supplier was not challenged for managerial time and effort as it was run professionally by L-X Chennai. The company had a core competency in warehousing and transportation including line feed. Further, they had competency in inventory forecasting and management, given the complexity of assembly operation! Figure 1 captures the sequence of transactions.

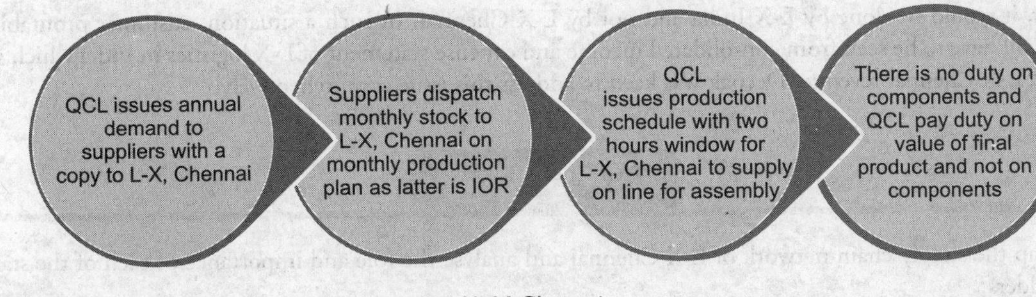

FIGURE 1 QCL order processing and role of L-X Chennai

Deepak mentioned the approximate value of these transactions on inventory alone to be ₹600 million and further, every order fill has a fee of about ₹1200. L-X Chennai had about four trucks dedicated to operating 24x7. Each truck could do about 10 fulfilment a day. If there was a surge in demand, L-X Chennai would deploy local trucks. If there was a fall in demand, inventory was not moving and hence fulfillment dropped! The risk of the drop-in business of QCL India could be due to seasonality and temporary phenomenon. The stock-based revenue had more certainty.

Cost Analysis

Warehouse was on their land when the government promoted this part for developing into Special Economic Zone. The other assets like building, equipment handling, trucks, and IT infrastructure were depreciable. The warehouse operated with the best of technology for shelving and order picking. The access was easy and seamless. It employed on rotation about 40 employees for picking and kitting for delivery. A temporary workforce was added as and when required.

Exhibit 2 in the annexure shows the income and expense statement of the operations of the QCL fulfilment. Deepak once mentioned in a review meeting that, "The business is giving a decent margin on its operations. Even if there is volatility, warehouse operations will give adequate margin to have a decent net profitability from this operation. QCL will have business in India and possibly, export from this plant. Domestic and international opportunities are adequate. The company has been the leader in the global market and the potential of the Indian market is naturally high as it is an aspirational product." Customer profitability was established. Seasonality or fluctuating trends could affect the quantum of transportation revenue and contribution. But the overall quality of revenue and margin was likely to support this operation. Hence, Deepak said, "When QCL grows, then L-X Chennai will also grow in proportion".

Operating on a Customer-focussed Approach

Deepak viewed that the operations over the last twelve years had been going smooth, and have reached a saturation point. They were neither likely to be attracting new investment opportunities nor improving margins. Growth was solely dependent on QCL plans. It was a service centre and might have to operate efficiently at this level to keep the customer satisfied. There was a limited chance that QCL India would bring additional investment and turn aggressive in this market. Deepak was convinced of the operations strategy to be focussed and performed consistently. The scope for growth and challenges was limited. At the same time, it gave the opportunity to globally integrate with the customer.

Deepak was of the view that he could discuss with Rajan about the possibility of trying downstream business of QCL India. Though delivery of orders might not be possible as QCL India has a tie-up with an international package service provider, it could give a share of its reverse logistics during warranty or parts replacement market.

However, it would be done by L-X India and not by L-X Chennai. In such a situation, customer profitability analysis will have to be seen from consolidated income and expense statement of L-X logistics in India which will aggregate L-X Chennai revenue. Deepak was keen to address this issue comprehensively!

QUESTIONS

1. Map the supply chain network of L-X Chennai and analyse the role and importance of each of the stake-holders.
2. What is IOR? How does it fit with inventory management, vendor managed inventory concepts and facilitate JIT?
3. What would be the difference between operating a shared warehouse and supporting transportation for suppliers and IOR? Why should IOR as a policy be supported by the government and a company like QCL India deploy?
4. Analyse L-X Chennai business in an operations strategy framework of operations perspective and market requirement and put forth your arguments for Deepak.
5. Discuss QCL capacity allocation between domestic and international markets. Would change in capacity allocation affect L-X Chennai operations? If so, how?

REFERENCE

1. https://definitions.uslegal.com/i/importer-of-record/ accessed on 9 July 2019

ANNEXURES

EXHIBIT 1 Demand of components for assembly of units

	In thousands		
	2016-17	2017-18	2018-19
April	128	128	128
May	115	135	115
June	200	198	185
August	90	128	120
September	95	125	110
October	200	225	225
November	180	200	195
December	165	185	190
January	150	150	135
February	100	105	85
March	90	100	92
Total	1723	1899	1778

EXHIBIT 2 Estimated Income and Expense statement

No of units produced (million units)	1.8
Approximate value of inputs served from WH (₹ in Million)	30000
Value of goods shipped (₹ in Million)	5400
Value of stock based on one-month requirement (₹ in Million)	450
Revenue at inventory held at 15% of value (₹ in Million)	67.5
Number of shipments in a day	40
Fee per load of shipment charged to QCL	1200
Transportation revenue (₹ in Million)	17.52
Revenue from value added service like IOR, kitting and order processing (₹ in Million)	23.3
Total revenue (₹ in Million)	108.32
Cost of operations:	
Fixed salary of employees (₹1 million per month)	12
Salary of managerial staff and planners (₹0.8 million per month)	9.6
General overheads including electricity (₹ in Million)	4.8
Vehicle and machinery related maintenance and charges (₹ in Million)	2.56
Total fixed expenses (₹ in Million)	28.96
Variable cost for transportation (estimated) (₹ in Million)	11.68
Average cost of temporary workforce (₹ in Million)	10.68
Total expenses (₹ in Million)	51.32
Margin from IOR and fulfilment (₹ in Million)	57

L-X Logistics India: Time-sensitive spares and uptime service of automatic teller machines

(**Disclaimer:** This case is based on common knowledge and discussions in forums about such business. The company name is not real and not relating to any company which operates in this business. The figures are illustrative and neither supported by factual records nor verified. The objective of this case is to discuss academic discussions to apply the concepts and framework for a similar business situation.)

Abstract

L-X Logistics was one of the operators of third-party service providers to ATM consumable spares and maintaining uptime by delivery at ATM location. There are service technicians from other third-party service contractors who jointly facilitate uptime of ATMs. The challenges for L-X Logistics are that of aligning spares at different cities for disturbed location of ATMs, the varying window of service time for the upkeep of ATMs across the country and reducing the number of ATMs in the country due to regulatory factors and digitalisation. The case raises questions from an operations strategist perspective on whether the company should integrate vertically for the sustainability of its existence.

Learning Objective: To understand the operations strategist perspective of a time-sensitive spares management business where uptime management is critical for the customer, especially when there is a need to align with a partner service provider in fulfilment responsibility.

Key Words: Time sensitive supply chain; Spares management; Managed service; Aligning with partner; Customer service.

Case

Deepak Sahu, Chief Financial Officer at L-X Logistics, was preparing for a strategic meeting with Rajan Saxena, CEO of the company, on (automatic teller machines) ATM spares business. He was looking at recent reports on pressure towards this business because of many environmental factors. L-X Logistics was one of the operators of third-party service providers and maintaining uptime by delivering ATM consumable spares to service technicians at ATM location.

Deepak was worried as the number of ATMs was reported to be reducing in the last one year. He felt that the situation could be a temporary phase, as he thought that India has a youth population that would increasingly go to work. Since the salaries were paid through banks, employees withdrew cash through ATMs. Such transactions were bound to increase. Hence, even if the rate of growth could be limited, the volume of transactions should have increased in absolute numbers.

Rajan's interest was more to see from overall business management. Given this perspective, one had to understand whether in short to medium term, the service margin could be maintained. Second, the future of this business was key to share fixed overheads of the company, as it served an important business of spares management for ensuring uptime of ATMs by working with partners.

L-X Logistics (Global)

The company was founded with a focus on the cargo transportation business, which subsequently grew to include extended supply chain and logistics services, such as warehousing and freight management. Over the years, L-X Logistics (Global) grew to be a global supply chain solutions provider mainly focussed on the East and South East region of the globe. It was the largest home-grown supply chain solutions company and leading regional supply chain management partner to many of the world's leading brands across Asia-Pacific region.

The company's strengths were the location of key hubs, deep-rooted understanding of local terrains, and in-depth presence. Such advantages helped in providing a wide range of specialised services, such as strengths and ability to deliver customer value through its technology, processes, and people. Such strengths empowered its customers to achieve a comprehensive footprint and seamless global connectivity across the region.

The company established regional connectivity by setting up greenfield operations in emerging markets. It expanded its scope of services in the supply chain from the design of solutions to implementation for a client. It had, thereby, expanded its scope of service and products from vendor managed inventory in the electronics and technology industry to temperature-controlled and cold storage solutions. It increased its offering to sectors like electronics, chemicals and healthcare, consumers and the retail sector and e-commerce. The company had innovated supply chain solutions which was an app for vehicle efficiency and commuter ease of movement. This demonstrated its ability in offering an innovative solution in the supply chain domain.

The company had grown across geographies using its ability to develop, design and deliver solutions and business models in the space of supply chain whether it was cargo transportation, storage and inventory management for business to business segment or transportation in people movement segment in different places.

L-X Logistics, India

L-X Logistics first entered India in 2004 providing freight, customs clearance services, and finished goods distribution across India. Over the years, the company delivered customised end-to-end supply chain solutions. It was operating one of the country's largest service parts network across more than 81 forward serving locations and satellite hubs. Working closely with its last-mile partners, L-X Logistics, India was also able to leverage on its pan-India network to achieve time-specific deliveries for its clients. L-X Logistics, India built one of the first green warehouses in India.

ATMs in India

By the end of the year 2018, the total number of ATMs in India was about 2,05,201. This included ATMs of public sector banks, private sector banks, and foreign banks. While onsite ATMs were about 52 per cent, offsite were about 48 per cent. Further, public sector branches to ATMs ratio was less than 1, whereas private-sector branches to offsite ATMs ratio was 1.5. This was due to more presence of the public sector banks in rural and remote areas.

EXHIBIT 1 Number of ATMs in India as of 28 December 2018

Banks by ownership	Branches					ATMs		
	Rural	Semi - Urban	Urban	Metro	Total	On-site	Off-site	Total
Public Sector	29,201	25,397	17,677	18,546	90,821	83,259	61,839	1,45,098
Private Sector	6,160	9,242	5,926	7,477	28,805	23,564	35,601	59,165
Foreign	9	10	36	231	286	214	724	938
Total	35,370	34,649	23,639	26,254	1,19,912	1,07,037	98,164	2,05,201

Source: https://www.rbi.org.in/scripts/PublicationsView.aspx?id=18752

It can be seen in Exhibit 2 that about 88 per cent of ATMs were outsourced and banks on their own managed about 12 per cent. In the case of managed service ATMs, banks leased the site where the ATM was located. This was also done in case of off-site ATMs. Typically, a bank bought ATMs and in total gave operating lease to the third party or even to ATM equipment supplier. The banks provided only cash for loading ATMs, while the service providers were responsible for the uptime and operation of the ATMs. They were paid a fixed fee for the services. The key condition of outsourcing was the uptime of ATMs.

EXHIBIT 2 Types of ATMs

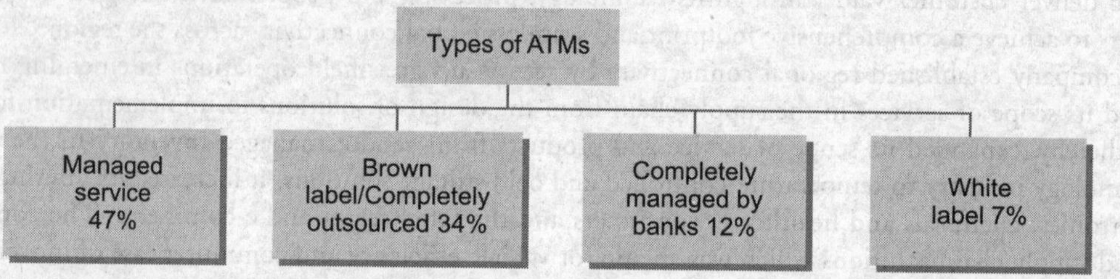

In the case of ATMs other than those managed completely by banks, types of operating contracts were focussed on uptime after a failure. ATMs managed by banks also entered into similar contracts. Deliverable was the same, but the terms of the contract varied.

Some of the operating issues of this business are captured with the help of industry analysis and given in Exhibit 3.

EXHIBIT 3 Cash withdrawal from ATMs in India using debit card

	Financial year ending				CAGR
Cash withdrawal (Debit cards)	2015	2016	2017	2018	
Number of transactions (in million)	6995.8	8072.5	8563.1	8602.3	7%
Amount in ₹million	2,22,08,651	25357945.5	23602725.6	28987611	9%
Average amount per transaction in ₹	3174.6	3141	2756	3370	2%

It can be seen from Exhibit 3 that the compound annual growth rate in using debit cards for withdrawal from ATMs was at seven per cent and the amount withdrawn in total had gone up by nine per cent. Further, the average amount per transaction had also gone up, which means that the uptime efficiency was to be higher.

However, an article in *Business Today* (May 2019) mentions that the number of ATMs had gradually shrunk in the past two years. This was not because of a decline in demand of cash but more due to tighter regulations which were making maintenance of ATM quite a costly affair. Further, it mentioned that chip cards were made mandatory by the central bank. This was as per the international standards. Improvement in hardware and software was mandated to check fraudsters as a part of the global agreement. Confederation of ATM industry (CATMi) predicted that adhering to the upgrade rules could cost the ATM industry about ₹3,000 crore.

There were certain trends predicted, which include:

The government added 355 million to the banking system, since 2014. Demonetisation of currency in 2016 to the extent of 86 per cent of notes increased the amount of opening of bank accounts, use of ATMs and digital payments and money.

It was reported that the use of mobile banking went up by 65 per cent. This would have harmed the number of ATMs that might be required. Since it was on a small base, the growth in mobile banking was high. The fact was that it would likely impact the number of ATMs and bring stress on uptime efficiency as close to 100 per cent on available ATMs.

India had a low proliferation of ATMs to the population. The ratio might have to improve. Urbanisation was expected to continue, as semi-urban towns would urbanise over time. Such a trend would increase the demand for ATM services. It was expected that the rate of increase would be influenced by urbanisation factors and population growth rate, especially the income-earning band of the demography.

One limiting factor for ATM operators was the service charge paid per transaction. It was low at ₹15 per transactions and banks were finding it increasingly difficult to pass it on to the customers. And alternatively, they rationalised through a reduction in operating costs of branches and ATMs. They were likely to be reducing the number of redundant ATMs mainly in urban India and improving branch level cost to avoid customers demanding in-person services. Such employees are relatively costly compared to per customer service cost while using ATMs. More than one ATM can be found in many metropolitan branches (onsite ATMs), mainly to improve customer service level and cost of operations.

ATM is typically made up of the following devices or components:

- CPU which controls the user interface and transaction devices
- Swipe card reader
- Display screen
- Speaker
- Receipt printer
- Tactile keyboard integrated braille
- Cash dispenser

Earlier, ATMs have used custom hardware architectures using microcontrollers or application-specific integrated circuits. They adopted the hardware architecture of a personal computer, such as USB connections for peripherals, Ethernet and IP communications, and use personal computer operating systems.

Types of consumables shown in Exhibit 4 are those which were to be replaced or serviced while ensuring ATMs were operational. Some of these were mechanical, electronics or mechatronics and sensor-based.

Though the list had about 16 components, depending upon ATM manufacturer and design, SKUs ran into hundreds of numbers. Further, failure rate followed Poisson distribution and was linked to factors like frequency of use, power fluctuations and few other factors like handling by customers, dust, the menace of rodents and so on.

EXHIBIT 4 List of consumables for an ATM

Belts	Pick lines	LCD	Card reader heads
Gears	Power supply unit	Rollers	RAM
Air filters	Vacuum cups	Vacuum pumps	EOP glass
Spacers	Anti-vandal glass	FDK (Custom)	Shutters

Then, major players in India's ATM Managed Services Market included NCR Corporation, Diebold Nixdorf, AGS Transact Technologies, Brinks, CMS Info System, Euronet, FIS, FSS, Hitachi Payments, SIS India, SIS Prosegur and Writer Corporation Ltd. These were hardware suppliers like ATM itself, software vendors and cash loading service providers.

L-X Logistics Role

Under managed service, these vendors, especially for hardware maintenance, tie-up with third-party service providers like L-X Logistics. They were responsible for stocking based on failure estimates and the type of consumables that might be required. Thus, it invested in inventory of spares and maintained them in such a way that there was no stockout or overstock. Stockout would have led to a penalty of service failure, and excess stock to an increase in holding costs and component aging costs. Hence, the first key competency required was that of spare estimation and efficient stock maintenance in a distribution centre.

Second, when a failure occurred, the bank got an automatic message with a failure error. Bank server mapped the error messages with those who were to address the issue. All messages related to components failure were sent to ATM's vendor and managed service provider. Managed service provider (MSP) would instantaneously sent auto messages to the respective service providers. For a service call, the managed service provider had a third party logistics service provider (LSP) carrying the component reaching the ATM location. LSP was not authorised service and Technical service provider (TSP). TSPs had engineers and technicians on their employment who were trained in maintaining ATMs by way of overhauling and component replacements. LSP coordinated with TSP and both needed to be available together at any site for fulfiling the service call. MSP entered into separate contracts with LSP and TSP for the fulfilment of uptime requirements. The uptime was primary responsibility of the LSP who was expected to coordinate with the TSP.

MSP had a high penalty on non-adherence to committed time for retrieval and ensuring that the ATM was back in service after a reported failure. This was typically 4 to 6 hours in metropolitans; 12 hours in urban areas, 18 hours in semi-urban areas and 36 hours in rural areas.

L-X Logistics Operations in Spares Support for ATMs

The company had two large distribution centres (DCs) — one at Noida in NCR and the other in Bengaluru. These two centres could also do refurbishment of parts for those companies which were responsible for it. In such a case, MSPs authorised L-X Logistics to do the same for it. After refurbishment, the part was taken into spares stock so that it could be used later. There were times when a part could not be completely recovered and had to be scrapped and was replaced by a new one. There were timelines for the reverse flow of repaired parts. Typically, it reached DC in a day if it was urban and semi-urban location; and in the case of rural areas, it took one and a half days. Spare stock-flow to forward stocking and satellite locations followed similar timelines.

To fulfil its commitment to uptime, at places like Mumbai and few others, LSP had a moving van with stock. It could not serve from DC or forward fulfilment centres which were localised DCs, as the intracity movement could not ensure service level at the tight timeline. There were about 56 warehouses of forwarding spare parts across India for supporting this business.

Spare parts movement which was billed annually averages to ₹600 million. The company had an inventory turnover of 2.33. The total value of stock was ₹257.5 million. The cost of holding including the funding of spare parts by value and DCs was about 20 per cent on average inventory held. The company on top of each transaction incurred an expense, including overheads. The typical income and expense statement of this business is as shown in Exhibit 5.

EXHIBIT 5 Income and Expense Statement of Spare Parts Business (Estimated)

Description	₹ (in millions)
No. of ATMs serviced	30000
Average ATM parts value per annum	20000
Overall billing of value of parts (in Mn)	600
Average inventory (in Mn)	257.51
Inventory turnover ratio	2.33
Cost of holding	20%

Cost of inventory holding (in Mn)	51.50
Overheads expenses field service person (in Mn)	67.20
Managerial salary (in Mn)	10
Other overheads (in Mn)	20
Servicemen movement cost (in Mn)	90
Total cost (in Mn)	238.70
Per ATM cost of spares and uptime in ₹	7,956.74
Mark up per ATM in ₹	2,043.26
Total mark up in 30000 ATMs (in Mn)	61.30
Total revenue (in Mn)	300

According to the opinion of an expert industry analyst on Exhibit 5, "It is understood that a 20 per cent drop in the number of ATMs served will lead to drop in mark up by 52 percent at the current operating level." The company's management team felt that inventory of parts is scientifically arrived at by following the Poisson Distribution and many inventory, staff cost, and overheads of field staff expenses could proportionately be reduced. Mark up would have come down from 25 percent to 18 percent. The analyst was of the view that, "Such a reduction is not possible because though ATMs may reduce service level, demand is more determined by the number of transactions which is increasing marginally. Further, this business needs a revised operating strategy."

Deepak wanted to review this business from a strategic perspective from both operations and as a strategic business unit.

QUESTIONS

1. With increased use of digital transactions, mobile transactions and payment banks through mobile, can ATMs be in service in the long term? Will customer's dependence on ATMs reduce drastically forcing LSP to relook at its service offering? Is there a scope of merging TSP and LSP together and aggregate margins so that some of the overheads can be saved? For example, is it possible to upskill technicians to carry and manage inventory or LSP employees be technically trained?
2. What are the supply chain alliance/partner relationships that can be thought of to overcome changing industry conditions?
3. Map the operating parameters and market requirements like cost, quality, speed, dependability, and flexibility and relate your recommendations.

REFERENCES

https://www.rbi.org.in/scripts/PublicationsView.aspx?id=18752 Accessed on 12 July 2019

http://www.marketsguruji.com/report-on-atm-industry-in-india/ Accessed on 12 July 2019

https://www.businesstoday.in/current/economy-politics/atms-number-india-reducing-transactions-continue-grow/story/346843.html Accessed on 12 July 2019

Aligning Supply Chain of Sweet Corn Processor for Growth

(**Disclaimer:** The case is prepared for academic discussions with the support of the company and financial inputs here are for academic discussions and not exactly reflective of the business. The author and the company would not be responsible for any liability towards commercial decision based on the material shared.)

Abstract

Sweet corn is a niche product and its supply chain is complicated by the need to collaborate with farmers and then involve in farming. Further product has complexity in terms of its challenges in maintaining quality due to natural limitations of ability to gather heat and deteriorate in a short period. On forward linkages, there are requirements to strengthen the market segments. Each of the segments is unique. Rajesh Kumar, promoter of the company is ambitious to grow into a large pan India market with brand recall. Establishing a supply network requires addressing issues of centralisation and decentralisation of the location of farms and processing units. Further, it also requires evaluating outbound transportation and localisation of farming and processing with strategic orientation of achieving growth aspiration by the promoter.

Learning Objective: To understand about niche agribusiness supply chain and application of strategic thinking towards managing growth, especially in an uncommon product category in India.

Key Words: Agribusiness; Supply chain; Strategy; Supplier development; Agro-based product processing; Distribution network; Corporate growth.

Aligning supply chain of sweet corn processor for growth

Introduction

Looking at the changing food habits and evolution of standardised retail formats in urban areas, Rajesh Kumar, in October 2014, drew a strategic plan to increase his turnover (projected based on the first six months' performance) from ₹33.5 crore in the current financial year to ₹100 crore in 5 years. He understands that it is a highly ambitious growth which requires strong brand recall and establishing a synchronised supply chain from farm to customer. He has called in one of the top four management consultants to advise him on establishing a supply chain network for achieving this task. He has to prepare a background note to be shared with the consultant.

Sweet corn is commonly consumed as a vegetable, either fresh or processed. Though sweet corn is popular in the United States of America, Europe, and other developed countries as a commonly used food item, it is gaining acceptance in terms of consumption in India, especially among the urban population. With fast foods like pizza, ready to eat foods and Indian traditional recipes, it is growing at a galloping rate because of increasing westernised lifestyle. There are many first-generation and smaller medium size entrepreneurs in processed food segment business who are looking for seizing opportunities to establish high growth firms with good brand identity. Someone with a decent awareness of sweet corn cultivation can enter into this business. He then needs to organise the cultivation of sweet corn, set up a processing unit and further establish a downstream to reach institutional customers.

Rajesh Kumar, who is a management graduate, hails from a family running successfully retail stores over generations in Salem, Tamil Nadu. After a visit abroad to understand processed food business as a business delegate through an industry association, he figured out opportunities for entering into the sweet corn business. It took nearly two years for him to evaluate the working of the technology and identify a suitable vendor for process equipment. During this period, he also spoke to several farmers around the Salem district who have wetlands to produce sweet corn. He also engaged in conversations with marketing experts and set up distribution channels for his products.

Outline on Sweet Corn

Sweet corn belongs to the fam ily of Maize, with a variation of high level of sugar content. Maize is commonly consumed by people in the lower economic strata as it gives high energy at a fairly low price. The crop is also grown across different regions in India and by and large consumed in the local terrain. However, sweet corn is considered to be more as a product for urban youth who can consume fresh cob or processed corn. The high level of sweetness and moisture in sweet corn results in lower storability. The normal duration of storage is within 3 days from the day of harvest. Corn in India is grown in small inland pockets throughout the country. Sweet corn and baby corn are grown in the state of Gujarat, Maharashtra, Karnataka and Tamil Nadu throughout the year.

Sweet corn requires little preparation of the land. As mentioned earlier, wetlands with good irrigation facilities are ideal. Normally, three cropping seasons in a year is possible in a plot. Typically, a farmer would go for a cycle of production of 2 years and rotate with alternative crops for 1 year with short term crops. Normally, the number of days till maturity for harvesting ranges from 65-95 days depending on variety. However, sweet corn which is marketed at the high end as done by the company Green Land Farms owned by Rajesh Kumar requires 90 days for harvesting.

Farm-level Perspectives at Green Land Farms

Green Land Farms currently commands over 1000 acres of land around an 80 km radius from the Salem processing unit. Ideally, it is important to have contiguous tracks of land registered in the command area by the company for promoting cultivation. The company first registers a list of farmers who are willing to grow sweet corn. It then draws up an annual plan for plantation based on its business plan. Green Land Farms then details plot-wise registration based on farmer's current crop cycle. The field workers organise the preparation of the plot for plantation of seeds. The company organises high quality certified seeds for distribution to farmers. Under their supervision, the seeds are planted. The field workers continuously monitor the growth of the plant and provide all extension services and supply of growth nutrients like fertilizers, micronutrients, and pesticides to ensure high yield and healthy growth of the crop. On an average, an acre plot yields about 5 tonnes, and farmers realise about ₹50,000 – ₹60,000 per acre (refer Annexure 1). Green Land Farms must ensure this kind of return to farmers for continued patronage by the farmers to grow in this business.

Rajesh understands the challenge to get the product from "plot to processing unit" as rapidly as possible. Once it is picked, sucrose in sweet corn cob immediately begins to turn into starch. As it happens, sweet corn will start losing its flavour. Hence, from the field, it needs to be moved to sheds where it should be immediately sorted, packed and cooled. Sweet corn should not be handled in bulk unless it is copiously iced. The maximum time that can be allowed in a heap is about two hours within which Green Land Farms tries to get the product to the processing centre. Otherwise, the produce would gather heat throughout the pile and natural conversion into starch could happen. It may be noted here that fresh sweet corn with a cob without processing cannot be in marketable condition even if it is kept in cold storage at 32 degrees F for more than 5 days.

At the farm level, Green Land Farms identifies and registers lands for cultivation, arranges seeds, facilitates sowing, ensures crop growth and then harvests and moves to process unit. This involves supply chain challenges of supplier development, input management, operation management at the field level, harvest and transporting (inbound) to the processing centre.

Inbound movement is by trucks and ideally of four-tonne vehicle. This is better for two reasons—one, as it is harvested, one lot of four tonnes can be brought to the processing centre. Second, it improves the quality of the final products. The disadvantage would be that when in a nine-tonne truck, inbound transport cost is ₹3600 per trip, inbound transportation by four-tonne is about ₹2400 per trip. Currently, 60 percent is by four-tonne vehicles and balance by nine-tonne vehicles. Rajesh Kumar feels that though this is higher unit cost-wise, but realisation is better as well as desired quality. Hence, reduced losses on produce and market realisation pay for the same. However, it increases the challenge of operation.

Processing

Fresh sweet corn cobs from the fields are marketed in the following product varieties:

- **Fresh Sweet Corn** Either as corn cob or kernels
- **Frozen Fresh Corn** Either as corn cob or kernels
- **Ready to Eat** Kernels are processed to extend shelf life of 1 year without refrigeration
- **Vending Kiosks** These kiosks serve corn in cups and steamed corn cobs – frills-free and flavoured and also takeaway corn kernel packs.
- **Canned Corn**

For the first product, sweet corn produce is peeled, washed and graded and then airtight vacuum packing is enabled even for marketing in a short period of 5 – 7 days. Packing cost for product marketed per tonne equivalent in packs of 300 grams is ₹4500.

The next variant of the product is the same fresh sweet corn which is frozen. However, as mentioned earlier, frozen sweet corn also has lesser life compared to processed sweet corn products. It is mainly done for the export market. Green Land Farms exports a substantial quantity to the Middle East and Far East countries. Today, the export volume is about 10 per cent of business. It has a huge potential and the company targets to achieve 20 per cent of export in total business in five years. Typically, cold storage and supply chain-related expenses would be ₹7,500 per tonne.

Cooling is usually done by:

- Hydrocooling – consists of precooling by either showering the corn or immersing it in cold water. It is the most popular method of precooling.
- Vacuum cooling
- Package icing
- Cold storage
- Cooling in transit is done by blowing finely crushed ice over the top and through the corn crates, as the trucks are loaded. This method of icing keeps temperatures low during transit but provides little or no additional cooling.

Green Land Farms does vacuum cooling and adheres to further process to be on cold chain till the product reaches retail point or institutional customers who buy it in bulk packs of a kg and above.

Ready to eat Corns: The company brands ready to eat corn as "Farm Harvest" which are ready to eat sweet corn packs. The raw materials used are sweet corn cobs, water, salt, and sugar. The shelf-life of the products is 12 months. Technology used is retort technology.

The objective of processing is to increase the shelf life of sweet corns from few days to 12 months using retort technology.

Preparation: Freshly harvested sweet corns are graded manually in the factory. Generally, grading happens depending upon defined parameters, such as size, maturity, etc. Once graded, the sweet corns are forwarded to the next stage called "Husk-removing". The "husks" or leaves" are removed by slitting the surface using knives. Then these sweet corns are made into halves using semi-automatic cutting machines and the kernels are manually removed from the cob so that they are used as a whole.

Packing: The sweet corn kernels are filled into retort-grade pouches. Simultaneously, brine solution is added to the kernels through automatic liquid fillers. These retort-grade pouches are imported from China, as it is made up of multilayers. This multi-layer structure prevents the retort pouch from being recycled into other retort pouches or food packaging. Then these pouches are sealed using band sealers, vacuum sealers, and rotary sealers depending upon the SKUs.

Processing: The sealed pouches are sent into "steam retorts" for processing. Retort processing is a process of eliminating all forms of transmissible agents in the retort pouches so that its shelf life has been increased. The retort processing is carried out as a combined process of multiple machinery, such as boiler for producing steam, reverse osmosis plant and a softener plant for supplying soft water, and compressor for producing uniform air circulation.

TABLE I Ready to eat sweet corn products marketed by Green Land Farms

	Retail pack Corn Kernal	Institutional pack Corn Kernel	Sweet Corn Cob	Cup O Corn
Qty (Gross)	300 gm	1.35 kg	1 No	110 gm
Qty (Nett.Drain)	225 gm	1 kg	1 No	85 gm
Shelf Life	12 Months	12 Months	6 Months	6 Months
Refrigeration	Not Required	Not Required	Not Required	Not Required
Microwave Heating	Yes	Yes	Yes	Yes
Pan Heating	Yes	Yes	Yes	Yes
Flavours	Natural	Natural	Natural	Natural
Additional Seasonings	No	No	No	Spice Butter add on available
Accessories	No	No	Sticks to hold the corn cob	Spoon, Paper Napkin & Seasonings Sachet

Marketing and Distribution

Currently, the company's domestic sales (90 per cent of total sales) are 80 per cent ready to eat sweet corn and 20 per cent green cobs. In terms of geography wise sales, 70 per cent from Tamil Nadu and 30 per cent from Kerala. The company sells around a radius of 500 km from Salem. It has 400 kiosks in Tamil Nadu. This contributes to 60 per cent of retail sales in Tamil Nadu. Kiosks give a margin of 20 per cent higher than that through retail outlets. In terms of segment, about 95 per cent of sales are through retail and 5 per cent is institutional sales. The latter has the potential to go up to 15 per cent in five years at the targeted sales. The company sells 20 per cent of domestic sales as green cobs which will come down to 10 per cent on the five years sales target. Within ready to eat segment, corn o cups are 20 per cent, 15 per cent are cobs and balance is corn kernels.

Since Green Land Farms does not have intermediaries, currently they sell direct by loading kiosks and delivering to retail points. The outbound transportation cost on an average is ₹6 per tonne per km and including handling, it is about ₹7.50 per tonne per km. Typically, the retail price of sweet corn cob of ready to eat segment is ₹80 per kg, kernels are ₹100 per kg and cup o corn is ₹150 per kg. The company enjoys a margin of 20 per cent overall costs but before taxes. The company incurs channel cost at 25 per cent of realisation. Apart from these, the company incurs overhead expenses to the tune of ₹14,500 per tonne. This includes expenses of managers, corporate office and that of marketing including promotions. Once the company scales up in five years, overheads may come down to ₹9,000 per tonne. The company has a working capital facility for ₹1 crore at the cost of 15 per cent and long-term capital on 1:1 at 12 per cent. The company sells all export volume at ₹120 per kg to an agent and there is no difference in cost between domestic and export sales.

Plan

Green Land Farms wants to go on the pan India market with a focus on Delhi and other northern parts, Karnataka, Telangana, Andhra Pradesh, and Western India, especially Maharashtra and Gujarat. The company would focus on the Middle East and Far East for exports.

The company is evaluating the following options:

1. One of the options is through centralised processing in Salem and reaching out to other markets in India. New markets require setting up stockists and distribute from stock points. This will change the supply chain network. Stockists could ideally cover a 500 km radius. The current level of cost in the existing set up would be the basis for scaling up. But the cost of filling stock points and service charges to stockists must be added. Typically, the stockiest charge including storing and handling would be at a fixed cost of ₹1,00,000/- per month and variable cost of ₹1000/- per tonne. Considering the current infrastructure and scope for expansion in the existing facility, for achieving the target turnover in five years, the company may have to invest another ₹18 crore.
2. Another option is through decentralised processing by creating plants as nodes. This would require establishing local sweet corn cultivation and processing unit at each node to achieve service level at 500 radius. The operating costs would be at the service level to these markets under the current cost of operation. Typical process facility at the current level which can handle up to ₹10 crores of sales is ₹3 crores. This option would require an additional investment of ₹27 crores.
3. Decentralised processing and distribution through outsourced partners enjoying brand value. This would reduce the capital investment, but the outsourced partner would charge ₹7500 per tonne.
4. All the options would require promotional expenses through digital marketing media to the tune of ₹2 crore per annum.

Evaluation of Alternatives

Rajesh Kumar wants to understand the four perspectives, namely role, responsibility, reward, and risk of supply chain network partners. He wants to design a suitable supply chain strategy with the vision of Pan India presence achieving ₹100 crore in five years. He wants to understand the key parameters and develop a balanced scorecard for implementing performance measurement for the chosen supply chain strategy.

QUESTIONS

1. Map the supply chain network of sweet corn processor, Green Land Farms.
2. Using financial data given in the case, facilitate strategic thinking towards managing growth of the firm to achieve the vision of ₹100 crore.

3. How would you design a suitable supply chain strategy with the vision of Pan-India reach?
4. Develop a balance scorecard for implementing performance measurement for the chosen supply chain strategy. What are the key parameters for each of the perspectives and justify the same.

REFERENCES

1. http://articles.economictimes.indiatimes.com/2012-04-20/news/31373994_1_sweet-corn-wheat-cultivation-quality-seeds. Accessed on 10 December 2014.
2. http://farmharvest.in/

Notes

(1) Author would like to thank Mr. Rajesh Kumar for the opportunity and insights into Sweet Corn processing and marketing business.

(2) Authors of this case are Dr. N. Chandrasekaran and Dr. Ramasubramaniam M., Associate Professor, Loyola Institute of Business Administration, Chennai. The case was earlier published in the www.thecasecentre.org and reference number is: 615-047-1).

Annexure I: Sweet Corn Production at Sonipat

Farmers in Sonipat are shifting to sweet corn farming. Low-income levels and high investment in paddy farming are forcing farmers to cultivate sweet corn rather than paddy. Around 350 such farmers are generating about ₹3.5 crore per annum from about 1,000 acres in the region as of March 2014. This is achieved in 10 years. Sweet corn farming started quite late in Sonipat but in just one decade, the farmers have established their processing units so that they are not exploited by the mandi (market) players or other buyers.

According to one farmer, "I cultivate sweet corns on the land where my ancestors used to cultivate paddy. But, because of the lowering water table in the region, paddy becomes a loss-making crop where my input had almost matched my income. Today, one requires around ₹8,000 per acre as investment for sweet corn farming that gives you returns in the range of ₹20,000 to ₹80,000 per acre depending on the mandi price".

According to a report, the Yamuna bed of Sonipat is the most suitable land for sweet corn cultivation and one can harvest the crop thrice in a year. Some recommend that farmers should take two crops of sweet corn and one crop of wheat in between cycles.

Initially, it was difficult to get the quality seeds for sweet corn because there were few suppliers. But, in the past few years, these seeds have become readily available in the market like any other traditional crop. There are high yielding seeds available in the market that grow around 50 to 60 quintals of sweet corn from one acre of land.

At Sonipat, farmers have Azadpur Mandi, Reliance Fresh, and Mother Dairy as the major buyers of sweet corn. Normally, a farmer gets from ₹6 to ₹18 per kg of sweet corn depending upon the mandi price. However, to safeguard the interests of the farmers, the association of sweet corn farmers have set the lowest selling price at ₹6 per kg. This was done after consultations with the mandi representatives.

Source: http://articles.economictimes.indiatimes.com/2012-04-20/news/31373994_1_sweet-corn-wheat-cultivation-quality-seeds

Sapthagiri Street Food Vending: Positioning and entrepreneurial clarity

(**Disclaimer:** This case is based on common knowledge and discussions about this company. The figures are illustrative and neither supported by factual records nor verified. The objective of this case is to discuss academic discussions to apply the concepts and framework.)

Abstract

Sapthagiri Street Food vending is into retail roadside food eatery in a populous locality in the central business district of Chennai in the place called T. Nagar. They started off their business about forty years back selling snacks during the evening time. This was mainly for students who were coming to coaching classes and those who came for shopping in the adjoining area. The customers were happy; the incidental growth of tutorial business and the business at the central business district increased the footprints and nature of demand for food at all-time windows. This led Sapthagiri Vendors to sell food from a cart at the popular junction.

They started the business for livelihood and employees were all a part of the business. They were more like partners and associates rather than salaried employees. They retained their unique positioning and lived daily by doing business forecasting and with limited growth. They had split locations where the kitchen was in the neighborhood and most of the food items were served from there. Over the years, they ran into crisis because of the challenge of continuing at the location. They moved after two years of search for a new location. Extreme weather conditions and disruptions affect the business. On 30 November 2016, when "Varda" storm was predicted to cross over Chennai, promoters of Sapthagiri Street Food Vending were compelled to revisit their model!

Learning Objective: To understand the importance of livelihood business operations, supply network and ensure its business success despite low capital and customer loyalty.

Key Words: Supply chain network; Service operations and delivery; Strategic options; Livelihood entrepreneurship; Strategic options in small businesses.

Case

Sapthagiri Street Food Vending: positioning and entrepreneurial clarity

Introduction

Prakash and Balraj were on their routine review meeting along with Baby on 30 November 2016. They had now understood that the weather report was almost precise – "Varda cyclone was to cross over Chennai on 1 December 2016." They were serving about 1500 – 2000 plates of food every day at the cart. There were customers coming from 30 kilometers away in their best of the cars to eat "dosa" at the "Sapthagiri" cart! Everyone might have been informed about the then-impending cyclone. Probably, they would have had a huge drop on 30 November night sale and could not have any sales for a couple of days afterwards. What could they have done with the batter that was prepared? How would they manage loss of revenue till the city gained normalcy? Already during the rainy season, they had lost a few days and had huge drop in sales. Prakash raises the question, "Are we doing the right things towards our business model during the last forty years? Are we used to this volatility in our business and be happy serving at 30 – 35 percent of price to our customers who value us for our quality and not just price alone? Is that what we want, or could we not avoid this? May be we can built our business on a regular model of brick and mortar and brand-driven physical service center? Why others found it difficult to replicate our current model? Could we have used the opportunity when an investor wanted to recreate this model in an umbrella brand across the city, say, in 100 different centers?" Balraj and Baby replied, "Prakash, we are happy the way we are! You have not asked this as an owner of this setup. Every one of us is enjoying what we are doing because it is the way it is. Forty years of experience have helped us to sway through the tides of volatility comfortably. This would also pass! Enjoy your tea!"

Genesis

Balraj came to Chennai in 1969 searching for a livelihood. He stayed at then busy part of Chennai, T. Nagar and became close to Prakash. This was the time when IIT and IIM education became popular. Also, tutorials for different examinations were conducted at a popular centre named "Brilliant Tutorials". This was located at Masillamani Street, T. Nagar. This was close to the shopping hub of Pondy bazaar. Even today T. Nagar continues to be the shopping hub. Further, there were a few theatres, which exhibited movies featuring popular actors within a kilometer radius. Looking at these, three men, namely Balraj, Prakash and Baby who were in the early twenties started selling snacks for those students and the rest of the potential customers. They were selling quick snacks that were of good quality and priced reasonably. Even if someone had only a rupee, he could have had a snack with his friend and went back to his classes at Brilliant Tutorials. Parents also liked the idea and encouraged these children to focus on class with quick bites at Sapthagiri Cart vending at Masillamani Street.

Years of Growth and Success

In a matter of few years, they stabilised demand. They were able to adequately estimate demand for every stock keeping unit (SKU) and started making profits. Customers' loyalty and "word of mouth" marketing became significant factors contributing to their growth. Further, their growth got coupled with the growth of Brilliant Tutorials and the latter started experiencing exponential growth driven in turn by ambitious students. Classes ran round the clock.

This made Prakash and team to start full-fledged service at the cart. They started off with a breakfast between 7 am and 10 am. Then, they started off afternoon lunch, which would be a choice of variety like rice and chapatis and so on. They closed by 3.30 pm. The evening service started at 5 pm going on late into midnight. On an average, about 1500 to 2000 people dined there every day. But these numbers needed to be analysed and seen in the context of operating focus and challenges.

Location

The choice of location to place the cart for vending food was a masterstroke of this team. The captive customer prospects at Brilliant Tutorial, shoppers at T. Nagar and small establishments and bachelors living around the area were one set of customer groups at the road adjoining Brilliant Tutorials. This was not all! The road was the widest at this junction. Any number of cars could be parked along the three sides of the road where this vending cart was placed. Yes! this cart attracted the best of customers in swanky cars driving in, especially during late evenings, to their joint to have dinner. It is common to hear tales of guys, who had studied at Brilliant's and had food at Sapthagiri visiting on weekends and on their sojourn to Chennai either from any other city in India or from abroad. This became a meeting point during their visits and was on their "To do list". This was the brand loyalty. Balraj mentions, "Even today some customers from High Income Group travel 30 km to have podi dosa (a delicacy in this place)! They are our ambassadors"!

This speaks volumes about their acumen in choice of this location.

Location Advantage Lost!

There were several developments happening over the years. First, the coaching industry became competitive. Several players started to emerge at multiple locations and even through cyberspace. Better-ranked institutes started attracting students. However, this development did not affect Prakash and his team business. This was because of the simple fact that the coaching center was one that triggered the business but sustainability and growth depended on performance and appeal! Footprints and sticky customer base took care of growth. Second, T. Nagar shopping intensity increased when more large retail formats in clothing, jewelry and so on started appearing. This increased the catchment potential for the Sapthagiri business. This also attracted a large number of food retailers like Saravana Bhavan and many others who invested in this area. However, it did not take away the business of Sapthagiri.

In fact, their business and popularity was growing. More cars and vehicles started coming in there. It was generally believed that street vending led to traffic congestion. There is a study that contradicts this, as quoted in one of the papers of "Transparent Chennai" by IFMR Trust. However, there were a few rumblings on Sapthagiri's ability to attract vehicles and possible congestion.

Balraj and the team ensured that the vehicles do not obstruct traffic. They helped them by guiding to appropriate parking zones. They took orders and served to the passengers in their cars. They made every effort to balance the traffic flows and avoided congestion by guiding on a voluntary basis. The local authorities, at times, commended about their phenomenal commitment to local people and ensured that business was normal and was not adversely impacting local movements.

From 2007 to 2012, there were several national and state level regulations on street vending and this included the need for licenses. One set of arguments would be to support street vending as it provides livelihood to a segment of society who are entrepreneurial and make the best use of available resources. The contrarian view had been that they have been congesting the places and crowding away pedestrians' space and, possibly bringing unhealthy practice and socially irrelevant practices. However, the government had by then set up several directions and guidelines for the operation of street vendors, including the food quality. In fact, food vending came under severe surveillance for quality of eatery, for good health of consumers, sanitation and traffic congestion in terms of an overall impact on the surrounding.

It may be interesting to note that Prakash and the team lost advantage during this period. It was not because of any regulatory moves but due to an organisational crisis. The first time in nearly four decades of operation, they got into a crisis. The culture of the unit was more morally carrying ownership of business together in one or any part of the business. There was a core management team with Prakash, Balraj and Baby and a couple of others. Everyone believed that they were a part of the business. When the external crisis came in, some of the employees ripped apart the business and led to inherent failure to hold together by the core team. In this tussle, Prakash and the team lost the location where they were for nearly thirty-eight years!

Local administration soon notified the area as a "no vending" zone as well and street vendors around were removed.

Dissipation of the Crisis!

Prakash, Balraj and Baby team went through this crisis for two years. The customers were reportedly saddened. There were reports in local newspapers and a television channel about their conspicuous absence in the busy area of T. Nagar shopping hub. Thus, on one end of the spectrum in the supply chain network, namely ultimate customers were longing for Sapthagiri fast food on the cart. But the focal firm, namely Sapthagiri could not find a cart space. There are certain things that one must note here on the business limitations. These normal limitations or characteristics of this business include cash management, revenue drain, cannibalisation, volatile nature of business and seasonality, which are discussed in later section of this case.

Somewhere around 2009, Prakash, Balraj and Baby found a place near Natesan Park off Venkat Narayana Road, a place where they resume their sale in their cart as a street vendor. It brought back cheer to the residents and commuters at T. Nagar. They went back quickly to 1500 – 2000 serving all three times a day. It took them two years to restart the raised level of flexibility and durability of the business and its model! It raises the question, Were they right in running the business the way they were doing for so long? Could they have not pursued a different model for stability? What are the key success factors in this business? Is there somewhere in the supply chain network wherein all the role agents were thrilled by challenges it offered as being small, roadside and livelihood driven rather than panning out into a robust business model of different scale or distributed through a common shared brand across the city? For that matter, was a brick and mortar food outlet a possibility?

Intricacies of the Street Vending Retail Food Business

1. Ownership: It is a low capital business wherein a person owns the cart, a number of plates, cooking stove with gas connections, grinders, mixtures, a rented place to prepare batter and food, crockery and mobile power service. Importantly, it needs to have a protective canvas over the cart, especially during winter. Hence the amount of capital required to start the business is low if not paltry! But nobody lends this money, as the assets cannot be securitised.
2. Investment: Investment in true sense is on people. The business requires every one of the employees to be truly carrying the shared vision of serving quality food at a reasonable price. The customers are conceivably taking a risk by eating at a roadside cart. They are also from different strata like children of middle to high-income groups; people who come by two wheelers and cars to eat and common man. Since there is no common denominator on their economic and social status, one will have to ensure that the food served meets the highest standard. Balraj mentions, "Even if there is a slightest complaint about quality, the batch which is running would be thrown away and replenished from kitchen with a new batch"! To avoid losses due to such wastages, employees must be ever vigilant and consciously aware of ensuring that no spoilage or foreign particles come in the vessels where food is stored at the cart.

   Second, it is somewhat of a distributed leadership model because service runs nearly for 18 hours in a day. There is a need for change in guard. Further, night service requires two persons from Prakash's team at the cart cash counter for collecting payments. This is true throughout the day and night in the weekends. Given the hands-on nature of the business, unless all employees take ownership, the business would fail.

   Imagine a roadside eatery where there are no order books, no billing system and no oversight of staff! It is estimated that there is a likelihood that 10 percent of the revenue is lost by customers under-reporting their consumption, especially at peak serving time. It is next to impossible to track orders and consumption, especially of group orders. Trust is what holds the business together. Hence employees must ensure that there are no leakages in revenue.

   Further, any kind of roadside eatery would have people coming to eat there during late evening after a few rounds of liquor, especially from TASMAC (government liquor outlets). These people may be inebriated and impatient. Sapthagiri eatery attracts families wherein men with their family eat alongside all other customer groups. Balraj and the team ensure that the setting is not disturbed by the misbehavior of a few! They handle this with patience by taking them away a few steps and serving them so that they are convinced that they are being attended to. Balraj mentions, "It is important that we show our understanding of their state of mind and ensure peace for all present around the place! Every member of my team is trained to handle this".

   Another important investment for the team is respect among the local community. They keep the place clean and ensure food is not littered around. They use turmeric and other material to ensure that there are no insects, rodents and foul smells in and around the place. Further, all wastes are disposed of carefully. Sewage is handled carefully and let into common sewage to maintain hygiene of the place. As mentioned earlier, they ensure that traffic moves smoothly by regulating the same as and when required.

These are the key investments that the owner has to make which Prakash has done in abundance. Once beaten twice shy! Yet Prakash, Balraj and Baby along with Santosh, Badrinath, Vijay, and Bhaskar run as a team wherein each other's fortune is recreated every day and lived through. Balraj mentions, "I am standing the way I started in 1969 to date. No change! But I am happy that my livelihood is taken care of. My family has also accepted this. Likewise, families of each one of us accept this. We cherish this togetherness. The ability to hold together like this is fundamental to our existence".

3. Profit margins: The price of the serving is conservative. For the quality, the price can be benchmarked to about 30 – 40 percent of what is sold is in a decent restaurant. The question is that if all of them earn a similar kind of margin, does the balancing percentage reflects the overheads of a standard restaurant? Does Sapthagiri follow a kind of "limit pricing" concept of economists where a firm makes it uncompetitive for others to engage in competitive warfare?

   Other issues in margins include inability to transfer the cost of inputs and material to the customers as they expect stickiness of price. Prakash and team never compromise on the quality of inputs as output is directly related to the input that goes in preparation. Second, markup for risk of revenue leakage by under-reporting of consumption is not possible as customers are sensitive and can easily relate through conversations. Third, provision for risk coverage by way of natural calamities and vagaries of nature is impossible. In fact, it may be interesting to note that there is no rate card or display of rates. But everyone who eats there is familiar, and trust runs high in this business. Any increase in price needs to be seeded among customers before it is being implemented.
4. Working capital and cash management: Prakash and team buy inputs on cash and daily basis. They neither have any bank facility nor storage system to carry on the stock based on demand estimate. They have a simple principle of buying for cash on a daily basis so that they get the best price. They also do day end profit statement intuitively and carry on business with customer orientation. Balraj mentions, "If I were to buy provisions for ₹12,000 to ₹15,000 on a credit basis, it is natural that I do not get to buy inputs at fair price. Further, it gives us flexibility, as this is livelihood business wherein I run it like a vegetable hawker who stocks early morning and completes sale by the end of the day. He counts the margin at the end of the day's sale. This works better for us. Also, this enforces a discipline among all of us that we do not give any credit sale and are disciplined in cash counter without any fund diversion."
5. Demand estimation and refill: Balraj mentions, "We do a day-to-day demand estimate based on a number of factors like weather condition, seasonality in shopping at T. Nagar, day of the week, festive times and so on. We have a standard demand of, say, 250 servings as base for every mealtime and top it up from our kitchen that is close by. This is critical from different standpoints, namely cost savings, reduction of wastage of cooked food and freshness of stock at the sale counter. On average, we have a seasonality of four months of low demand spread over two times in a year. Second, we have weekday versus weekend variations". Though the business is suited for chase strategy in terms of workforce, they have a fixed number of workforce, as they are keen to provide livelihood for associates!
6. Disruptions: Apart from the business risk, street vending faces loss of revenue days of four to six days in a year because of severe disruptions due to rain and flooding, socio-political factors like strikes by hawkers, parties and so on. Balraj mentions, "We have the agility to recover quickly from disruptions as our kitchen is close by. Normal rains do not affect us. If there are heavy rains, we try to see how well we could serve to minimal customers who show up. Generally, customers also do not show up many times before normalcy arrives. They are connected through their whatsapp group and we are up in full steam in the least possible time".
7. Succession: Since it is a livelihood business, the team is not deeply involved in a succession plan. They feel that it would go on as long as their entrepreneurial spirit is carried through.

An Opportunity to Differentiate!

Sapthagiri Tiffin Centre is now set up in Sivagnanam Road, Pondy Bazaar-Thyagaraya Nagar, Chennai as an outlet encompassing a clinic/hospital there. It is a small outlet, started in 2014. A hospital came up opposite to Local Head Post office at Pondy bazaar. This is close to the end of the road where they were operating. For the convenience of many who visit there, a small space was provided to Prakash and the team to run an eatery. This was found to be ideal by the hospital management and Prakash and team because they had a split location principle in operation for many years. Here also there would be more customers dining as they stand comfortably keeping plates on a running table. Hence model is a limited variant from what they have been doing all along!

Generally, Sapthagiri prepared food, side dishes and snacks in a common kitchen that would be about hundreds of meters away from their street cart vending location. This helped them in the following ways:

1. Better management of site, as Sapthagiri, prepared only "dosa" made from rice batter at the location point of sale, as it needs to be served steam.
2. Balancing demand and supply in a perishable business with a shorter window of time to respond. Such centralisation of the facility helps instead of making the "made to stock" process work.
3. Most importantly, customers perceive food to be fresh and clean.

Balraj adds, "Customers who come to street cart vending are unique and continue to come there. There is a different segment, which visits the new set up. However, a new set up sells a sizeable volume as "to carry".

Conclusion

Prakash and team sustained during the storm with closure of outlet for a few days. There was also a political crisis as the then Chief Minister of Tamil Nadu passed away. The city returned to normalcy after a couple of weeks. The team was going about their usual business accepting their punishing routine. But Prakash is bewildered by the commitment of purpose towards the livelihood business of street food vending by his team and is not keen on rocking the boat through innovative and disruptive plans!

Note: Authors are Dr. N. Chandrasekaran and Dr. C. R. Rajan, Professor, Great Lakes Institute of Management. The case was earlier published in the www.thecasecentre.org and reference number is 317-0118-1.

QUESTIONS

1. Define the business which Saptahgiri is into and explain key success factors and challenges they faced.
2. Discuss the entrepreneurial challenges in livelihood business which Prakash and his team faced.
3. Explain supply chain network defining nodes and flows of physical, financial and information for this business.
4. If one was to convert the business into an organised business with brick and mortar restaurant, how could one go about it? What were the challenges in your opinion that dissuaded them to pursue the same?
5. What are the chances that the business can be taken in a single brand with multiple outlets across the city with common serving nodes on a "hub and spoke" model?

Management of Pharmaceutical Drugs in Resource-constrained Not-for-profit Healthcare in Uttar Pradesh

Case authored by: Vijaya Chebolu-Subramanian, Gaurav Kumar Singh
IFMR-GSB, KREA University

(**Disclaimer:** This case is based on common knowledge and discussions about a Trust which is into not-for-profit service. The name of the Trust is disguised to avoid assessment of any such Trust that may exist in the geography. The figures are illustrative and neither supported by factual records nor verified. The objective of this case is to discuss academic discussions to apply the concepts and framework for a similar business situation. Authors of the case confirm that the material is prepared for this book and has not been published elsewhere.)

Abstract

Anik Sinha joined a not-for-profit primary healthcare facility as Manager in a remote part of Uttar Pradesh state in India. He soon realised that the facility was riddled with issues and inefficiencies abounded, and the absence of any system to manage drugs meant that wastage was immense. The situation was compounded by the low resource setting, especially common to Not-for-Profit organisations operating in the developing world. Anik undertook a holistic review of the facility and utilised fundamental operations management methods to streamline the handling of drugs at the facility. This case illustrates the operational challenges faced by organisations serving sections of the population at the "bottom of the pyramid". It also demonstrates in a simple but effective manner how forecasting demand and inventory planning can be used in a resource-constrained setting to achieve greater efficiency and savings.

Learning Objective: To understand the relevance of forecasting and scope of inventory management in service sector.

Key Words: Forecasting; Inventory management; Resource-based; Efficiency; Cost management.

Case

Introduction

Anik was an idealistic young man who wanted to combine his training in Management with his love for the offbeat and passion for charity. As he arrived at the end of his MBA education, unlike his friends who took up coveted job offers, Anik dreamt of spending a few years working at the grassroots. This led to his meeting the Director and couple of board members of Mansi Lal Trust, a Not-for-Profit in the state of Uttar Pradesh in India. "We started this facility in one of the remote regions of the state intending to provide quality, timely and primary healthcare services to the people there. But we find that the facility does not have a system in place and is chaotic", said the Director. He further added, "The typical budget crunches faced by an organisation such as ours and the escalating costs of the facility has put a hold to our plans of scaling and setting up similar facilities in other parts of the state. Though we have a dedicated team of doctors and staff, they are ill-equipped to manage the place".

Anik decided that this opportunity provided the challenge he was looking for, and he accepted a position as Healthcare Facility Manager at the Trust's Primary Healthcare facility.

Organisation

Mansi Lal Trust was a charitable organisation with about 250 employees, headquartered in the city of Lucknow. The mission of the organisation was to serve the needs of the poor and socially marginalised sections of society. The Trust specifically worked in the areas of health and education. It also advocated with the National and State Governments on these issues.

As a part of its healthcare initiative, the Trust ran a primary healthcare center with an attached pharmacy in Siddharth Nagar in the Himalayan foothills in India. Siddharth Nagar is among India's 250 most backward districts and is below the national average on socio-economic and healthcare indicators and receives funds from the Backward Regions Grant Fund Program of the government (Ministry of Panchayati Raj, 2007).

The facility was focussed on addressing the primary healthcare issues of the population in a radius of approximately five kilometers, covering 10,000 people on an average. It treated common illnesses, and patients in need of advanced medical services were referred to tertiary centers. The healthcare facility has an overall staff strength of 10–12 at any given time, including the doctors, administrative, and nursing staff. Given the limited resources, each employee was responsible for multiple tasks.

The facility provided drugs free of cost or at a subsidised rate to the patients. It aimed to have a very high service level, as the availability of medicines in the required quantities at all times was the driving philosophy behind the organisation.

However, as Anik started his job, reality slowly set in, and he discovered that there were several inefficiencies in the management of pharmaceutical drugs in the facility, which placed huge stress on the already limited resources of the organisation and undermined its noble intentions.

Organisational Issues

Anik soon understood that the functioning of the facility was fraught with issues compounded by the limited human resources, lack of infrastructure due to its not-for-profit nature and remote location.

As Anik made his daily rounds, observing the working of the organisation, he realised that one of the major issues plaguing the facility was the purchase and management of drugs, which was random and unplanned. He would often walk into the Pharmacy store to find it overflowing with stock and disposal of drugs past expiry date was frequent. The organisation did not have a central authority to oversee the purchasing of medicines. This, coupled with the absence of proper forecasting and planning mechanisms, meant that the drug purchasing was done on an ad-hoc basis.

Additionally, the staff lacked awareness about current management practices and the use of technology and data to manage drug inventory. The lack of even a basic computer to track drugs was a significant constraint. Instead, the old fashioned logbooks were still used, and random ordering of medicines without any central authorisation meant that the pharmacy did not have an accurate estimate of the drug availability or their expiry dates. This led to the theft, misplacement, and misuse of drugs.

The doctors and staff were focussed on adhering to the mission of the organisation. They always wanted to provide drugs to the patients in the required quantities. In their zeal to make sure that patient needs were fulfiled, they went by their intuitive understanding of disease prevalence and placed frequent orders with the pharmacy. These orders were fulfiled without checking the stock availability leading to over-ordering of drugs and subsequent wastages.

As Anik was about to leave the facility at the end of a tiring day, he ran into Dr. Gauri, a general practitioner. She was rushing into the pharmacy to place an emergency order for drugs to treat some common gastrointestinal infections.

Dr. Gauri explained, "I walked into the clinic today to find a stream of patients pouring in with gastro issues, I anticipate an outbreak".

"Hmm....but I bumped into Dr. Gautam placing an order for gastrointestinal related drugs just yesterday", said Anik.

"Oh..well better to be safe than sorry. Most of these patients are daily wage workers and forgo a part of their wages to make clinic visits. We don't want them to make multiple trips to the Pharmacy to pick up the drugs", said Dr. Gauri.

Some drugs required special storage as they were light or temperature-sensitive. The facility had limited space and storage capabilities aggravated by the intermittent supply of electricity. A small refrigerator or cooling unit was available, which ran on a generator unit in the absence of electricity. The over-ordering of drugs coupled with limited infrastructure and improper storage of medicines resulted in rampant wastage and subsequent shortages when requirements came in.

Anik also observed that the pharmacy staff spent an excessive amount of time in trying to implement the conventional method of First in First out (FIFO) to use drugs in the order of their decreasing shelf life. Also, the complete focus was on implementing the FIFO system in exclusion to addressing other problems such as over-ordering.

Current System

The pharmacy purchased drugs from Gorakhpur, the nearest town from the facility. Gorakhpur is an important medical destination for people from other states, such as Bihar and even the neighboring country of Nepal. It is a hub for pharmaceutical drugs and medical facilities with numerous drug distributors, and therefore the availability of drugs was not an issue encountered by the organisation.

The pharmacy preferred to purchase drugs from a specific set of trusted distributors for the sake of simplicity, convenience, and long-term relationships. These distributors provided discounts varying from 5–7 per cent, and orders were placed in advance through mobile phone. Order fulfilments were delivered by the distributors or collected by the staff, as and when available.

Most of the drugs are available with a lead time of 3–4 days. The facility planned for ordering medicines in bulk once every 4–6 months. However, this was rarely implemented in practice due to the lack of proper planning, and several weekly orders were a standard feature.

The Way Ahead

Anik decided to tackle issues by undertaking a series of steps focussed on streamlining the drug ordering process. He communicated with the Director and the Board of the Trust to get them aboard his plan of action. He also convinced them to invest in a basic computer and training of a young staff member in necessary IT skills to facilitate his plan of action.

He was also designated as the authority for approving the purchase of drugs. Though others could recommend the purchase of certain drugs, the final approval authority lay with the manager, and all requests and purchases were recorded in a database.

Though FIFO is a time-tested method in inventory management, Anik posited that since most of the drugs had an average shelf life of 18 to 24 months, an effective demand management system was the need of the hour. This combined with rapid drug turnover, may reduce the need for concerted efforts to maintain a FIFO system. He also made efforts to streamline the drug list and replace high priced branded drugs with lower-priced generics.

Over the years 2014 and 2015, these efforts were implemented and in 2016, it was seen that there was a decrease in the amount of drug purchases made (Table 2a-2d, Annexure).

From a long-term perspective, Anik realised that demand estimation was key to negate the need for individual ad-hoc ordering except in emergencies.

He interacted extensively with the doctors at the facility to chalk out a plan on how to go about recording disease prevalence. Dr. Gautam, who had been working with the facility since its inception provided his perspective, "We have a small area of focus, and the diseases we commonly treat can be broadly classified under four categories – skin, eye, gastro-intestinal, and respiratory infections. Rarely do we encounter diseases outside these categories, and even if we do, such cases are referred to tertiary centers.

Based on this information, Anik set up a simple system to capture monthly occurrences of diseases under these four categories, which were recorded by the pharmacy staff (Table 1, Annexure).

Drugs purchased and the price was also recorded for April to June for each year (Table 2a-2d, Annexure). The drugs were then grouped based on the category of disease they were prescribed for, ensuring that there were no overlaps. The price of the drugs did not fluctuate majorly over the period. Hence price was assumed to be the same.

The drugs are also sold under different brand names. However, the data list only the generic name along with the purchase price, while the brand name is ignored.

With these changes in place, Anik believed that he was indeed on the path to streamlining the system though there was still a lot to be done.

QUESTIONS

1. What type of inventory management system and measures will you suggest for the organisation?
2. Are there any unique features to the demand experienced by the organisation, and if so, can the organisation leverage it to its advantage utilising forecasting techniques?
3. What are some of the unique challenges that a non-profit organisation with limited resources faces, and how can these be minimised through the principles of operations management?

Annexure

TABLE 1 Number of monthly occurrences under each infection type for the years 2013-2015

Infection Type	Skin			Eye			Gastro Intestinal			Respiratory		
Year	'14	'15	'16	'14	'15	'16	'14	'15	'16	'14	'15	'16
Month												
January	12	13	16	2	7	4	6	8	8	12	14	10
February	10	15	18	3	4	4	14	12	13	6	5	14
March	6	8	11	7	1	11	21	15	14	3	6	7
April	8	9	9	9	12	16	15	13	19	5	4	6
May	5	0	9	3	4	7	13	18	23	5	4	7
June	4	4	7	2	1	15	17	20	16	10	11	9
July	7	7	9	4	8	5	15	23	22	10	9	10
August	8	13	15	5	7	5	24	21	29	10	14	11
September	8	10	18	6	7	0	12	16	13	7	14	13
October	11	11	10	9	12	9	8	8	9	7	8	11
November	13	14	11	11	13	12	11	10	10	9	9	13
December	14	16	14	13	4	10	5	9	6	10	10	12

TABLE 2A Drugs purchased for treating skin infection

Drug Type	Name	Cost/ Unit* (₹)	Number of Units Purchased During April–June period		
			2014	2015	2016
Topical	Benzyl Benzoate 25%	23	5	8	4
Topical Cream	Butenafine 1%	52	4	10	4
Injection	Cefotaxim	15	3	15	2
Topical	Cetrimide	41	2	10	6
Tablet/Capsule	Gatifloxacin	25	20	10	3
Cream	Neomycin	40	15	1	1
Topical	Ketoconazole 2%	130	10	1	3
Tablet	Ketoconazole 200mg	150	5	3	3
Cream	Miconazole	14	7	1	1
Powder	Clotrimazole	38	20	3	1
Topical gel/cream	Metronidazol	24	5	3	2
Topical Cream	Beclomethasone + Miconazole +Gentamycin	23	4	7	4
Topical Cream	Beclomethasone + Neomycin +Clotrimazole	34	3	5	2

TABLE 2B Drugs purchased for treating eye infection

Drug Type	Name	Cost/Unit* (₹)	Number of Units Purchased During April- June period		
			2014	2015	2016
Eye drop	Carboxy methyl cellulose 0.5mg	140	5	3	2
Eye drop	Moxifloxacin 0.5% w/v	90	4	8	4
Eye drop	Gentamicin 0.3% w/v	238	3	9	10
Tablet	Cefditoren 200mg tab	240	2	2	2
Eye drop	Gatifloxacin 0.3% w/v	18.5	20	6	8
Eye drop	Idoxuridin 0.1%w/v	16	15	10	5
Eye drop	Gatifloxacin 0.3 % w/v with Dexamethasone 0.1 % w/v.	30	10	15	8
Eye drop	Homatropin 2%w/v	49	5	4	3
Eye drop	Ketorolac0.5%w/v	42	7	5	0
Eye drop	Ciprofloxacin0.3% w/v	10	20	20	15

TABLE 2C Drugs purchased for treating gastrointestinal infection

Drug Type	Name	Cost/Unit* (₹)	Number of Units Purchased During April- June period		
			2014	2015	2016
Injection	Ranitidine(H2)Blockers	5	10	7	3
Tablet/Capsule	Famotidine	8	4	4	2
Tablet/Capsule	Omeprazole	30	5	3	2
Tablet/Capsule	Clarithromycine	350	3	2	1
Tablet/Capsule	Metronidazole 400 mg	10	7	8	5
Tablet/Capsule	Amoxcicyllin 250 mg	43	10	6	4
Tablet/Capsule	Amoxcicyllin 500mg	65.5	10	7	4
Tablet/Capsule	Tetracycline	8	4	4	2
Tablet/Capsule	Oxytetracycline (ointment)	20	5	7	5
Tablet/Capsule	Oxytetracycline 500mg	15	9	8	6
Tablet/Capsule	Ciproflaxacine 250mg	34	4	2	2
Tablet/Capsule	Ofloxacin + Ornidazole	36	6	4	4
Tablet/Capsule	Ciproflaxacine 500mg	66	5	4	4
Tablet/Capsule	Doxycycline	28	5	4	3
Tablet/Capsule	Domperidom	70	5	4	2

TABLE 2D Drugs purchased for treating respiratory infections

Drug Type	Name	Cost/Unit* (₹)	Number of Units Purchased During April- June period		
			2014	2015	2016
Inhaler	Salbutamol(inhalation)	83	5	8	4
Inhaler	Triatropium bromide 9mcg	410	5	15	2
Inhaler	Salmetarol + Flucticasone	450	20	10	3
Capsule	Amoxcycilline	65.5	1	1	1
Capsule	Erythromycine 250mg	33	2	1	3
Capsule	Erythromycine 500mg	38	3	3	3
Capsule	Cefuroxim 250mg	280	2	1	1
Capsule	Cefuroxim 500mg	520	4	3	1
Capsule	Paracetamol 500mg	22	5	3	2
Capsule	Paracetamol 650 mg	13	7	7	5
Syrup	Paracetamol Oral Syrup	34	5	5	2
Tablet	Mefinamic acid/Drotaverin	122	6	4	2
Cream	Gentamicin	21	40	30	24
Tablet	Aceclofinac 100mgs	25	8	5	4

**Unit may refer to a strip of tablets, injection or syrup depending on the drug type*

Index

K

L

M

N

T

U

V

W